ADAM SMITH TODAY

AM SMITH TODAY

An Inquiry into the Nature and Causes of

THE WEALTH OF NATIONS

Simplified, Shortened and Modernized

BY

ARTHUR HUGH JENKINS

KENNIKAT PRESS, INC./PORT WASHINGTON, N. Y.

ADAM SMITH TODAY

Copyright 1948 by the Richard R. Smith Co. Inc.
Reissued 1969 by Kennikat Press by arrangement

Library of Congress Catalog Card No: 68-8231
Manufactured in the United States of America

CONTENTS

CONTENTS

BOOK II

CONTENTS

EDITOR'S INTRODUCTION

In 1776, just as the tension between England and her American colonies was reaching the breaking point, the solitary Scotchman in Kirkaldy finished and published his book. In the course of the next fifty years it was literally to change the world.

His name was Adam Smith, and he called his work "An Inquiry Into the Nature and Causes of the Wealth of Nations." The publisher was W. Strahan.

This is no story of the starving genius in the garret. The father of the science of economics was a man of the world, Oxford-trained, widely-traveled, a friend of the greatest philosophers of Great Britain and France, himself a university lecturer and writer, and in comfortable circumstances.

All of Adam Smith's experience and reflection went into the ten years of work on the book in the house of his mother in Kirkaldy. He saw a world tormented with the selfishness of individuals and the well-meant stupidities of law-makers. Steam power was just ahead; the machine was taking an ever-more-important place in the processes of production.

Adam Smith saw clearly that these forces are controllable by human wisdom. He saw that human greeds tend to cancel each other out; that they are dangerous only when the state interferes on one side or another; above all, that human nature is a constant, and the laws of human behavior unchangeable. He set out to persuade his generation of these truths, and succeeded in making over the world.

The purpose of this book is to present to American readers, in modern language, a condensation of "The Wealth of Nations." Its aim is to remove as many as possible of the obstacles to the reading of the book.

That those obstacles are serious, everyone must agree. "The Wealth of Nations" appears in every list of classics, of books "every educated person must read"; yet like most other classics, from the plays of Sophocles to "Paradise Lost," it is as a matter of fact all but unreadable, and for the most part is unread.

As if the length and the mere appearance of the closely-packed pages were not enough, the popular misconception of economics as "the dismal science" is against it. Thus it has always been the exceptional individual—barring of course the economist and the student of economics—who looks inside these covers.

Even with its length reduced more than half, its language simplified and Americanized, it is scarcely to be hoped that "The Wealth of Nations" can be converted into a best-seller. It will still present something of a mental obstacle to the general reader.

Yet the difficulty, or improbability, of popularizing Adam Smith ought not to discourage the attempt. The publication of the book in 1776, as innumerable writers have agreed, was an event comparable in importance to the Declaration of Independence in the same year. With the exception of the books of the Bible, and possibly the Koran, no single literary work has so powerfully affected the thoughts and lives of so' many people, directly or indirectly.

"Well may it be said of Adam Smith," wrote Buckle, "that this solitary Scotchman has, by the publication of one single work, contributed more toward the happiness of man than has been effected by the united abilities of all the statesmen and legislators of whom history has presented an authentic account."

Almost anyone, and certainly any economist, surveying the degree of economic illiteracy of the 20th Century, will conclude that something ought to be done about it.

Confusion is piled on confusion. The simplest and most just and reasonable of economic principles are commonly ignored by legislators, as they are apparently unknown to great masses of people. Perhaps the world is actually, in Herbert Spencer's phrase, in the process of re-barbarisation.

Some years ago, Professor Edwin Cannan, himself one of the most able editors of Adam Smith, remarked sadly that the combined labors of the Fellows of the Royal Economic Society had not succeeded, in forty-two years, in producing any considerable enlightenment in the mind of the public on the subject of the employment of labor.

That is a phenomenon painfully familiar to economists. The public seems to learn little if at all. On the other hand, truth itself is invincibly tenacious, if only it can be preserved and not forgotten. While "The Wealth of Nations" and the works of the other great economists survive, we need not despair of this muddle-headed world.

Thus it appears that this is a continuing battle, like bathing. The believer in economic truth should seek ways to make the weapons of truth more effective, and should direct his assault on the defenses of economic ignorance and error at the point where they are strongest, in the minds of the uninformed and misinformed.

The first step is obviously to clear the approaches for the attack. Before the truths of "The Wealth of Nations" can be understood, or believed, or acted upon, they must be read. And this volume represents a determined effort to remove as many as possible of the obstacles to a reading of the book.

It seems a little difficult to classify this work; it is not exactly a re-editing, nor a paraphrase, nor an abridgement, but something of all three. It started out as an attempt to re-write "The Wealth of Nations," as Adam Smith might be supposed to have written it in the United States today. But this, as I soon discovered, was an impossible formula. Insoluble problems arose.

The consequence has been that this book will be found to have none of the unities. The reader will pass from 1947 to 1776 and from the British Isles to the United States to India and back again as the subject seems to require. I have done what I could, of course, to make the transitions as inconspicuous and painless as possible.

The idea of shrinking "The Wealth of Nations" to a manageable size is by no means new; I know of five such attempts, and doubtless there have been others.

The earliest, of which copies probably could be found in England, is an abridgement by Jeremiah Joyce. It was followed by a similar work, the editor being Professor Wolseley P. Emerton of Oxford, in 1881. This is a condensation in which all chapters of "The Wealth of Nations" are briefly summarized, primarily for a classroom text. Some excellent notes and appendices are supplied.

An abridgement by Sir W. J. Ashley in 1895, consists merely of a selection of chapters, not too well chosen, using Adam Smith's full original text. In 1904 appeared a "new and condensed" edition of "The Wealth of Nations," with notes by Mr. Hector C. Macpherson; I have had no success in finding a copy.

A recent work is called "The Synthetic Wealth of Nations," by Malcolm K. Graham. Under this somewhat ambiguous title Mr. Graham presents the text of Adam Smith, so extremely compressed as to be not much more than an abstract or syllabus. Into this text he introduces his own criticisms, comments, and views on money, gold, the protective tariff principle, and much more; on the whole, a book not without interest and value.

The present work differs from all of these, in that it not only undertakes to discriminate between the more important and the less important, for the general reader of 1947, but simplifies and Americanizes Adam Smith's 18th Century vocabulary. It rearranges and regroups the chapters; and finally, it does away with duplicated material, of which there is a good deal.

Of all the difficulties of the task, the most formidable has naturally been that of shortening Adam Smith's 370,000 words, more or less—I have not counted them; those who care to may— to little more than a third of that total. This was possible only through the drastic paraphrasing of long passages, for very little in the book has been altogether left out. It has compelled the condensation of every page and paragraph, almost every sentence.

As very little has been omitted, so very little has been added; that little consisting in an occasional phrase or sentence for clarity or amplification. All other added text appears in footnotes.

Since Adam Smith had the habit of treating a single topic in several widely-separated places, in different connections—the book is indeed a marvel of disorderly arrangement—considerable parts of it will be found far from their original positions.

I have made no attempt to identify this transplanted tissue as the reader comes to it. It can generally be traced to its proper spot, if anyone cares to do that, by referring to Dr. Cannan's excellent index, or any standard edition.

In making selections I have sometimes, I confess, followed my own fancy. I eliminate a very tedious section on the Scottish herring fisheries, for example, but have retained Adam Smith's caustic observations on the stupidities and perversities of lawmakers; I have cut to the bone the account of the prices of coarse woolen goods in the 12th Century, while retaining the explanation of the reason for the beauty of Irish prostitutes in London.

The text is divided into five books, as in the "Wealth of Nations," and each book into chapters; but so inconsistent and incoherent is Adam Smith's arrangement that I have abandoned any attempt to make the chapter numbers coincide with his. The classic analysis of the so-called "Mercantile System," which constitutes Book IV in "The Wealth of Nations," becomes Book V; this is the one major change in arrangement.

As compared with the standard editions of the book, the innovations in typography will, I hope, be welcome to readers. Dr. Cannan in his edition is quite apologetic for a liberty he had taken: he dared to start a new chapter at the top of a new page, although there was still space at the bottom of the last.

The whole purpose of this edition is to make Adam Smith readable and better-read. The newspapers long ago learned that not only must their pages be readable, but they must *look* readable, and following their example, I have broken up Adam Smith's long paragraphs into many, possibly too many, short ones. Spacings and margins are liberal. The pages, I hope, look as if they could be read.

It will be noticed that there are three types or classes of reading matter. Much the largest of these is the text of Adam Smith, with the elisions and word changes which seem most suitable for American readers.

The second class, introduced by this symbol ℭ, consists of connecting and explanatory matter of my own; for the most part it summarizes chapters, or large parts of chapters, which have little or no contemporary importance.

The third class, in a distinctive type face, consists of a number of verbatim quotations from "The Wealth of Nations," which for their unusual significance, or celebrity, or humor, or some other particular reason, I wish to single out for the attention of readers.

In this edition, I have thought it unnecessary to include the biographies of Adam Smith, the discussions of variations in texts, and the voluminous notes which are easily available in the standard editions. I omit even a bibliography. A thorough index I regard as indispensable, and I hope it will be found adequate.

Since it is necessary to repeat the names of Adam Smith

and "The Wealth of Nations" many times, I abbreviate them in most cases to "A. S." and "W. N."

Wherever possible, I have resolutely suppressed all statistics. This may disappoint the statistically-minded; it will be apt to dampen the interest of that wing of economists to whom the science appears as a wonderland of tabulations, graphs, and algebraic equations.

These have their function, and an essential function. But the general inquirer, who cares nothing for equations as such, will I think be grateful to be given only the conclusions, with the assurance that the supporting figures are to be had if wanted.

It is to be expected that my judgment as to modernizing of the text, and as to printing or omitting particular passages, will often be questioned, and doubtless in some cases it will be wrong. My sole aim has been to present Adam Smith's thoughts without any change in meaning, in a form most understandable to American readers. I have consciously favored those passages which apply directly to the economic and politico-economic problems of today.

These problems, with two or three important exceptions, are not new, but very old. Adam Smith did not invent the solutions—indeed did not discover them, but in part learned them from Turgot, from Hutcheson, and from many others. It is his great distinction to have been the first to recognize the nature of the problems, to have seen what the solutions were, to have reduced them to a generally consistent whole, and to have written them down with unique clarity and force.

The late 18th and 19th Centuries saw the beginning of the so-called "industrial revolution," for which Adam Smith lived too soon. While there is no industrial problem in 1947 that did not in 1776 exist in essence, if on a smaller scale, there are developments which Adam Smith could not clearly foresee. As the so-called heavy industries have vastly increased in size, under corporation ownership and professional management, they have progressively withdrawn the tools of production from the workman's possession. They have required more and more specialized skills. They have, by mere size and concentration of capital, made it more difficult to establish the new competition constantly necessary for the restraint of monopoly.

The result has been to increase the dependence of the

worker on tools he does not own and could not operate; because of greater specialization of skills, it has caused a further retreat from that perfect fluidity of the labor supply on which a just and efficient production system relies.

To many this seems evil, and calls for some extension of state intervention, and certainly none who believe in the intervention of the state to restrain by law the constant tendency toward monopoly are in any position to complain of this.

The second development not foreseen in "The Wealth of Nations" is the great change in the nature and use of money, which has produced such wonderful improvements, along with so many painful perplexities.

Adam Smith's "money" was silver and gold, coins and bullion, with some few paper bank notes, and a still smaller amount of miscellaneous paper currency. He could not foresee a time when paper money makes only a small part of the money supply, and metal coinage a still smaller, while the expanding and contracting deposits of commercial banks provide the circulating medium with which most of the transactions of the industrial nations are carried on.

Such notes as are supplied—and their number could have been multiplied many times—are confined chiefly to criticisms of Adam Smith's ideas and statements. Where no contradiction appears, it may be presumed that his ideas are generally approved by the economists of all countries and ages; it is only when they disagree that I note that fact.

This arrangement has the effect of making the notes as a whole seem unduly critical—the dissents greatly outnumber the agreements; but this would be to create a false impression.

170 years of analysis and debate have brought most economists to agreement on these points: that the great body of fact and deduction and conclusion found in "The Wealth of Nations" stands substantially intact; that some slight modifications in Adam Smith's ideas must be made, and some were in fact made by Smith himself before his death; that the age of steam, electricity, and mass-production has raised some social problems to which "The Wealth of Nations" does not provide wholly satisfactory answers; that the book itself is of loose texture, defective in arrangement, but framed on a consistent principle, and, in the words of David Hume, of "depth, solidity, and acuteness, and so

much illustrated by curious facts that it must at last attract the public attention."

That attention has not, of course, been wholly favorable. In addition to the professional economists, whose dissent from Adam Smith's "wage-fund" and "unproductive capital" theories, and others, will be pointed out in footnotes to the text, the whole basic principle of "The Wealth of Nations" has been attacked from sources which it may be useful to identify.

These assailants of "The Wealth of Nations" nearly all ignore the objective basis of the book. They still speak of "classical economics," of "the outworn theory" or system of laisser-faire, of the "barren abstraction of the economic man," of the "assumptions" on which the "system" is based. No attack could be worse conceived. For "The Wealth of Nations" contains few theories, few assumptions, no systems, and no abstractions.

In particular, it is impossible to find in "The Wealth of Nations" any such doctrine as pure "laisser-faire." Some followers of Adam Smith later took this extreme position, but such a theory seems to lead ultimately to simple anarchy, and Adam Smith's severely practical mind rejected such an idea, if he ever entertained it. He specifically lists cases where intervention of the state is beneficial, and even essential to justice and prosperity. Yet the myth persists, even among those who should know better.

"Smith allows several departures from the let-alone policy," writes Dr. Lewis H. Haney, whose "History of Economic Thought" is valuable and comprehensive, "although he does not seem to suspect that he is disturbing the harmony of his system."

One asks: "what harmony of what system?" for Adam Smith nowhere claims harmony for his ideas. If he exposes the absurdities and injustices of most government regulation, yet admits the necessity of it in some specified cases, this is surely not inconsistency—it is just good sense. His years of observation and reflection resulted, not in a set of economic theories, but in the most objective analysis of actual human behavior the world had known up to that time. One wonders if the critics have ever read the book.

It is not difficult to identify the animus of most of these attacks. First of all we may rule off all the Marxists, whose unreal world of the class struggle and what we are learning to call

Statism must be forever impossible in a society that understands the values of economic freedom.

Adam Smith says many times that the laborer should enjoy the fruits of his labors, and that great moral principle is implicit in all his writings. The laborer ought to enjoy what his labors have produced, all he has produced, and no part of what has been produced by another; if he obtains what he has not produced, it must be through dishonesty or the fiat of an unjust government.

Between this moral principle and the Socialists' arbitrary and capricious distribution of wealth by a coercive state there is an impassable gulf. No compromise is possible, no accommodation, no middle ground, scarcely a *modus vivendi*. One or the other must perish. Hence the deadly feud of the Marxists and their fellow-travelers with "The Wealth of Nations."

In his introduction to a recent American edition of "The Wealth of Nations," Mr. Max Lerner categorically denies the objective nature of the book. Adam Smith did not, he says, "start with truths about human behavior and the natural order, and arrive at economic liberalism," but the other way about.

The unbiased reader of "The Wealth of Nations" will not, I think, reach any such conclusion; but the Marxist must if possible show that the science of economics evolves out of the personal history, background, prejudices, and predilections of the economist, not out of the unvarying laws of human conduct.

That Adam Smith's "personal sympathies were not entirely with the capitalist," Lerner admits somewhat grudgingly. Through "The Wealth of Nations" there runs "a strain of partisanship for apprentices and laborers, for farmers, for the lowly and oppressed everywhere, and a hostility to the business corporations, . . . the ecclesiasts and the aristocrats."

There are examples of such a feeling in "The Wealth of Nations." No one who reads the last chapter of Book I will accuse Adam Smith of partiality toward capitalists. He minces no words in his strictures on particular practices, selfish policies, and abuses of power, but these are applied indiscriminately to all the selfish and short-sighted.

Thus we shall meet with "the desperate violence, folly, and extravagance" of workmen who are "incapable of understanding their own interests," are "as stupid and ignorant as it is possible for a human creature to become," and "incapable of bearing a part in any rational conversation."

But we shall also hear of "the insolent outrage of furious and disappointed monopolists," who have "on many occasions both deceived and oppressed the public"; of great land-owners devoted to "violence, rapine, and disorder," and later to "the gratification of the most childish, the meanest and most sordid of all vanities"; and of "the folly and presumption" of "that insidious and crafty animal, vulgarly called a politician."

How well we know them all! But there is one class of men for whom Adam Smith has only kind words—the men who cultivate the soil. It is the farmer whom he openly admires, and singles out as at once the most serviceable to society, the most intelligent, the most upright, and the most abused of mankind. In all "The Wealth of Nations," there is scarcely one word of criticism of him.

Nowhere in "The Wealth of Nations" will the reader find any trace of anything resembling the Marxist theory of the class struggle.

The Marxist sees all economic and social phenomena in terms of partisanship and personal conflict, and with these the science of economics surely has nothing to do. Strictly speaking, there seems no more reason why the economist-scientist should feel sympathy or partisanship toward the lowly against the capitalist, or vice versa, than the chemist-scientist's heart should bleed for sodium as against calcium.

Political assailants are less dangerous than the Socialists, because less doctrinaire, and less bitter. Indeed, their attitude is apt to be indifference and expediency rather than hostility. It is only when sound economic truths tend to interfere with some special interest of his constituents that the run-of-mine legislator finds it useful to abuse Adam Smith.

A third attack, more subtle and therefore more dangerous than either of the foregoing, appears from time to time in the ranks of the economists themselves. Here the most rigorous scrutiny and harsh criticism are not only natural but necessary. And it is far and away the strongest evidence of the soundness of Adam Smith's work that his book emerges from this 170-year ordeal almost intact.

The most mischievous of the modern critics among the

economists are those of the type of the late Lord Keynes, who admit the truth of most of "The Wealth of Nations," but who claim to have discovered serious divergences between the behavior of society as it actually is, and what it should be according to Adam Smith. Their speculations are largely in the most difficult and least understood branch of economics—that dealing with the institution of money and public and private finance.

More particularly, they are concerned with the "business cycle"—that disconcerting succession of booms and depressions that seems inseparable from an economic system based on free prices and the profit motive. It is a phenomenon not noticed by Adam Smith, although it could hardly have been unknown to him.

Of the teachings of the Keynes school it is enough to say that their monetary heterodoxy appears to be directed toward advocating and justifying the same type of Statism that we find so obnoxious in the Marxists and their Fascist cousins. Their theories are contradicted in whole and in detail by the great body of economists, here and abroad.

The mischief achieved by these economists and pseudo-economists—Veblen, Keynes, Hansen, Chase and the rest—is therefore not so much in their doctrines, for the principles of economics will in the long run take care of themselves. It is rather in the minds of the lay public, who have read neither attack nor rebuttal, but tend to gain the fixed impression that the economists are fighting among themselves. It is common knowledge that this is a common attitude: "There can be no truth in economics—the economists themselves can't agree." It is a convenient alibi for many an uneasy economic conscience.

The truth is, that the area of agreement among contemporary economists is very large, the points of dispute small and for the most part of only technical importance. But it is to the interest of many people, not all Socialists, constantly to exaggerate these differences.

The question is, therefore, is or is not economics an exact and objective science? I am of the opinion—a layman's opinion, to be sure—that it is. And on this supposition I venture to suggest here a more precise definition of the science—a definition that will make it clear that economics deals not with wealth and its production and exchange, but with human beings and their normal or average behavior.

Except for an off-hand reference to "political economy" in the introduction to Book IV, by which he means the economic policies of governments, Adam Smith does not define the general subject he is writing about. He does use habitually such phrases as "natural law," the "laws of justice," and "the natural order of things," and by this he obviously means the natural laws of human behavior and of fundamental justice. He calls it "this very important science."

One of the first to define economics was Ricardo, who called it "the laws which determine the division of the produce of industry amongst the classes who concur in its formation."

If economics is actually a science, it must have laws, and these must be stable and unvarying. They must depend on some natural and universal principle, and that principle may readily be found, I believe, in the constant and unvarying character and conduct of the mass of human beings.

It is Winwood Reade who remarks that while any individual man is an insoluble puzzle, in the mass he becomes a mathematical certainty.

Gresham's law is universally recognized as a constant, and this is because it is not a law of money, but of human behavior in handling money.

On this principle I propose a new definition of economics, in substantially these terms: the science that observes and records the actual behavior of human beings in the production, exchange, and consumption of wealth.

This, it seems to me, puts the whole matter on an unassailable basis. It shows why the "laws" of economics, being the observed course of actual historical human conduct, cannot be challenged as long as human nature and behavior remain constant. It disposes at a single sweep of the notion that Adam Smith "invented" an economic system, laisser-faire or any other. If there is any "inventor" of economics, it is *pithecanthropus erectus* at the moment he became *homo sapiens*.

There are, to be sure, traces of this idea in many of the innumerable definitions in the text-books and dictionaries. Thus the able Irish economist Cairnes defined economics as "the science which, accepting as ultimate facts the principles of human nature, and the physical laws of the external world, as well as the conditions, political and social, of the several communities of men, investigates the laws of the production and distribution of wealth, which result from their combined operation."

That is very nearly the nub of the matter; but I prefer my own definition as more explicit and concise.

It cannot reasonably be charged that such a change in the definition of economics is merely a play upon words—a distinction without a difference; nor that the standard definitions imply clearly enough that laws of production and exchange are laws of human activities. This may be true for economists; but for others it is demonstrably false. The public mind has no such conception. And this is a case where the image in the public mind is the important thing.

In the end, if the public mind absorbs the idea that economic law does not rely on the say-so of Adam Smith, Malthus, Ricardo, Mill, Karl Marx, Lord Keynes, or any other authority, but on something quite impersonal and absolutely dependable, I am sure the result must be extraordinarily good.

"The Wealth of Nations" has been criticized on other grounds, notably on its "wage-fund" idea, to which I have already alluded, and by the so-called "Austrian school" on its theory of value, or rather its lack of a theory of value. All economists criticize Adam Smith's handling of the principles of rent as expressed in price. Minor criticisms are innumerable.

All of these are what may be called, without disrespect, economists' squabbles; whichever way they are settled (and it may be remarked in passing that defenders of Adam Smith have more than held their own) they need not concern the general reader of this book.

Dr. Haney says of one of these disputations: "One puts down the 'pure political economy' with the feeling that little if anything has been added to real knowledge"; and the same may be said of most of these controversies.

Of Adam Smith Dr. Haney lists these general criticisms:

That his philosophy was over-individualistic, tending toward too much restriction of government intervention in economic affairs;

That he was at bottom a materialistic thinker, giving too little weight to considerations of social welfare;

That this trait was made more harmful by his absolutism of theory.

[21]

Whether these criticisms are considered valid will depend, I think, on the extent to which one thinks of economics as distinct from and independent of social considerations. My own feeling is that they are mutually exclusive; but I am satisfied to let the question go unanswered here.

This is an introduction to this volume, not to the science of economics; but the reader should be warned that it is necessary to familiarize himself with certain words in the slang—or let us say technical vocabulary—of the economists.

In particular, a clear understanding of the word "wealth," as used by economists, is indispensable. That word is ordinarily associated in the public mind with large personal possessions or income; but its proper use in modern economics is as the generic term for all useful, desirable, and/or enjoyable goods.

Wealth is everything that is produced to meet any human need or demand, from matches to yachts, from bobby pins to country estates. Many natural products are wealth, provided only that they are limited in amount—water, for example, in an arid country.

One school of economists thinks that even services could well be classed as wealth. Under such a definition the postman delivering letters is producing wealth; so is the barber shaving customers.

But this is a strictly modern development in economic definition. Adam Smith did not use the word in this sense. By "wealth" in the title of his book he meant the "opulence and prosperity" of nations.

A second essential word is missing in the English language. For lack of a better, the economist uses the French "entrepreneur" —one who undertakes to carry on some economic activity. The English equivalents are "enterpriser" or "undertaker"; but the former has never gained favor, and the latter is out of the question for an obvious reason, although Adam Smith uses the word in both its economic and mortuary senses.

Finally, the reader should accustom himself to the concept of the "general welfare," or "common good," or "public interest," as distinguished from and often opposed to private interest. This should be obvious to everybody, but so frail is human nature, and so easily are all of us blinded by our own wants and ambitions, that we cannot always make the distinction, much less act on the altruistic plane that sometimes seems to be required.

This seems to take us into the field of morals and ethics, but in truth it is the sole foundation of economic health. Nine-tenths of the economic woes of nations come about through violation of the concept of the general good as superior to any private interest.

A few further remarks as to the use of words in this volume:

For the benefit of American readers, certain of Adam Smith's common words are replaced by the American equivalent. Thus "corn," which here would mean maize, is replaced by "grain." Adam Smith's "stock" becomes "capital." "Corporation," which in America is uniformly a limited liability joint-stock company, had quite a different meaning in 1776. This is the subject of an explanatory footnote at an appropriate point.

American readers should also bear in mind that the organization of agriculture in England and generally in Europe in 1776 was not that with which they are familiar. (Indeed, the organization of American agriculture is in some respects unique.)

In England in 1776 the last vestiges of the feudal tenure system had been abolished nearly ninety years before. But the typical organization of English agriculture was unchanged—the landlord, the entrepreneur farmer, the farm laborer. The "landed aristocracy" still owned vast areas; freehold tenure of land by a working farmer, the ideal of American agriculture, was the exception in England, not the rule.

Again, a far larger proportion of the population was engaged in agriculture then than now. Not in value of output, but in the relative number of people it employed, farming in England was a far more important element in the economy.

In condensing and re-writing the text of Adam Smith's classic, my work has necessarily been closely circumscribed; it has been that of an editor or specialist in language, not an economist.

But this introduction and the footnotes to the text are quite another matter; there it has been necessary to turn to the professional economists for guidance. Grateful acknowledgments are due to Dr. Thomas N. Carver, long my economic mentor, who ignored medical advice in reading and criticizing all the original material.

Still more am I indebted to Dr. Herbert F. Fraser, who generously gave the entire work the benefit of his experienced advice and criticism.

Finally, a word of thanks, at least, to Mr. Robert West Howard, in the course of an intense argument with whom the idea of the book was born, and who went so far as to promise to try to read it when printed.

Arthur H. Jenkins

Philadelphia
1948

PREFACE AND PLAN OF THE WORK

THE SCIENCE OF ECONOMICS may be separated into two general divisions, which may be named natural economics and political economics.

The first observes and records the behavior of the human race in obtaining its necessary subsistence, as it could reasonably be expected to be when not interfered with nor diverted by any outside force.

This, however, is a state which does not actually exist anywhere in the civilized world. The organization of a civilized society supposes some impairment of individual rights, and some restraint of natural individual impulses and desires. Until human nature becomes perfect, such restraints are necessary; the problem is to keep them within the narrowest possible limits.

The extent to which the members of the society can be left free to seek the betterment of their condition may be expected to be the measure of the happiness and prosperity of the whole society. For while almost any society can survive, in spite of the most absurd and pernicious political regulation, it will always remain less happy and prosperous than it might otherwise be.

In the first three books I shall therefore explain the productive powers of labor, the accumulation and employment of capital, and the relationships between the production of raw materials, commerce, and industry, as they must exist when interference of the state is not a determining factor.

The forces which often prevent human activities from following their natural direction are for the most part the efforts of law-makers, laudable in themselves, to promote the general welfare. Such political economics proposes two separate objects: first, to provide the state or commonwealth with a revenue sufficient for the public services; and secondly, to guide the people into activities which will provide a plentiful income or subsistence for themselves. It aims to enrich both the state and the people.

[25]

In the former effort, governments have been generally successful; in the latter, they have almost always failed.

In the fourth book I shall therefore explain the necessary expenses of the state, and the various methods which governments have devised for meeting these expenses.

In the fifth book, I shall examine the Mercantile System, under which particular classes of the people have persuaded legislatures to adopt absurd and unjust measures which, while intended to enrich the whole society, have generally enriched only those particular classes, to the injury of the whole.

In the last chapter of this book, I shall examine another system, which may be called the system of agriculture, and which, notwithstanding some faults, may be considered to be the most nearly sound of any which rests upon the interference of governments. This system, however, arose only from the speculations of a few men of great learning and ingenuity in France, and has never been adopted by any nation.

BOOK 1

How wealth is produced and distributed through the use of money, all income arising either from the wages of labor, the profit or interest of capital, or the rent of land; what causes fluctuations in and eventually fixes wages, profit, and rent; money and its price; and an explanation of value.

CHAPTER I

The division of labor (as illustrated in the making of pins) and how it is the basis of all improvement in industry and agriculture; how the vastly greater production of commodities resulting from this divison, and the exchange of them one for another, produces the wealth of the society.

THE GREATEST IMPROVEMENTS in the productive powers of labor, as well as the skill, dexterity, and judgment with which it is applied, seem to have been the effects of the division of labor.

This may be more easily understood, by considering how it operates in the manufacture of some particular article.

I take an example, therefore, from a very minor manufacture; but one in which the division of labor has very often been noted—the trade of pin-making.[1]

A workman not educated to this business, nor acquainted with the use of the machinery used, could scarcely, perhaps, with his utmost industry, make one pin in a day, and certainly could not make twenty. But in the way in which this business is now carried on, it is divided into a number of branches, of which the greater part are special skills.

One man draws out the wire, another straightens it, a third cuts it, a fourth points it, a fifth grinds it at the top for receiving the head; to make the head requires two or three distinct operations; to put it on is a skilled job, to whiten the pins is another; it is even a trade by itself to put them into the paper; and the making of one pin is thus divided into about eighteen distinct operations.

---

[1] While the manufacture of pins has advanced far beyond this description of A. S., it seems to illustrate his point sufficiently well, and I retain it.

I have seen a small pin factory where only ten men were employed, and where some of them consequently performed two or three of the operations. But though they were very poor, and their machines inferior, they could, by hard work, make among them about twelve pounds of pins a day.

There are in a pound upwards of four thousand pins of medium size. Those ten workmen, therefore, could make among them upwards of forty-eight thousand pins a day. Each man, therefore, might be considered as making four thousand eight hundred pins a day.

But if they had all worked separately and independently, they certainly could not have made twenty, perhaps not one pin a day apiece—not a thousandth part of what they are at present capable of turning out, through a proper division and combination of their different operations.

In every other art and manufacture, the effects of the division of labor are similar, although in many of them the labor cannot be so much subdivided nor simplified. The separation of different trades and employments from one another, seems to have been the result of this improvement. It is generally carried furthest in those countries which enjoy the highest degree of industry and improvement.

The labor which goes into the production of any single article is almost always divided among a great number of hands. How many different trades are employed in each branch of the linen and woolen manufactures, from the growers of the flax and the wool, to the bleachers and smoothers of the linen, or to the dyers and dressers of the cloth.

The nature of agriculture, indeed, does not admit of so many subdivisions of labor, nor of so complete a separation of one business from another. It is impossible to separate the business of the stock-raiser from that of the grain-grower so completely, as the trade of carpenter is commonly separated from that of the blacksmith. The spinner is seldom the same person as the weaver, but the man who plows, harrows, sows and harvests, is often the same man.

This impossibility of making so complete a division between the different branches of labor employed in agriculture, is perhaps the reason why the improvement of the productive powers of labor in this field does not always keep pace with its improvement in industry and trade.[2]

The wealthiest nations, indeed, generally excel all their neighbors in agriculture, as well as in manufactures; but they commonly are more superior in the latter than in the former. Their lands are in general better cultivated, and having more labor and expense put into them, produce more in proportion to the extent and natural fertility of the soil.

❦ A. S. here makes the first of his many digressions, to explain, not too clearly, why a highly-developed country like England or France can not produce and market grain any more cheaply than a backward country like the Poland of 1776. An important reason for this—the fact that in a thinly-populated country only the most fertile soils will be cultivated—A. S. does not mention.

This great increase of production, which, because of the division of labor, the same number of people can make, is owing to three different circumstances; first, to the increase of skill in each workman; secondly, to the saving of the time which is commonly lost in passing from one type of work to another; and lastly, to the invention of machinery which replaces hand labor, and enables one man to do the work of many.[3]

The greater skill of the workman necessarily increases the quantity of work he can perform; and the division of labor, by reducing every man's business to some one simple operation, and making this his sole employment, necessarily increases very much his dexterity.

A common smith, who, though accustomed to handle the hammer, knows nothing of making nails, if for some reason he has to attempt it, will scarce, I am assured, be able to make more than two or three hundred nails in a day, and those, too, very bad ones. Yet I have seen boys under twenty years of age who had never made anything but nails, who, when they exerted themselves, could each make upwards of twenty-three hundred nails a day.

The rapidity with which some of the operations of nail-

---

[2] Thorold Rogers questions this. Improvement of agriculture does keep pace, he says, when land is plentiful, labor scarce.

[3] A fourth advantage of the division of labor, not mentioned by A. S., is that it makes it possible to pay differing rates of wages for different operations, thus, on the whole, reducing the cost of production.

making and other manufactures are performed, has to be seen to be believed.

Secondly, the advantage which is gained by not having to shift from one sort of work to another, is much greater than one would suppose. It is impossible to pass very quickly from one kind of work to another, carried on at a different place, and with different tools. A country weaver,[4] who cultivates a small farm, must lose a good deal of time in passing from his loom to the field, and from the field back to his loom. When two trades can be carried on in the same room or building, the loss of time is no doubt much less, but even in this case, it is very considerable.

A man commonly saunters a little in turning his hand from one sort of employment to another. When he first begins the new work he is seldom very keen and hearty; his mind, as they say, does not go to it, and for some time he rather trifles than applies himself to good purpose.

This habit of sauntering and of indolent careless application, which is naturally, or rather necessarily, acquired by every country workman who has to change his work and his tools every half hour, and to apply his hand in twenty different ways every day, renders him almost always slothful and lazy. Not counting his lack of skill, this cause alone must always reduce considerably the quantity of work he can do.[5]

Thirdly, and lastly, everybody must be sensible how much labor is facilitated and abridged by the design and use of proper machinery. It is unnecessary to give examples.

I shall only observe, therefore, that the invention of all those machines seems to have been originally the result of the division of labor. Men are much more likely to discover easier and readier methods of doing something, when their whole attention is directed towards that single object, than when it is dissipated among many objects. But in consequence of the division of labor, the whole of every man's attention comes naturally to be directed towards some one very simple object.

It is only natural, therefore, that one or another workman

[4] The force of this illustration is partly lost since weaving ceased to be a one-man trade, carried on in the home; but many other examples will occur to the reader.

[5] Mill thinks that A. S. somewhat exaggerates the advantages of continuity of work.

should soon find out easier and readier methods of performing his own particular work, wherever the nature of it makes such improvement possible.

Whoever has been accustomed to visit factories where labor is highly subdivided, must frequently have been shown very pretty machines, which were the inventions of such workmen, in order to make their own work easier and quicker.

In the first steam engines, a boy was constantly employed to open and shut alternately the valve between the boiler and the cylinder, according as the piston went up or down. One of those boys, who preferred to play with his companions, observed that, by tying a string from the handle of the valve to another part of the machine, the valve would open and shut by itself, and leave him at liberty to divert himself with his play-fellows. Thus one of the greatest improvements that has been made upon this machine, since it was first invented, was the discovery of a boy who wanted to save his own labor.[6]

Not all the improvements in machinery, however, have been the inventions of those who used it. Many improvements have been made by the ingenuity of the machine-builders, when that trade came into being; and many others by those who are called philosophers or men of speculation, whose trade it is not to do anything, but to observe everything; and who, upon that account, are often capable of combining together the powers of the most distant and dissimilar objects.

In the progress of society, philosophy or speculation becomes, like every other employment, the sole or principal trade and occupation of a particular class of citizens. Like every other employment, too, it is subdivided into a great number of different branches, each of which gives occupation to a peculiar tribe or class of philosophers; and this subdivision of employment in philosophy, as well as in every other business, improves dexterity, and saves time.[7]

[6] This engaging story is, alas, largely mythical; if boy-power ever opened and closed the steam valve, it must have been in the earliest days of the steam engine, about 1700. But the point A. S. makes is valid.

[7] Cannan remarks that A. S. ignores here, and denies later on, that the division of labor permits workers to engage in tasks for which they have a natural aptitude. Some disadvantages of such specialization we shall have occasion to consider in another place.

It is the immense increase in the production of goods and services, resulting from the division of labor, which creates in a well-governed society, that universal prosperity which extends itself to the lowest ranks of the people.

Every workman has a great quantity of his own product for sale beyond what he himself consumes; and every other workman being in exactly the same situation, he is enabled to exchange a great quantity of his own goods for a great quantity, or, what comes to the same thing, for the money that will buy a great quantity of theirs.

He supplies them abundantly with what they have use for, and they recompense him as amply with what he has use for, and a general plenty diffuses itself through all the different ranks of society.

Observe the living conditions of the most common workman or day-laborer in a civilized and thriving country, and you will note that the number of people of whose industry a small part has been employed in supplying him, exceeds all computation.

The woolen coat, for example, which covers the day-laborer, coarse and rough as it may appear, is the produce of the joint labor of a great multitude of workmen. The shepherd, the sorter of the wool, the wool-comber or carder, the dyer, the scribbler, the spinner, the weaver, the fuller, the dresser, with many others, must all join their different arts in order to complete even this homely production.

How many merchants and carriers, besides, must have been employed in transporting the materials from some of those workmen to others over long distances! how much commerce and navigation, in particular, how many ship-builders, sailors, sail-makers, rope-makers, must have been employed in order to bring together the different drugs made use of by the dyer, which often come from the remotest corners of the world!

What a variety of labor is necessary, too, in order to produce the tools of the meanest of those workmen! To say nothing of such complicated machines as the ship of the sailor, the mill of the fuller, or even the loom of the weaver, let us consider only what a variety of labor is required to form that very simple machine, the shears with which the shepherd clips the wool.

The miner, the builder of the furnace for smelting the ore, the lumberman, the burner of the charcoal to be used in smelting, the brick-maker, the bricklayer, the workmen who attend the furnace, the mill-wright, the forger, the smith, must all of them join their different arts in order to produce them.

We might examine, in the same manner, all the different parts of the workman's dress and household furniture, the shirt which he wears next his skin, the shoes which cover his feet, the bed which he lies on, and all the different parts which compose it, the electric range [8] at which he prepares his victuals, the coal from which the current is made, dug from the bowels of the earth, and brought to him perhaps by a long sea and a long land carriage, all the other utensils of his kitchen, all the furniture of his table, the knives and forks, the plates upon which he serves up and divides his victuals, the different hands employed in preparing his bread and his beer, the glass window which lets in the heat and the light, and keeps out the wind and the rain, with all the knowledge and art requisite for preparing that beautiful and happy invention, without which these northern parts of the world could scarcely have afforded a very comfortable habitation, together with the tools of all the different workmen employed in producing those different conveniences!

If we examine, I say, all these things, and consider what a variety of labor is employed about each of them, we shall see that without the assistance and co-operation of many thousands, the very meanest person in a civilized country could not be provided, even according to what we falsely imagine the easy and simple manner in which he commonly lives.

Compared, indeed, with the more extravagant luxury of the great, his circumstances must no doubt appear extremely plain; and yet it may be true that the accommodation of a European prince does not always exceed that of an industrious and frugal peasant, as much as the accommodation of the latter exceeds that of many an African king, the absolute master of the lives and liberties of ten thousand naked savages.

[8] "the kitchen-grate"—W. N.

CHAPTER II

It is because of the natural human propen-
sity to trade and barter that the division of
labor probably arose in the beginning; it is
not found in any other animal.

THIS DIVISION OF LABOR, from which so many advantages are derived, is not originally the effect of any human planning.

It is the necessary, though very slow and gradual,
consequence of a certain propensity in human nature
which has in view no such extensive utility; the propensity to truck, barter, and exchange one thing for another.

Whether this propensity be ingrained in human nature, or
whether, as seems more probable, it be the necessary consequence
of the faculties of reason and speech, is not material. It is common
to all men, and is found in no other animals, which seem to have
no idea of such a thing as a voluntary contract.

Nobody ever saw a dog make a deliberate exchange of one
bone for another with another dog. Nobody ever saw one animal
indicate to another, this is mine, that yours; I will trade you this
for that.

When an animal wants to obtain something, either from a
man or from another animal, it has no other means of persuasion
but to gain the favor of those whose service it desires. A puppy
fawns upon its mother, and a spaniel tries by a thousand wiles to
attract the attention of its master at dinner, when it wants to be fed.

Man sometimes uses the same arts, and when he has no

other means of getting what he wants from his brethren, tries by every servile and fawning attention to obtain their good will. But this method will answer only part of the time. In civilized society he always needs the co-operation and assistance of great multitudes, while his whole life is not long enough to gain the friendship of more than a few.

Among almost all other animals each individual, when grown to maturity, is entirely independent, and in its natural state needs the assistance of no other living creature. But man has almost constant need for the help of his brethren, and it is in vain for him to expect it from their good-will only.

He will get along much better if he can interest their self-love in his favor, and show them that it is for their own advantage to do what he asks. Whoever offers to another a bargain of any kind, does exactly this. Give me what I want, and you shall have what you want, is the meaning of every such offer; and it is thus that we obtain from one another most of those good offices which we need.

It is not from the benevolence of the butcher, the brewer, or the baker, that we expect our dinner, but from their care for their own interest. We appeal not to their humanity but to their self-interest, and never talk to them of our own necessities, but of their advantages.

Thus nobody but a beggar chooses to depend chiefly upon the benevolence of his fellow-citizens, and even a beggar does not depend upon it entirely.

℃   As it is by negotiation, by barter, and by purchase, that we obtain from one another most of those mutual good offices which we need, so it is this same disposition to bargain which originally gives rise to the division of labor.

℃   In a tribe of hunters or shepherds a particular person may make bows and arrows, for example, with more ease and skill than do others. He finds he can exchange them for cattle or for venison, and eventually discovers that he can in this manner get more cattle and venison, than if he himself went to the field to catch them.

Merely out of his own interest, therefore, the making of bows and arrows grows to be his chief business, and he becomes a sort of armorer. Another excels in making the frames and covers of huts or tents. For this his neighbors reward him in the same manner with cattle or venison, until at last he finds it most profitable to devote himself entirely to this employment, and to become a sort of carpenter.

In the same manner a third becomes a smith; a fourth a tanner of hides or skins. And thus the certainty of being able to exchange his surplus production (over what he himself needs) for other goods and services, encourages every man to apply himself to a particular occupation, and to cultivate and bring to perfection whatever talent or aptitude he may possess for that calling.[1]

The difference of natural talents between different men is, in reality, much less than we usually think. The inequalities in genius which appear to distinguish men of different professions, is often not so much the cause as the effect of the division of labor. The difference between the most dissimilar characters, between a philosopher and a ditch-digger,[2] for example, seems to arise not so much from nature, as from habit, custom, and education.

When the two came into the world, and for the first six or eight years of their existence, they were, perhaps, very much alike, and neither their parents nor playfellows would notice any remarkable difference.

About that age, or soon after, they take up very different occupations. The difference of talents is then apparent, and widens by degrees, until at last the vanity of the philosopher is willing to acknowledge scarcely any resemblance.

But without the disposition to truck, barter, and exchange, every man must have supplied all his own wants by his own labor, and all laborers must have toiled at the same tasks.

As it is this disposition to bargain and exchange which forms those striking differences of talents, so it is this same disposition which renders that difference useful.

By nature a philosopher is not half so different from a ditch-digger, as a mastiff is from a greyhound, or a greyhound from a spaniel, or this from a shepherd's dog. Those different tribes of animals, however, though all of the same species, are of scarcely any use to one another. The strength of the mastiff is not

---

[1] M'Culloch thinks that A. S. underestimates the part that common sense and observation play in the division of labor. An intelligent savage who had no particular skill in tanning could hardly fail to notice that in a particular tribe the demand for tanned hides was large and the supply small, and would conclude that it would pay him to learn to be a tanner.

[2] "a common street porter."—W. N.

[38]

in the least aided or increased by the swiftness of the greyhound, the sagacity of the spaniel, or the docility of the shepherd's dog.

The effects of those different talents, for want of the power or disposition to barter and exchange, cannot be brought into a common stock, and do not in the least contribute to the better accommodation and convenience of the dog world. Each animal is still obliged to support and defend itself, separately and independently, and obtains no sort of advantage from that variety of talents with which nature has provided its fellows.

Among men, on the contrary, the most dissimilar geniuses are of use to one another. The different products of their different talents, by their general propensity to truck, barter, and exchange, are thrown, as it were, into a common stock, where every man may purchase whatever part of the produce of other men's talents he needs.

CHAPTER III

The larger the market, the more the great benefits of the division of labor have scope to operate; and the breadth of the market is largely determined by the quality of transportation.

It is the power to exchange and desire to exchange that results in the division of labor, but the extent of this division can never go further than the available market. Thus when the market is very small, no person can confine himself entirely to one occupation, because there would be no market for the surplus production he has for sale.

There are some occupations, therefore, which can be carried on only in large cities. A porter, for example, can make a living in no other place. A village is much too narrow a sphere for him; even an ordinary county-seat is scarcely large enough to keep him busy.

In the lone houses and very small villages which are scattered about in so desert a country as the Highlands of Scotland, every farmer must be butcher, baker, and brewer for his own family. Here we can scarcely expect to find even a smith, a carpenter, or a mason, within less than twenty miles of another of the same trade. The scattered families living eight or ten miles from the nearest of them, must learn to do many little pieces of work, for which, in more populous areas, they would call in those workmen.

Country workmen are almost everywhere obliged, therefore, to carry on all the different branches of industry that employ about the same materials. A country carpenter does all kinds of wood-work; all kinds of iron-work is done by a country smith.

It is impossible for this reason that there should be such a trade as a nail-maker in the remote parts of the Highlands of Scotland. At the rate of a thousand nails a day, a workman could make three hundred thousand nails in the year; but he could not sell a thousand nails a year—one day's work.

As by means of water transportation a more extensive market is opened up, so it is upon the sea-coast and along navigable rivers, that industry of every kind naturally begins to subdivide and improve itself. It is frequently not until much later that those improvements extend themselves inland.

Water transportation is cheaper, although not necessarily quicker. Six or eight men can transport by boat as much freight between London and Scotland in a given time as two hundred men and four hundred horses could do by land. Indeed, land transportation is so much more expensive that only commodities whose price is high in relation to bulk can move at all.[1]

As for distant parts of the world, there could be little or no commerce with them except for ships. What goods could bear the expense of land-carriage between London and Calcutta? Or if there were any so valuable as to be able to pay the cost, with what safety could they be transported through the territories of so many barbarous nations?

Those two cities, however, carry on a very considerable commerce with each other by sea, and by mutually affording a market, encourage each other's industry.

Since water-carriage is thus so superior, it is natural that the first improvements of art and industry should be made where this type of transportation opens the whole world for a market.

The inland parts of any country can for a long time have no other market for most of their products than the country which lies round about them, and separates them from the sea-coast, and the great navigable rivers. The extent of their market, therefore, can never be greater than the riches and populousness of that area permit.

In our North American colonies the plantations have constantly followed either the sea-coast or the banks of navigable rivers, and have scarcely anywhere extended themselves far from one or the other.

---

[1] This superiority of water-borne freight, where speed is not a factor, still continues, though perhaps not so markedly as in 1776.

❡   On the same principle, the most civilized nations of ancient times were on the shores of the Mediterranean. Egypt in particular enjoyed not only the commerce of the sea, but also of the many waterways of the lower Nile.

❡   It was so also in India and in China; but Africa, the interior of Western Asia, and in Europe such nations as Bavaria, Austria and Hungary, lagged behind, largely because their commerce had to move by land.

CHAPTER IV

As soon as men began to bargain and barter,
it immediately became necessary to find
some suitable material or substance by
which different values could be compared
and measured; hence the invention of metal
money, which by trial and experience was
found to be the most suitable and convenient
commodity for this purpose. And how gov-
ernments since the beginnings of history
have always dishonestly debased their own
money.

WHEN THE DIVISION OF LABOR has once been thoroughly established, it is but a very small part of a man's wants which his own
labor can directly supply. He supplies nearly all of them by exchanging that surplus part of his product, whatever it is, for such
parts of the products of other men as he needs.

But when the division of labor first began, this power of
exchanging must frequently have been very much clogged and em-
barrassed in its operations. One man, no doubt, would have more
of a certain commodity than he himself needed, while another had
less. The former consequently would be glad to sell, and the latter
to purchase, this surplus.

But if this latter should happen to have nothing that the
former stands in need of, no exchange could be made.

Let us say that the butcher has more meat in his shop than
he himself can eat, and the brewer and the baker would each of
them be willing to purchase a part of it. But they have nothing
to offer in exchange, except beer and bread, and the butcher already

has all of these he needs. No exchange can, in this case, be made between them, and they are all of them thus mutually less serviceable to one another.

In order to avoid such awkward situations, every prudent man must naturally have tried to so manage his affairs as to have at all times at hand, besides his own product, a certain quantity of some one commodity or other, such as he found by experience few people would be likely to refuse in payment for what they had for sale.

Many different commodities, it is probable, were successively thought of and tried for this purpose. In the rude ages of society, cattle are said to have been the common instrument of commerce; and, though they must have been a most inconvenient one, yet in ancient times we find things were frequently valued according to the number of cattle which had been given in exchange for them.

The armor of Diomede, says Homer, costs only nine oxen; but that of Glaucus cost a hundred oxen.[1]

Salt is said to be the common medium of exchange in Abyssinia; sea shells in some parts of the coast of India; dried cod at Newfoundland; tobacco in Virginia; sugar in some of the West Indies; hides or dressed leather in some other countries; and there is to this day a village in Scotland where it is not uncommon, I am told, for a workman to carry nails instead of money to the baker's shop or the ale-house.

In all countries, however, men seem at last to have been influenced by irresistible reasons to give the preference, for this purpose, to metals above every other commodity. Metals can not only be kept with as little loss as any other commodity—scarcely anything being less perishable than they are—but they can likewise, without any loss, be divided into any number of parts, and by melting those parts can easily be reunited again. And these are qualities which no other equally durable commodities possess, and which more than anything else make them fit to be the instruments of commerce and circulation.

The man who wanted to buy salt, for example, and had nothing but cattle to give in exchange for it, must have been

---

[1] In the time of Homer it is more likely that the armor was paid for with coins stamped with the figure of an ox; but in still earlier days the cattle themselves were probably used.

obliged to buy salt to the value of a whole ox at a time. He could seldom buy less than this, because he could hardly divide one ox without loss. But if he had some metal to give in exchange for it, he could easily proportion the quantity of the metal to the precise quantity of salt he needed.

Different metals have been used by different nations for this purpose. Iron was the common medium of exchange among the ancient Spartans; copper among the ancient Romans; and gold and silver among all commercial nations since Roman times.

Those metals seem originally to have been used in the form of bars, or ingots, without any stamp or marking. Thus we are told by Pliny that until the time of Servius Tullius, the Romans had no coined money, but used unstamped bars of copper. These rude bars, therefore, performed at that time the function of money.

The use of metals in this rude state had two very serious inconveniences; first to find their weight, and second their purity or fineness. In the precious metals, where a small difference in the quantity makes a great difference in the value, even the business of weighing requires very accurate weights and scales. The weighing of gold in particular is an operation of some nicety.

In the coarser metals, indeed, where a small error would matter less, accuracy is not so important. Yet we should find it exceedingly troublesome, if every time a poor man had occasion to buy or sell a nickel's worth of goods, he had to weigh the nickel.

The operation of assaying is still more difficult and tedious, yet equally important. But unless both these operations were performed, people must always have been liable to the grossest frauds, and instead of a pound weight of pure silver, or pure copper, might receive, in exchange for their goods, an unknown weight of some adulterated mixture of the coarsest and cheapest metals.

To prevent such abuses, to facilitate exchanges, and thereby to encourage industry and commerce, it was found necessary to affix a public stamp upon particular quantities of particular metals.

Hence the origin of coined money, and of those public offices called mints.

The first public stamps of this kind placed on the current metals, seem in many cases to have been intended to certify only what it was both most difficult and most important to find out, the goodness or fineness of the metal. It thus resembled the sterling mark which is at present affixed to silverware.

Being stamped only upon one side of the piece, and not covering the whole surface, it guarantees the fineness, but not the weight of the metal. Abraham weighs to Ephron the four hundred shekels of silver which he had agreed to pay for the field of Machpelah.

The revenues of the ancient Saxon kings of England are said to have been paid not in money but in kind, that is, in food and provisions of all sorts. William the Conqueror introduced the custom of paying them in money.[2] This money, however, was for a long time received at the English treasury by weight and not by tale.

The inconvenience and difficulty of weighing those metals with exactness eventually brought the invention of coins, of which the stamp, covering entirely both sides of the piece, and sometimes the edges too, was supposed to certify not only the fineness, but the weight of the metal. Such coins, therefore, were received by tale as at present, without the trouble of weighing.

The denominations of those coins seem originally to have expressed the weight or quantity of metal contained in them. In the time of Servius Tullius, who first coined money at Rome, the Roman *as* or *pondo* contained a Roman pound of good copper. It was divided like our Troyes pound into twelve ounces.

The English pound sterling in the time of Edward I., contained a pound, Tower weight, of silver of a known fineness. The Tower pound seems to have been somewhat heavier than the Roman pound, and lighter than the Troyes pound.

The French livre contained, in the time of Charlemagne, a pound, Troyes weight, of silver of a known fineness. The fair of Troyes in France was at that time frequented by all the nations of Europe, and the weights and measures of so famous a market were generally known and esteemed.

English pennies originally contained a real pennyweight of silver, the twentieth part of an ounce, or one two-hundred-and-fortieth of a pound. The shilling, too, seems originally to have been the denomination of a weight.

The proportion, however, between the shilling and the penny on the one hand, and the pound on the other, seems

2 "Absurd statement"—Cannan.

[46]

not to have been constant and uniform. But since the time of Charlemagne among the French, and from that of William the Conqueror among the English, the relation between the pound, the shilling, and the penny, seems to have been uniformly the same as at present, though the value of each has been very different.

This difference is the result of the avarice and injustice of princes and sovereign states, who, in every country, I believe, abusing the confidence of their subjects, have by degrees reduced the quantity of metal which had been originally contained in their coins.

The Roman *as*, in the latter ages of the Republic, was reduced to the twenty-fourth part of its original value, and, instead of weighing a pound, came to weigh only half an ounce. The English pound and penny contain at present about a third only; the Scots pound and penny about a thirty-sixth; and the French pound and penny about a sixty-sixth part of their original value.[3]

By those operations the governments concerned were enabled, in appearance, to pay their debts and fulfil their obligations. It was indeed in appearance only; for their creditors were really defrauded of a part of what was due them.

All other debtors in the nation were allowed the same privilege, and might pay with the same debased coin whatever they had borrowed in the old. Such operations, therefore, have always proved favorable to the debtor class, and ruinous to creditors.

It is in this manner that money (which in the modern world will include not only metal coins, but paper money and bank checks and drafts, used as substitutes for and symbols of money) has become in all civilized nations the universal instrument of commerce, by which goods of all kinds are bought and sold, or exchanged for one another.

[3] As will be shown in the last chapter of Book IV, this debasement of the coinage has generally been the result of piling up in warfare an unmanageable debt. Temporary debasement in wartime is almost universal. The last campaign of the Seven Years' War was fought by Frederick the Great, so-called, with debased metal money; the American Revolution with nearly worthless paper, much of it counterfeit; the French Revolution with paper assignats, convertible into nothing; the war between the States with greenbacks on both sides; both World Wars were fought principally on pen-and-ink entries in the books of commercial banks.

CHAPTER V

*A somewhat abstruse and rather long but
exceedingly important chapter explaining
the concept of "value." "The real price of
everything, what everything really costs, is
the toil and trouble of acquiring it. Labor
is the only universal and accurate measure
of value." Value that is measured in money
is not accurate, for money itself fluctuates
in price.*

THE WORD VALUE, it is to be observed, has two different meanings.
Sometimes it expresses the utility of some particular object, and
sometimes the power of obtaining other goods by its exchange.
The one may be called "value in use;" the other, "value in exchange."

The things which have the greatest value in use have
frequently little or no value in exchange; and on the other hand,
those which have the greatest value in exchange have frequently
little or no value in use.

Thus nothing is more useful than water; but it will
purchase scarcely anything; scarcely anything can be had in exchange for it. A diamond, on the contrary, has scarcely any value
in use; but a very great quantity of other goods may frequently
be had in exchange for it.

Value in use requires little explanation. But in order to
explain the principles which regulate the "value in exchange" of
commodities, I shall try to show first; what is the real measure of
this exchangeable value; or in other words what is the real price
of any commodity.

Secondly, what are the different parts of which this real price is composed.

And, lastly, what are the causes which sometimes hinder the market price, that is, the actual price of a commodity, from coinciding exactly with what may be called its natural price.[1]

In this explanation I must very earnestly entreat both the patience and attention of the reader: his patience in order to examine a detail which may perhaps appear unnecessarily tedious; and his attention in order to understand what may, perhaps, after the fullest explanation I am capable of giving it, appear still obscure. For the matter is of the greatest importance.

Every man is rich or poor according to the degree in which he can afford to enjoy the necessaries, conveniences, and amusements of human life.

But in a civilized country, where the division of labor has once thoroughly taken place, a man's own labor can supply him with only a very small part of these wants. The far greater part of them he must obtain from the labor of other people, and he will be rich or poor according to the quantity of that labor which he can command, or which he can afford to purchase.

The value of any commodity, therefore, to the person who owns it, but does not intend to use or consume it himself, is equal to the quantity of labor which it enables him to purchase or command.

---

[1] It is all too easy to become confused among the three closely-related words "cost," "price," and "value," particularly the last two.

Let us suppose that a misguided manufacturer decided that there was a market for a bustle, an article of feminine re-design much used about 1885. With the assistance of workmen and materials, he might produce a bustle at an outlay of $5.00; this is "cost." He might then advertise the bustle for sale for $12.50, allowing for overhead and selling costs and his profit; this is the "price." But since no human being could be induced to buy the contraption, its "value" (or "value in exchange") is zero.

The idea of cost is relatively simple, since cost can be expressed in money. It represents the wages and rent that have gone into making a given article or commodity, together with some other charges such as the interest on borrowed money.

Price, or real price, or natural price, is the sum of these costs, plus whatever profit the seller expects to make on the sale. It is what a thing ought to sell for. (Price is also expressed in terms of money, hence money has no price, though it has value.)

Value, or value in exchange, is what a thing will actually sell for; it may be the same as, or above or below the natural price; what it is, in money, determines whether the seller makes a large, a normal, or a small profit, or even sells at a loss.

Labor, therefore, is the real measure of the exchangeable value of all commodities.[2]

The real price of everything, what everything really costs to the man who wants to acquire it, is the toil and trouble of acquiring it.

What everything is really worth to the man who owns it, and who wants to dispose of it or exchange it for something else—or in other words its real "value in exchange"—is the toil and trouble which it can save to himself, and which it can impose upon other people.

What is bought with money or with goods is purchased by labor, as much as what we acquire by the toil of our own body. Labor was the first price, the original purchase-money that was paid for all things.

It was not by gold or silver, but by labor, that all the wealth of the world was originally purchased; and its value, to those who possess it, and who want to exchange it for something else, is precisely equal to the quantity of labor which it enables them to purchase or command.

But though labor is the real measure of the exchange value of all commodities, that value is commonly expressed not in quantities of labor but in money.

It is often difficult to determine the proportion between

[2] Thorold Rogers and other critics think that this famous sentence and the paragraphs that follow are, to say the least, unfortunately phrased, and confuse rather than enlighten. Labor, says Rogers, is one cause of value, but not the sole cause, and still less the measure of value. In the next sentence A. S. means "the real value of anything," not the real "price," he says; the price is the value of a given object at a given moment in relation to money.

All that is quite true, and these criticisms are valid, if one assumes that A. S. is here defining a theory of value; it is no doubt partly on this passage that critics classify him as a labor-cost-value economist.

But I find it hard to believe that A. S. had any such purpose. Here he is merely trying to show that exchanges of goods are exchanges of labor; the use of money, and the expression of value in terms of money, are only a useful human invention for purposes of convenience.

Probably these sentences might be better worded. But the idea is surely clear enough—when you sell a thing, you are really selling your own past labor; when you buy, you are buying somebody else's past labor; the cost of what you buy is the labor you put into what you exchange for it.

This has nothing to do with any definition or theory of value. Indeed, A. S. is here indulging in a philosophic discussion, rather than a precise proposition in economics.

two different quantities of labor. The time spent in two different sorts of work will not always determine this relationship. The different degrees of hardship endured, and of ingenuity exercised, must likewise be taken into account.

There may be more labor in an hour's hard work than in two hours' easy business; or in an hour's application to a profession which it took ten years to learn, than in a month's industry at an ordinary and obvious trade. It is hard, too, to find any accurate measure of hardship or ingenuity.

In exchanging the different products of different sorts of labor for one another, some allowance is commonly made for both. This is done, however, not by any accurate measure, but by the higgling and bargaining of the market, according to that sort of rough equality which, though not exact, is close enough for carrying on the business of common life.

But this comparison of one quantity of labor with another, to determine exchange values, is so difficult that it is rarely done. It is far easier to compare a commodity with a certain quantity of another commodity; which is what we know as barter. And barter, in turn, is greatly inferior to the exchange of the commodity for a known quantity of a certain other commodity, which is money.

Thus the butcher does not carry his beef or his mutton to the baker, or the brewer, in order to exchange them for bread or for beer; but he carries them to the market, where he exchanges them for money, and afterwards exchanges that money for bread and for beer.

It is natural and obvious to him, therefore, to estimate their value by the quantity of money, the commodity for which he immediately exchanges them; he expresses it by saying that his butcher's meat is worth threepence or fourpence a pound, not that it is worth three or four pounds of bread, or three or four quarts of beer.

Hence it follows that the exchange value of every commodity is generally estimated by the quantity of money which can be had in exchange for it, not the quantity of another commodity, much less the quantity of labor.

But money itself varies in its value, like all other commodities. Even gold and silver vary in their value, are sometimes cheaper and sometimes dearer, sometimes easier to buy and sometimes more difficult. This always depends upon the productivity of the mines which happen to be known at that particular period.

The discovery of the abundant mines of America, in the 16th Century, reduced the exchange value of gold and silver in Europe to about a third of what it had been. As it cost less labor to bring those metals from the mine to the market, so when they arrived they could purchase less labor; and this depreciation in their value, though perhaps the greatest, is by no means the only one known to history.

But as a measure of quantity, such as a yard or pound, which continually varied in its own quantity, could never be an accurate measure of the quantity of other things, so a commodity which is itself continually varying in its own value, can never be an accurate measure of the value of anything else.

But equal quantities of labor, at all times and places, may be said to be of equal value *to the laborer*. He has only one life to live, only so many total hours of productive labor to exchange for what he needs and wants

Labor alone, therefore, never varying in its own value, is alone the ultimate and real standard by which a person can estimate and compare the value of all commodities at all times and places.[3] It is their real price to him; money is their nominal price only.

But though equal quantities of labor are always of equal value to the worker, yet to the person who employs him they appear sometimes to be worth more, and sometimes less. He buys them sometimes with a greater and sometimes with a smaller quantity of goods, and to him the price of labor seems to vary like everything else. In reality, however, it is the goods which are sometimes cheap and sometimes dear.

In this popular sense, therefore, labor, like commodities, may be said to have a real and a nominal price. Its real price will be the quantity of the necessaries and conveniences of life which are given for it; its nominal price, the wages paid. The laborer is

---

[3] But while labor does not vary in value to the laborer himself, it fluctuates widely in its value in exchange; an hour's labor of one man may not produce the hundredth part of the value produced by another man in the same time. Thus a unit such as a man-hour could not possibly be used as a measure of value to replace money. Nor could the quantity of labor in an object be used to set the price, or value in exchange.

rich or poor, in proportion to the real, not the nominal price of his labor.

This exceedingly important distinction between nominal prices and real prices of goods and labor has sometimes led to surprising results.

The wide advance in nominal prices, following the discovery of the mines of America, has been noted above, and in general the value of gold and silver has tended to fall, while the quantity used in a given coin has also diminished.

Thus in England ancient rents which were payable in shillings and pounds have greatly fallen in real value. In Scotland and France, where the value of money has fallen still further, some old rents are now practically worthless.

℃ For this reason, old rents payable in grain or other commodities have preserved much more of their value, (and may even rise in real value), although they are subject to violent fluctuations from year to year.

Labor, therefore, it is evident, is the only universal, as well as the only accurate measure of value—the only standard by which we can compare the values of different commodities at all times and at all places.[4]

We cannot estimate, to be sure, the real value of different commodities from century to century by the quantities of money which were given for them, nor from year to year by the quantities of grain. But by the quantities of labor we can, with the greatest accuracy, estimate both from century to century and from year to year.

From century to century, grain is a better measure than gold and silver, because from century to century, equal quantities of grain will command the same quantity of labor more nearly than equal quantities of the precious metals. From year to year, on the contrary, money is a better measure than grain, because equal quantities of it will more nearly command the same quantity of labor.

But the matter of land rents is of much less importance than that of day-to-day buying and selling—the ordinary and universal transactions of human life. For these, value expressed in

[4] No, not even labor is an accurate measure. An hour of labor is the same hour in all places and in all centuries; but the productivity of an hour's labor may and does vary widely. Probably there is no really accurate and universal measure.

money is sufficient, being perfectly accurate at a given time and place, and the only thing that need be considered in transactions between distant places.

The merchant who ships goods from one market to another has nothing to consider but their money price, or the difference between the quantity of money for which he buys them, and that for which he hopes to sell them.

Half an ounce of silver at Hong Kong may command more labor and the necessaries and conveniences of life, than an ounce at London. A commodity, therefore, which sells for half an ounce of silver at Hong Kong may there be really dearer, of more exchange value to the man who owns it there, than a commodity which sells for an ounce at London is to the man who owns it at London. If a London merchant, however, can buy at Hong Kong for half an ounce of silver, a commodity which he can afterwards sell at London for an ounce, he gains 100% by the bargain, just as much as if an ounce of silver was at London exactly of the same value as at Hong Kong. And this is all he wants.

As it is the nominal or money price of goods, therefore, which finally fixes the profit or loss in all purchases and sales, and thereby regulates almost the whole business of common life in which price is concerned, we cannot wonder that most people pay far more attention to the money price than to the real price.

In the course of history, commercial nations have coined their money out of several different metals—gold for large payments, silver for purchases of moderate value, and copper, or some other coarse metal, for those still smaller.

They have always, however, considered one of those metals as more peculiarly the measure of value than others; and this preference seems generally to have been given to the metal which they first happened to make use of as a medium of exchange. Having once begun to use it as their standard, they have generally continued to do so, even after conditions had changed.

The Romans are said to have had nothing but copper money till within five years before the first Punic war, when they first began to coin silver. Copper, therefore, appears to have continued always the measure of value in that republic.

The northern nations which arose upon the ruins of the Roman empire, seem to have had silver money from the first beginning of their settlements, and not have known either gold or copper coins for several ages thereafter. There were silver coins in England in the time of the Saxons; but there was little gold coined until the time of Edward III, nor any copper until that of James I of Great Britain.

In England, therefore, and for the same reasons, I believe, in all other modern nations of Europe, all accounts are kept, and the value of all goods is generally computed in silver; so that when we mean to express the amount of a person's fortune, we seldom mention the number of gold guineas, but the number of pounds sterling which we suppose it is worth.

Originally, in all countries, I believe, a legal tender or offer of payment could be made only in the coin of the standard metal. In England, gold was not considered as a legal tender for a long time after it was coined into money.

The proportion between the values of gold and silver money was not fixed by any public law or proclamation; but was left to be settled by the market. If a debtor offered payment in gold, the creditor might either reject such a payment altogether, or accept it at such a valuation of the gold as he and his debtor could agree upon. Copper is not at present a legal tender, except in change for the smaller coins.

When this was the rule, the distinction between the metal which was the standard, and that which was not, was something more than a nominal one.

In process of time, and as people became gradually more familiar with the use of the different metals in coin, and consequently better acquainted with their respective values, it has in most countries, I believe, been thought necessary to fix by law the relationship between the metals. When this is done, the distinction between the metal which is standard, and that which is not, becomes little more than nominal.

If this legally-fixed ratio is changed, however, the change will cause some dislocation in buying and selling, and particularly in the settlement of contracts payable in fixed amounts of one or the other metal.

In reality, as long as any given ratio is maintained, the value of the most precious metal regulates the value of all coins.[5]

[5] No, says M'Culloch; even if the legal ratio was correctly calculated in the beginning, it soon becomes wrong as the real values of the metals fluctuate. Whereupon the undervalued metal is universally used, and the overvalued metal disappears.

Twelve copper pence contain half a pound, avoirdupois, of rather poor copper, which, before it is coined, is seldom worth sevenpence in silver. But as by the regulation twelve such pence are ordered to exchange for a shilling, they are in the market considered as worth a shilling, and a shilling can at any time be had for them.[6] The regulations of 1774 brought English gold coin as near perhaps to its standard weight as it is possible to bring the current coin of any nation; and the order to receive no gold at the public offices but by weight is likely to preserve it so, as long as that order is enforced.

The silver coin still continues in the same worn and degraded state as before the reformation of the gold coin. In the market, however, 21 shillings of this degraded silver are still considered as worth a guinea of this excellent gold coin.

℄ A. S. now proceeds to describe in detail the market price of silver in England, where in 1776 it was undervalued in relation to gold. The silver could not be given its full weight, for it would then be melted down for bullion; but it ought to be rated higher. In this case, if properly valued, silver bullion would fall below the mint price, since coins, both silver and gold, because of their convenience, are always worth a little more in the market than an equal weight of bullion.

The continual fluctuations in the market prices of gold and silver bullion arise from the same causes as similar fluctuations in other commodities. The frequent loss of those metals from various accidents by sea and by land, the disappearance in gilding and plating, in lace and embroidery, in the wear and tear of coin, and in that of silverware, require, in all countries without mines, a continual importation, in order to repair this loss and waste.

The merchant importers, like all other merchants, try to adjust their importations to what, they judge, is likely to be the immediate demand. With all their care, however, they sometimes over-do the business, and sometimes under-do it.

When they import more bullion than is wanted, rather than incur the risk and trouble of exporting it again, they will sometimes sell a part of it for something less than the ordinary or

[6] This is giving a little too much credit to government "regulation"; the real reason why overvalued copper and silver maintain their legal relationships is that the government itself will at all times accept them in payment of taxes, postage, or as loans, at the values set.

average price. When, on the other hand, they import less than is wanted, they get something more than this price.

But these fluctuations are temporary. When the market price of gold or silver bullion continues for several years together steadily above or below the mint price, we may be assured that this steady and constant divergence is the effect of something in the state of the coin, which renders a certain quantity of coin either more or less valuable than the precise quantity of bullion which it ought to contain.

The metallic currency of any country which uses such money extensively will be a good standard of value only when it is itself good, containing the precise quantity of metal it is supposed to. When there is any considerable loss of weight, the prices of commodities are obliged to adjust themselves to the quantity of metal which the coins are found, by experience, actually to contain.[7]

[7] It should be repeated here that the all-but-universal use of paper money and bank checks and drafts in this country makes the foregoing discussion of metal coinage of limited value in 1947. We have developed a better system. A gold eagle in circulation may be subject to the same physical vicissitudes as the English guinea; but a draft on a solvent bank, representing an enforceable claim on ten dollars of paper money, representing in turn an enforceable claim on a given number of grains of gold in a secure vault, can suffer no such inconvenience and loss.

CHAPTER VI

The money price of anything is made up of one or more of three elements—the wages of the labor that went into it, the profit (or interest) on the capital that was used, and the rent of land. All income therefore arises from one or two or all three of these sources.

IN THE EARLY and rude state of society, what fixed the relative values of different things must have been the relative amount of labor it cost to acquire them.

If among a nation of hunters, for example, it usually cost twice the labor to kill a beaver as to kill a deer, one beaver should naturally exchange for or be worth two deer. It is only reasonable that what is usually the product of two hours' labor should be worth double the product of one hour's labor.

If however, one type of labor should be more difficult or severe than the other, some allowance will naturally be made for this greater hardship; and the product of one hour's labor in the one way might frequently exchange for that of two hours' labor in the other.

Or if one type of labor required unusual dexterity and ingenuity, the esteem which men have for such talents would naturally give a higher value to their product than the mere time spent on it would justify.

In an advanced state of civilization, allowances of this kind, for superior hardship or superior skill, are commonly made in the wages of labor; and something of the same kind must probably have been found even in its earliest and rudest period.

In those days the whole produce of labor would belong to

the laborer; and the quantity of labor commonly employed in acquiring or producing any commodity would be the only rule that could fix its value in exchange.[1]

But as soon as capital has accumulated in the hands of individuals, some of them will naturally employ it in hiring other people, whom they will supply with materials and subsistence, in order to make a profit by the sale of their work, or by what their labor adds to the value of the materials.

In selling the article—that is, in exchanging it for money, for labor, or for other goods—over and above what is necessary to pay the cost of the materials, and the wages of the workmen, something must be included to compensate the undertaker of the work who risks his capital in this adventure.[2]

The value which the workmen have added to the materials, therefore, resolves itself into two parts, of which the one pays their wages, the other the profits of their employer on the materials he bought and the wages which he advanced.

He could have no interest and would not have bothered to employ them, unless he expected from the sale of their work something more than enough to replace his capital; and he could have no interest to employ much capital rather than little, unless he expected his profit to be large in proportion.

The profit of capital, it may perhaps be thought, is only a different name for the wages of a particular sort of labor, the labor of inspection and management. But profit is regulated altogether by the value of the capital employed, and under ordinary circumstances is greater or smaller in proportion to the extent of this stock.

℄   A. S. here proceeds to explain (not too clearly, indeed) that a business employing a given number of workmen, working with cheap materials, may take as much supervision and management as another business with the same payroll, but dealing in very expensive materials. In the two cases the labor of management will

[1] Yes, says Thorold Rogers, but only if the product is in *demand*. It is the strength of the demand that will determine whether any more labor will be employed in producing any more of it after that.

[2] Here, on the first occasion on which A. S. uses the term "undertaker," let us recall that such a person is the "entrepreneur" of modern economics. He is the "enterpriser," the man who undertakes some enterprise, at his own risk, collecting the profit if there is any, shouldering the loss if the enterprise fails. Hereafter, since no better word exists, he will be called "entrepreneur."

be the same, but in the case of the latter business, since it may require many times greater investment of capital for materials, the owner of the capital will expect a much greater profit. Plainly, in such a case, the extra profit (or interest) is paid not for the labor of extra management, but as a return on the extra capital employed.

❡ Sometimes, and this generally is the case in great modern corporations, the management, which is a form of highly-trained labor, is almost wholly separate from the owners of the capital, or stockholders.

In the price of commodities, therefore, the profits of capital form an element entirely different from the wages of labor, and regulated by quite different principles.

As soon as capital begins to be used in production, therefore, the produce of labor ceases to belong wholly to the laborer. He must share it with the owner of the capital which employs him, and the price of the commodity must include an additional amount to cover this profit.

Besides the wages of labor and the profit of capital, most commodity prices include a third element, the rent of land.[3]

As soon as the land of any country has all become private property, the landlords, like all other men, love to reap where they never sowed, and demand a rent even for its natural produce. The wood of the forest, the grass of the field, and all the natural fruits of the earth, which, when land was in common, cost the laborer only the trouble of gathering them, come, even to him, to have a price fixed upon them.

The man who cultivates the land must give up to the landlord a portion of what his labor collects or produces. This portion, or, what comes to the same thing, the price of this portion, constitutes the rent of land which must be included in the price of most commodities.[4]

---

[3] They do actually, but they need not necessarily, as Thorold Rogers points out. The price at which a commodity actually sells must exceed the labor cost and the profit on capital, before any rent will be collected or collectible.

[4] It should be emphasized here that these three elements—wages, profit, and rent—are found in the theoretical price (what A. S. calls the "natural price") of any article or commodity, and on the average will be found in the actual price, or exchange value; for unless these costs are repaid, on the average, the commodity will soon cease to be produced. But the actual selling price of a particular article at a particular time and place may not be the same as the theoretical price, because of variations in demand and supply.

The real value of all the three component parts or elements of price, it must be observed, is measured by the quantity of labor which they can, each of them, purchase or command.

In every society, however rude, the price of every commodity finally breaks down into one or another, or all three of those parts; and in every improved society, all three enter more or less into the price of most commodities.

In the price of grain, for example, one part pays the rent of the landlord, another pays the wages or maintenance of the "hired hands" employed in producing it, and the third pays the profit of the farmer.

In the price of flour or meal, we must add to the price of the grain, the profits of the miller, and the wages of his workmen; in the price of bread, the profit of the baker, and the wages of his workmen; and in the price of both, the labor of transporting the grain from the farm to the mill, and from the mill to the baker, together with the profits of those who advance the wages of that labor.

In the case of commodities of intricate nature and design, that part of the price which consists of wages and profit comes to be greater in proportion than that which consists of rent. In such a case, not only does the number of profits increase, but every subsequent profit is greater than the last, because the capital from which it is derived must always be greater.

The capital which employs the baker, for example, must be greater than that which employed the millers, because it not only replaces that capital with its profits, but pays, besides, the wages of the bakers, and the profits must always bear some proportion to the capital.[5]

Even in the most highly-developed countries, however, there are always some commodities of which the price consists of only two or even one of the three elements. There is no rent element, or almost none, in the price of deep-sea fish. The price of the little variegated pebbles picked up on the beaches of Scotland and sold for ornaments contains a labor element only.

But the whole price of any commodity must still finally resolve itself into some one or another, or all three of those

[5] This is not necessarily true in all cases; if by the nature of the business the machinery and plant of the last manufacturer is small, he may need no more capital in his business than the others.

elements, as whatever part of it remains after paying the rent of the land, and the price of the whole labor employed in raising, manufacturing, and bringing it to market, must necessarily be profit to somebody.

Furthermore, as the price or exchange value of every separate commodity is made up of these three elements, or some of them, it follows that the whole annual product of all labor in all countries (at least the salable part) must also be made up of the same three elements.

Wages, profit, and rent, are the three original sources of all income, as well as of all exchange value. All other income is ultimately derived from some one or other of these.

Whoever gets an income from a fund which is his own, must draw it either from his labor, from his capital, or from his land. The income derived from labor is called wages; that derived from capital, is called profit. That derived from capital by a person who does not employ it himself, but lends it to someone else, is called interest. It is the compensation which the borrower pays to the lender, for the profit which he has an opportunity of making by the use of the money.

Part of that profit naturally belongs to the borrower, who runs the risk and takes the trouble of employing it; and part to the lender, who has made it possible for him to make this profit.

The income which proceeds altogether from land, is called rent, and belongs to the landlord. The income of the farmer arises partly from his labor, and partly from his capital.[6] To him, land is only the instrument which enables him to earn the wages of this labor, and to make the profits of this capital.

All taxes, and all the revenue which is founded upon them, all salaries, pensions, and annuities of every kind, are ultimately derived from some one or other of those three original sources of income, and are paid either directly or indirectly from the wages of labor, the profits of capital, or the rent of land.

When those three different sorts of income are received by three different persons, it is easy to recognize and distinguish them; but when one person receives two or three kinds of income, they are often confused with each other.

[6] This is particularly the case in the United States, where the farmer is generally both capitalist and laborer; his earnings are partly profit and partly wages—what our economists call his "labor income."

For example, a gentleman farmer who farms part of his land may receive both rent and profit, but his whole income is generally considered as profit. If he does some of his work with his own hands, a part of his income is really wages.

A small gardener who does all his own work similarly receives rent, profit, and wages; but his income is more often called wages only. A very small manufacturer who does all his own work receives the same three kinds of income, but that income is commonly called profit.

Since in a civilized country the exchange value of nearly all commodities includes labor, rent, and profit, and not simply labor, so the whole annual produce will always be sufficient to purchase or command a much greater quantity of labor than what was employed in producing it and bringing it to market.

If the country were thereupon to employ all the labor which it could annually purchase, the quantity of labor employed would increase greatly every year, and the produce of every succeeding year would be vastly greater than the last.

But there is no such country; nowhere is the whole annual produce employed in maintaining the industrious. The idle everywhere consume a great part of it; [7] and according to the proportion in which it is divided between the industrious and the idle, its ordinary or average value must either increase, or diminish, or continue the same from one year to another.

[7] Not only the voluntary idle, of course, but the babies, the sick, and the aged.

CHAPTER VII

*The natural price of anything is the cost of
the labor, profit, and land rent that went
into bringing it to market; but what can
actually be got for it is quite another matter.
The actual market price or exchange value
may be below or above its natural price; it
is more often above it than below it.*

THERE IS IN EVERY COMMUNITY an ordinary or average rate both
of wages and profit in every different employment of labor and
capital. This rate is naturally regulated, as I shall show hereafter,
partly by the general circumstances of the community, its prosperity or poverty, its advancing, stationary, or declining condition;
and partly by the particular nature of each employment.

The same principles apply to the ordinary or average rent
of land, which is regulated partly by the general circumstances of
the community, partly by the fertility of the land itself.

These ordinary or average rates may be called the natural
rates of wages, profit, and rent, at that particular time and place.

When the selling price of any commodity is what is just
enough to pay the rent of the land, the wages of the labor, and the
profits of the capital employed in raising, preparing, and bringing
it to market, the commodity is then sold for what may be called
its "natural" price.

The commodity is then sold precisely for what it is worth,
or for what it really costs the person who puts it on the market;
and this includes his own profit. For if he sells it at a price which
does not allow him the ordinary rate of profit in his neighborhood,
he is evidently a loser by the trade; since by employing his capital
in some other way he might have made that profit.

His profit, besides, is his income, the proper source of his living. Just as, while he is preparing and bringing the goods to market, he advances to his workmen their wages, for their subsistence, so he advances to himself, in the same manner, his own subsistence, which he will generally adjust to the profit which he may reasonably expect from the sale of his goods. Unless the sale price yields him this profit, therefore, it does not repay him what the goods may very properly be said to have really cost him.

Though the price, therefore, which leaves the seller this profit, is not always the lowest at which he may sometimes sell his goods, it is the lowest at which he is likely to sell them for any considerable time; at least where there is liberty to change his trade as often as he pleases.

The actual price at which any commodity is commonly sold is called its "market price," and this may be above, or below, or exactly the same as its "natural" price.

The market price of every particular commodity is determined by the relation between the quantity which is actually brought to market, and the demand of those who are willing to pay the natural price of the commodity—that is, the total cost of the rent, labor, and profit, which must be paid in order to put it on the market.

Such people may be called the effective demanders, and their demand the effective demand; since it will be sufficient to attract the commodity to that market.

But the effective demand is not the same as the absolute demand. A very poor man may be said in some sense to have a demand for an expensive automobile; [1] he might like to have it; but his demand is not an effective demand, as the commodity can never be brought to market at a price he can pay.

When the quantity of any commodity which is brought to market falls short of the effective demand, not all of those who are willing to pay the whole value of the rent, wages, and profit, which must be paid in order to bring it thither, can be supplied. Rather than go without, some of them will be willing to pay more. A competition will immediately begin among them, and the market price will rise more or less above the natural price, according as the shortage, or the wealth and wanton luxury of the competitors, happen to affect the eagerness of the competition.

[1] "a coach and six."—W. N.

Among competitors of equal wealth and luxury the same shortage will generally cause a more or less eager competition, according as the acquisition of the commodity happens to be of more or less importance to them. Hence the exorbitant price of the necessaries of life during the blockade of a town, or in a famine.

When the quantity brought to market exceeds the effective demand, it cannot all be sold to those who are willing to pay the natural price. Some part must be sold at a lower price, and this low price must reduce the average price of the whole. The market price will sink more or less below the natural price, according as the surplus increases more or less the competition of the sellers, or according as it happens to be more or less important to them to get rid of the commodity quickly.

A surplus of perishable goods will cause much greater competition to sell than durable commodities; in the importation of oranges, for example, than in that of old iron.

When the quantity offered on that market is just sufficient to supply the effective demand and no more, the market price naturally comes to be approximately the same as the natural price. The whole quantity on hand can be disposed of for this price, and cannot be sold for more. The competition of the different sellers obliges them all to accept this price, but does not oblige them to accept less.

In the long run, the quantity of every commodity brought to market adjusts itself naturally to the demand. It is the interest of all sellers that the quantity never should exceed the effective demand; and it is the interest of everybody else that it never should fall short of supply.

If at any time supply exceeds the effective demand, some of the component parts of its price must be paid less than their natural rate. If it is rent, the interest of the landlords will immediately prompt them to withdraw a part of their land; and if it is wages or profit, the interest of the laborers in the one case, and of their employers in the other, will prompt them to withdraw a part of their labor or capital from this particular line of business. The quantity brought to market will soon decline, all the different parts of its price will rise to their natural rate, and the whole price to its natural price.

If, on the other hand, the supply should fall short of the demand, some of the component parts of its price must rise above their natural rate. This will increase production, and the quantity brought to market will soon be sufficient to supply the demand. All the different parts of its price will soon sink to their natural rate, and the whole price to its natural price.

The natural price, therefore, is, as it were, the central price, to which the prices of all commodities are continually gravitating. Different accidental circumstances may sometimes keep them supported a good deal above it, and sometimes force them down even somewhat below it.

But whatever may be the obstacles which keep them from this center of repose, they are constantly tending towards it.[2]

The whole total of industry annually employed in bringing a particular commodity to market, naturally adjusts itself in this manner to the demand. It naturally aims at bringing always that precise quantity which may be just enough, and not too much.

But in some lines of business the same quantity of industry will in different years produce very different quantities of the commodity, while others will produce always the same, or very nearly the same.

The same number of farmers, for example, will, in dif-

---

[2] This is as good a place as any to finish up the discussion of "value" and "marginal utility," already touched upon in Chapter V. It is, perhaps, hardly worth the space; the "marginal utility" theory occupies an area in economic literature out of all proportion to its practical importance.

But A. S. is often called a "labor-cost-value" economist, and I propose to devote some paragraphs to his defense. I suspect that those who make this charge cannot have read this chapter up to this point. But let us see what the economists are driving at.

Stated simply, the question is: supposing a thing has value-in-exchange, because it is scarce and somebody will buy it, how do you arrive at that value? If somebody will buy it, what determines the price they will pay? Why may a thing have different values at different times? In general, what measures value?

The effort of a whole school of economists, including Jevons in England, the "Austrian School," and others, was to find a formula to define and explain this amount of value. The result is the modern theory of "marginal utility," which says—again stated simply—that the value of any one unit of goods (or commodities) is fixed by and limited by its utility to the buyer; as he buys additional units, their utility to him decreases. The last unit he will buy does not attract him much—it has only "marginal utility." After that, he will not buy at all.

Now it will be seen that this explanation of value is by no means complete. Utility to the buyer explains *demand*, but it says nothing about *supply*; and it is the balance of demand and supply, like the two blades of a pair of scissors, that determines value. (*Footnote continued on following page.*)

ferent years, produce very different quantities of grain, milk, fruit, etc. But the same number of spinners and weavers will every year produce the same or very nearly the same quantity of cloth.[3]

It is only the average produce of the former type of industry which can be adjusted to the effective demand; its actual produce is frequently much greater and frequently much less than the average. Even though that demand should continue always the same, therefore, the market price will be liable to great fluctuations, will sometimes fall a good deal below, and sometimes rise a good deal above, the natural price.

In the latter species of industry, the production of equal quantities of labor being generally about the same, it can be more exactly suited to the demand. As long as that demand continues the same, therefore, the market price of the commodities is likely to do so too, and will not vary far from the natural price.

That the price of cloth is liable neither to such frequent nor to such great variations as the price of grain, every man's experience will testify. The price of the former varies only with the variations in the demand: that of grain varies not only with the

---

Mr. Martin Dooley, the sage of Archey Road, put the case neatly in his argument with the hat-maker. "The value of the hat," declared the workman, "is the six hours of work it took me to make it, at two dollars an hour." "The value of the hat," retorted Mr. Dooley, "is how much I want it."

Both were partly right. If Mr. Dooley at that moment had all the hats he wanted, he had passed the point of marginal utility as to hats. Another hat would be worth very little to him. But the same day his crony Mr. Hennessey might need and want a hat. And Mr. Dooley himself, when his best hat blew into the Chicago River that evening, might find utility in a new one next day.

In other words, "marginal utility" does explain *demand*, for that particular buyer, at that particular moment, very well. That is all there is to it. It is not a complete explanation of value.

The "marginal utility" explanation of demand, I have little doubt, would have been perfectly acceptable to A. S. There is nothing in W. N. that contradicts it. Emphatically, there is nothing in W. N. to indicate that A. S. agreed with the hat-maker, that the value of the hat was solely the labor that went into making it.

A. S. assumes that most things have value-in-exchange because of demand plus a degree of scarcity. He explains at length why the market price or sale value of anything that is in demand tends to move toward the natural or cost-of-production price. Value will be determined by the demand, as related to the supply, which in turn is related to the cost of production.

That is all A. S. has to say on the subject, but what more need be said?

[3] This is hardly true under 20th Century conditions, as spinning and weaving are carried on wholly in factories.

variations in the demand, but with the much greater and more frequent variations in the supply.

The fluctuations in the market price of any commodity fall chiefly upon those parts of its price which represent wages and profit. That part which represents rent is less affected by them.[4]

A rent paid in money is not in the least affected by them, but rent paid "in kind" or "on shares" fluctuates in value, according to all the occasional and temporary fluctuations in the market price. In settling the terms of the lease, the landlord and tenant endeavor, according to their best judgment, to adjust the rent, not to the temporary and occasional, but to the average and ordinary price of the produce.

But price fluctuations affect both the value and the rate of wages or profit, according as the market happens to be either overstocked or under-stocked with commodities or with labor; with work done, or with work to be done. A public mourning raises the price of black cloth (with which the market is almost always understocked upon such occasions), and augments the profits of the merchants who happen to have a good stock of it. It has no effect upon the wages of the weavers, for the market is under-stocked with cloth, not with labor; with work done, not with work to be done.

But it raises the wages of journeymen tailors, because the market is here under-stocked with labor. There is an effective demand for more labor, for more work to be done, than can be had.

Finally, it sinks the price of colored silks and cloths, and thereby reduces the profits of the merchants who have any considerable stock of them on hand. It sinks, too, the wages of the workmen employed in preparing such commodities, for which all demand is stopped for six months, perhaps for a year. The market is here over-stocked, both with commodities and with labor.

But though the market price of every particular commodity is in this manner continually gravitating, so to speak, towards the natural price, yet sometimes particular causes, sometimes natural, and sometimes regulations of law, may keep up the market price, for a long time together, a good deal above the natural price.

[4] Thorold Rogers remarks that occasional or unusual fluctuations in price affect profit directly; but frequent or habitual fluctuations take the character of a foreseeable risk, and count as a cost of production.

When by an increase in the demand, the market price of some particular commodity happens to rise a good deal above the natural price, those who supply that market generally try to conceal this change. If it became known, their abnormal profit would tempt so many new rivals into the field, that the market price would soon be reduced to the natural price, and perhaps for some time even below it.

If the market is at a great distance from the residence of those who supply it, they may sometimes be able to keep the secret for several years together, and may during that time enjoy their extraordinary profits without any competition.

Secrets of this kind, however, it must be acknowledged, can seldom be long kept; and the extraordinary profit can last very little longer than they are kept.

Secrets in manufacturing are capable of being kept longer than secrets in trade. A dyer who has developed a particular color with materials which cost only half the price of those commonly used, may, with good management, enjoy the advantage of his discovery as long as he lives, and even leave it as a legacy to his posterity.

His extraordinary gains arise from the high price which is paid for his private labor, and properly consist in the high wages of that labor. But they are commonly considered as extraordinary profits of capital.[5]

Such enhancements of the market price are evidently the effects of accidental circumstances, of which, however, the operation may sometimes last for many years together.

Some natural products require such peculiarities of soil and situation, that all the suitable land in a great country may still not be sufficient to supply the demand.

The whole supply, therefore, may be sold to those who are willing to give more than the natural price. Such commodities may continue for whole centuries together to be sold at this high price; and that part of the price which represents the rent of land is in this case the part which is generally paid for above its natural rate. Such are the rents of some vineyards in France which have special qualities of soil or climate. As such advantages sometimes cannot

---

[5] This point seems hardly worth stressing; for as M'Culloch points out, such profits arise from a simple monopoly, by which the dyer sells "at the market" a dye that only he can produce cheaply.

be duplicated, the high market price and abnormally high rent which results may continue indefinitely.

A monopoly granted to an individual or to a trading company by law has the same effect as a secret in trade or manufacture. The monopolists, by keeping the market constantly undersupplied, by never fully meeting the effective demand, sell their commodities much above the natural price, and raise their emoluments, whether they consist in wages or profit, greatly above their natural rate.

A monopoly price is always the highest which can be got.[6] The natural price, or the price under free competition, on the contrary, is the lowest which can be accepted, not for every individual transaction indeed, but for any considerable time together. The one is the highest which can be squeezed out of the buyers, or which, it is supposed, they will consent to pay; the other is the lowest which the sellers can commonly afford to take, and at the same time stay in business.

The exclusive privileges granted by law to trade associations, statutes of apprenticeship, and all those laws which in particular employments limit the competition to a smaller number than might otherwise go into them, have the same tendency, though in a less degree.

They are a sort of enlarged monopolies, and may frequently, for ages together, and in whole classes of business, keep up the market price of particular commodities above the natural price, and maintain both the wages of the labor and the profits of the capital employed in them somewhat above their natural rate.

By contrast, the market price of any particular commodity, though it may continue long above, can seldom continue long below, its natural price. Whenever the price fell below the natural rate, the persons whose interest it affected would immediately feel the loss, and would immediately withdraw either so much land, or so much labor, or so much capital, from being employed in it, that the supply would soon be no more than suf-

---

[6] Not always, but generally.—M'Culloch. Thorold Rogers agrees and adds that government monopolies, (being neither flexible nor particularly intelligent) may at times even charge less than the price that could be got. On the other hand, he says, it is doubtful that unlimited competition will always produce the lowest prices; it is likely that London cab fares would be cheaper if there were not such an excessive number of cabs.

ficient to supply the demand. Its market price, therefore, would soon rise to the natural price. This at least would be the case where there was perfect liberty.

The same statutes of apprenticeship and other trade laws indeed, which, when a manufacture is prosperous, enable the workman to raise his wages a good deal above their natural rate, sometimes oblige him, when it decays, to let them fall a good deal below it. As in the one case they keep many people out of his trade, so in the other they keep him out of other trades.

The effect of such regulations, however, is not nearly so durable in sinking the workman's wages below, as in raising them above, their natural rate. Their operation in the one way may endure for many centuries, but in the other it can last no longer than the lives of some of the workmen who were bred to the business in the time of its prosperity.

When they are gone, the number of those who are afterwards educated to the trade will naturally adjust itself to the effective demand.

It would be only a government with powers as violent as those of India or ancient Egypt (where every man was bound by a principle of religion to follow the occupation of his father, and was suppose to commit a horrid sacrilege if he changed it for another), which could in any particular employment, and for several generations together, sink either the wages of labor or the profits of capital below their natural rate.

The natural price itself varies with the natural rate of each of its component costs—wages, profit, and rent; and these costs vary according to the prosperity or depression of the community, and its advancing, stationary, or declining condition.

I shall, in the following chapters, endeavor to explain, as fully and distinctly as I can, the causes of these variations.

CHAPTER VIII

What regulates wages? Originally the laborer, working only for himself, received as wages the whole product; but when the laborer works for someone else, he receives only a part of the product; that part is determined by fixed laws of human behavior, and not (as sometimes appears) by bargaining or by government intervention. In a prosperous nation real wages tend to **rise.**

RETURNING ONCE MORE to the original state of things, before land was privately owned or capital began to accumulate, the whole product of labor belonged to the laborer himself. He had neither landlord nor employer to share it with him.

If this state had continued, the wages of labor would have increased steadily, as production became more efficient through the division of labor. All things would gradually have become cheaper —that is, would have been produced by a smaller quantity of labor.

But though all things would have become cheaper in reality, being produced more easily and quickly, some things might appear to have risen in price.

Let us suppose, for example, that in most occupations a day's labor could produce ten times the quantity of work which it had done originally; but that in one particular occupation a day's labor could produce only twice the quantity it had done before.

In exchanging the product of a day's labor in the majority of occupations for that of a day's labor in this particular one, ten times the total work in the former would exchange for only twice as much of the latter it formerly did. The latter product would be twice as cheap, but the former, being ten times as cheap, would appear to have fallen to a fifth of its value in comparison.[1]

But the original state of things, in which the laborer collected the whole product of his own labor, came to an end with the private appropriation of land and the accumulation of capital. It ended, therefore, long before the chief improvements were made in the productive powers of labor.

As soon as land becomes private property, the landlord demands a share of whatever the tenant makes out of it. His rent makes the first deduction from the product of the labor employed upon land.[2]

It often happens that the person who tills the ground has not enough reserves to maintain himself till he reaps the harvest. His maintenance must therefore be advanced to him by someone with capital, and the profit on this advance makes a second deduction from the product.

The product of almost all other labor is liable to the same deduction of profit. In all arts and manufactures most workmen stand in need of a master to advance them the materials of their work, tools to work with, a building to work in, and their wages and maintenance, until the product is finished and sold. The employer shares in the product of their labor, or in the value which it adds to the materials upon which it is bestowed; and in this share consists his profit.

An independent workman using his own capital only, receives both wages and profit, but such cases are rare. In every part of Europe, twenty workmen are employed for one that is independent.

The common wages of labor are generally the result of a contract or agreement between the workman and the owner of capital, whose interests are by no means the same. The workmen

---

[1] The point is abstruse, and perhaps of no great importance anyway.

[2] The landlord may demand rent, says Thorold Rogers, but will not necessarily get it. No rent can be paid (except out of savings) unless the sale price of the product exceeds the labor and capital cost of production. In other words, rent is paid only out of gross profit, realized or expected.

wish to get as much, the employers to pay as little as possible. The former are disposed to combine in order to raise, the latter in order to lower wages.

It is not, however, difficult to foresee which of these two parties will usually have the advantage in the dispute, and force the other into a compliance with their terms. Employers, being fewer in number, can combine much more easily; and the law, besides, authorizes, or at least does not prohibit their combinations, while it prohibits those of the workmen.[3]

In all such disputes the employers can hold out much longer. A landlord, a farmer, a master manufacturer, a merchant, though they did not employ a single workman, could generally live a year or two upon the stocks which they have already acquired.

Many workmen could not exist a week, few could exist a month, and scarcely any a year without employment. In the long run, the workman is as necessary to his employer as his employer is to him, but the necessity is by no means so urgent.[4]

We rarely hear, it ·has been said, of combinations of employers, though frequently of those of workmen. But whoever imagines that employers rarely combine, is as ignorant of the world as of the subject. Employers are always and everywhere in a kind of tacit, but constant and uniform agreement not to raise wages of labor if they can help it. To violate this understanding is everywhere most unpopular, and a sort of reproach among his neighbors and equals.

We seldom, indeed, hear of such combinations, because they are so common as to be taken for granted. There are even secret combinations to depress wages.

Such combinations, however, are frequently resisted by a defensive combination of the workmen; who sometimes combine of their own accord to raise the price of their labor. Their usual claims are, sometimes the high price of food; sometimes the great profit which their employers are making.

[3] The British anti-union laws were repealed in 1824.

[4] In this discussion and that which immediately follows, it is obvious that the positions of employers and employed have been almost exactly reversed since the day of A. S. In the United States in 1947, it is employers who are forbidden by law to combine, and workmen who are encouraged by law to do so. Probably this is on the whole a gain; a much greater gain would be for the government to abandon such interference altogether.

But whether their combinations are offensive or defensive, they are always abundantly heard of. In order to bring the dispute to a speedy decision, they always have recourse to the loudest clamor, and sometimes to the most shocking violence and outrage. They are desperate, and act with the folly and extravagance of desperate men, who must starve or frighten their employers into an immediate compliance with their demands.[5]

The employers upon these occasions are just as clamorous upon the other side, demanding protection of the courts, and the rigorous execution of those laws which have been enacted with so much severity against combinations of servants, laborers, and journeymen. The workmen, accordingly, very seldom derive any advantage from the violence of these tumultuous combinations.

But though in disputes with their workmen, employers must generally have the advantage, there is a certain level below which it seems impossible to reduce, for any considerable time, the ordinary wages even of the lowest grade of labor.

A man must always live by his work, and his wages must at least be sufficient to support him. They must in most cases do more than that; for otherwise it would be impossible for him to bring up a family, and the nation would quickly begin to lose population.

It seems fairly certain, that, in order to bring up a family, the labor of the husband and wife together must, even in the lowest grades of common labor, be able to earn something more than what is precisely necessary for their own support; but how much more, I cannot say.

Under some conditions, however, the laborers have an advantage, and can raise their wages considerably above this absolute minimum.

When in any country the demand for those who live by wages is continually increasing, when employment grows year by year, workmen have no occasion to combine in order to raise their wages. The scarcity of hands creates competition among employers, who bid against one another, and thus voluntarily break through the usual gentlemen's agreement not to raise wages.

The demand for wage-earners, it is evident, can increase only in proportion to the increase of the money available for the

[5] A. S. here exceeds his customary moderation and good humor; labor disputes are not "always" noisy, desperate, foolish, and extravagant.

payment of wages. This money, or "wage-fund," is of two kinds—surplus income and surplus capital.[6]

When a wealthy man has more income than he thinks sufficient to maintain his own family, he employs the surplus or part of it in maintaining servants. Increase this surplus, and he will naturally increase the number of those servants.

When an independent workman, such as a shoemaker, has more capital than he needs to buy the materials of his own work, and to maintain himself until he can sell, he naturally employs one

[6] Here we meet for the first time the celebrated "wage-fund," considered by economists one of three major theories of W. N. which criticism has demolished. An entire chapter of Dr. Haney's "History of Economic Thought" is given to "the downfall of the wage-fund theory."

Any controversy important enough to rate such attention from all top economists is important enough to be explained here, at least in outline.

Let me say at once that A. S. is not directly responsible for the wage-fund idea in its extreme form; he was more the innocent bystander; and if the general reader wishes to drop the subject at this point, I think he may do so with an easy conscience.

The form which the theory took, developed and expanded by later economic writers, was in brief that wages depend solely on a fixed fund of circulating capital. James Mill (father of J. S. Mill), expressed it thus: "Other things remaining the same, if the ratio which capital and population bear to each other remains the same, wages will remain the same; if capital increases in its ratio to population, wages will rise."

This sounds harmless enough, but the logical conclusion to be drawn is that it is useless for the society to concern itself with wages at all. If capital is increased at the highest possible rate, and population does not increase in proportion, wages will automatically rise as far as they can, without further effort or attention.

The harm of the doctrine, in other words, was not in the formula but in its practical application. But the critics pounced on the theory itself, as well they might.

The fund, they pointed out, in the form of money or goods available for maintaining labor while it is producing, need not necessarily be used for that purpose; there is a demand for a certain quantity or volume of labor, but no one is anxious to expend a certain amount of capital for wages simply for the sake of spending it; the employer hires as many men as he thinks he can use profitably, and pays them what he must; in continuous production, much the largest part of the capital paid in wages comes from the sale of the product previously produced, hence wages are really dependent not on any fixed wage-fund, but on the demand for the product and the wealth available for buying it; furthermore, a fixed wage-fund is impossible anyway, since it is the aggregate of the resources of many employers, all of which fluctuate; the productivity of labor, as well as the number of workmen, affects the amount of money that must be paid out in wages; finally, an increase in fixed capital—buildings, machinery, and equipment—may greatly reduce the wage expenditure.

All of these criticisms have force, and James Mill's wage-fund theory, as stated, simply will not hold water.   *(Footnote continued on following page.)*

or more helpers, in order to make a profit by their work. Increase this surplus, and he will naturally increase the number of his workmen.

The demand for wage-earners, therefore, necessarily increases with the increase of income or capital, or both, and cannot possibly increase without it.

But an increase of income and capital is only another name for the increase of national wealth. Hence the demand for wage-earners naturally increases with the increase of national wealth, and cannot possibly increase without it.

It is not the actual greatness of national wealth, but its continual increase, which causes high wages. It is not, accordingly, in the richest countries, but in the most thriving, or in those which

---

Let us see what A. S. says. In this particular chapter he develops the wage-fund idea principally to show that in different countries wages are high, moderate, or low, according as the countries are themselves flourishing, stationary, or declining. Later he takes up, in various places and connections, the relationships between capital and wages. He refers ten or a dozen times to a fund "destined for the payment of wages," or for "the maintenance of labor." What does he mean by that?

I am of the opinion that the chief difficulty in construing these passages in W. N. arises not from faulty reasoning, but from a fortuitous shift in the use of words.

After all, it is undeniable that there is some aggregate of capital, made up from a variety of sources, from which wages are actually advanced to workmen, pending the sale of their product; there seems no reason why this should not be called a wage-fund; the size of that fund certainly bears some relation to the total volume of employment. But a question remains; what does A. S. mean by a fund "destined" for the payment of wages?

If he means a sum of money or equivalent goods *set aside on the books and certain to be used for that purpose,* that is one thing. If he means something else, that is another story.

What he actually meant, I think, is a fund "available" for such payment, as we would put it; I think we in 1947 give "destined" a more restricted and specific meaning than it had in A. S.'s vocabulary.

At all events, wherever A. S. wrote "destined," throughout the book, I have changed the word to "available," and I find no passage where the argument is not thereby made clearer and more reasonable.

On the whole, the reader will be safe in assuming, here as elsewhere, that A. S. knew exactly what he meant, and was not far from the truth. The worst that can be said is that his use of words is archaic, or careless, or both.

As Professor F. W. Taussig says in summing up the wage-fund controversy, there is certainly some connection between real capital and real wages; wage earners do get their money wages, and hence their share of real income, from what the capitalist-employer finds it profitable to himself to turn over to them. Most of the wage-fund theory in W. N. boils down to just that.

are growing rich the fastest, that the wages of labor are highest.

England is certainly, at present, a much richer country as far as capital is concerned than any part of North America. The wages of labor, however, are much higher in North America than in any part of England.

In the province of New York, common laborers as well as skilled workmen earn higher wages than in London, and wages are said to be as high in the other colonies as in New York.

By contrast, the price of food is everywhere in North America much lower than in England. A shortage has never been known there, and even in the worst seasons, they have always had enough for themselves, though less for export.

If the money price of labor, therefore, be higher than in the mother country, its real price, the real command of the necessaries and conveniences of life, the "real wages," must be higher still.

But though North America is not yet so rich as England, it is much more thriving, and advancing much faster in the further acquisition of riches.

This can easily be shown by the increase in population, which is the most decisive measure of the prosperity of any country.

In Great Britain, and most other European countries, the population is not supposed to double in less than five hundred years. In the British colonies in North America, it has been found that it doubles in twenty or twenty-five years.

℃ This A. S. attributes to the early marriage and large families usual in new countries, where children and their labor are regarded as assets. But no matter how fast the population increases, the demand for labor, and the wage-fund available for paying it, increases still faster.

Though the capital of a country should be very large, yet if it has been long stationary, we must not expect to find the wages of labor very high in it. If the funds available for the payment of wages, the incomes and capital of its inhabitants, have continued for several centuries about the same, the number of laborers employed each year could easily supply, and even more than supply, the number wanted the following year.

There could seldom be any labor shortage, nor would employers be obliged to bid against one another in order to get them.

[79]

Workmen, on the contrary, would, in this case, naturally multiply beyond the available jobs. There would be a constant scarcity of jobs, and the laborers would be obliged to bid against one another in order to get them.

China has been long one of the richest, that is, one of the most fertile, best cultivated, most industrious and most populous countries in the world.[7] It seems, however, to have been long stationary.

Marco Polo, who visited it about 1275, described its cultivation, industry, and swarming population, almost in the same terms in which they are described by travelers today. These all agree as to the very low wages of labor, and as to the extreme difficulty which a laborer finds in bringing up a family in China. The poverty of the rank and file of Chinese far surpasses that of the most beggarly nations in Europe. Marriage is encouraged in China, not because children are profitable, but because they can so easily be got rid of.

In all great towns several are every night exposed in the street, or drowned like puppies in the water. The performance of this horrid office is even said to be the avowed business by which some people make their living.

China, however, though it may perhaps stand still, does not seem to go backward. Its towns are not deserted, its cultivated lands are not neglected.

The same or very nearly the same annual labor must therefore continue to be performed, and the wage-fund must not, consequently, be sensibly less.

But it would be otherwise in a country where the surplus income and capital available for the maintenance of labor were sensibly decaying. Every year the demand for servants and workmen in all lines would be less than it had been the year before.

Many who had been bred in the upper classes, not being able to find employment in their own professions, would be glad to seek it in the lowest.

The lowest classes, being not only overstocked with its own workmen, but with the overflowings of all the other classes, the

---

[7] It is doubtful if the word "richest" is the proper one to use here. China is rich neither in income nor fixed capital, and it is these that make a "rich" country, not the population or production per acre of land.

competition for jobs would be so great as to reduce the wages of labor to a miserable minimum.

Many would not be able to find employment even on these hard terms, but would either starve, or be driven to begging or crime. Want, famine, disease, and high mortality would immediately result, and thence would extend themselves to all the upper classes, until the number of inhabitants in the country was reduced to what could easily be maintained by the income and capital which remained, and which had escaped the calamities which had destroyed the rest.

This is perhaps nearly the present state of India, and of some of the other English settlements in the East Indies.

The contrast between the genius of the British constitution which protects and governs North America, and that of the mercantile company which oppresses and domineers in the East Indies, cannot perhaps be better illustrated than by the different state of those countries.[8]

The liberal reward of labor, therefore, as it is the necessary effect, so it is the natural symptom of increasing national wealth. The scanty living of the laboring poor, on the other hand, is the evidence that things are at a stand, and their starving condition that things are fast going backwards.

℄ A. S. here proceeds to appraise the situation in Great Britain. There, in 1776, wages were above the bottom rate, as proved by the fact that (1) there was a difference between wages in summer and in winter; (2) that wages did not fluctuate with changes in the price of food; (3) that wages varied more from place to place than did the price of food; and (4) that wages frequently fluctuated in the opposite direction from the price of food.

℄ He devotes several pages to examples of these movements of wages and food prices in various parts of England and Scotland, including the calculation of Gregory King in 1688 that the annual income of a workman's family of 3½ persons was about fifteen pounds.

The price of labor, it must be observed, cannot be ascertained very accurately, different prices being often paid at the same place and for the same kind of labor, not only according to the

[8] A. S. was no friend of the great East India Company, which he detested both as a monopoly and as an evil and corrupt monopoly.

[81]

different abilities of the workmen, but according to whether the employer is easy-going or hard-boiled.[9]

Where wages are not regulated by law, all that we can pretend to determine is what are the most usual; and experience seems to show that law can never regulate them properly, though it has often claimed to do so.

The real income of labor, the real quantity of the necessaries and conveniences of life which it can buy the laborer, has increased perhaps in a still greater proportion than its money price, in the last century. Not only grain has become somewhat cheaper, but many other foods have become a great deal cheaper. Potatoes, for example, do not at present cost half the price which they used to do thirty or forty years ago. The same thing may be said of clothing and furniture.

Soap, salt, candles, leather, and fermented liquors, indeed, cost a good deal more, chiefly as a result of the taxes which have been laid upon them. The quantity of these which the working class will consume, however, is so very small, that the increase in their price does not neutralize the lower prices of other things.

The common complaint that luxury extends itself even to the lowest ranks of the people, and that the poor will not now be contented with the same food, clothing and lodging which satisfied them in former times, may convince us that it is not the money price of labor only, but its real wages, which have advanced.

Is this improvement in the circumstances of the poor to be regarded as an advantage or a disadvantage to the whole community?

The answer seems abundantly plain. Servants, laborers and workmen of all kinds, make up by far the greatest part of every great political society. But what improves the circumstances of the great majority can surely never be injurious to the whole. Surely no society can be called flourishing and happy as long as the far greater part of the members are poor and miserable.

The population of a nation is closely related to its wealth or poverty.

Poverty, though it no doubt discourages marriage, does not always prevent it. It seems even to be favorable to generation. A half-starved Highland woman frequently bears more than twenty children, while a pampered fine lady is often incapable of

[9] "The easiness or hardness of the masters."—W. N.

[*82*]

bearing any, and is generally exhausted by two or three. Barrenness, so frequent among women of fashion, is very rare among those of lower station.

℃   But poverty is unfavorable to the successful rearing of children, and the high birth-rate is thus balanced by an equally high death-rate, particularly among babies. Thus a very low standard of subsistence sets definite limits to the normal increase of population.[10]

High real wages, by enabling parents to provide better for their children, and consequently to bring up more of them to maturity, naturally tend to widen and extend those limits. It deserves to be remarked, too, that it necessarily does this very nearly in the proportion which the demand for labor requires.

If this demand is continually increasing, the reward of labor must necessarily so encourage the marriage and multiplication of laborers, that it enables them to supply that continually increasing demand by a continually increasing population. If the reward should at any time be insufficient for this purpose, the shortage of workers would soon raise it; and if it should at any time be more, their excessive multiplication would soon lower it to this necessary rate.

It is this demand for labor which regulates and determines the rate of propagation throughout the world, in North America, in Europe, and in China; which renders it rapidly progressive in the first, slow and gradual in the second, and altogether stationary in the last.

The liberal reward of labor, therefore, as it is the effect of growing wealth, so it is the cause of growing population. To complain of it, is to lament over the necessary effect and cause of the greatest public prosperity.

It is in the progressive state, while the society is advancing in prosperity, rather than when it has already reached its peak, that the condition of the laboring poor, of the great body of the people, seems to be the happiest and the most comfortable. It is hard in the stationary community, and miserable in the declining one.

The liberal reward of labor, furthermore, increases the industry of the common people, just as every human quality im-

[10] The population tends to increase to the limit of subsistence, but subsistence itself is a relative term. Furthermore, as in highly civilized countries like modern France, other factors may hold the population far below subsistence limits.

proves in proportion to the encouragement it receives. Where wages are high, accordingly, we shall always find the workmen more active, diligent, and expeditious, than where they are low; in England, for example, more than in Scotland; in the neighborhood of large towns, more than in remote country places.

Some workmen, indeed, when they can earn in four days what will maintain them through the week, will be idle the other three. But these are a minority.

Workmen who are on piece-work at high rates, are very apt to over-work themselves, and to ruin their health and constitution in a few years. A carpenter in London, for example, is not supposed to last in his full vigor more than eight years. Almost every class of workers is subject to some peculiar infirmity resulting from excessive application to their particular work.

It is often the excessive application during four days of the week that is the real cause of the idleness of the other three, so much and so loudly complained of.

If employers would listen to the dictates of reason and humanity, they would often hold their workmen back, rather than to drive them. It will be found, I believe, in every sort of trade, that the man who works moderately, so that he is able to work continuously, not only preserves his health the longest, but, in the course of the year, turns out the greatest quantity of work.

In years of low prices, it is claimed, workmen are generally more idle than normal, and in years of high prices more industrious. That a little more than ordinary prosperity may render some workmen idle, cannot well be doubted; but that it should have this effect upon the majority, or that men in general should work better when they are ill-fed than when they are well-fed, when they are disheartened than when they are in good spirits, when they are frequently sick than when they are generally in good health, seems not very probable.

In years of prosperity,[11] servants frequently leave their

[11] The phrase used by A. S. is "years of plenty," by which he means specifically abundance and cheapness of food. There is no exact equivalent in the United States, where for centuries a dearth of food has been all but unknown. Here every year is a year of plenty. Hence it is a little difficult for us to picture the England of 1776, when England's food was for the most part home-grown, and when production was so little above the minimum requirement that a bad crop season inevitably brought scarcity and distress among the poor.   (*Footnote continued on following page.*)

masters, and trust their subsistence to what they can make by their own industry. But the same cheapness of food, by increasing the fund which is available for the maintenance of servants, encourages employers, especially farmers, to employ a greater number.

At such times farmers expect more profit from their grain by maintaining a few more hired men than by selling it at a low price in the market. The demand for men increases, while the number of those who offer to supply that demand diminishes. The price of labor, therefore, frequently rises in prosperous years.

In years of depression, this process is exactly reversed. More people want employment than can easily get it; many are willing to take jobs at reduced wages, and the wages of both servants and workmen thus frequently sink at such times.

Employers of all sorts, therefore, frequently make better bargains with their servants in bad times than in good, and find them more humble and dependent. They naturally, therefore, prefer the former, as more favorable to industry.

Landlords and farmers, besides, two of the largest classes of employers, have another reason for being pleased with years of high prices of food. The rents of the one and the profits of the other depend very much upon these prices.

Nothing can be more absurd, however, than to imagine that men in general will work less when they work for themselves, than when they work for other people. An independent workman will generally be more industrious than even an employe on piecework. The one enjoys the whole product of his own industry; the other shares it with his employer. The one, in his separate independent state, is less liable to the temptations of bad company, which in large factories so frequently ruin the morals of the other.

The superiority of the independent workman over those who are hired by the month or by the year, and whose wages and maintenance are the same whether they work much or little, is likely

---

In the budget of a British workman's family, too, food was relatively a much larger item in 1776. Nowadays food prices fluctuate far less from year to year, and food costs make a considerably smaller part of the annual expenditure of the workman.

For this reason, and in order to make the argument somewhat more intelligible to modern readers, I make A. S. speak of "good times" and "bad times," rather than years of "plenty" or "scarcity."

to be still greater. Good years tend to increase the proportion of independent workmen, and bad years to diminish it.

While the alternation of good years and bad thus has direct effects upon the employment of labor, and the rates of wages, it does not seem to have much effect, from year to year, on the total amount of manufactured products which come to market.

This is partly because a considerable proportion of manufactured goods are destined for distant markets, where the demand depends upon other circumstances. But there may be more correspondence than appears on the surface, since much work done and goods produced do not appear in public records and statistics at all.

Though the variations in the price of labor not only do not always correspond with those in the price of food, but are frequently quite the opposite, this must not lead us to suppose that the price of food has no influence upon that of labor.

The money price of labor is necessarily regulated by two factors—the demand for labor, and the price of the necessaries and conveniences of life.

The demand for labor, according as it happens to be increasing, stationary, or declining, determines the quantity of the necessaries and conveniences of life which must be furnished to the laborer; and the money price of labor is determined by what it takes to buy this quantity.

Though the money price of labor, therefore, is sometimes high where the price of food is low, it would be still higher, the demand remaining the same, if the price of food were high.

It is because the demand for labor increases in years of sudden and extraordinary plenty, and decreases in those of sudden and extraordinary scarcity, that the money price of labor sometimes rises in the one, and sinks in the other.

In a year of sudden and extraordinary plenty, there are funds in the hands of many employers, sufficient to maintain and employ a greater number of workers than had been employed the year before; and this extraordinary number cannot always be found. Those employers, therefore, who want more workmen, bid against one another, in order to get them, which sometimes raises not only the money price of their labor, but its real price.

The reverse of this happens in a year of sudden and extraordinary scarcity. The funds available for employment of labor are less than they had been the year before. A considerable number of people are thrown out of work, and these bid against one another for jobs, which sometimes lowers both the real and the money price of labor.[12]

In the ordinary variations of the price of food, those two opposite causes seem to counterbalance each other, which is probably (in part at least) the reason why the wages of labor are everywhere so much more steady and permanent than the prices of food.

Any increase in the wages of labor necessarily increases the price of many commodities, by increasing that part of it which resolves itself into wages, and to that extent tends to reduce their consumption. The same cause, however, which raises the wages of labor—the increase of the wage-fund available for paying wages—tends to increase its productive powers, and to make a smaller quantity of labor produce a greater quantity of work.

The owner of the capital which employs a great number of laborers necessarily tries to make such a proper division and organization of the work as will secure the maximum output. For the same reason, he supplies them with the best machinery obtainable.

What takes place among the workmen in a particular plant, takes place, for the same reason, among those of a great society. The greater their number, the more they naturally divide themselves into different classes and subdivisions of employment. More brains are devoted to devising or obtaining the best machinery, and improvements are thus more likely to be invented.

There are many commodities, therefore, which by improved machines or methods, come to be produced by so much less labor than before, that the increase of cost through high wages is more than compensated by the smaller labor force required.

[12] The increase of capital not only employs more labor, but the use of the capital makes the labor more productive, hence cheaper per unit of product; although money wages may be higher.

CHAPTER IX

What fixes the profit on capital? It fluctuates much more than do wages, but it is likewise fixed by natural laws; and in point of fact the average rate of profit in a prosperous nation tends to fall.

FLUCTUATIONS IN THE PROFITS of capital depend upon the same causes as fluctuations in the wages of labor and the increasing or declining state of the wealth of the community; but these causes affect the two very differently.

An increase of capital which raises wages, tends to lower profit. When the capital of many rich merchants is turned into a single trade, their mutual competition naturally tends to lower its profit; and when there is a like increase of capital in all the different trades carried on in the same country, the same competition must produce the same effect on them all.[1]

It is not easy, as I have remarked, to ascertain what are the average wages of labor even in a particular place and time. We can seldom determine, even in this case, more than what are the most usual wages—the so-called "going wage." But the profits of capital are quite as difficult to determine. Profit is so very variable that the person who carries on a particular trade cannot himself always tell what he makes in an average year.

His profit is affected, not only by every variation in the

---

[1] Competition carried to the ultimate point—so-called "pure competition"— would force prices down to a point where they merely covered costs; there would then be no profit except interest. Fortunately, pure competition is an abstraction and never exists. M'Culloch points out that the average rate of profit is depressed by the wearing out of soils, increases in taxes, and advances in real wages; and does in fact nearly always fall as a community progresses. Thorold Rogers says that oppressive taxes must raise the rate of profits, not lower it, because they reduce the capital employed.

price of his product, but by the good or bad fortune both of his rivals and of his customers, and by a thousand other accidents, to which goods are liable in transit, and even when stored in a warehouse.

Profit varies, therefore, not only from year to year, but from day to day, and almost from hour to hour.

To ascertain what is the average profit of all the different trades carried on in a great nation must be still more difficult; and to judge of what it may have been formerly, or in the remote past, with any degree of precision, must be altogether impossible.

But though these uncertainties exist, we can get a fair idea of the variations in the profits of capital by observing the rates of interest on money.

It may be laid down as an axiom, that wherever a large profit can be made by the use of money, a high price will commonly be paid for the use of it; and that wherever little can be made by it, less will commonly be paid. According as the usual market rate of interest varies in any country, we may be assured, therefore, that the ordinary profits of capital must vary with it. The progress of interest, therefore, may give us a fairly accurate idea of the progress of profit.

Before the time of Henry VIII (1509–1547) the common rate of interest may have exceeded 10 per cent, as it was reduced to this legal maximum during his reign. Religious scruples resulted in a law of his son Edward VI, abolishing interest entirely; but this being unenforceable (as such laws always are), interest was again made lawful under Elizabeth.

The legal rate was reduced successively to 8 per cent, to 6 per cent, and under Queen Anne to 5 per cent, which was then rather above the ordinary going rate. By 1750 the common rate for the best loans was 3½, 4, or 4½ per cent.

During all this time the wealth and income of England were steadily increasing; wages continually increased; but the profits of capital steadily decreased.

It generally requires more capital to carry on any sort of trade in a large city than in a country village. The great concentrations of money, and the number of rich competitors, generally reduce the rate of profit in cities. But the wages of labor are generally higher in the city than in the village.

City employers must often bid against each other for workmen, whereas in villages the supply of labor often exceeds the demand, wages are lower, and the rate of profit higher.

In Scotland, though the legal rate of interest is the same as in England, the market rate is rather higher. And this in spite of the fact that Scotland is a poorer country, with a lower wage rate. Business can therefore be carried on there with less capital, and the rate of profit is higher.

℃   The same principle is illustrated in France, a poorer country than England. There the legal rate of interest has usually been low, but the actual market rate higher than in England; for as in all countries, there are several safe and easy methods of evading the law. French wages are lower than in England, the profits of capital are higher.

℃   Again, in Holland, a richer country than England, interest rates are low, wages higher than here, and business profits the lowest in all Europe.[2]

On the other hand, in our North American and West Indian colonies, not only the wages of labor, but the interest of money, and consequently the profits of capital, are higher than in England. But this is exceptional, and is a situation peculiar to new and growing colonies. As a general rule, high wages of labor and high profits of capital are scarcely ever found together.

As the colony progresses, the profits of capital gradually diminish. When the most fertile and best-situated lands have been all occupied, less profit can be made by the cultivation of poorer lands, and the borrowed capital so employed can pay less interest. In most of our colonies, accordingly, both the legal and the market rate of interest have been considerably reduced during the course of the present century.

The wages of labor do not sink with the profits of capital. The demand for labor increases with the increase of capital, whatever be its profits; and after these are diminished, capital may not only continue to increase, but to increase much faster than before.

Industrious nations which are advancing in the acquisition of riches follow the same course as industrious individuals. A large capital, though with small profits, generally increases faster than a small capital with great profits. Money, says the proverb, makes money. When you have got a little, it is often easy to get more. The great difficulty is to get that little.

[2] Due almost entirely, thinks M'Culloch, to heavy and oppressive taxation.

The acquisition of new territory, or of new branches of trade, may temporarily raise the profits of capital, and with them the interest rate, even in a country which is rapidly growing rich. The capital of the country not being sufficient for the whole accession of new business, it is naturally put into those particular branches which offer the greatest profit. Part of what had before been employed in other trades, is necessarily withdrawn from them, and turned into some of the new and more profitable ones.

In all those old trades, therefore, the competition is not so keen. There are smaller supplies of many different sorts of goods. Their price necessarily rises more or less, and yields a greater profit to those who deal in them, who can, therefore, afford to borrow at a higher interest.

It is quite otherwise in countries which are going backward. The great fortunes so suddenly and so easily acquired in Bengal and the other British settlements in the East Indies, may satisfy us that, as the wages of labor are very low, so the profits of capital are very high in those ruined countries. The interest of money is correspondingly so.

In Bengal, money is frequently lent to the farmers at 40, 50, or 60 per cent, and the succeeding crop is mortgaged for the payment. As the profits which can afford such an interest must eat up almost the whole rent of the landlord, so such enormous usury must in its turn eat up the greater part of those profits.

Before the fall of the Roman republic, usury of the same kind seems to have been common in the provinces, under the ruinous administration of their proconsuls. Even the virtuous Brutus lent money in Cyprus at 48 per cent, as we learn from the letters of Cicero.

In a country which was as rich and populous as it possibly could be, doubtless profits and wages would both be very low. But as there is no such country, there is no way of proving this. China seems to have been long stationary, and probably long ago became as rich as it could under its peculiar laws and institutions. But it may be far less rich than it could be, considering its soil and climate, under other laws and institutions.

A country which neglects or despises foreign commerce, and which admits the vessels of foreign nations into only one or two of its ports, must be much restricted in business.

Furthermore, in a country where, though the rich enjoy a

good deal of security, the poor have very little, but are liable, under the pretense of justice, to be pillaged and plundered at any time by their local rulers, the quantity of capital employed can never be equal to what it might otherwise be. In such countries the oppression of the poor must establish the monopoly of the rich, who by monopolizing the whole trade will be able to make very large profits. 12 per cent is said to be the common interest of money in China, and the ordinary profits of capital must be sufficient to pay this high rate.

Defects in the laws or in their enforcement may sometimes raise the rate of interest considerably above what the wealth or poverty of the country would naturally require. When the laws do not enforce the performance of contracts, all borrowers are put nearly upon the same footing with bankrupts or people of bad credit in better-regulated countries. The uncertainty of recovering his money makes the lender exact the same usurious interest that is usually demanded from bankrupts.

Among the barbarous nations who over-ran the western provinces of the Roman Empire, the fulfillment of contracts was left for many ages to the faith of the contracting parties. The royal courts of justice took no notice of it. The high rate of interest current in those ancient times and nations may perhaps be partly accounted for thus.

When the law prohibits interest altogether, it still does not prevent it. Many people must borrow, and nobody will lend without such an inflated consideration for the use of their money as will cover not only its legitimate use and profit, but the difficulty and danger of evading the law.

The high rate of interest among all Mohammedan nations is accounted for by Montesquieu, not because of their poverty, but partly from the risk and danger of violating the law, and partly from the difficulty of recovering the loan.

The lowest ordinary rate of profit must always be somewhat more than enough to cover the occasional losses to which every employment of capital is exposed. It is this surplus only which is clear or net profit.

What is called gross profit usually includes not only this surplus, but what is retained for compensating such extraordinary losses. The interest which the borrower can afford to pay is in proportion to the actual net profit of the business.

The lowest ordinary rate of interest must, on the same principle, be somewhat more than enough to compensate the occasional losses to which lending, even prudent lending, is exposed. If this were not so, no one would ever lend except out of charity or friendship.

In a country which has become as rich as it can possibly be, where no more capital can be employed in any business, as the ordinary rate of profit would be very small, so the usual interest rate would be so low that only the very wealthiest people could live upon the interest of their money. It would be necessary that almost every one else should be a man of business, or engage in some sort of trade.

The province of Holland seems to be approaching this state. It is there unfashionable *not* to be a man of business. As it would be ridiculous not to dress, so it is considered somewhat absurd not to be employed, like other people.

The highest ordinary rate of profit may be so high that it eats up the whole of what should go to the rent of the land, and leaves only enough to pay the labor of preparing and bringing the commodities to market, at a bare subsistence wage for labor.

The workman must always have been fed and supported in some way or other while he was about the work; but the landlord may not have been paid at all.

The profits of the trade which the East India Company carries on in Bengal may not perhaps be very far from this rate.

The proportion which the usual market rate of interest ought to bear to the ordinary rate of net profit necessarily varies somewhat. Double the interest is reckoned a good, moderate, reasonable profit by merchants in Great Britain.

In a country where the ordinary rate of profit is 8 or 10 per cent on capital, it may be reasonable that one half of it should go to interest, if the business is carried on with borrowed money. The capital is at the risk of the borrower, who, as it were, insures it to the lender; and 4 or 5 per cent may, in most lines, be both a sufficient profit upon this insurance risk and a sufficient recompense for the trouble of employing the capital.

But the proportion between interest and profit might not be the same in countries where the ordinary rate of profit was either a good deal lower, or a good deal higher. If it were a good deal lower, one half of it perhaps could not be afforded for interest; and more might be afforded if it were a good deal higher.

In countries which are rapidly getting rich, the low rate of profit may, in the price of many commodities, compensate for the high wages of labor, and enable those countries to sell as cheaply as their less thriving neighbors, among whom the wages of labor may be lower.

In reality, high profits tend much more to raise the price of goods and services than do high wages. If in the linen manufacture, for example, the wages of the different workers—the flax-dressers, the spinners, the weavers, etc.—should all be advanced five cents a day, it would be necessary to raise the price of a piece of linen only by the same number of nickels as the number of people employed, multiplied by the number of days they had worked.

That part of the price of linen which was wages would rise only in arithmetical proportion to this rise of wages.

But if the profits of all the different employers should be raised 5 per cent, that part of the price of the commodity which was profit would, through all the different stages of manufacture, rise in geometrical proportion.

In other words, in raising the cost or natural price of commodities the rise of wages operates in the same manner as simple interest does in the accumulation of debt. The rise of profit operates like compound interest.[3]

Our merchants and master-manufacturers complain much of the bad effects of high wages in raising costs and prices, and thereby lessening the sale of their goods both at home and abroad. They say nothing concerning the bad effects of high profits. They are silent with regard to the pernicious effects of their own gains. They complain only of those of other people.

[3] This is, to put it mildly, very doubtful. Market prices, at least, are determined by many factors, of which wage costs and profits are only two. Prices will be nearly the same, whether wages or profits are high or low. A. S.'s example is itself defective. He supposes wages to be advanced only a nickel a day, but appears to double the rate of profit. If on the contrary wages were doubled, and profits advanced only 5 per cent instead of 100 per cent, the advance in the price of the commodity would, by his own computation, be far greater. But this passage in W. N. is not clear.

CHAPTER X

In a society that was perfectly free, wages would still be unequal among different trades, for five good reasons; and the rate of profit on capital would also be unequal, but not so much so. There is, however, no society that is perfectly free.

THE ADVANTAGES AND DISADVANTAGES of the different employments of labor and capital must, in the same neighborhood, always tend toward equality if they are not actually equal. If there was any one employment obviously more or less profitable than the rest, so many people would crowd into it in the one case, or would desert it in the other, that its advantages would soon return to the level of other employments.

This at least would be the case in a community where things were left to follow their natural course, where there was perfect liberty, and where every man was perfectly free to choose what occupation he thought proper, and to change it as often as he thought proper.

But this is far from the case, at least in Europe, where wages and profits vary widely in different occupations and businesses.

Such differences arise partly from certain circumstances in the occupations themselves, which make up, or in imagination seem to make up, for differences in money rewards, which may be large or small; and partly because there is no perfect liberty in Europe.

In the first category, there seem to be five principal reasons why one employment seems more or less attractive than others. These are (1) the pleasantness or unpleasantness of the occupation itself; (2) the easiness and cheapness, or the difficulty and expense of learning it; (3) the regularity or irregularity of employment; (4) the responsibility involved in the work; and (5) the probability or improbability of success.[1]

The wages of labor vary with the ease or hardship, the cleanliness or dirtiness, the honorableness or dishonorableness of the employment. Thus in most places a tailor earns less than a weaver. His work is much easier. A weaver earns less than a blacksmith. His work is not always easier, but it is much cleaner. Even a skilled blacksmith seldom earns as much in twelve hours, as a coal-miner, who is only a laborer, does in eight. His work is not quite so dirty, is safer, and is carried on in daylight and above ground.

Public esteem makes a great part of the reward of all honorable professions. In point of money income, all things considered, they are generally under-paid. Other occupations which are looked down upon are often more profitable.

The trade of a butcher is a brutal and an odious business; but it is generally more profitable than most other common trades. The most detestable of all employments, that of public executioner, is, in proportion to the quantity of work done, better paid than any ordinary trade whatever.

It may be observed, by contrast, that hunting and fishing, the most essential employments of mankind in early days, become in civilized times their most agreeable and popular amusements. Men eagerly pursue for pleasure what they once followed from necessity.

In an advanced society, therefore, only very poor people follow as a trade, what other people pursue as a pastime. Fishermen have been poor men since the time of Theocritus, and the licensed hunter is not in a much better condition. The natural taste for those occupations makes more people follow them than can live comfortably by them.

Disagreeableness and low social esteem affect the profits of capital in precisely the same way. The keeper of an inn or saloon, who is never master of his own house, and who is exposed to the brutality of every drunkard, has neither a very agreeable nor a very respected business. But there is scarcely any common business in which it is easier to make money with little capital.

[1] Thorold Rogers remarks that the 1st, 3d, and 5th of these reasons should be classified as *risk;* the 2d and 4th as *cost.*

Wages vary also with the easiness and cheapness, or the difficulty and expense of learning the business.

When some expensive machine is erected, it is expected that its efficiency will replace the capital laid out upon it, with at least the ordinary profit, before it wears out.

A man educated at the cost of much labor and time to any of those employments which require extraordinary dexterity and skill, may be compared to one of those expensive machines. The work which he learns to perform should replace to him the whole cost of his education, with at least the ordinary profits of equally valuable capital.

Indeed, it must do this in a reasonable time, as well, considering that the duration of human life is much less certain than the life of a machine. And skilled labor is always better paid, for this reason.

❦ It is this principle, too, which accounts for the almost universal difference between the earnings of labor in the cities and in the country. The workman must usually pass through the stage of apprentice, which may be costly, while the farm laborer learns the hard parts of his business while performing the easier parts, and is paid for doing so. The difference in earnings seems to be wholly accounted for by the difference in the cost of training.

Education in the arts and in the liberal professions is still more tedious and expensive. The money reward of painters and sculptors, of lawyers and physicians, ought reasonably to be much more liberal; and it is so accordingly.[2]

The profits of capital, however, seem to be very little affected by the easiness or difficulty of learning the trade in which it is employed. One business in which capital is employed seems to be about as easy (or as difficult) to learn as another.

Employment is much more constant in some trades than in others. In most manufactures conducted indoors, a workman may be reasonably sure of employment almost every day in the year that he is able to work.

A mason or bricklayer, on the contrary, can not work in very bad or cold weather, and his employment depends upon the uncertain calls of his customers. What he earns, therefore, while he is working, must not only maintain him while he is idle, but

[2] It is so, at least, for the top artists and professional men—certainly not for all. The rank-and-file of artists are notoriously ill-paid.

make up to him for those anxious and desponding moments which the thought of his precarious situation must sometimes cause.

❡ These trades are not particularly hard to learn, but wages are relatively high, and the difference must be a payment for irregularity of employment, not for special skill. The trade of a carpenter, more highly skilled but less liable to interruption by the weather, is not so well paid as bricklaying.

❡ In some trades, which combine hardship, danger, and dirt with irregular employment, such as that of the men who unload coal from ships at London, wages are abnormally high—about four times the rate for common labor.

Regularity or irregularity of employment cannot affect the ordinary profits of capital in any particular trade. Whether the capital is or is not constantly employed usually depends, not upon the business, but upon who is running it.

Again, wages will vary according to the small or great trust which must be reposed in the workmen.

The wages of goldsmiths and jewelers are everywhere higher than those of many other workmen who may be far more skilled and ingenious, because of the precious materials with which they work.

We trust our health to the physician; our fortune and sometimes our life and reputation to the lawyer. We could not place such confidence safely in people of a very mean or low condition. Their reward must be such, therefore, as may give them that standing in society which so important a trust requires. The time and heavy cost of their education, when combined with their positions of trust, necessarily raises still further the price of their labor.

When a person employs only his own capital in trade, there is no element of trust; and the credit which he may get from other people depends, not upon the nature of the business as much as upon their opinion of his resources, integrity, and prudence. The different rates of profit, therefore, in different branches of trade, cannot be attributed to the different degrees of trust reposed in the traders.[3]

[3] Except, remarks Cannan, that a profession like that of banking, calling for a quite unusual reputation for integrity, sometimes raises the banker's compensation because people with that quality are rare.

Finally, the wages of labor vary according to the probability or improbability of success in that trade.

This element of probability varies widely in different occupations. In most mechanical trades, success is almost certain; train your son to repair shoes, and there is little doubt of his learning to do the work. But send him to study law, and it is at least twenty to one that he will never reach such proficiency as will enable him to live by this profession.

The lawyer who, perhaps, at forty years of age, begins to make money by his profession, ought to receive the reward not only of his own tedious and expensive education, but of that of twenty others who are never likely to make a success of it. No matter how exorbitant a successful lawyer's fees may seem, they are never as high as this standard.

Taking all mechanical trades together, you will find that the workers earn a larger total than they spend. But take all lawyers and law students together, and you will find their aggregate income is far less than their expense. It may be taken as a general principle that the law, as well as other liberal professions, is as a whole underpaid.

Notwithstanding these discouragements, all the most generous and liberal spirits are eager to crowd into these professions, attracted by the high reputation which follows great success in them, and the natural confidence which every man has, more or less, in his own abilities and good luck.

To reach the top in any profession, in which few individuals are more than mediocre, is the most decisive proof of what is called genius or superior talents. The public admiration which follows is always a part of the compensation. It makes a considerable part of that compensation for the doctor, and still more for the lawyer; in poetry and philosophy it makes almost the sole reward.

The case of the dramatic and musical world is perhaps unique. Here the exorbitant earnings of actors, dancers, singers and movie stars are due partly to the rarity and beauty of their talents, and partly to a subconscious sense of contempt for the persons themselves.

It may be absurd at first glance to despise the individuals, and yet reward them so richly; but it will be seen that it is because of the first that we must do the second.

The over-weening conceit which most men have of their own abilities, is an ancient evil remarked by philosophers and moralists of all ages.

Their absurd faith in their own good fortune has been less remarked, but it is, if possible, still more universal. There is no man living who, when in tolerable health and spirits, has not some share of it. The chance of gain is always more or less over-estimated, and the chance of loss under-estimated.

That the chance of profit is naturally over-estimated, we may learn from the universal success of lotteries. The world has never seen nor will ever see a perfectly fair lottery, in which the whole gain compensated the whole loss, because in such a case those who ran it could make nothing by it.

℃   The soberest people will risk a dollar for the chance of gaining fifty thousand, although they know as a matter of mathematics that even that dollar chance is worth no more than seventy or eighty cents.

℃   As for those who in hopes of improving their chances buy additional tickets, they ignore the mathematical fact that the more they buy, the more certain they are to lose; for if they bought all the tickets, they must necessarily take out less than they put in, and the greater the number of tickets, the nearer they approach this mathematical certainty.

That the chance of loss is frequently under-estimated, and scarcely ever valued more than it is worth, we may learn from the insurance business. Here the premiums paid must be sufficient to compensate for all losses, to pay the expense of management, and to pay as much profit on the capital as in other businesses.

Moderate as the cost of insurance commonly is, however, many people despise the risk too much to care to pay it. Taking the whole of England, nineteen houses in twenty, perhaps ninety-nine in a hundred, are not insured from fire.

Sea risk is more alarming to most people, and the proportion of ships insured is consequently much higher.[4]

The contempt of risk and the presumptuous hope of success, are in no period of life more active than at the age at which young people choose their professions. How little the fear of mis-

---

[4] The status of insurance of all kinds has changed greatly since A. S. wrote. Nowadays it is perhaps ninety-five houses out of a hundred that are insured; and no ship sails without this protection.

fortune is then capable of balancing the hope of good luck, appears in the readiness of common people to enlist as soldiers or sailors, and the eagerness of higher classes to enter into what are called the liberal professions.

℄   It is with romantic hopes of honor and distinction that a young man enters the fatiguing and dangerous trade of a soldier, where he will be worse paid than a common laborer. Other people may think he would fare better by going to sea; nobody but himself can see any future in the army.

℄   Sailors, in a trade calling for greater skill and knowledge, but even more hazardous, are not much better paid.

The dangers and hair-breadth escapes of a life of adventure, instead of disheartening young people, seem frequently to attract them.

A tender mother is often afraid to send her son to school at a seaport town, lest the sight of the ships and the conversation and adventures of the sailors should entice him to go to sea. The distant prospect of hazards which we can hope to surmount by courage and address, is not disagreeable to us, and certainly does not raise the wages of labor employed.

It is quite otherwise with those occupations in which courage and address can be of no use. In trades which are known to be very unhealthful, the wages of labor are always remarkably high.

In the employment of capital, the ordinary rate of profit varies more or less with the certainty or uncertainty of the returns. These are in general less uncertain in the domestic than in overseas trade, and in some branches of foreign trade than in others.

The ordinary rate of profit always rises more or less with the risk. It does not, however, seem to rise exactly in proportion to it, for bankruptcies are most frequent in the most hazardous trades.

The most hazardous of all trades, that of a smuggler, is the infallible road to bankruptcy, even though success is always highly profitable.

The presumptuous hope of success seems to act here as upon all other occasions, and to entice so many adventurers into those hazardous trades, that their competition reduces the rate of profit below what is necessary to cover the risk.

Of the five circumstances, therefore, which cause the wages

of labor to vary, two only affect the profits of capital; the agreeableness or disagreeableness of the business, and the risk or security with which it is attended. In point of agreeableness or disagreeableness, there is little or no difference between different lines of business—much less than between different kinds of labor.

The rise in the return on capital as a result of greater risk, does not seem to be as great in proportion.

It should follow from all this, that in a particular community, the average and ordinary rates of profit in the different employments of capital should be more nearly upon a level than the wages of the different sorts of labor. They are so accordingly.

℃   There are particular instances where the rate of profit on capital may seem far higher than the average. Such cases are those of the apothecary, or the grocer in a small village.

℃   The apothecary may sell drugs at an apparent profit of five hundred or a thousand per cent. But he is a skilled worker, the physician of the poor and (when the distress or danger is not very great) of the rich as well. His income is thus to be classed as wages rather than profit.

℃   Similarly, the grocer is a skilled specialist in his trade, with the same qualifications and abilities as a great merchant, differing only in the capital he can command. It is these qualities that are paid for as wages, and if deducted from the apparent profit on his stock, would probably leave no more than the ordinary return on capital.

The difference between the apparent profit of the retail and that of the wholesale trade, is much less in a great city than in small towns and country villages. Where fifty thousand dollars can be employed in the grocery trade, the wages of the grocer's labor make but a very trifling addition to the real profits of so much capital. The apparent profits of the wealthy retailer, therefor, are in cities more nearly upon a level with those of the wholesale merchant.

It is for this reason that goods sold at retail are generally as cheap, and frequently much cheaper, in the large cities than in small towns and country villages.

Though the rate of profit on capital is generally less in a great city than in small towns and country villages, yet great fortunes can only be made there.

In small towns and country villages, on account of the narrowness of the market, trade cannot always be expanded. In such places, therefore, though the rate of profit may be very high, the sum or total of them can never be very great.

In big cities, on the contrary, trade can be extended almost indefinitely, and the credit of a frugal and thriving man increases much faster than his capital. His trade can expand in proportion to the amount of both, and the sum of his profits and his annual accumulation, will ordinarily be in proportion.

The greatest fortunes are made, even in cities, in consequence of a long life of industry, frugality, and attention. Sudden fortunes, indeed, are sometimes made by what is called speculation. The speculative merchant exercises no one regular, established, or well-known business, but enters into every trade when he foresees that it is likely to be more than commonly profitable, and quits it when he foresees that its profits are likely to fall.

A bold adventurer may sometimes acquire a considerable fortune by two or three successful speculations; but is just as likely to lose one by two or three unsuccessful ones.

This trade can be carried on nowhere but in large cities, for it is only in such places that the necessary intelligence and wide information can be found.

The five circumstances above mentioned, though they cause considerable inequalities in the wages of labor and profits of capital, make no real inequality in the relative attractiveness of different trades or uses of capital. All they do is to equalize, in the money reward, other advantages or disadvantages of the employment.

But this equalizing process can take place only under what may be called normal circumstances, and specifically under three conditions:

In the first place, the business must be well-known and long-established. Where all other circumstances are equal, wages are generally higher in new than in old trades. When a pioneer attempts to establish a new manufacture, he must first entice his workmen away from other employment by higher wages, and a considerable time must pass before he can venture to reduce them.

Manufactures for which the demand arises altogether from fashion and fancy are continually changing, and seldom last long enough to be considered well-established. Those for which the demand arises chiefly from use or necessity, change much less, and the same article may continue in demand for whole centuries together. The wages of labor, therefore, are likely to be higher in the former case, lower in the latter.

As wages are higher in a new line of business, so the profit of capital is expected to be higher.

The establishment of any new manufacture, of any new branch of commerce, or of any new practice in agriculture, is always a speculation, from which the entrepreneur promises himself extraordinary profits. These profits sometimes are actually very large, but more frequently, perhaps, are quite otherwise; in general they bear no fixed relation to those of other old trades in the neighborhood.

If the project succeeds they are usually at first very high. If and when the trade or practice becomes thoroughly established and well-known, competition reduces them to the level of other trades.

In the second place, the equalizing process can take place only when the trade or business is itself in a normal or natural condition, and not affected by some accident or emergency.

The demand for farm labor is greater at haytime and harvest than during the rest of the year; and wages rise with the demand. In time of war, the demand for sailors to man ships necessarily causes a shortage and a rise in wages.[5]

In a business that is drying up, on the contrary, many workmen, rather than quit their old trade, will accept smaller wages than they would otherwise demand and obtain.

The profits of capital vary for the same reasons, but also according to the prices and volume of production of the commodities in which it is employed. All commodities are more or less liable to variations of price, but some are much more so than others.

The same quantity of labor will, in different years, produce very different quantities of grain, cotton, sugar, tobacco, etc. The prices of such commodities, therefore, vary not only with the variations of demand, but with the much greater and more frequent variations of volume produced, and consequently fluctuate widely.

[5] A sudden scarcity of labor, says Thorold Rogers, causes a rise in wages, which will be greatest in the cheapest unskilled grades. After the Great Plague in 1348, "the most instructive economic event in history," the wages of women doubled, and the wages of common labor went far above those of skilled artisans.

The profit of some of the dealers must necessarily fluctuate with the price of the commodities.

The operations of the speculator are principally in such commodities. He endeavors to buy them up when he foresees that their price is likely to rise, and to sell them when it is likely to fall.

Finally, the equalizing process can take place only where labor or capital is employed "full time"—where the employment is not a secondary or part-time one.

When a person makes his living from one employment, which does not take up all of his time, he is often willing to work at another for less than the going wage in that trade.

℃ The "cotters," or cottagers, of Scotland were such part-time workers, and in ancient times they seem to have been common all over Europe.

In prosperous countries the market is generally so extensive that any one trade is sufficient to employ the whole labor and capital of those who occupy it. Instances of people's living by one employment, and at the same time picking up a little income from another, occur chiefly in poor countries.

But there are instances even in wealthy countries. There is no city in Europe, I believe, in which house-rent is more expensive than in London, and yet I know no capital in which a furnished apartment can be hired so cheaply.

Lodging is not only much cheaper in London than in Paris; it is much cheaper than in Edinburgh, for equal accommodations; and what may seem extraordinary, the dearness of house-rent is the cause of the cheapness of furnished rooms.

The dearness of house rent in London arises, not only from those causes which make it dear in all great cities—high wages, high building costs, high rents—but partly from the peculiar manners and customs of the Londoners, which oblige every head of a family to rent a whole house from top to bottom.

A dwelling house in England means everything that is contained under one roof. In France, Scotland, and many other parts of Europe, it frequently means no more than a single story.

A tradesman in London is obliged to rent a whole house in that part of the city where his customers live. His shop is upon the ground floor, and he and his family sleep in the garret; and he aims to pay a part of his house rent by sub-letting the two middle stories to lodgers.

[*105*]

In other words, he expects to maintain his family by his trade, and not by his lodgers, whereas at Paris and Edinburgh, the people who rent rooms have commonly no other means of subsistence; and the price of the lodging must not only pay the rent of the house, but must support the whole family.

CHAPTER XI

Another long chapter showing how all societies are more or less injured by restrictions sanctioned by law; how all of these tend toward some kind of monopoly, giving some persons an unjust advantage over others; capital is also somewhat restricted, but by no means so much as labor; and the worst injustices are those perpetrated by town people upon farm people.

THE INEQUALITIES THAT RESULT when a business is new, or under some temporary disadvantage, or when it is not the principal business of the person who runs it, are of some importance. But much greater inequalities result from the fact that employment is not perfectly free, but suffers from interferences and legal restraints of various sorts.

The three most injurious of these, either imposed by law or tolerated by law, operate thus: first, by restricting the competition in some employments to a smaller number than would otherwise enter them; secondly, by increasing it in others beyond what it naturally would be; and, thirdly, by obstructing the free circulation of labor and capital, both from one business to another and from place to place.

The exclusive privileges of corporations are the principal means for avoiding or minimizing competition.[1] These privileges

[1] As has been remarked in the Introduction, the American reader of this day would almost certainly be misled by the word "corporation" as used in W. N. To an American of 1947 the "corporation" is the limited-liability joint-stock company, operating under the laws of some state, and identified to many as "soulless," predatory, and generally evil. (*Footnote continued on following page.*)

necessarily restrain the competition, in the town where it operates, to those who are "free of trade." To have served an apprenticeship in the town, under a master properly qualified, is commonly the requirement for obtaining this freedom.

Thus the by-laws of the trade regulate sometimes the number of apprentices which any master is allowed to have, and almost always the number of years which each apprentice is obliged to serve.

The intention of both regulations is to restrict the competition to a much smaller number, both employers and workmen, than might otherwise try to enter the business. The limitation of the number of apprentices restricts it directly. A long term of apprenticeship restricts it more indirectly, but quite as effectively, by increasing the expense of training.

In Sheffield no master cutler can have more than one apprentice at a time, by a by-law of the trade. In Norfolk and Norwich no master weaver can have more than two apprentices, under pain of forfeiting five pounds a month to the government. And many other trade rules are just as oppressive.

Seven years seems to have been, all over Europe, the usual

The English corporation of 1776 was quite different, and indeed has no exact counterpart in our day. It was any body of men organized for some civilian purpose, and included the governing bodies of towns and cities. It was the "corporations" of London and many smaller towns which surrendered their ancient charters of rights and privileges to James II, to their sorrow. (A still earlier name for the town corporation was "university.")

But more particularly, the corporation was an incorporated trade in a particular city or town, including all of that business in that town, employers and workmen alike. Its by-laws were designed to promote the selfish interest of all, as A. S. goes on to show, by limiting the number of workmen, thus protecting the jobs of the present workers, and by limiting competition among the employers by various measures.

No such organization exists in this country, where the employers generally combine in trade associations, and the workmen in trade unions, so that the whole trade is divided against itself internally. There is no general overall organization of a whole trade in an American town.

It is a problem, in construing A. S., therefore, whether to retain a necessarily misleading word, or to invent one which, while not precisely accurate, will put the American reader on notice that A. S. is describing an organization which is unfamiliar to him. I have followed the latter course, and wherever A. S. writes "corporation" I usually make it "incorporated trade," or simply "trade." This seems sufficiently descriptive, and at least preserves A. S. from appearing to criticize the joint-stock company. He has something to say on joint-stock companies in a later book.

term for the duration of apprenticeships in most incorporated trades.

All such incorporations were in early times called universities; which indeed is the proper Latin name for them. The university of smiths, the university of tailors, etc., are expressions which we commonly meet with in the old charters of ancient towns.

When those educational incorporations which are now called universities were first established, the term of study, in order to obtain the degree of master of arts, apparently was copied from the term of apprenticeship in common trades, which was much older.

℃   The first statute of apprenticeship, enacted during the reign of Elizabeth, was intended for all trades in the whole kingdom, but in practice was confined to the larger "market towns," and to those trades that existed when the law was passed.

℃   This gave rise to some absurdities, such as the rule that a carriage-builder could not make wheels, but must buy them of a wheelwright, because the latter trade was practiced when the law was passed; whereas a wheelwright was perfectly free to build carriages, which trade was not covered by the law.

℃   In France, the terms of apprenticeship were similar, although differing in detail, but in Scotland were far less rigid and oppressive.

The property right which every man has in his own labor, as it is the original foundation of all other property, so it is the most sacred and inviolable.

The estate of a poor man lies in the strength and dexterity of his hands; and to hinder him from employing his strength and dexterity in whatever manner he thinks proper without injury to his neighbor, is a plain violation of this most sacred property.

It encroaches upon the just liberty both of the workman and of those who might want to employ him. As it hinders the one from working at what he thinks proper, so it hinders the others from employing whom they think proper.

To judge whether he is fit to be employed, may surely be trusted to the discretion of the employers who are most concerned, and the affected anxiety of the law-makers lest they should employ an improper person is as impudent as it is oppressive.

℃   The institution of long apprenticeships is itself bad. It gives the customer no guarantee of good workmanship, and it has

no beneficial effect on the young apprentices themselves. The boys
who are taken from charitable institutions are usually made to
serve longer apprenticeships, and they generally turn out very idle
and worthless.

℀ The apprentice system was unknown to the ancients, and
long apprenticeship should be discarded. Were the trades to be
freed, competition would no doubt reduce the profits of employers
and the wages of workmen. But their goods and services being thus
somewhat cheapened, the public as a whole would be the gainer.

It is specifically to prevent this reduction of price, and consequently of wages and profit, by restraining that free competition
which would surely bring it about, that all incorporated trades and
most trade laws have been established.[2]

The trades were usually incorporated by the towns in which
they were located, and while in England a charter from the king
was likewise necessary, this seems to have been for the purpose of
extorting money rather than for the defence of the common liberty
against these oppressive monopolies.

The government of the incorporated towns was altogether
in the hands of traders and artificers; and it was plainly to the in-

[2] It is hardly necessary to repeat that the exclusive corporation of the 18th
Century has disappeared. Or at least, as Thorold Rogers remarks, it survives only in
the close monopolies of doctors and lawyers, where, because of the special skills of
these classes, monopoly might possibly be justified.

But economic man is a natural monopolist; as the hart panteth after the
water brooks, so man's soul panteth after such a restriction of his competition as will
enable him to raise the exchange value of his product or his labor. Hence we live in
a world of semi- or would-be monopolies, from plumbers who will let no workmen
from another town use a wrench or cut a thread in their territory, and barbers who
conspire to establish and enforce a uniform scale for shaves and hair-cuts, to the tight
little monopolies of photo-engravers, electrotypers, and other highly-skilled trades.

These are the classes of workmen who, as A. S. says, are able to maintain
their selling prices above their natural levels for long periods at a time. Their operations are too local to come under the Federal laws against conspiracies in restraint of
trade; and state and local laws, where they exist, are universally ignored. There is not
even a pretense of enforcement.

There is a kind of rude justice when the conspirators rob each other, as
when the electrotyper is robbed by the barber with each Saturday night hair-cut, the
barber plundered by the plumber when his water pipes burst, and the plumber by the
electrotyper when he plans to get out some printed advertising.

But the great body of consumers, farmers in particular, unable to form defensive monopolies of their own, are plundered indiscriminately by all who can, and
there seems no sufficient remedy when the state will not act.

terest of all of them to prevent the market from being over-supplied, as they commonly express it, with their own particular goods and services. By which, in reality, they mean to keep it always under-supplied.

Each trade was eager to establish regulations that would accomplish this purpose, and, provided it was allowed to do so, was perfectly willing that every other trade should do the same.

The effect of such regulations, indeed, was that each class was obliged to pay more for the goods they needed, within the town, than they might otherwise have done. But to compensate them, they were enabled to sell their own just so much dearer; so that it was as broad as it was long, as they say; and in the dealings of the different trades within the town with one another they were neither better off nor worse.

But in their dealings with the surrounding countryside they were all great gainers; and in these latter dealings consists the whole trade which supports and enriches all towns.

Every town draws its whole subsistence, and all the raw materials of its industry, from the country. It pays for these chiefly in two ways; first, by selling back to the country part of those materials worked up and manufactured, in which case their price is increased by the wages of the workmen, and the profits of their employers; and secondly, by selling the country other goods from distant places. In this case, too, the original price of those goods is augmented by the cost of transport, as well as wages and profits.

In the profits upon the first of those two activities consists the advantage which the town makes by its industries; in what it makes upon the second, the advantage of its commerce.

Whatever artificial measures, therefore, tend to increase those wages and profits beyond what they otherwise would be, enable the town to purchase, with a smaller quantity of its labor, the product of a greater quantity of the labor of the country. They give the dealers and workmen in the town an advantage over the landlords, farmers, and laborers in the country, and break down that natural equality which would otherwise exist in the commerce which is carried on between them.

The whole annual product of the labor of the country is divided between these two different sets of people. By artificial means, a greater share of it is given to the townspeople than would otherwise fall to them; and a smaller share to country people.

[*113*]

That towns are on the whole more prosperous than the country we may, without entering into any very nice computations, convince ourselves by one very simple and obvious observation.

In every country in Europe we find at least a hundred people who have acquired great fortunes from small beginnings by trade or manufacture, for one who has grown rich by that which properly belongs to the country, the raising of raw products by the improvement and cultivation of land. Industry, therefore, must be better rewarded, the wages of labor and the profits of capital must evidently be greater in the towns. But capital and labor automatically seek the most advantageous employment. They naturally, therefore, resort as much as they can to the town, and desert the country.[3]

But the particular advantage of the townspeople is in their opportunity to combine. Being collected in one place, even the most insignificant trades have accordingly, in some place or other, been incorporated. And even where they have never been incorporated, yet the monopolistic spirit, the jealousy of strangers, the aversion to take apprentices, or to let the secrets of their trade become known, generally prevail in them, and often enable them, by voluntary associations and agreements, to prevent that free competition which, being unorganized, they cannot legally enforce.

Trades which employ but a small number of workers run most easily into such combinations. Half a dozen photo-engravers,[4] perhaps, are necessary to keep a thousand printers at work. By combining they can not only monopolize the employment, but reduce the whole business into a sort of slavery to themselves, and raise the price of their labor above what is due to the nature of their work.

The inhabitants of the country, widely separated as they are, cannot easily combine together. They have not only never been incorporated, but the trade spirit never has been strong among them.

No apprenticeship has ever been thought necessary to

[3] M'Culloch and Cannan both question this thesis. Cannan thinks A. S. does not sufficiently consider the numerous failures in towns; M'Culloch says that industry is not really better rewarded in the towns, but only that opportunities for the employment of large capital are greater. But there can be no argument as to where most rich men made their fortunes.

[4] "Wool-combers."—W. N.

qualify for agriculture. Next to what are called the fine arts, and the liberal professions, however, there is perhaps no trade which requires so great a variety of knowledge and experience.

The innumerable books which have been written upon it in all languages, may satisfy us, that even among the wisest and most learned nations, it has never been regarded as a matter very easily understood.

And from all those volumes we shall in vain attempt to collect that knowledge of its various and complicated operations, which even the common farmer knows—notwithstanding the contempt with which the very contemptible authors of some of them may sometimes affect to speak of him.

There is scarcely any common mechanical trade, on the contrary, of which all the operations may not be as completely and distinctly explained in a pamphlet of a very few pages, as it is possible for words and illustrations to explain them.

Not only the art of the farmer, the general direction of farm operations, but many farming details, require much more skill and experience than most mechanical trades. The man who works with brass and iron, works with tools and upon materials of which the temper is always the same, or very nearly the same.

But the man who plows the ground works with tools of which the health, strength, and temper are very different upon different occasions. The materials he works with are as variable as his tools, and both require to be managed with much judgment and discretion.

How much the lower levels of country people are really superior to those of the town, is well known to every man whom either business or curiosity has led to converse much with both.[5]

The farmer is less accustomed, indeed, to social intercourse than the mechanic who lives in a town. His voice and language are uncultivated. His understanding, however, being accustomed to consider a greater variety of objects, is generally much superior to that of a city workman, whose whole attention from morning till

[5] M'Culloch denies this with some heat; in 1838, at least, he says, the superiority is with the town workmen. Probably, taking a broad average, there is not much difference one way or the other.

Dr. T. N. Carver says that the farm operator should be compared only with the small business man of the town, and the farm "hired man" with the wage-earning workman in the shops and factories.

night is commonly occupied in performing one or two very simple operations.

The advantage which the industry of the towns always has over that of the country is not entirely owing to the incorporated trades and their rules. It is supported by many other regulations.

The high duties upon foreign manufactures and upon all goods imported by alien merchants, all tend in the same direction. The trade laws enable the townspeople to raise their prices, without danger of being under-sold by the free competition of their own countrymen. National laws secure them equally against that of foreigners.

The excessive prices caused by both are everywhere finally paid by the landlords, farmers, and laborers of the country, who, oddly enough, seldom oppose the establishment of these monopolies. They have commonly neither inclination nor ability to enter into similar combinations; and the clamor and sophistry of merchants and manufacturers easily convince them that the private interest of a part of the community (and that a small part) is the general interest of the whole.

In Great Britain the superiority of the industry of the towns over the country seems to have been greater formerly than it is now. This change may be regarded as the necessary, though very much delayed, consequence of the extraordinary encouragement given to the industry of the towns.

The capital accumulated there comes in time to be so large that it can no longer earn its usual profit, and forces out capital to the country, where, by creating a new demand for country labor, it necessarily raises its wages.

It then spreads itself, so to speak, over the face of the land, and thus is in part restored to the country, at the expense of which, very largely, it had originally been absorbed by the town.

People of the same trade seldom meet together, even for merriment and diversion, but the conversation ends in a conspiracy against the public, or in some contrivance to raise prices.[6]

[6] M'Culloch denies that it can have this effect over any considerable period. But no one can deny that this is the universal tendency; that prices may be raised temporarily; and that if the attempt is made frequently, the effect is almost as pernicious as if prices were always excessive.

It is impossible indeed to prevent such meetings, by any law which could be enforced, or would be consistent with liberty and justice. But though the law cannot hinder people in the same line of business from sometimes assembling together, it ought at least to do nothing to make such meetings easy, much less to make them necessary.

Any regulation which obliges all those in the same trade in a particular town to register their names and addresses, facilitates such assemblies. Individuals meet who might never otherwise be known to one another, and every man in the trade learns where he can find all the others.

An ordinance which authorizes those of the same trade to tax themselves in order to provide for their poor, their sick, their widows and orphans, by giving them a common fund to manage, renders such assemblies necessary.

Incorporation of a trade not only renders meetings necessary, but makes the act of the majority binding upon the whole. An effective combination cannot be established without incorporation, except by the unanimous consent of every single trader, and it can last only as long as every single trader continues of the same mind.

. The pretense that incorporated trades are necessary for better government is without any foundation. The real and effective discipline over a workman is not that of his trade, but of his customers. It is the fear of losing their accounts which restrains his frauds and corrects his negligence.

An exclusive organization necessarily weakens the force of this discipline. A particular set of workmen must then be employed, whether they behave well or ill, and it is for this reason that in many large towns no competent workmen are to be found, even in some of the most necessary trades.

If you would have your work tolerably done, it must be taken to the suburbs, where the workmen, having no exclusive privilege, have nothing but their character to depend upon, and you must then smuggle the work back into the town as best you can.

It is in this way that regulations and laws sometimes restrict competition. In other ways, they sometimes increase competition beyond what is necessary or proper.

It has been considered as of so much importance that a

proper number of young people should be educated for certain professions, that many pensions, scholarships, etc., have been founded, both privately and by governments, thus attracting many more people into those trades than could otherwise hope to follow them. In all Christian countries, I believe, the education of most clergymen is paid for in this manner. Very few of them are educated altogether at their own expense.

The long, tedious, and expensive education, therefore, of those who pay their own way, will not always secure them suitable compensation, the church being crowded with people who, in order to get employment, are willing to accept much smaller salaries than what such an education would otherwise have entitled them to.

It would be indecent, no doubt, to compare a clergyman with a workman in any common trade, but the pay of a clergyman may surely be considered as of the same nature with the wages of a workman.

In England, the pay of the parish curate has generally been much below that of skilled labor. Whenever the law has attempted to regulate the wages of workmen, it has always been to lower rather than to raise them. But the law has often attempted to raise the wages of curates, and for the dignity of the church, to force the rectors of parishes to pay more than the curate himself might be willing to accept.

In both cases the law seems to have been equally ineffective, because of the excessive competition in the latter case, and the lack of it in the former. The curate must work for less, and the workman demands and gets more, than the legal rate.

In professions in which there is nothing corresponding to the great religious foundations, such as law and medicine, if an equal proportion of people were educated at public expense, the competition would soon be so great as to make them unprofitable. They would be entirely abandoned to such as had been educated by public institutions, and their numbers and necessities would oblige them in general to content themselves with a very miserable recompense, very degrading to the now respectable professions of law and medicine.

That unprosperous race of men commonly called men of letters is just about in the situation which lawyers and physicians probably would be, in the case just mentioned. Most of them have been educated for the church, and have generally, therefore, been educated at the public expense, and their numbers are everywhere so great that their usual earnings are very paltry.

Before the invention of the art of printing, the only way by which a man of letters could earn anything by his talents, was to be a teacher—to pass along to other people the curious and useful knowledge which he had acquired himself. And this is still surely a more honorable and useful, and in general even a more profitable occupation than that other of writing for publication, to which the art of printing has given occasion.

The time and study, the genius, knowledge, and diligence requisite to qualify an eminent teacher of the sciences, are at least equal to what is necessary for the greatest practitioners in law and medicine. But the usual reward of a famous teacher bears no proportion to that of the lawyer or physician, because the trade of the one is crowded with indigent people who have been brought up to it at the public expense; whereas the other two professions are encumbered with very few who have not paid for their own education.

Before the invention of the art of printing, a scholar and a beggar seem to have been terms very nearly synonymous. Many governors of universities before that time appear to have often granted licenses to their scholars to beg.

In ancient times, indeed, before any charities of this kind had been established for the wholesale education of indigent people to the learned professions, the rewards of famous teachers appear to have been much greater. Many records of the ancient Greek teachers and philosophers indicate that they were highly paid.

But the relatively poor earning power of teachers is upon the whole, perhaps, rather advantageous than hurtful to the public. It may somewhat degrade the profession of a public teacher; but cheapness of education is surely an advantage which greatly over-balances this trifling inconvenience.[7]

Private and governmental laws and regulations cause even greater inequalities and injustices, by obstructing the free passage of labor and capital from place to place, and from one employment to another.

In England it often happens that high wages and low wages exist side by side in a certain town, because one trade is prospering

[7] "Trifling" to whom? the teachers? But A. S. was himself a professor.

and needs workers, while the other is declining and has a surplus. Yet no shift of workers occurs, because the laws of apprenticeship and trade privileges do not permit it.

Where such a condition occurs, workers thrown out of employment have no choice but to work as ill-paid common labor, or to "come upon the parish," [8] and this is what they generally do.

Whatever obstructs the free movement of labor from one employment to another, obstructs that of capital as well, as the capital which can be employed in any branch of business depends very much upon how much labor can be employed in it.

There is, however, rather less obstruction to the free circulation of capital from one place to another than to that of labor. It is everywhere much easier for a wealthy merchant to obtain the privilege of trading in an incorporated town than for a poor artisan to obtain that of working in it.

℃ Wherever trade regulations exist, which is everywhere in Europe, workmen find difficulty in moving from place to place. In England they have an additional difficulty, peculiar to this country, in the operation of the poor laws, which oppress common labor and skilled artisans alike.

℃ This results from the legal obligation that each parish support its own poor, to be financed from a parish tax. The question as to which parish should support a certain individual, therefore, became a matter of importance and dispute. A natural result was that every parish resisted the settlement of a newcomer who had no visible means of support but his hands, and was therefore likely to increase the parish poor tax, and wherever possible it would attempt to deport such a person to some other parish.

℃ All kinds of subterfuges and chicanery were common, and many times these parish disputes reached a pitch resembling a state of war against the poor and against one another.

℃ The result of this poorly-contrived system, in general, was to increase the difficulty, and discourage the free movement of all classes of labor from place to place.[9]

---

[8] That is, to take advantage of what we call the "poor laws," claiming support from the local government.

[9] It was largely because of the thorough and devastating analysis of the working of the parish poor laws in W. N., covering several pages, that the worst features of the system were abolished in 1795, and the system further reformed and improved in 1834.

The very unequal price of labor which we frequently find in England in places at no great distance from one another, is probably owing to the obstruction which the poor laws offer to free movement from parish to parish.

The scarcity of hands in one parish, therefore, cannot always be relieved by their superabundance in another, as is constantly done in Scotland and, I believe, in all other countries.

In such countries, though wages may sometimes rise a little in the neighborhood of a large city, or wherever else there is an extraordinary demand for labor, yet we never meet with those sudden and unaccountable differences in the wages of neighboring places which we sometimes find in England.

Here it is often more difficult for a poor man to pass the artificial boundary of a parish, than to cross an arm of the sea or a ridge of high mountains, natural boundaries which sometimes sharply separate differing rates of wages in other countries.

To remove a man who has committed no crime from the parish where he chooses to reside, is a plain violation of natural liberty and justice. The common people of England, however, so jealous of their liberty, but like the common people of most countries never rightly understanding wherein it consists, have now for more than a century allowed themselves to be thus oppressed without a remedy.

CHAPTER XII

*A mercifully short chapter dealing with
some attempts to regulate wages and prices
by law; why these are ineffective and have
for the most part been abandoned.*

ALTHOUGH IN FORMER TIMES it was usual to fix wage rates, first
by general laws extending over the whole kingdom, and afterwards
locally by orders of the justice of the peace, both these practices
are now entirely abandoned.

Particular acts of Parliament, however, still attempt [1]
sometimes to regulate wages in particular trades and in particular
places. Thus one law prohibits under heavy penalties all employing tailors in London, and five miles round it, from paying, and
their workmen from accepting, more than two shillings and sevenpence halfpenny a day, except in the case of a public mourning.

Whenever the legislature attempts to adjust the arguments
between employers and their workmen, it is the employers whose
advice is taken. When the regulation, therefore, is in favor of the
workmen, it is always just and equitable; but it is sometimes otherwise when in favor of the employers.

Thus the law which obliges the employers in several different trades to pay their workmen in money and not in goods, is
quite just and equitable. It imposes no real hardship upon the
employers. It only obliges them to pay the real value in money,
which they pretended to pay, but did not always really pay, in
goods. This law favors the workmen.

When employers combine to reduce the wages of workmen,
they commonly enter into a private agreement not to pay more
than a certain wage under a certain penalty. Were the workmen
to enter into a similar combination, not to accept a certain wage

[1] In 1776, be it remembered.

[*120*]

under a certain penalty, the law would punish them very severely; and if it dealt impartially, it would treat the employers in the same manner.[2]

As our ancestors vainly tried to fix wages, so they long tried to regulate the profits of merchants and other dealers, by fixing the prices of food and other goods. The regulation of bread is, as far as I know, the only remnant of this ancient usage.

Where there is a baking monopoly, it may perhaps be proper to regulate the price of the staff of life. But where there is none, competition will regulate it much better than any law.[3]

A final note as to inequalities of wages and profits: The proportion between the different rates of wages and profit in different employments does not seem to be much affected, as has already been observed, by the riches or poverty, the advancing, stationary, or declining state of the nation. Such fundamental changes in the public welfare, though they affect the general rates both of wages and profit, must in the end affect them equally in all different employments. The proportion between them, therefore, must in general remain the same.

[2] Again, this was England in 1776, not 1947 in the United States.

[3] "The new is that which has been forgotten," observes Carver. What is now regarded as progressive—wage-fixing, hours-fixing, price-fixing, profit-fixing—were long ago tried, called out of date and discarded. And not once but many times. "There is no new thing under the sun."

CHAPTER XIII

The rent of land, the third source from which all income arises, is also subject to natural laws of human behavior; how rent first arose, and why its laws differ greatly from those of wages and profits.

I HAVE ALREADY EXPLAINED the nature of the wages of labor, and the profits of capital, two of the three sources from which men receive their support. The third source, the rent of land, differs in many respects from the other two, and seems to follow a different set of principles.[1]

Rent, which may be defined as the price paid for the use of land, is naturally the highest which the tenant can afford to pay in the actual circumstances of the case. In adjusting the terms of a lease, the landlord aims to leave him no more of the produce than enough to keep up the stock from which he furnishes the seed, pays the labor, and purchases and maintains the livestock and implements, together with the ordinary rate of profit on farm operations in the neighborhood.

This is obviously the smallest share with which the tenant can get along, and the landlord seldom means to leave him any more.

[1] This chapter, and the three which follow, are not as clear and complete as could be wished. The theory of the origin and nature of rent has been further developed since W. N., notably by Ricardo, who laid down the basic rule: rent of land is a payment for "the original and indestructible powers of the soil"; it arises when all free and fertile land is taken up, and recourse must be had to land less fertile or less favorably situated.

Critics agree, however, that the basic principles of rent are about as A. S. outlines them. Thorold Rogers says that the account of the origin of rent in W. N. has its blemishes, but only because A. S. used insufficient facts. "As usual, A. S. is much more in the right than his critics."

Whatever part of the produce, or, what is the same thing, whatever part of its selling price, is over and above this share, he naturally tries to collect as the rent of his land, and this will be the most the tenant can afford to pay in the actual circumstances.

Sometimes, indeed, the liberality, or more frequently the ignorance, of the landlord, induces him to accept somewhat less than his portion; and sometimes, too, though more rarely, the ignorance of the tenant makes him undertake to pay somewhat more, which means that he will receive somewhat less than the ordinary profits of farming capital in the neighborhood.

The rent of land, it may be thought, is frequently no more than a reasonable profit or interest for the capital invested by the landlord in its improvement. But such a case is rare, if not altogether unknown.

The landlord will demand rent even for unimproved land, and if he makes improvements he will demand additional rent. Those improvements, besides, are not always made by the landlord, but sometimes by the tenant. But when the lease comes to be renewed, the landlord is pretty sure to demand the same increase in rent as if he himself had paid for them all.

He sometimes demands rent for what is altogether incapable of human improvement. Kelp is a species of sea-weed, which yields an alkaline salt, useful for making glass, soap, and for several other purposes. It grows on rocky coasts where it is twice every day covered with the tide, and where human industry has nothing to do with its production. The landlord, however, whose estate is bounded by a kelp bed of this kind, demands rent for it just as he does for his fields.

The sea about the Shetland Islands abounds in fish, which make a great part of the subsistence of the islanders. But in order to profit by the produce of the sea, they must have a habitation upon the adjacent land. The rent of the landlord is in proportion, therefore, not only to what the tenant can make by the land, but to what he can make both by land and sea.

This rent is partly paid in sea-fish; and one of the very few instances in which rent makes a part of the price of that commodity, is to be found in those islands.

The rent of land, therefore, considered as the price paid for the use of the land, is naturally a monopoly price. It is not at all proportioned to what the landlord may have invested in the improvement of the land, or to what he can afford to take; but to what the traffic will bear.[2]

There are cases in which the traffic will bear no rent charge at all. Some products which reach the market can find so little demand that their price will cover only the bare cost of bringing them there; there is no surplus from which the landlord could collect rent.

On the other hand, there are some products for which the demand must always be large enough to command a price higher than what is sufficient to bring them to market; and there are still other cases where the demand may or may not be such as to command this higher price. The former must always yield rent to that landlord. The latter sometimes may, and sometimes may not, according to the circumstances.

Rent, it may therefore be observed, enters into the composition of the price of commodities in a different way from wages and profit. High or low wages and profit are the principal causes of high or low price; high or low rent is not a cause but the effect of it.

It is because high or low wages and profit must be paid, in order to bring a particular commodity to market, that its price is high or low. But it is because its selling price is high or low—whether it is a great deal more, or very little more, or no more, than what is sufficient to pay those wages and profit—that it yields a high rent, or a low rent, or no rent at all.

[2] "to what the farmer can afford to give."—W. N. It is not brought out clearly here, nor elsewhere in W. N., that the rent of land is what is paid for the natural or inherent productive powers of the soil, or in towns, for its site value. What is paid for the use of improvements of any kind is not rent but the profit or interest on capital.

CHAPTER XIV

*Explaining that some land always yields
rent, because its product, human food,
always brings a price high enough so that
the landlord receives a share.*

TAKING UP FIRST those commodities of which the price is always
high enough to yield rent to the landlord, these are all included
in one class—human food.

As men, like all other animals, naturally multiply in proportion to the means of their subsistence,[1] food is always more or
less in demand. It can always purchase or command labor, whether
more or less, and somebody can always be found who is willing to
do something in order to obtain it.

But almost any land produces more food than what will
maintain all the labor necessary for bringing it to market. The surplus, too, is always more than enough to replace the capital which
employed that labor, together with its profits. Something, therefore, is always left over for rent to the landlord.

Even the most desert moors in Norway or Scotland produce
some sort of pasture for cattle, of which the milk and the increase
are always more than enough, not only to maintain all the labor
necessary for tending them, and to pay the ordinary profit to the
farmer or owner of the herd or flock, but to yield some small rent
to the landlord.

The rent then increases in proportion to the productiveness
of the pasture. The acreage not only maintains more cattle, but
as they are brought within a smaller compass, less labor is needed

[1] As already observed, they tend to do so in many countries, but not in some
of the oldest and most highly civilized, such as France.

to tend them, and to collect their produce. The landlord gains both ways: by the increase of production, and by the smaller amount of labor which must be maintained out of it.

The rent of land varies not only according to its fertility, but according to its situation, regardless of its fertility. Land in the vicinity of a town rents for more than land equally fertile in a distant part of the country.

Though it may cost no more labor to cultivate the one than the other, it must always cost more to bring the produce of the distant land to market. A greater quantity of labor, therefore, must be maintained out of it; and the surplus, from which are drawn both the profit of the farmer and the rent of the landlord, must be reduced.

But in remote parts of the country the rate of profit, as has already been shown, is generally higher than near a large town. A still smaller proportion of this surplus, therefore, remains for the landlord.

Good roads, railroads, and canals,[2] by reducing the cost of transportation, put the remote parts of the country more nearly on a level with those nearer town. They are for that reason the greatest of all improvements.[3]

They are an advantage to the town, by breaking down the monopoly of the surrounding country. They are advantageous even to that area, for although they introduce some competing commodities into the market, they open many new markets to its produce.

Monopoly, besides, is a great enemy to good management, which depends wholly on that free and universal competition which forces everybody to manage efficiently in sheer self-defense.

Within the last fifty years, some of the counties in the neighborhood of London petitioned the Parliament against the extension of the turnpike roads into the remoter counties. Those remoter counties, they asserted, because of their cheaper labor, would be able to sell their hay and grain cheaper in the London market than farmers nearby, and would thereby reduce their rents, and ruin their cultivation.

[2] "canals and navigable rivers"—W. N.
[3] Carver says that improved transportation may reduce the differences in site value, and thus reduce the rent of land—certainly of some land, possibly the total rent of all land.

The turnpikes, nevertheless, were built, and since then their rents have risen, and their cultivation has been improved.

℃   Land used for growing grain crops produces much more human food per acre than pasture land. Although cultivation takes much more labor, the surplus remaining after that labor is maintained and the seed replaced is nevertheless greater than what remains from the products of grazing.

℃   In the early stages of agriculture, meat is plentiful and cheap, and bread relatively expensive. But when land is more cultivated, and less is available for pasture, the price of meat rises, and eventually there is little difference in the rental value of crop land and pasture.[4]

This equality, however, between the rents and profits of hay and those of grain, of the land of which the immediate product is food for cattle, and of that of which it is food for men, must be understood to be the general rule only. In some particular local situations it is quite otherwise, and the rents and profits of pasture are much higher than what can be made in grain-growing.

Thus in the vicinity of a large city, the demand for milk and for forage for horses, frequently raises the value of hay and grass above what may be called its natural proportion to that of grain. This local advantage, it is evident, cannot be enjoyed by land at a distance.[5]

In some very populous countries, the whole territory, like the lands near a large city, has not been sufficient to produce both the pasture products and the grain necessary for their inhabitants. Their lands, therefore, have been principally employed in the production of grass, the more bulky commodity, and which cannot be so easily brought from a distance; the grain, the food of the great body of the people, has been chiefly imported from foreign countries.

Holland is at present in this situation, and a considerable part of ancient Italy seems to have been so during the prosperity of the Romans. Tillage, indeed, in that part of ancient Italy which

[4] Pasture generally commands a higher rent than tilled land, writes Thorold Rogers, in 1880.

[5] All these relationships in agriculture are intricate, and the successful farmer has to weigh his alternatives carefully. In the dairy districts of England, observes Carver, wheat is sometimes grown at a cost higher than the value of the grain, solely to obtain the straw as bedding for cows.

lay around Rome, must have been very much discouraged by the distributions of grain which were frequently made to the people, either free, or at a very low price.[6]

This low price must necessarily have sunk the price of what could be brought to the Roman market from Latium, or the ancient territory of Rome, and must have discouraged its cultivation in that country.

In an open country, too, of which the principal product is grain, a well-fenced piece of grassland will frequently rent higher than any grain field in its neighborhood.

But where there is no local advantage of this kind, the rents and profits of grain, or whatever else is the common vegetable food of the people, must naturally control the rents and profits of pasture land.

The use of the artificial grasses, of turnips, carrots, cabbages, and the other expedients which have been devised to make an equal quantity of land feed a greater number of cattle, should somewhat reduce the price of meat as compared with bread, and it has in fact generally done so.

In all great countries most of the cultivated lands are employed in producing either food for men or feed for livestock. The rent and profit of these lands regulate the rent and profit of all other cultivated land. If any particular product was less profitable, the land would soon be turned into grain or pasture; and if any was more so, some part of the lands in grain or pasture would soon be turned to that product.

In such a case as a truck or vegetable farm, or fruit orchards, both the rent of the landlord and the profit of the farmer are generally greater than in the field and pasture crops. But to bring such properties into production is more expensive, and hence a greater rent becomes due to the landlord.

It requires a more attentive and skilful management, as well; hence a greater profit becomes due to the farmer.

The circumstances of gardeners, generally poor, and never more than moderate, may satisfy us that their great ingenuity is

[6] Professor Simkhovitch traces all the ills of ancient Rome, including the distributions of grain which corrupted the Roman proletariat, to the loss of fertility of the Italian soil, which made profitable agriculture impossible. Distributions of free grain were the result, not the cause, of the ruin of Italian tillage. (*Rome's Fall Reconsidered.*)

not commonly over-paid. Their delightful art is practiced by so many rich people for amusement, that little advantage is to be made by those who practice it for profit; because the persons who should naturally be their best customers, frequently supply themselves with all their most precious productions.

℃   The same principle applies to home vegetable gardens and vineyards; where the higher profits realized (whether real or imaginary) are probably no more than a fair profit on the additional investment and labor expense.

The rent and profit of those products, therefore, although often much higher than those of grain and pasture, yet when they do no more than compensate such extraordinary expense, are in reality regulated by the rent and profit of those common crops.

It sometimes happens, indeed, that the quantity of land which is peculiarly adapted to grow a particular product is too small to supply the demand. The whole output can be disposed of to those who are willing to pay somewhat more than enough to pay the whole rent, wages and profit necessary for growing and bringing it to market, according to their ordinary rates.

This is, in effect, a monopoly of a particular type of land, and the greater part of this monopolistic price naturally goes to the rent of the landlord.

℃   The lands in vineyards which produce unusually choice wines, certain sugar plantations, and to a lesser extent the lands which in North America are used to grow tobacco, are examples of these natural monopolies of soil, which bear no fixed relation to the ordinary rental value of ordinary cultivated land.

In Virginia and Maryland the cultivation of tobacco is preferred, as more profitable, to that of grain. Tobacco might be cultivated with advantage in many parts of Europe; but in almost every part of Europe it has become a principal subject of taxation, and to collect a tax from every individual farm where this plant might be cultivated would be more difficult, it has been supposed, than to levy a customs duty upon its importation.

The cultivation of tobacco has upon this account been most absurdly prohibited in most of Europe, which necessarily gives a sort of monopoly to the countries where it is allowed; and as Virginia and Maryland are the largest producers, they share largely, though with some competitors, in the advantage of this monopoly.

Although the present price of tobacco is probably more

than sufficient to pay the whole rent, wages and profit necessary for preparing and bringing it to market according to the rate at which they are commonly paid in crop land, our tobacco planters have shown the same fear of the super-abundance of tobacco, which the proprietors of the old vineyards in France have of the super-abundance of wine.

They have accordingly tried to restrict its production by law, and have, I am told, sometimes burnt in plentiful years a considerable amount.[7]

If such violent methods are necessary to keep up the present price of tobacco, the advantage of its culture over that of grain, if it still has any, will probably not continue very long.

It is in this manner that the rent of cultivated land, which produces human food, regulates the rent of the greater part of other cultivated land. No particular product can long pay less rent, for in this case the land would immediately be turned to some more profitable use. And if any particular product commonly pays more, it is only because the quantity of land fitted for its cultivation is too small to supply the effective demand.

In Europe wheat is the principal product of land which serves immediately for human food. Except in particular situations, therefore, the rent of wheat land regulates in Europe that of all other cultivated land.

Britain need envy neither the vineyards of France nor the olive groves of Italy. Except in particular situations, the value of these is regulated by that of grain, in which the fertility of Britain is not much inferior to that of those two countries.

℃ But wheat is by no means the principal food of all countries and races. The rice crop, for example, produces a much larger volume of human food to the acre, although its cultivation requires many times more labor than does wheat. Another such crop is the potato, and in Scotland and some other regions oatmeal is said to be preferred to wheat flour.

℃ Wherever a greater surplus of food is produced through cultivation of these crops, the share of the landlord will always maintain a greater quantity of labor, and consequently will enable him to purchase or command a greater quantity of it.

℃ Hence, the real value of his rent—not necessarily his money

---

[7] As the Brazilians do to this day, with surplus coffee, and with similar results.

rent, but his real power and authority, his command of the necessaries and conveniences of life will necessarily be much greater.

The common people in Scotland, who are fed with oatmeal, are in general neither so strong nor so handsome as the same rank of people in England, who are fed with wheaten bread. They neither work so well, nor look so well; and as there is not the same difference between the people of fashion in the two countries, experience would seem to show, that the food of the common people in Scotland is not so suitable to the human constitution as that of their neighbors of the same rank in England.

But it seems to be otherwise with potatoes. The chairmen, porters, and coal-heavers in London, and those unfortunate women who live by prostitution, the strongest men and the most beautiful women perhaps in the British dominions, are said to come, for the most part, from the lowest class of people in Ireland, who are generally fed with this root.

No food can afford a more decisive proof of its nourishing quality, or of its being peculiarly suitable to the health of the human constitution. It is only its perishable nature that discourages potato cultivation, and is, perhaps, the chief obstacle to its ever becoming, in any great country, the principal vegetable food of all classes of people.

CHAPTER XV

More about rent; land producing clothing and shelter sometimes yields rent, sometimes does not; the same may be said of fuels, metals, and minerals; why this is.

As I HAVE shown in the last chapter, human food seems to be the only commodity which always and necessarily affords some rent to the landlord. Other kinds of produce sometimes may and sometimes may not, according to different circumstances.

After food, clothing and shelter are the two great necessities of mankind.

In its original rude state land can afford the materials of clothing and shelter to a much greater number of people than it can feed. In its improved state it can sometimes feed more people than it can supply with those materials; at least of a kind and quality for which they are willing to pay.

In the one state, therefore, there is always a super-abundance of those materials, which are frequently, for that reason, of little or no value. In the other, there is often a scarcity, which necessarily auguments their value.

In the one state these materials are commonly thrown away as useless, and the price of what is used is considered as equal only to the labor and expense of fitting it for use; it can, therefore, afford no rent to the landlord.

In the other they are all made use of, and there is frequently a demand for more than is for sale. Somebody is always willing to pay more than enough to pay the expense of bringing them to market, and their price, therefore, can always yield some rent to the landlord.

Among nations of hunters and shepherds, whose food consists chiefly in the flesh of those animals, every man, by providing himself with food, provides himself at the same time with more clothing than he can use, in skins and hides.

This was probably the case among the hunting nations of North America, before their country was discovered by the Europeans. Their surplus skins, which were doubtless thrown away as worthless, can now be exchanged for other goods, and have thus acquired value. But because there is no land property among these Indians, there is no rent.

When most of the cattle of the Scottish Highlands were consumed on their own hills, the exportation of their hides formed the chief article of the commerce of that country, and what they were exchanged for added something to the rent of the Highland estates.

The materials of shelter cannot always be transported to so great a distance as those of clothing, and so do not enter much into foreign commerce. When they are super-abundant in the country which produces them, it frequently happens that they are of no value to the landlord. A good stone quarry close to London would yield a considerable rent, but in many parts of Scotland and Wales it affords none. Timber for building is of great value in a populous and well-cultivated country, and the land which produces it yields considerable rent. But in many parts of North America the landlord would be much obliged to anybody who would cut and carry away some of his large trees.

The population of a country depends on how much food is available, not on the supply of clothing and shelter. In a barbarous country a family can often clothe and shelter itself by three days' work, but it takes the rest of the year to provide its food.

But when by improvement of land and other improvements one family can produce enough food for two families, obviously half the whole population is freed for other productive work. And this work generally produces clothing, shelter, household furniture, and what may be called equipage.

The rich man consumes no more food than his poor neighbor. In quality it may be very different, and to select and prepare it may require more labor and art; but in quantity it is very nearly the same.

But compare the spacious palace and great wardrobe of the one, with the hovel and few rags of the other, and it is evident that the difference between their clothing, lodging, and household furniture, is almost as great in quantity as it is in quality. The desire for food is limited in every man by the narrow capacity of the human stomach; but the desire for the conveniences and ornaments of building, dress, equipage, and household furniture, seems to have no fixed limit or boundary.

Those, therefore, who have the command of more food than they themselves can consume, are always willing to exchange the surplus, or, what is the same thing, the price of it, for other gratifications. What is over and above satisfying the limited desire, is given for those desires which cannot be satisfied, but seem to be altogether endless.

These desires and fancies of the rich open an inexhaustible market for the labor of others, and for every sort of material which human invention can employ, usefully or ornamentally, in building, dress, equipage, or household furniture; for the fossils and minerals contained in the bowels of the earth; the precious metals, and the precious stones.

Food is, in this manner, not only the original source of rent, but all other commodities obtain a part of their rent-paying value from the improvement of the powers of labor in producing food, by means of the improvement and cultivation of land.

Those other commodities, however, do not always yield rent.

℃ Whether a coal mine, for example, can afford any rent, depends partly upon its richness, and partly upon its location. A mine of average productivity near the great markets will pay both profit to the operator and rent to the landlord.

℃ But a mine that is a poor producer, or far from market, while it may pay its operator, will not yield rent. It can be worked to advantage only by the landlord himself, who can live by thus collecting both profit and rent. Many small mines in Scotland can be worked on this basis, and on no other.

℃ It may be noted here, that the price of coal is in many places kept down by the price of fuel wood, which varies according to the state of agriculture, in nearly the same way, and for precisely the same reasons, as the price of cattle.

Coal, in coal-producing areas, is much below the highest theoretical price. If not, it could not pay the expense of transportation to market. A small quantity only could be sold, and the owners and operators find it more to their interest to sell a great quantity at a price somewhat above the lowest, than a small quantity at the highest.

The most productive mine regulates the price of coal at all the other mines in its neighborhood.[1] Both the owner and the operator find, the one that he can get a higher rent, the other that he can get a greater profit, by somewhat under-selling all their neighbors. Their competitors are soon obliged to sell at the same price, though they cannot so well afford it, and though it always cuts down, and sometimes wipes out both rent and profit. Some mines are abandoned altogether; others can pay no rent, and can be worked only by the proprietor.

The lowest price at which coal can be sold for any considerable time is, like that of all other commodities, the price which is barely sufficient to replace, together with its ordinary profits, the capital which must be employed in bringing it to market. At a coal mine for which the landlord can get no rent, but which he must either work himself or shut it down, the price of coal must be somewhere near this level.

For these reasons, rent generally forms a smaller part of the price of coal than of most other raw materials. How much rent a coal mine pays to its owner depends as much upon its location as upon its richness.

℮ This is not true of other minerals, particularly the metals. These are so valuable in proportion to their weight, even the basest, that their price will bear the cost of transportation from great distances. The location of the metal mine is therefore much less important that its richness or cost of production.

℮ As metals are drawn from all parts of the world, their prices compete with each other in all markets. The element of rent, accordingly, plays a very small part in setting the price of the coarse metals, and still less in the price of gold and silver. Labor and profit are almost the only elements in these prices.

---

[1] While A. S. undoubtedly understood the general principle of prices, as shown in the next paragraph, and elsewhere in W. N., this statement is clearly erroneous, as all editors agree. The price of coal (as of all commodities) is fixed in the long run by the cost of production of the "marginal producer"—the poorest, or highest-cost and least profitable mine that can find a market for its coal and keep operating. If this mine and the others in its class closed down, the total production of coal would drop, until rising prices again made it just worth someone's while to reopen these mines.

❡ The rent of the tin mines in Cornwall and of some lead mines in Scotland is figured at 16⅔ per cent of the gross output. But the silver mines of Peru, although they belong to the government, and consequently are encouraged, now pay a rent or tax of only 10 per cent of the gross, and profits are small. The gold mines pay only 5 per cent.

Gold is much more liable to be smuggled than silver, not only on account of the higher value of the metal in proportion to its bulk, but on account of the peculiar way in which nature produces it.

Silver is very seldom found in pure form, but, like most other metals, is generally in combination with some other mineral, from which it can only be separated by a very laborious and tedious process, and by means of machinery.

Gold, on the contrary, is almost always found virgin. It is sometimes found in nuggets of some bulk; and even when mixed in small and almost insensible particles with sand, or gravel, it can be separated by a very short and simple operation, which can be carried on in any private house by anybody who has a small quantity of mercury.

If the tax, therefore, is but ill-paid upon silver, it is likely to be much worse paid upon gold; and rent must make a much smaller part of the price of gold, than of silver.

The lowest price at which the precious metals can be sold—the smallest quantity of other goods for which they can be exchanged during any considerable time—is regulated by the same principles which fix the lowest ordinary price of all other forms of wealth. The capital which must be employed, the food, clothing and shelter which are used up in bringing them from the mine to the market, fix the price. It must at least be sufficient to replace that capital, with the ordinary profits.

The highest price of these metals, however, seems to be not necessarily determined by anything but the actual scarcity or plenty of those metals themselves. It is not determined by the price of some other commodity, as the price of coal is by that of wood.

Increase the scarcity of gold to a sufficient degree, and the smallest bit of it may become more precious than a diamond, and exchange for a greater quantity of other goods.

The demand for those metals arises partly from their utility, and partly from their beauty. If you except iron, they are perhaps more useful than any other metal.[2] A silver boiler is more cleanly than an aluminum, copper, or tin one; and the same quality would render a gold boiler still better than a silver one.

The principal merit of the precious metals, however, arises from their beauty, which renders them peculiarly fit for the ornaments of dress and furniture. No paint or dye can give so splendid a color as gilding.

The merit of their beauty is greatly enhanced by their scarcity. With most rich people, the chief enjoyment of riches consists in the parade of riches, which in their eyes is never so complete as when they obviously possess those decisive marks of opulence which nobody can afford but themselves. In their eyes the merit of any object, useful or beautiful, is greatly enhanced by its scarcity, or by the great labor which is necessary to collect any considerable quantity of it, a labor which nobody can afford to pay for but themselves.

Such objects they are willing to purchase at a higher price than other things much more beautiful and useful, but more common.

These qualities of utility, beauty, and scarcity, are the original foundation of the high price of gold and silver, or of the great quantity of other goods for which they can everywhere be exchanged.

This value was antecedent to and independent of their being employed as coin, and was the quality which fitted them for that employment.

Their use in coinage, however, by creating a new demand, and by reducing the quantity which could be used in other ways, may have afterwards contributed to keep up or increase their value.

The demand for precious stones arises altogether from their beauty and scarcity. They are of no use except as ornaments. Wages and profit accordingly make up, as a rule, almost the whole of their high price. Rent comes in but for a very small share; frequently for no share; and only the richest mines yield any considerable rent.

[2] Steel is still the most valuable metal to mankind; but with the metallurgists every day finding new uses for even the rarest metals, with constantly expanding employment for copper, for nickel, for aluminum, magnesium, tungsten, it is not clear in these days that we need these less than gold and silver.

The most abundant mines of precious metals or of precious stones could add little to the real wealth of the world. When the value of a commodity is principally derived from its scarcity, it necessarily is worth less when abundant. To be sure, silverware, and the other frivolous ornaments of dress and furniture, could be bought for a smaller quantity of labor, or for a smaller quantity of other commodities; and this is the only advantage which the world could derive from that abundance.

It is otherwise in land that is above ground. The value of its product and of its rent is in proportion to its absolute, not to its relative fertility. The land which produces a certain quantity of food, clothing and shelter can always feed, clothe, and lodge a certain number of people; and whatever may be the proportion of the landlord, it will always give him a proportionate command of the labor of those people, and of the commodities with which that labor can supply him.

The value of the most barren lands is not diminished by being close to the most fertile. On the contrary, it is generally increased by it. The great number of people maintained by the fertile lands affords a market for much of the produce of the barren, which they could never have found among those whom their own produce could maintain.

It is for this reason that whatever increases the fertility of land in producing food, contributes likewise to increase that of many other lands, by creating a new demand for their produce.

That abundance of food, of which many people have the disposal beyond what they themselves can consume, is the true cause of the demand for the precious metals and precious stones, as well as for every other convenience and ornament of dress, lodging, household furniture, and equipage.

Food not only constitutes the principal part of the riches of the world, but it is the abundance of food which gives the principal part of their value to many other forms of wealth. The poor inhabitants of Cuba and Santo Domingo, when they were first discovered by the Spaniards, used to wear little bits of gold as ornaments in their hair and other parts of their dress. They seemed to value them as we would do any little pebbles of somewhat more than ordinary beauty, and to consider them as just worth the picking up, but not worth the refusing to anybody who asked for them.

They gave them to their new guests willingly, without seeming to think that they had made them any very valuable present, and were astonished to observe the eagerness of the Spaniards to obtain them. They had no notion that there could anywhere be a country in which many people had the disposal of so great a surplus of food, so scanty always among themselves, that for a very small quantity of those glittering trifles they would willingly give as much as might maintain a whole family for many years. Could they have been made to understand this, the greed of the Spaniards would not have surprised them.

CHAPTER XVI

*As food becomes more plentiful, its value in
exchange tends to fall, and that of other
commodities, clothing, shelter, etc., therefore tends to rise.*

THE INCREASING abundance of food, which results from improvement and better cultivation, must necessarily increase the demand
for all other products of land, whether for use or ornament. It
might be expected, therefore, that as a country progresses, the
value of these other commodities, which sometimes do and sometimes do not afford rent, should constantly rise in proportion to
food, which always yields some rent.

As art and industry advance, the materials of clothing and
shelter, the useful fossils and minerals of the earth, the precious
metals and the precious stones should gradually come to be more
and more in demand, should gradually exchange for a greater and
a greater quantity of food, or in other words, should gradually
become more and more expensive.

In fact, this is exactly what has happened, except on some
occasions when particular circumstances have interrupted the
process.

The value of a stone quarry, for example, will necessarily
increase with the increasing improvement and population of the
neighborhood, especially if it should be the only one in the area.
But the value of a silver mine, even though there should not be
another within a thousand miles of it, will not necessarily increase
with the improvement of the country in which it is located.

The market for building stone can seldom extend more
than a few miles round about it, and the demand must generally
be in proportion to the improvement and population of that small

district. But the market for silver may extend over the whole known world.

Unless the world in general, therefore, be advancing in improvement and population, the demand for silver might not be at all increased by the improvement even of a large country in the neighborhood of the mine.

Contrariwise, even though the world in general were improving, yet if new mines should be discovered, much richer than any which had been known before, though the demand for silver would be increasing, yet the supply might increase so much faster that the real price of that metal might gradually fall.

In other words, any given quantity, a pound weight of it, for example, might purchase or command a smaller and a smaller quantity of labor, or exchange for a smaller and a smaller quantity of grain, the principal part of the subsistence of the laborer.

The relationship between the price of silver and the price of grain is one of great interest, and will be considered more fully in another place. It is sufficient here to point out that the money price of grain—that is, the amount of silver for which a given amount of grain will exchange—seems to depend on the supply-and-demand situation as to silver.

If the market for silver should improve, as a result of the general progress of the community, while for any reason the supply did not increase as fast, the value of silver would rise, and the money price of grain would fall.

If, on the contrary, the production of silver should rise faster than the demand, the average money price of grain would go higher.

Finally, if the supply and demand for silver remained approximately in balance, silver would continue to buy or exchange for nearly the same quantity of grain, and, in spite of all improvement, the average money price of grain would continue about the same.

CHAPTER XVII

*High prices and low prices of goods and
services alike have to be measured, or at least
are generally measured, in money; when a
price changes, the change may be in the
value of the thing, or in the value of the
money; it could be either, and many people
confuse one with the other; a country where
prices are low is not necessarily a poor country, nor a country with high prices a rich
one.*

Most writers who have collected the money prices of things in
ancient times, seem to have considered the low money price of
grain, and of goods in general, or, in other words, the high value
of gold and silver, as a proof, not only of the scarcity of those
metals, but of the poverty and barbarism of the country at the time
when it took place.

This notion is connected with the system of political
economy which represents national wealth as consisting in the
abundance, and national poverty in the scarcity, of gold and silver;
a system which I shall endeavor to examine and explain at great
length in the fifth book of this inquiry.

I shall only observe here, that the high value of the
precious metals can be no proof of the poverty or barbarism of any
particular country at a particular time. It is a proof only of the
barrenness of the mines which happened at that time to supply
the commercial world. A poor country can neither buy more gold
and silver than a rich one, nor pay more for it; and the value of

those metals, therefore, is not likely to be higher in the former than in the latter.

As the wealth of Europe, indeed, has increased greatly since the discovery of the mines of America, so the value of gold and silver has gradually diminished. This lowered value, however, has not been due to the increase of the real wealth of Europe, but to the accidental discovery of more productive mines than any that were known before.

The increase of gold and silver in Europe, and the increase of its manufactures and agriculture, are two phenomena which, though they have appeared during the same period, have arisen from very different causes, and have hardly any connection with each other. The first has arisen from a mere accident, in which neither foresight nor policy had or could have any share. The second from the fall of the feudal system, and from the establishment of governments which give to industry the only encouragement it needs—some tolerable security that it shall enjoy the fruits of its own labor.

Poland, where the feudal system still survives, is to this day as beggarly a country as it was before the discovery of America. The money price of Polish grain, however, has risen; the real value of the precious metals has fallen, just as it has in other parts of Europe. Their quantity, therefore, must have increased there as in other places, and nearly in the same proportion to the annual produce of its land and labor.

Spain and Portugal, both mining countries, are, next to Poland, perhaps the two most beggarly countries in Europe. The value of the precious metals, however, must be lower in Spain and Portugal than in any other part of Europe, since they are sold to all the other parts of Europe, loaded not only with the cost of freight and insurance, but with the expense of smuggling, their exportation being either prohibited, or subject to an export duty.

In proportion to the annual produce of the land and labor, therefore, gold and silver must be more plentiful in those countries than in any other part of Europe; but those countries are among the poorest in Europe. Though the feudal system has been abolished in Spain and Portugal, the system that has followed it is not much better.

℃   It is not possible to prove that a country is flourishing, therefore, merely because gold and silver are low-priced; nor does their high price, nor the cheapness of commodities, necessarily prove its poverty and barbarism. A much better test is the relationship in price between different classes of commodities; low prices for cattle, poultry, game, etc., as compared with grain, indicate with a degree of probability approaching certainty that most of its lands are unimproved, and that it is a poor country.

❡ A rise in prices of goods which resulted from a fall in the value of silver would naturally affect all commodities equally. All would advance in proportion. But this is not the case. During the present century grain has risen much less than several other foods, so that these increases certainly cannot be blamed on the falling value of silver.

The opinion, therefore, that silver is constantly sinking in value, seems not to be founded upon any solid evidence.

❡ It may be said, perhaps, that it is after all not a matter of consequence whether we say that silver has fallen in value, or that goods and services have risen in price, since whichever it is, a man with only a certain sum of money to spend will be able to buy less with it than before. If he knew which was which, he still could not buy anything more, or anything cheaper.

❡ But it appears to me that a correct understanding of the matter is valuable in appraising the condition of the country, and in shaping national policy. It may be used to judge whether the salaries of government employes should be increased, as they should be if the value of money has actually fallen.

❡ But if the increase in prices of some foods is a real increase, this does not necessarily mean that the whole cost of living has risen, for a rise in price of some foods means that the prices of others will fall. Indeed, the condition of poor people is much more apt to be impaired by artificial increases in the cost of other commodities, resulting from taxes and import duties on their production or sale.

CHAPTER XVIII

While the progress of a country raises the real price of all materials, it is particularly favorable to agricultural prices; but these prices rise unequally, according to the amount of additional capital which must be employed to increase the supply.

THE PROGRESS and improvement of a country, as has been said, tends to raise not only the money price, but the real price of many raw materials; while silver continues to buy about the same amount of labor as before, these raw materials come to buy a great deal more.

℃ The first class of such commodities, tending to rise in price, are those of which the quantity cannot easily be increased by human industry. Such are game and some kinds of fish. If woodcock should become fashionable enough to sell for a hundred dollars apiece, no human effort could greatly increase the supply that came to market.

℃ We read in Pliny that Sico gave the Empress Agrippina a white nightingale, which cost him 6000 *sestertii*, the equivalent of fifty pounds of English money. And indeed, considering the higher real value of silver in Roman times, the price was actually a third higher than that.

℃ Other commodities, such as cattle and poultry, can be multiplied according to the demand. In countries not much cultivated, these products are abundant and cheap, but as agriculture progresses, they become fewer, while the demand increases. Their price, consequently, tends to rise, until eventually it becomes high enough to make it profitable to cultivate land to grow feed for them.

℃   Their price cannot go much higher, for if it did, more land would be converted to this use. On the other hand, the price of livestock must reach this ceiling in order to secure the cultivation of all land capable of it.[1]

℃   The increase of livestock and the improvement of the land are two things which must go hand in hand, and neither can much out-run the other. It is for this reason that new colonies are commonly ill-cultivated, and Kalm, the Swedish naturalist, found this to be the case in the North American colonies in 1749.

℃   The colonists would exhaust a piece of ground by continuous cropping, having no manure, and would then abandon it and clear and cultivate a new plot until this too was exhausted. Meanwhile, what few cattle there were wandered in the woods or waste land, half-starved, stunted, unproductive, and deteriorating from year to year.

℃   The production of poultry follows much the same course, except that a considerable amount of poultry can be raised on any farm from ordinary farm wastes, and the point where land must be specially cultivated for food is not reached so quickly.

℃   The hog, which is a general scavenger, is originally kept, like poultry, for this purpose. Pork, therefore, is originally much cheaper than beef. But when the demand increases, and it becomes necessary to turn land to the production of feed for swine, the price necessarily rises.

℃   Eventually the price will compare with other meats, on the average, according as the nature of the country and the state of its agriculture happens to make hog-raising more or less expensive than other livestock.

℃   The price of milk and other dairy products follows much the same course. It tends to rise to a point where, if the increase went further, it would cause more land to be devoted to this branch of agriculture, and the surplus production would soon reduce the price to its proper relationship.

℃   In dairy products, however, the variations in quality are much greater than in meat. Superior quality, therefore, will sometimes command a price somewhat above average; but in England

[1] A. S. elaborates this thesis at some length. But as he wrote at a time when agriculture was still "rude," when the principal plant food was animal manure, and when the transportation of livestock feed over long distances was unknown, his argument is not now important enough to give in full.

th dairy business is not regarded as more profitable than the growing of crops or the fattening of livestock.

℄ If the complete improvement and cultivation of a country be, as it most certainly is, the greatest of all public goods, the rise in price of these commodities ought, instead of being considered a public calamity, to be regarded with the greatest satisfaction.

℄ It is, too, a real increase in price, not the result of any degradation in the value of silver. These commodities have become worth, or can exchange for, not only a greater amount of money, but a greater quantity of labor and subsistence.

℄ A third and last class of commodities are those where human industry sometimes can, and sometimes can not, increase the quantity in response to an increase in demand.

℄ Such commodities are wool and hides, which are commonly obtained as a by-product of mutton and beef. In countries ill-cultivated and thinly inhabited, the wool and hides, being of use for clothing, are more valuable than the meat, which in some provinces of Spain, I am told, is left to rot on the ground. But in advanced and highly cultivated countries the reverse is true.

℄ In the progress of a country, wool and hides should rise in value, but not so much as meat, so that relatively their value should fall. But in England their price has fallen not only relatively but absolutely, over several hundred years. This has been the effect of certain artificial laws and regulations, which may be called the effect of violence and artifice.

℄ The price of hides is now rather above than below the price of several centuries ago. And this is perhaps because the tanners have not been so successful as the cloak-makers in convincing the law-makers that the safety of the commonwealth depends solely upon the prosperity of their particular business.

℄ Whatever laws tend to sink the prices of wool or raw hides below what they would naturally be, must have some tendency toward raising the price of meat.

℄ The price of all livestock, at least that grown on cultivated and improved land, must be enough to pay the rent and profit which the landlord and farmer have reason to expect. Whatever part of this price is not paid by the wool or hide, must be paid by the meat. The less paid for one, the more must be paid for the other.

℄ This would not be true in an unimproved country, where

little capital was invested in land. It was not true, therefore, in early England, nor in Scotland.

℄   Other commodities in this uncertain class are fish, minerals and metals, the supply of which may or may not be capable of increase as a country progresses.

CHAPTER XIX

*A brief chapter showing that in a country
that is prospering, the real price of manufactured commodities tends to fall.*

WHAT THE improvement and advancement of a country always
does, is to diminish gradually the real price of almost all manufactures. Through better machinery, greater skill, and a more
proper division and organization of work, all of which are the
natural effects of improvement, a much smaller quantity of labor
goes into a particular product. And though, in consequence of the
flourishing circumstances of the society, the real price of labor
should rise very considerably, yet the smaller quantity necessary
will generally much more than compensate for the higher wage
rate.

There are, indeed, a few manufactures in which improvements in methods cannot compensate for higher prices of materials.
In carpenter work, and in the coarser sort of cabinet work, the
necessary rise in the real price of lumber, in consequence of the improvement of land, will more than wipe out any advantage that
can be derived from better methods and machines.

But in all cases in which the real price of the materials does
not rise at all, or not very much, that of the manufactured commodity sinks very considerably.

℃ Probably the most striking example is in the case of manufactures made from steel and the other non-precious metals.
Watches and cutlery, in particular, are far better and cheaper than
they used to be. There is no branch of manufacture, perhaps,
where the division of labor and the improvement of machines and
methods has been carried so far.

℃ By contrast, clothing is not much cheaper than a century
ago, and may be no cheaper, because of variations in the quality of
wool used. As compared with more remote times, however, even

clothing is much cheaper; fine cloth is less than a third of the real price charged in 1487, although not so much lower than the money price. Coarse cloth is also cheaper, although not by as great a margin.

℃   The manufacture of coarse cloth was in former times a household task, with crude and inefficient machines. The labor cost was therefore very low. The invention of far better methods of spinning, weaving, and fulling, with the introduction of power machinery in factories, requiring still less labor, somewhat reduced the cost of bringing cloth to the market. As it required less labor to produce, so it could be exchanged for a smaller quantity of labor in the form of other goods.

℃   Fine cloth, however, was largely imported from Flanders, where it was a regular manufacture instead of a part-time job for the family. Its price, therefore, was always naturally higher, and was capable of greater reduction as methods improved.

℃   It was for these reasons, most likely, that the difference in price between coarse and fine woolen cloth was so much greater in former times than it is now.

CHAPTER XX

*Why every improvement in the society
tends to raise the rent of land, and every
retrogression tends to lower it.*

I SHALL conclude this study of the principles regulating the rent of
land by observing that every improvement in the circumstances of
the community tends directly or indirectly to raise the real rent
of land, to increase the real wealth of the landlord, and his power
of purchasing the labor, or the produce of the labor of other people.

The extension of improvement and cultivation tends to
raise it directly, for the landlord's share of production necessarily
increases with the increase of the produce.

A rise in the real price of the products of land—a rise in
the price of cattle, for example—also tends to raise the rent of land
directly, and in a still greater proportion.

The real value of the landlord's share, his real command
of the labor of other people, not only rises with the real value of
what is produced, but his share of the whole produce is larger in
proportion. That produce, after the rise in its real price, requires
no more labor to collect it than before. A smaller part of it will,
therefore, be sufficient to replace, with the ordinary profit, the
capital which employs that labor. A greater proportion of it must
consequently be left over, and will belong to the landlord.

All those improvements in the productive powers of labor,
which tend directly to reduce the real price of manufactured goods,
tend indirectly to raise the real rent of land. The landlord exchanges his share of the production of his land, or what comes
to the same thing, the price of that part of it, for manufactured
produce.

Whatever reduces the real price of the latter, raises that
of the former. An equal quantity of the former becomes thereby
equivalent to a greater quantity of the latter; and the landlord is

able to buy a greater quantity of the conveniences, ornaments, or luxuries, than before.

Every increase in the real wealth of the society, every increase in the quantity of useful wealth of the society, every increase in the quantity of useful labor employed, tends directly to raise the real rent of land. A certain proportion of this labor naturally goes to the land. More men and equipment are employed in its cultivation, production increases with the increase of the capital which is thus employed in raising it, and the rent increases with the produce.

As the above favorable changes raise the real rent of land, so their opposite lower it. The neglect of cultivation and improvement, a fall in the real price of products of land, a rise in the real price of manufactures, a decline in the real wealth of the community, all tend to lower the real rent of land, to reduce the real wealth of the landlord, and to diminish his purchasing power.

CHAPTER XXI

Why the landlords, the workmen, and the capitalists have conflicting interests; and why any proposal of a law from capitalist sources must be viewed with suspicion.

THE WHOLE annual production of the land and labor of every country, or what comes to the same thing, the whole price of that production, naturally divides itself, it has already been observed, into three parts: the rent of land, the wages of labor, and the profits (or interest) of capital.

These three forms of production make up the incomes of three different orders of people: those who live by rent, those who live by wages, and those who live by profit. These are the three great original and constituent orders of every civilized society, from whose incomes those of every other order are ultimately derived.

The interest of the first of those three great orders, the landlords, as indicated in the last chapter, is strictly and inseparably connected with the general interest of the community. Whatever promotes or obstructs the one, necessarily promotes or obstructs the other.

When some law or regulation is being considered, the proprietors of land never can mislead public opinion in their own interest—at least not if they have any tolerable knowledge of that interest; which, indeed, is too often not the case.[1]

Landlords are the only one of the three orders whose revenue costs them neither labor nor care, but comes to them, as it were, of its own accord, and independent of any plan or project

---

[1] A sentence that begins with fine optimism and ends in quite a different vein. Indeed, landlords in England and elsewhere have never been more notable than other people for understanding where their true interest lies.

of their own. That indolence, which is the natural effect of the ease and security of their situation, too often renders them not only ignorant, but incapable of that application of mind which is necessary to foresee and understand the consequences of a given law.

The interest of the second order, that of those who live by wages, is as strictly identified with the interest of the community as that of the first. The wages of the laborer, it has already been shown, are never so high as when the demand for labor is continually rising.

When this real wealth of the society stops growing, wages are soon reduced to what is barely enough to enable the workman to bring up a family. When the society declines, they fall even below this.

Landlords may, perhaps, gain more by the prosperity of the community than do workmen; but the workman suffers more cruelly than anyone else from its decline.

Although the interest of the laborer is exactly the same as that of the community, he is generally incapable either of comprehending that interest, or of understanding its connection with himself.[2] His condition leaves him no time to obtain the necessary information, and his education and habits are commonly such as to render him unfit to judge, even though he were fully informed.

In the public deliberations, therefore, his voice is little heard and less regarded, except upon some particular occasions, when his clamor is animated, set on, and supported by his employers, not for his, but for their own particular ends.

These employers constitute the third order, that of those who live by profit. It is the capital that is employed for the sake of profit which puts into motion the greater part of the useful labor of civilized communities.

The plans and projects of the employers of capital regulate and direct all the most important operations of labor, and profit is the end aimed at by all those plans and projects.

But the rate of profit does not, like rent and wages, rise with the prosperity of the community, and fall with its decline. On the contrary, it is naturally lowest in rich, and highest in poor

[2] The word "generally" is inserted; A. S. makes no qualification at all. His opinion of the mentality of the laborer of 1776 was low, perhaps with reason.

[154]

countries, and it is always highest in the countries which are going fastest to ruin.[3]

The interest of this third order, therefore, has not the same connection with the general interest of the community as that of the other two.

Merchants and manufacturers are, in this order, the two classes of people who commonly employ the largest capital, and who by their wealth draw to themselves the greatest share of public deference. As during their whole lives they are engaged in plans and projects, they have frequently more acuteness of understanding than rural people.

. But as they are apt to be much more concerned with their own affairs than with those of the country, their judgment, even when given with the greatest candor (which it has not always been) is much more to be depended upon with regard to the former of those two objects, than with the latter.

Their superiority over the landlord class is not so much in their knowledge of the public interest as in having a better understanding of their own interest than the landlord has of his. It is by this superior knowledge of their own interest that they have frequently imposed upon his generosity, and persuaded him to injure both his own interest and that of the public, from a very simple but honest conviction, that their interest was the same as the interest of the public.

The interest of the dealers in any particular branch of trade or manufacture, however, always diverges from that of the public, and may directly oppose it.

To widen the market and to narrow the competition, is always the interest of the dealers. To widen the market may frequently be in the interest of the public; but to narrow the competition must always be against it, and can serve only to enable the dealers, by raising their profits above what they naturally

[3] "A most erroneous statement," says M'Culloch. "Profits are always highest in those countries that are improving fastest." But A. S. is speaking of the *rate* of profit, or the rate of return on capital, a different thing. It is true that this high rate in poor countries includes an element of insurance against abnormal risk, which is not true profit.

Thorold Rogers makes a distinction here; in countries going to ruin the rate of interest is high, he says, because of risk, but the profit on capital is not. Carver says that it is true that the rate of profit is low in rich countries, the reason being that it is only in rich countries that capital is abundant.

would be, to levy an absurd tax upon the rest of their fellow-citizens.

The proposal of any new law or regulation of commerce which comes from the capitalist class ought always to be listened to with great skepticism, and ought never to be adopted until it has been examined, not only with the most scrupulous, but with the most suspicious attention.

It comes from an order of men, whose interest is never exactly the same as that of the public, who have generally an interest to deceive and even to oppress the public, and who accordingly have, upon many occasions, both deceived and oppressed it.

BOOK II

Capital being necessary to every advancing society—regardless of who owns it—its laws are important and should be understood; this book shows how all classes of people are dependent upon capital for their subsistence and prosperity.

CHAPTER I

The nature and accumulation of capital ex-
plained; what it is, what it does, and why;
and the distinctions between fixed and cir-
culating capital.

IN THE NINTH AND TENTH chapters of the previous book I have
already examined and explained the reasons for the differing rates
of profit which may be made on the use of capital in different employments. It is now time to examine the nature of capital itself,
to trace its origin and describe how it is accumulated.

In a rude state of society in which there is no division of
labor, in which exchanges are seldom made, and in which every
man provides everything for himself, it is not necessary that any
capital should be accumulated or stored up beforehand, in order
to carry on the business of the community.

Every man endeavors to supply by his own industry his
own wants as they occur. When he is hungry, he goes to the forest
to hunt; when his coat is worn out, he clothes himself with the skin
of the first large animal he kills; and when his hut begins to go to
ruin, he repairs it, as well as he can, with the trees and the turf
that are nearest.[1]

But when the division of labor has once been thoroughly
introduced, the product of a man's own labor can supply only a few
of his wants. Much the largest part of them are supplied by the
product of other men's labor, for which he exchanges what he himself has produced, or (what is exactly the same thing) for the

---

[1] It might almost be said that man became human at the moment when he
became a capitalist. When the savage first fashioned a spear or a stone hammer, and
saved up enough food for a day's hunting, he began accumulating capital. For that
matter, even a squirrel stores up nuts, and a robin builds a nest.

money he has received by the sale of it. For it is evident that this exchange cannot be made until such time as the product of his own labor has not only been completed, but sold.

A stock of goods of different kinds, therefore, must previously have been stored up somewhere sufficient to maintain him, and to supply him with the materials and tools of his work, until such time, at least, as he has finished his product and sold it. A boat-builder cannot apply himself entirely to his peculiar business, unless there is beforehand stored up somewhere, either in his own possession or in that of some other person, a stock sufficient to maintain him, and to supply him with the materials and tools of his work, until he has not only completed but sold his boat.

It is this previous accumulation of food, clothing, shelter, raw materials, tools, and other goods, that we call collectively by the name of capital.

As the accumulation of capital must, in the nature of things, come before the division of labor, so labor can be divided and subdivided only as fast as capital is previously more and more accumulated. The quantity of materials which the same number of people can work up increases very rapidly as labor comes to be more and more subdivided; and as the operations of each workman are gradually simplified, new machines come to be invented for facilitating and speeding up those operations.

As the division of labor advances, therefore, in order to give constant employment to the same number of workmen, the same stock of provisions, together with a much larger stock of materials and tools than would have been necessary in a ruder state of things, must be accumulated beforehand.

As the accumulation of capital necessarily precedes this great improvement in the productive powers of labor, so that accumulation naturally leads to this improvement. The person who employs his capital in maintaining labor, necessarily tries to employ it so as to produce as much work as possible.

He endeavors both to organize the work efficiently, and to furnish his workmen with the best machines which he can buy or build. His abilities in both these respects are generally in proportion to the extent of his capital, or to the number of people whom it can employ.

The volume of industry, therefore, not only increases in every country with the increase of the capital which employs it, but, in consequence of that increase, the same quantity of industry produces a much greater output.

When the possessions of a certain man are so small that they will maintain him for only a few days or weeks, he seldom thinks of deriving any income from them. He consumes them as sparingly as he can, and endeavors by his labor to acquire something to replace them before they are consumed altogether. His income is, in this case, derived from his labor only. This is the state of the greater part of the laboring poor in all countries.

But when he has accumulated food and other possessions sufficient to maintain him for months or years, he naturally begins to think of putting the surplus to work to derive some additional income from it.

His whole supply of food and commodities, therefore, divides itself into two parts. That part which, he expects, is to earn him this income, is called his capital. The other is that which supplies his immediate wants; and this may include not only food, clothing, household furniture, and the like, but some part of his income as it comes in.[2]

There are two different ways in which capital may be employed so as to yield a revenue or profit to its owner.

First, it may be employed in raising, manufacturing, or purchasing goods, and selling them again at a profit. The capital employed thus yields no income until its product is sold. The goods of the merchant yield him no profit till he sells them for money, and the money yields him no real income until it is again exchanged for goods.

His capital is continually going from him in one shape, and returning to him in another, and it is only by means of such circulation, or successive exchanges, that it can yield him any profit. Such capital, therefore, may very properly be called circulating capital.

The other use of capital is in the improvement of land, in

[2] A. S. does not consider such possessions as capital, but modern economics is unwilling to make such a distinction; if it did, the total of the capital of individuals, including only a part of their possessions, would be smaller than the capital of the whole country, which includes everything—a manifest absurdity. Much of this chapter and the next must be read with this fundamental difference of opinion between A. S. and later economists in mind. It is, however, another dispute over definitions; and the definitions of A. S. do not, as a rule, lead to any very erroneous conclusions.

[*161*]

the purchase of useful machines, equipment, and buildings, or in such-like things as yield a revenue or profit without changing owners, or circulating any further. Such capital, therefore, may very properly be called fixed capital.

Nearly all occupations require both kinds of capital, but different occupations require them in very different proportions.

The capital of a merchant, for example, is altogether a circulating capital. He has occasion for no machines or instruments of trade, unless his shop, or warehouse, be considered as such.[3]

Some part of the capital of every master artisan or manufacturer must be fixed in the implements of his trade. This part, however, is very small in some, and much larger in others. A tailor requires no other instruments of trade but a parcel of needles.

Most of the capital of all such artisans, however, is circulated, either in the wages of their workmen, or in the price of their materials, and repaid with a profit by the sale of the product.

In other businesses a much greater fixed capital is required. In a great steel plant, for example, the blast furnaces, the forges, the rolling mills, are instruments of trade which cannot be erected without a very heavy investment.

That part of the capital of the farmer which is invested in implements is fixed; that which is employed in the wages and maintenance of his hired men is circulating. He makes a profit of the one by keeping it in his own possession, and of the other by parting with it.

The price or value of his horses and oxen is a fixed capital in the same class with his tools; his dairy cow is fixed capital, but not the milk; his livestock being fattened for sale is circulating capital; his seed is properly fixed capital, for he does not sell the seed, but only its increase.

The general stock of possessions of any country is the same as that of all its inhabitants or members, since it is merely the sum total of the possessions of individuals. Hence it divides itself into the same three portions, each of which has a distinct function or office.

The first I do not call capital at all; it is that portion which must be reserved for immediate consumption, and of which the characteristic is that it affords no direct revenue or profit. It consists in the stock of food, clothing, household furniture, etc., which

[3] Which, of course, it really is.

have been purchased by their proper consumers, but which are not yet entirely consumed. The whole number of dwelling houses in the country, too, make a part of this first portion.

It is true that a house that is rented will yield income to the owner; but it produces no money income to the tenant, who must pay the rent out of some other source of income. Hence even a rented house is not a part of the circulating capital of the country, and the total income of the whole population is not increased by it in the smallest degree.[4]

The second of the three portions into which the general stock of the population divides itself, is the fixed capital; of which the characteristic is, that it affords a revenue or profit without circulating or changing ownership. It consists chiefly in the four following categories:

First, all useful machines and instruments of trade which make labor more efficient and productive;

Second, all those profitable buildings which are the means of earning an income, not only to the owner who may rent them out, but to the person who occupies them and pays that rent for them; such as shops, warehouses, workhouses, farmhouses, with all their necessary buildings, stables, granaries, etc. These are very different from mere dwelling houses. They are a sort of instruments of trade, and may be considered in the same light;

Third, the improvements of land, the money that is invested in clearing, draining, enclosing, fertilizing and conditioning it. An improved farm is equally advantageous and more durable than any industrial machine, frequently requiring no other repairs than the most profitable applications of the farmer's capital employed in cultivating it;

[4] A house is very often indirectly a source of income, says M'Culloch. A paperhanger could no more carry on his trade without a house to live in than without his ladders and paste-brushes. The real nature of dwelling houses and equipment, indeed, is more important than is usually realized, and is one often overlooked. For example, there was in England during the 1930's a vast investment in new and improved dwelling houses. Delightful as this was to those able to occupy them, it is a question whether England would not have been far better off in the end to have used the money to modernize her productive industrial equipment.

All the "better housing" and "slum clearance" schemes have something of this defect. People should be housed as well as possible; but there is such a thing as a proper division of available capital between investments which are productive and those which are unproductive of income or new wealth—what A. S. calls "not capital at all."

Fourth, the acquired and useful abilities of all the inhabitants or members of the community. The acquisition of such talents always costs money, and hence is capital fixed and realized, as it were, in his person. Those talents, as they make a part of his private fortune, so do they likewise of that of the whole community to which he belongs. The trained skill of a workman may be considered in the same light as a machine or instrument of trade which facilitates and abridges labor, and which, though it costs a certain expense, repays that expense with a profit.[5]

The third and last of the three divisions of stock is the circulating capital; of which the characteristic is, that it affords a revenue only by circulating or changing owners. It is composed likewise of four categories:

First, the money by means of which all the other three are circulated and distributed;

Second, the stock of provisions which are in the possession of the butcher, the grocer, the farmer, the grain-merchant, the brewer, etc., and from the sale of which they expect to derive a profit;

Third, the materials, whether raw or more or less manufactured, of clothes, furniture, and building, which are not yet made up into any of these shapes, but which remain in the hands of the growers, the manufacturers, the wholesalers of dry goods, the lumber yards, etc.

Fourth, and last, products which are made up and completed, but which are in the hands of the merchant or manufacturer, and not yet distributed or sold to the ultimate consumers; such as the finished work which we see in all the stores.

The last three of these four categories—provisions, materials, and finished work—are, either every year, or in a longer or shorter period, regularly withdrawn from it, and placed either in the fixed capital or in the stock reserved for immediate consumption.

All fixed capital is both originally derived from, and requires to be continually fed by circulating capital. All useful machines and instruments of trade are originally derived from circulating capital, which furnishes the materials of which they are

[5] Not consistent with a former chapter, where the extra income from unusual skill is called wages; here it is called profit on fixed capital. But hardly anyone, including the workman, cares much which it is called, as long as he gets it.

built, and the maintenance of the workmen who built them. And they must constantly have more capital of the same kind to keep them in repair.

No fixed capital can yield any income but with the help of circulating capital. The most useful machines and equipment will produce nothing without the circulating capital which supplies the materials they utilize, and the maintenance of the workmen who operate them. Land, however improved, will yield no income without circulating capital, which maintains the labor which cultivates and collects its produce.

But fixed and circulating capital, however important they may seem to be, and indeed are, are only means to an end, not ends in themselves. Their sole end and purpose is, by producing income, to maintain and increase those possessions which are for human consumption. The whole aim of the system is consumption, not production. The wealth or poverty of a country depends on how much consumption is achieved by the whole population as a result of its total activities.

So much of the circulating capital being continually withdrawn from it to be placed in the other two branches of the general stock of the society, it must have this deficiency continuously replaced, if it is to continue to exist.

Thus fresh supply is principally drawn from three sources, the produce of land, of mines, and of fisheries, which between them yield continual supplies of raw materials.

One of these sources, the mines, also provides that form of circulating capital which is metallic money. For though money is not, like other circulating capital, withdrawn and converted into something else, there is a certain loss by wear and tear, and by export and use in the arts, which has to be made up.

Land, mines, and fisheries, all require both fixed and circulating capital to operate them; and their product replaces with a profit, not only that capital, but all other capital in the country.

Thus the farmer annually replaces to the manufacturer the provisions which he had consumed and the materials which he had used up the year before; and the manufacturer replaces to the farmer the goods which he had wasted and worn out in the same time.

This is the real exchange that is made between those two classes of people, although it seldom happens that the produce of the one and the manufactured goods of the other, are directly bartered for one another. The farmer sells his product for money, with which he can purchase, wherever it is to be had, the manufactured goods he wants.

Land even may be said to replace, in part at least, the capital with which fisheries and mines are operated. It is the produce of land which draws the fish from the seas; and it is the produce of the surface of the earth which extracts the minerals from its bowels.

In all countries where there is tolerable security, every man of ordinary good sense will try to employ whatever possessions he can command, in procuring either present enjoyment or future profit.

If it is employed in procuring present enjoyment, it is a stock reserved for immediate consumption.

If it is employed in procuring future profit, it must procure this profit either by staying with him, or by going from him. In the one case it is fixed, in the other it is circulating capital.

A man must be completely crazy who, where there is tolerable security, does not employ everything he owns (or can command by borrowing), in some one or other of those three ways.

In those unfortunate countries, indeed, where men fear the violence of their superiors, they frequently bury and conceal what possessions they can, in order to have them always at hand to carry with them to some place of safety, in case of disaster. This is said to be a common practice in Turkey, in India, and, I believe, in most other governments of Asia. It seems to have been a common practice among our ancestors under the lawless violence of the feudal system.

CHAPTER II

A long chapter devoted partly to exploding the popular illusion that money is income, partly to explaining the true function of money in the production of wealth, partly in an outline of the sound principles of banking; including also examples of the beneficial use of paper notes for money, and some American colonial experiments with fiat paper.

As shown in the sixth chapter of the first book, the price of most commodities resolves itself into three parts, of which one pays the wages of labor, another the profits of the capital, and the third the rent of the land which had been employed in producing and bringing them to market.

We noticed that there are, indeed, some commodities of which the price is made up of only two of those parts—wages and profits; and a very few in which it consists altogether in wages; but that the price of every commodity necessarily resolves itself into some one or two, or all three of these parts; every part of it which goes neither to rent nor to wages, being necessarily profit to somebody.

Since this is true as to every single commodity, taken separately, it must be so with all the commodities which compose the whole annual production of the country, lumped together. Likewise, the total price or exchangeable value of that national production must resolve itself into the same three parts, and be parcelled out among the inhabitants of the country, either as the wages of their labor, the profits of their capital, or the rent of their land.

❰ But it must be noted that this whole gross national income is by no means the same as the net income. A large part of it must be devoted to keeping up the capital of the country, both fixed and circulating, if the community is to stay prosperous, and a still larger part if it is to continue to grow.

❡ It is only after these necessary expenses are taken care of that what remains may be considered as the net income of the people, available for their subsistence, convenience, and amusement.

The expense of maintaining the fixed capital in a great country may very properly be compared to that of repairs in a private estate. The expense of repairs may frequently be necessary for keeping up production, and consequently maintaining both the gross and the net rent of the landlord. When repair costs can be kept down by good management, the gross rent will be the same, but the net rent will be that much larger.

All fixed capital has to be kept up out of income. but as to circulating capital, the rule is different.

Of the four parts of which this latter capital is composed, money, provisions, materials, and finished work, the last three, it has already been observed, are regularly withdrawn from it, and placed either in the fixed capital of the society, or in their stock reserved for immediate consumption. Whatever portion of these goods is not employed in maintaining fixed capital is withdrawn for consumption, and makes a part of the net revenue of the country.

The circulating capital of the whole population is in this respect different from that of an individual. That of an individual is totally excluded from making any part of his net income, which must consist altogether in his profits. But though the circulating capital of every individual makes a part of that of the nation, it is not upon that account totally excluded from making a part likewise of their net revenue.

Though the goods in a merchant's shop must by no means be placed in his own stock reserved for immediate consumption, they may be so placed in the stock of other people, who may regularly replace their value to him, together with its profits, without causing any reduction of his capital or theirs.[1]

---

[1] There would be no necessity of pursuing this involved argument if A. S. had not in the beginning made his error of excluding consumption goods from the general capital of the country. See Note 2 of the previous chapter.

Metallic money, therefore, is the only part of circulating capital of which the maintenance can cause any reduction in the net national income. It thus resembles fixed capital, as far as both affect the income of the nation.[2]

Just as the machines of a country require the expenditure of labor to build and maintain them, so the money stock must be accumulated and maintained. The maintenance of the machines makes a part of the gross national income, but not of the net, and money does exactly the same thing.

Contrary to common opinion, money is not income. It is only because of the inexact use of words that this proposition may appear dubious, and when properly explained and understood, it becomes almost self-evident.

When we talk of any particular sum of money, we sometimes mean nothing but the metal pieces or paper of which it is composed; but sometimes we have obscurely in our minds not the money itself, but the goods which can be had in exchange for it, or the purchasing power which the possession of it confers.

Thus when we say that money in circulation is twenty billions of dollars, we mean only to express the amount of the metal or paper, as announced by the government.

But when we say that a man is worthy twenty thousand dollars a year, we mean commonly to express not only the amount of cash which is annually paid to him, but the value of the goods which he can buy with it.

Or if a man makes fifty dollars a week, he can in the course of the week buy with it a certain quantity of subsistence, conveniences and amusements. In proportion as this quantity is great or small, so are his real riches, his real weekly income. No one would say that his weekly income was equal both to the fifty dollars, and to what can be bought with it, but only to one or the other of those two equal values; and in reality it is the goods that we mean.

A payment in money may be considered as a due-bill upon all the tradesmen in the neighborhood for a certain quantity of necessaries and conveniences. The income of the person to whom it is paid does not so properly consist in the money itself, as in what he

[2] To tell the truth, the differences between fixed capital and money are barely discernible to the naked eye. In hardly any respect does money act like circulating capital.

can get for it, or in what he can exchange it for. If it could be exchanged for nothing, it would, like a bill upon a bankrupt, be of no more value than any other useless piece of paper or metal.

As this is true of every separate individual, so it is true of the whole community or sum of the individuals. The whole income of all of them taken together is obviously not equal to both the money and the consumable goods; but only to one or other of those two values, and to the goods more properly than to the money.

Indeed, this proposition is even clearer in the case of a nation than of an individual. The money income paid an individual is often exactly the same as his real income, which is the goods and services he buys with the money. But the real income of the whole community is ordinarily much larger than the whole amount of money in circulation. The national income may be a hundred billion dollars, while the money in circulation is not more than twenty billion.

Money, therefore, the great engine of production, the circulating medium, the great instrument of commerce, like all other machines and implements, though it makes a part and a very valuable part of the capital, makes no real part of the income of the society to which it belongs; and though the metal pieces of which it is composed, in the course of their annual circulation, distribute to every man the income which properly belongs to him, they themselves make no part of that income.

In the third place, and lastly, the machines and other fixed capital of a country bear this further resemblance to that part of the circulating capital which consists in money; that as every saving in the expense of erecting and maintaining those machines is an improvement of the net revenue of the society, so every saving in the expense of collecting and maintaining the stock of money is an improvement of exactly the same kind.[3]

It is sufficiently obvious, as I have already said, that every saving in the expense of supporting the fixed capital is an increase in the net income of the community.

The substitution of paper for gold and silver money replaces a very expensive instrument of commerce with one much cheaper and equally convenient. Production comes to be carried on by a new wheel, which it costs less both to erect and to maintain than the old one. But how this operation is performed is not altogether so obvious, and may therefore require some further explanation.

ℂ   There are several kinds of paper money, but of these bank notes are the best and most useful. A well-known and strong bank may issue $500,000 of its notes among its customers, and as the notes serve all the purposes of money, the borrowers pay the bank the same interest on them.

ℂ   But as all outstanding notes are never presented for payment at one time, the bank need keep on hand gold and silver (or certificates calling for gold and silver) for only a part of this total, let us say $200,000.

ℂ   The rest of the bank's reserve, $300,000, may be used for other purposes, abroad or at home, and if all banks do very much

[3] Here is the point, as A. S. starts to explain the great improvements in the use of money, to emphasize once for all that everything, or nearly everything, said about money hereafter should be understood as applying to bank checks and drafts as well as to gold, silver, paper money and bills of exchange.

The twin sciences of banking and finance have developed the demand deposit and checking systems, in the United States at least, to the point where by far the largest part of the circulating medium is the individual check on a commercial bank. Such an order-to-pay by an individual reasonably well known and respected, on a well-known and trusted bank, is in every important sense the same as money.

It passes at par, or nearly par, in every part of the country. It retains its value because it is generally known to be convertible on demand into paper or metal currency, which in turn is (or will hereafter be) convertible into gold, the ultimate standard in this country. It differs from other money only because it is generally used in only one transaction instead of many.

Thus gold, silver, paper money of several categories, and bank checks and drafts, now constitute the total stock of money in this country. And as the volume of bank checks is capable of expansion and contraction within wide limits, the modern state possesses a currency of a degree of flexibility far beyond anything dreamed of in the days of A. S.

the same thing, the whole business of the country may be carried on with only a third, a fourth, or a fifth of the gold and silver that would otherwise be necessary.

℃   When this surplus gold and silver is exported, it will be used to buy foreign goods of some sort, to be sold either at home or in some third country. Whichever it may be, it is an addition to the real income of the home country, either through the profit on buying and selling, or through the importation of raw materials, which in most cases will maintain and employ industrious labor. The importation of luxurious articles for consumption does not, indeed, help the community, but the proportion of such imports is relatively small.

When we compute the whole volume of industry which the circulating capital of any country can employ, we must always count only the provisions, materials, and finished work; the fourth part, which consists in money, and which serves only to circulate the other three, must always be deducted.

In order to put industry into motion, three things are necessary: materials to work upon, tools to work with, and the wages or payment without which no one will work. Money is neither a material to work upon, nor a tool to work with; and though the wages of the workman are commonly paid to him in money, his real income, like that of all other men, consists not in the money itself, but in the money's worth or what can be bought with it.

The quantity of industry which the whole capital of the country can employ, is certainly not equal both to the money which purchases, and to the materials, tools, and maintenance, which are purchased with it; but only to one or the other of those two values, and to the latter more properly than the former.

When paper is substituted for gold and silver money, the quantity of the materials, tools, and maintenance, which the whole circulating capital can supply, may be increased by the whole value of gold and silver which was previously employed in purchasing them. The whole value of the great wheel of production and distribution, is added to the goods which are produced and distributed by means of it.

It is not possible to calculate exactly what proportion exists between the volume of the circulating money and the whole value of the country's annual production. It may be a very small part. But that part of the country's production destined for the maintenance of industry is also a small part of the total. Accordingly, if the substitution of paper for gold and silver should reduce the use of the metals to a fifth of what it was, and most of the other four-fifths is used to maintain industry, the effect of the change on the volume of industry would be very considerable.

℃ In Scotland the establishment of many small banks issuing their notes had exactly this effect. The change from gold and silver to paper money doubled the trade of the city of Glasgow, I have heard it asserted, within fifteen years thereafter.

℃ This paper money was put into circulation chiefly by discounting bills of exchange—that is, by advancing money upon the notes of individuals before they are due. But the Scottish banks introduced another valuable invention by granting what they called "cash accounts."

℃ This was a system of granting credit to any individual who could produce two securities for his honesty, without his maintaining a deposit account with the bank.[4] By means of these cash accounts every merchant could safely carry on a considerably larger volume of trade than he otherwise could. An English merchant, not having this benefit, could not carry on so large a business on the same capital.

The whole paper money of every kind which can circulate in a country never can exceed the value of the gold and silver, which would have been used if there had been no paper. In other words, a bank issuing its notes can never keep in circulation more than is necessary for carrying on the business of the community.

If the banks issued more than this, many people would immediately notice that they had more of this paper than was necessary for transacting business, and as they could not send it abroad, they would immediately demand payment of it from the banks.

When this superfluous paper was converted into gold and silver, it could then be put to use by sending it abroad; but they could find none as long as it remained in the form of paper. There would immediately, therefore, be a run upon the banks to the whole

---

[4] What we would call a loan on an endorsed note. The chief advantage of the "cash account," however, A. S. does not mention at all. This was not the additional capital the merchant could employ, but the ease with which he could draw upon his balance at the bank. It was, in effect, an imperfect kind of checking system against a deposit of borrowed funds.

extent of this superfluous paper. And if the banks betrayed any difficulty or backwardness in payment, the alarm would greatly increase such a run.

℃   A. S. now enters into a detailed analysis of the practices of British banks (including the Bank of England) in issuing their paper notes, which they frequently did in excessive amounts.

℃   The banks did not always understand their own interest, but issued too much paper for over-expanded trading or speculation. They ignored the principle that they should not advance to a merchant more than he would be obliged to keep on hand in cash for his business. Discounting of bills of exchange and payments from cash accounts should both be limited to the amount the merchant ought to use, according to the bank's observation of his character and mode of doing business.

℃   The Scottish banks were very careful, at least at first, in requiring regular payments from their borrowers, this being the indication which shows with much accuracy how the borrower's business is progressing.

℃   A. S. goes on to point out that commercial banks should make loans only for moderate periods of time, and should above all refuse to advance money to anyone whatever to be invested in fixed capital.

℃   Some time before 1750 the Scottish banks had issued about as much paper money as the country could absorb and use. Indeed, they had gone a little beyond this point, and had brought upon themselves that loss, or at least that reduction of profit, that never fails to fall upon a banking enterprise when it exceeds the proper limits of its resources.

℃   But the traders and promoters of Scotland, having already received more than they should from the banks, wished to get still more. The banks, they seem to have thought, could expand credit indefinitely at no expense.

℃   They complained of the narrow minds and dastardly spirit of the bank directors, who would not extend credit in proportion to the extension of the trade of the country; by which they really meant the extension of their own trade or speculation beyond the capital they already had or could raise among their friends.

℃   When the banks persisted in this mean and backward-looking policy, the traders sometimes had recourse to the dangerous and expensive practice of drawing and redrawing bills of ex-

[*174*]

change, which was for a time effective in supplying them with the funds they thought they needed.

⁋ A. S. now explains at length the operation of the system of bills of exchange, which, while still in use, particularly in international trade, may perhaps be left to the special student of this branch of commercial finance.

⁋ The abuses of the system, already referred to, got many banks in London and Edinburgh into serious difficulties, and their efforts to escape the consequences of their own violations of sound banking principles alarmed and enraged the traders who had been supplying their alleged capital needs in this way.

Their own distress they called the distress of the country; and this distress of the country, they said, was altogether owing to the ignorance, pusillanimity, and bad conduct of the banks, which did not give sufficiently liberal aid to those who exerted themselves in order to beautify, improve, and enrich the country. It was the duty of the banks, they seemed to think, to lend for as long a time and to as great an extent as they might wish to borrow.

The banks, however, by refusing in this manner to give more credit to those to whom they had already given a great deal too much, took the only method by which it was now possible to save either their own credit, or the public credit of the country.

In the midst of this clamor, a new bank was established in Scotland for the express purpose of relieving the distress of the country.

⁋ The plan was generous; not understanding the nature of the disorder, it proposed to lend more money to men who had already borrowed too much. The inevitable result was that it was soon in difficulties, and within two years was insolvent. Its only accomplishment of any value was to "bail out" the other Scottish banks, which were enabled to collect their bad loans from debtors who borrowed from the new institution to pay them off.

⁋ Another plan urged at the time was to raise money on the securities pledged by borrowers. This plan, like that of John Law sixty-five years earlier, from which developed the famous and disastrous "Mississippi Bubble," was in reality an expedient for issuing more paper money than the community could utilize in its ordinary transactions. Like all other schemes of the sort, before or since, it was fore-doomed to failure for this reason alone.

⁋ All of these are examples of the splendid and visionary

[*175*]

schemes, based upon the possibility of multiplying paper money to almost any extent, which always have made and probably always will make a powerful impression on the minds of many people.[5]

℃ A. S. now gives a brief history of the Bank of England, which he calls "the greatest bank of circulation in Europe," and "a great engine of state"—both of which it was and no doubt still is. Upon one occasion, in 1763, it is said to have advanced to continental countries, in one week, about £1,600,000; upon other occasions, this great company was reduced to the necessity of paying in sixpences.[6]

It is not by increasing the capital of the country, but by making a greater part of that capital active and productive than it would otherwise be, that the operations of banking can increase the industry of the country.

That part of his capital which a dealer is obliged to keep by him in ready money for answering occasional demands, is so much dead stock, which as long as it remains in this situation, produces nothing either to him or to his country. The operations of banking, properly conducted, enable him to convert this dead stock into active and productive capital; into materials to work upon, into tools to work with, and into provisions and subsistence to work for; in a word, into capital which produces something both for himself and his country.

[5] "No more inveterate and recurrent fallacy can be found," says Thorold Rogers, "than that which conceives a government to be possessed of some inherent force of its own, by which it can issue a paper currency, and maintain it at full credit." This generation can testify that it is inveterate and recurrent—a generation which sees every civilized nation on a basis of "managed" paper currency, and is daily told by its politicians and their advisers that inconvertible paper is no longer a fallacy, and that they have solved the problem of maintaining it at full credit.

But "greenbackism" is always a product of war and depression, and the world has just had a fearful dose of both.

Rogers goes on to say, with more optimism than clairvoyance, that we have passed through the economic delusion of unlimited paper money, have banned the "impolicy" of inconvertible paper, and "can therefore turn a deaf ear to the most plausible theories of currency quacks, as mathematicians do to those who profess to square the circle, and mechanicians do to those who assert that they have discovered perpetual motion."

Some of the worst of today's currency quacks, alas, are in Rogers' own England and directing its clouded destinies.

[6] This was in 1745, when there were suspicions that Jacobite money was being drawn out to finance the expedition of the Young Pretender.

The gold and silver which circulates in a country without banks or paper money is, in the same manner as the ready money of the dealer, all dead stock. It is a very valuable part of the capital of the country, but it produces nothing to the country. The operations of banking, by substituting paper in place of much of this gold and silver, enables the country to convert a great part of this gold and silver, enables the country to convert a great part of this dead stock into active and productive capital which produces something to the country.

Gold and silver may very properly be compared to a highway, which, while it carries to market all the hay and grain of the country, produces itself not a single pile of either. The operations of banking, by providing, if I may be allowed so violent a metaphor, a sort of air-way,[7] enable the country to convert, as it were, a great part of its highways into good pastures and fields, and thereby to increase very considerably the annual produce of its land and labor.

℃ A. S. now proceeds to consider the manner in which the issuance of paper money in the form of bank notes can best facilitate the production and exchange of goods, particularly as to the size or denomination of notes to be issued, and the terms on which they would be redeemed.

℃ As bank notes are practically obsolete in this day in this country, I omit these passages. And indeed, much of the foregoing discussion is printed rather for its exposition of banking principles than for its relevance to conditions in the United States.

The paper currencies of the American colonies consisted, not in bank notes payable to the bearer on demand, but in government paper on which payment in coin could not be claimed until several years after it was issued. And though the colonial governments paid no interest to the holders of this paper, they declared it to be a legal tender of payment for the full value for which it was issued.

But even allowing the credit of the colony to be perfectly good, a hundred pounds payable fifteen years hence, for example, in a country where interest is at six per cent, is worth little more than forty pounds ready money. To oblige a creditor, therefore, to accept this as full payment for a debt of a hundred pounds actually paid down in coin was an act of such violent injustice, as has

---

[7] "a sort of wagon-way through the air"—W. N.

scarcely, perhaps, been attempted by the government of any other country which pretended to be free.

It bears the evident marks of having originally been, what the honest and downright Doctor Douglas assures us it was, a knavish scheme of fraudulent debtors to cheat their creditors.

The government of Pennsylvania, indeed, pretended, upon their first emission of paper money in 1722, to make their paper of equal value with gold and silver, by enacting penalties against any-one who made any difference in the price of their goods when they sold them for paper money, and when they sold them for gold and silver—a regulation as tyrannical as it was ineffective.

A positive law may render a dime legal tender for a dollar, since it can direct the courts of justice to discharge the debtor who has made that tender. But no positive law can force a person who sells goods, and who is at liberty to sell or not to sell, as he pleases, to accept a dime as equivalent to a dollar in the price he demands.

No law, therefore, could be more just than the act of Parliament, so unjustly complained of in the colonies, which declared that no paper currency to be issued there in future should be a legal tender of payment.

Pennsylvania was always more moderate in its emissions of paper money than any other of our colonies. Its paper currency accordingly is said never to have sunk below the value of gold and silver which was current in the colony before the first issue of paper money.

Previously the colony had raised the denomination of its coin, and had, by act of assembly, ordered five shillings to pass in the colony for six and three-pence, and afterwards for six and eight-pence. A Pennsylvania pound, therefore, even when that currency was gold and silver, was more than thirty per cent below the value of a pound sterling, and when that currency was turned into paper, it was seldom much more than thirty per cent below that value.

The pretext for raising the denomination of the coin was to prevent the export of gold and silver, by making equal quantities of those metals pass for greater sums in the colony than they did in England. It was found, of course, that the price of all imported English goods rose in price (in Pennsylvania currency) exactly in proportion as they raised the denomination of their coin, so that their gold and silver were exported as fast as ever.

The paper of each colony being received in the payment of provincial taxes, for the full value for which it had been issued, it necessarily derived from this use some additional value, over and above what it would otherwise have had. This additional value was greater or less, according as the quantity of paper issued was more or less above what was actually needed for taxes, and the quantity issued was in all the colonies very much above what could be thus used.

C   Indeed, almost any government can give a certain amount of value to paper money, even when it is not convertible into gold or silver, by making it receivable in taxes.

A paper currency which falls below the value of gold and silver coin, does not thereby depreciate the value of those metals, or cause them to exchange for a smaller quantity of other goods. The relation between the value of gold and silver and that of goods always depends not upon the nature or quantity of the paper money which may be current, but upon the richness or poverty of the mines, which happen at that particular time to supply the great markets of the commercial world with those metals.

In other words, it depends upon the proportion between the quantity of labor necessary to bring a certain quantity of gold and silver to market, and that which is necessary to bring thither a certain quantity of any other sort of goods.

It appears, therefore, that banks may be left perfectly free to issue their paper notes, and the establishment of more banks may be encouraged, if the issuance of small notes is prohibited, and all notes are made payable immediately and unconditionally on demand.

CHAPTER III

In which Adam Smith endeavors to make clear the differences between what he calls "productive" and "unproductive" labor, of which the former does, the latter does not, result directly in the accumulation of capital and the employment of more labor.

THERE IS ONE SORT OF LABOR which adds to the value of the subject upon which it is bestowed: there is another which has no such effect. The former, as it produces a value, may be called productive; the latter, unproductive labor.

Thus the labor of a factory workman adds something, as a rule, to the value of the materials which he works upon, that of his own maintenance, and of his employer's profit. The labor of a menial servant, on the contrary, adds to the value of nothing.

Though the workman has his wages advanced to him by his employer, he costs him no expense in reality, the value of those wages being generally restored, together with a profit, in the improved value of the subject upon which his labor is bestowed. But the maintenance of a menial servant never is restored.

A man grows rich by employing a multitude of workmen; he grows poor, by maintaining a multitude of menial servants.

It is true that the labor of the latter has its value, and deserves its reward as well as that of the former. But the labor of the manufacturer fixes and realizes itself in some particular object or salable commodity, which lasts for some time at least after that labor is past. It is, as it were, a certain quantity of labor stocked and stored up to be employed, if necessary, upon some other occasion.

The labor of the menial servant, on the contrary, does not fix or realize itself in any particular object or commodity. His services generally perish in the very instant of their performance, and seldom leave any trace or value behind them, for which an equal quantity of service could afterwards be procured.[1]

The labor of some of the most respectable orders in the society is, like that of menial servants, unproductive of any salable value, and does not fix or realize itself in any permanent object, or salable commodity, which endures after that labor is past, and for which an equal quantity of labor could afterwards be procured.

The head of the government, for example, with all the officers of justice and war who serve under him, the whole army and navy, are unproductive laborers. They are the servants of the public, and are maintained by a part of the annual production of the industry of other people. Their service, however honorable, useful, or necessary, produces nothing for which an equal quantity of service can afterwards be procured.

In the same class must be ranked some both of the gravest and most important, and some of the most frivolous professions: clergymen, lawyers, physicians, men of letters of all kinds; actors, comedians, musicians, opera-singers, ballet dancers, etc. The labor of the meanest of these has a certain value, regulated by the very same principles as every other sort of labor; but like that of the noblest and most useful, produces nothing which could afterwards purchase or procure an equal quantity of labor.

[1] Some distinction may well be made between what A. S. defines as "productive" and "unproductive" labor, but the choice of terms is not a happy one. To call some labor "unproductive" carries a kind of implication that there is something wrong, or at least useless and superfluous, about it, which is unfortunate.

A. S. means only, as he emphasizes several times, that the one kind of labor produces some tangible thing—something that can be seen, stored, and sold—and the other kind does not.

The modern tendency is to class all labor as "productive," if it produces any kind of wealth; wealth being defined as all forms of useful, desirable or desired or enjoyable goods *and services.* In this sense truly "unproductive" labor would be rare; although doubtless each of us can call to mind some examples that seem to fall in this class. The labor of a gambler is hardly productive in any sense.

A better name than "unproductive" for labor producing services might be "auxiliary"; for such labor as that of the doctor or postman is certainly essential for maintaining the efficiency of the "productive" worker. Indeed, this is strictly in conformity with A. S.'s basic principle of progress and prosperity through the proper division of labor.

The whole of this chapter should be read with this basic criticism of A. S.'s use of words in mind, and it will be referred to several times hereafter.

Like the declamation of the actor, the speech of the politician, or the tune of the musician, the work of all of them perishes in the very instant of its production.[2]

All laborers, in whatever field, as well as people who do not labor at all, are all equally maintained by the annual production of the land and labor of the country. This production, however large, can never be infinite, but must have certain limits. According, therefore, as a smaller or greater proportion of it is employed in maintaining unproductive hands, the more in the one case and the less in the other will remain for the productive. The next year's production will be greater or smaller, accordingly; the whole total, if we except the spontaneous productions of the earth, being the effect of productive labor.

℄ Of the total annual production of the whole country, some is set aside for one purpose and some for another. The first and probably the largest demand upon this production, is for replacing the capital used up in producing it—the subsistence of the workers, the materials, and the finished work.

℄ The rest must go to the owner of the capital, as profit, or to some other person, as the rent of his land. This part of the total annual production, not used for replacing capital, is revenue or income to someone; and may be used for maintaining unproductive labor, or people who do not work at all.

℄ Thus not only great land-owners and rich manufacturers and merchants maintain servants, but even a common workman, if his wages are high, may hire a helper for his wife; or he may and generally does go to the movies or the baseball game,[3] and so contribute his share toward maintaining one set of unproductive laborers; and he always pays some taxes, and thus helps maintain another set, possibly more honored and useful, but just as unproductive.

However, it is the rent of land and the profits of capital that form the principal sources from which unproductive hands derive their subsistence. These are the two sorts of income of which the owners have generally most to spare.

℄ Since the number of unproductive workers in a country depends on how much surplus revenue, profit or rent, is available

[2] If too many persons live by entertainment, the production of real wealth must tend to fall.
[3] "a play or a puppet-show"—W. N.

for supporting them, it will ultimately depend on how much of the total annual production is needed to replace capital, and how much is left for that profit and rent.

⟨ In former times very little capital was employed in production, and that small amount was easily replaced out of the annual product. The rest, although very small indeed, was a much larger proportion of the whole than it is in rich and civilized countries of today. As much greater amounts of capital are nowadays employed, a far greater proportion of the annual production is necessary to replace it, and this must all go to productive labor of some kind.

⟨ Of what is left over as income, some will employ productive labor; and the net result is that in a modern country the opportunities for productive labor are far greater than in feudal times, or in poor countries at this day.

The proportion between these different funds necessarily determines in every country the general character of the inhabitants as to industry or idleness. We are more industrious than our forefathers, who were idle for want of a sufficient encouragement to industry. It is better, says the proverb, to play for nothing, than to work for nothing.

In mercantile and manufacturing towns, where the lower classes are chiefly maintained by the employment of capital, they are in general industrious, sober, and thriving; as in many English, and in most Dutch towns. In those towns which are seats of government or of the courts, where the lower classes are chiefly maintained by the spending of revenue, they are in general idle, dissolute, and poor.

London, Lisbon, and Copenhagen, are, perhaps, the only three cities in Europe which are both the seat of government and important trading cities, or cities which trade not only for their own consumption, but for that of other cities and countries. The situation of each of the three is extremely advantageous, and naturally fits it to be the entrepot of a great part of the goods destined for the consumption of distant places.

There was little trade or industry in Edinburgh before the union of Scotland and England. When the Scottish parliament was no longer assembled there, when it ceased to be the necessary residence of the principal nobility and gentry of Scotland, it became a city of some trade and industry. It still continues, however, to be the residence of the principal courts of justice in Scotland, of the boards of customs and taxes, etc. A considerable revenue, therefore, still continues to be spent in it. But in trade and industry it is much inferior to Glasgow, of which the inhabitants are chiefly maintained by the employment of capital.

The inhabitants of a large village, it has sometimes been observed, after having made considerable progress in manufactures, have become idle and poor, in consequence of some very wealthy man's having taken up his residence in their neighborhood.

The proportion between capital and income not earned on capital, therefore, seems to regulate the proportion between industry and idleness. Wherever capital predominates, industry prevails; wherever revenue, idleness. Every increase or decrease of capital, therefore, naturally tends to increase or diminish the real quantity of industry, the number of productive workers, and consequently the exchangeable value of the annual produce of the land and labor of the country, the real wealth and income of all its inhabitants.

Whatever a person saves from his income he adds to his capital, and either employs it himself in maintaining an additional number of productive workers, or enables some other person to do so, by lending it to him at interest; that is, for a share of the profits. As the capital of an individual can be increased only by what he saves from his annual income or profits, so the capital of a country, which is the same as that of all the individuals who compose it, can be increased only in the same manner.

Frugality, and not industry, is the immediate cause of the increase of capital. Industry, indeed, provides the subject which accumulates. But whatever industry might acquire, if frugality did not save and store it up, the capital would never increase.

Frugality, by increasing the fund which is available for the maintenance of productive workers, tends to increase the number of those workers, whose labor adds to the value of the subject upon which it is bestowed. It tends therefore to increase the exchangeable value of the annual production of the land and labor of the country. It puts into motion an additional quantity of industry, which gives an additional value to the annual production.

That portion of his income which a rich man annually spends, is in most cases consumed by idle guests and servants, who leave nothing behind them in return for their consumption. Anything that he saves, as for the sake of the profit it is immediately employed as capital, is consumed in the same manner, and nearly in the same period, but by a different set of people—by laborers, manufacturers, and artificers, who reproduce with a profit the value of their annual consumption.

His income, we shall suppose, is paid him in money. Had he spent the whole, the food, clothing, and lodging which the money could have purchased, would have been distributed among the idle and unproductive.

By saving a part of it which would normally be invested, the food, clothing, and lodging which may be purchased with it, are necessarily reserved for the industrious and productive. The consumption is the same, but the consumers are different.

With what a frugal man annually saves, he not only maintains an additional number of productive workers, but, like the founder of a charitable institution, he establishes as it were a perpetual fund available for the maintenance of an equal number in all time to come.

The perpetual allotment and use of this fund, indeed, is not always guarded by any positive law, by any deed of trust or mortmain. It is always guarded, however, by a very powerful principle—the plain and evident interest of every individual to whom any share of it shall ever belong. No part of it can ever afterwards be employed to maintain any but productive workers, without an evident loss to the person who thus perverts it from its proper use.

But such savings are not always employed in such a frugal manner. The prodigal who lives beyond his income has to encroach upon his capital. Like one who diverts the revenues of some pious foundation to profane purposes, he pays the wages of idleness with those funds which the frugality of his forefathers had, as it were, consecrated to the maintenance of industry.

By diminishing the funds available for the employment of productive labor, he necessarily diminishes in some degree the quantity of that labor which adds value to the subject upon which it is bestowed, and, consequently, the real wealth and revenue of its inhabitants.

If the prodigality of some were not compensated by the frugality of others, the conduct of every prodigal, by feeding the idle with the bread of the industrious, would tend not only to beggar himself but to impoverish his country. And this is true even if all the prodigal's extravagance is for commodities and services produced in his own country.[4]

[4] Extravagant expenditure, observes Thorold Rogers, is "good for trade" only in the sense that it is good for some particular traders. It makes savings, which is new capital, less than they otherwise would be. But, as A. S. remarks later, the constitution of a healthy society is so strong, that it easily survives this and many other minor disorders.

CHAPTER IV

The money in a country will increase as prosperity increases, and fall as it declines; the savings of frugal men are a public benefaction, and the extravagance of others a public injury; and the general increase of prosperity may come in spite of the impertinent meddling of governments, who are themselves the greatest spendthrifts.

IN ANY COUNTRY in which the value of the annual production diminishes, a surplus of money soon appears. The sole use of money is to circulate consumable goods. By means of it, food, materials, and finished work are bought and sold, and distributed to their proper consumers.

The quantity of money, therefore, which can be employed in any country, must be determined by the value of the consumable goods within it. But money which is thrown out of domestic circulation will not be allowed to lie idle. The interest of its owner requires that it should be employed, and if it can find no employment at home, it will, in spite of all laws and prohibitions, be sent abroad, and employed in purchasing consumable goods which may be of some use at home.

This export of money and import of goods will continue for some time to add something to the annual consumption of the country, beyond the value of its own production. What in the days of its prosperity had been saved, and employed in purchasing gold and silver, will contribute for some little time to support its consumption in adversity.

The exportation of gold and silver is, in this case, not the cause but the effect of depression and decline in that country, and may even, for some little time, alleviate the misery of that decline.

Contrariwise, the quantity of money must in every country naturally increase as the value of the annual production increases. The value of the consumable goods produced and distributed within the community being greater, it requires a larger stock of money to circulate it. A part of the increasing production, therefore, will naturally be employed in purchasing, from some source, the additional quantity of gold and silver necessary for circulating the rest. The increase of those metals will in this case be the effect, not the cause, of the public prosperity.

Gold and silver are purchased everywhere through this process. The food, clothing, and shelter, the income and maintenance of all those whose labor or capital is employed in bringing them from the mine to the market, is the price paid for them in South Africa as well as in England.

The country which has this price to pay, will never be long without the quantity of those metals which it needs and can use; and no country will ever long retain a quantity which it no longer needs.

Whatever we may imagine the real wealth and income of a country to be, therefore—whether in the value of the annual produce of its land and labor, as plain reason seems to dictate; or in the quantity of the precious metals which circulate within it, as vulgar prejudices suppose—in any case it is clear that every prodigal must be a public enemy, and every frugal man a public benefactor.

The effects of bad judgment are often the same as those of extravagance. Every foolish and unsuccessful project in agriculture, mines, fisheries, trade, or manufacture, tends in the same manner to diminish the funds available for the maintenance of productive labor. In every such project, though the capital is consumed by productive workers only, yet because the enterprise itself is unwise, the workers do not reproduce the full value of their consumption, and there must always be some diminution in what would otherwise have been the productive funds of the community.

It can seldom happen, indeed, that the circumstances of a great nation can be much affected by either the prodigality or bad judgment of individuals; the profusion or imprudence of some, being always more than compensated by the frugality and ability of others.

With regard to extravagance, the principle which prompts

us to spend money is the passion for present enjoyment; which, though sometimes violent and very difficult to restrain, is in general only momentary and occasional. But the principle which prompts us to save is the desire of bettering our condition, a desire which, though generally calm and dispassionate, comes with us from the womb, and never leaves us until we go into the grave.

In the whole interval which separates those two moments, there is scarcely perhaps a single instant in which any man is so perfectly and completely satisfied with his situation, as to be without any wish of alteration or improvement of any kind.

An increase in his possessions is the means by which most men propose to better their condition. It is the most vulgar and the most obvious method; and the most likely way of accomplishing it is to save and accumulate, either regularly or upon some extraordinary occasion.

Though the principle of spending, therefore, prevails in almost all men at times, and in some men almost all the time, yet in most men, taking the whole course of their lives at an average, the principle of frugality seems not only to predominate, but to predominate by a wide margin.

With regard to bad judgment, the number of prudent and successful undertakings is everywhere much greater than that of foolish and unsuccessful ones. After all our complaints of the frequency of bankruptcies, the unhappy men who fall into this misfortune make but a very small part of the whole number engaged in business; not much more perhaps than one in a thousand.

Bankruptcy is perhaps the greatest and most humiliating calamity which can befall an innocent man. Most men, therefore, are sufficiently careful to avoid it. Some, indeed, do not avoid it, just as another small number do not avoid the gallows.[1]

[1] Thorold Rogers questions whether bankruptcy is as humiliating as A. S. suggests, to many people. In 1880, he says, bankruptcy in England is common, fraudulent compositions as common, shamelessness commoner still. He blames it on the laws put through by lawyers to gratify their rapacity; 75 per cent of bankrupt assets go for law costs.

Great nations are never ruined by private prodigality and business failure, but they sometimes are by these faults in the public service. The whole, or almost the whole public revenue, is in most countries employed in maintaining unproductive workers. Such are the people who conduct the departments and bureaus of the government, the courts, the army and navy. Such people, as they themselves produce nothing, are all maintained by the produce of other men's labor.

When multiplied, therefore, to an unnecessary number, they may in a particular year consume so great a share of national production as not to leave enough for maintaining the productive laborers, who should reproduce it next year. The next year's produce, therefore, will be less than that of the preceding, and if the same disorder should continue, that of the third year will be still less than that of the second.

Those unproductive workers, who should be maintained by a part only of the surplus income of the people, may consume so great a share and therefore oblige so great a number to encroach upon their capital, upon the funds available for the maintenance of productive labor, that all the frugality and hard and intelligent work of individuals may not be able to compensate the waste and loss occasioned by this violent and forced encroachment.

Frugality and good judgment, however, are in fact usually sufficient to compensate, not only for the private prodigality and misconduct of individuals, but the public extravagance of government. The uniform, constant, and uninterrupted effort of every man to better his condition, the principle from which public and national, as well as private opulence is originally derived, is generally powerful enough to maintain the natural progress of things toward improvement, in spite of the extravagance of government, and of the greatest errors of administration.

Like the unknown principle of animal life, it frequently restores health and vigor to the constitution, in spite not only of disease itself, but of the absurd prescriptions of the doctor.[2]

The total production of the land and labor of any nation can be increased in value by increasing either the number of its productive laborers, or the production per worker employed.

[2] Trying to improve on this phraseology is like gilding the lily. But Thorold Rogers adds that government interference "is as futile as it is impertinent; the inductions of the many are incomparably wiser than the edicts of the few."

The number of its productive workmen, it is evident, can never be much increased except through an increase of capital, or of the funds available for maintaining them. The productive powers of the same number of laborers cannot be increased except through some addition and improvement to those machines and instruments which facilitate and abridge labor, or of better organization and management. In either case additional capital is almost always required.

It is by means of additional capital only, that the entrepreneur can provide his workmen with better machinery, or organize the work of production more efficiently.

When therefore we compare the state of a nation at two different periods, and find that its annual production is evidently greater than at the former date, that its lands are better cultivated, its manufactures more numerous and more flourishing, and its trade more extensive, we may be assured that its capital must have increased during this period, and that more must have been added to it by the good conduct of some, than had been taken from it by the private misconduct of others, or by the public extravagance of government.

But we shall find this to be true of almost all nations, in tolerably quiet and peaceful times, even of those who have not enjoyed the most prudent and economical governments. To form a proper judgment of it, indeed, we must compare the state of the country at periods somewhat distant from one another. The progress is frequently so gradual, that, at a short view, the improvement is not only not apparent, but from the decline of certain branches of industry, or of certain districts of the country (things which sometimes happen even when a country is prosperous as a whole), there frequently arises a suspicion that the riches and industry of the whole are going backward.

The annual produce of the land and labor of England, for example, is certainly much greater than it was, a little more than a century ago, at the restoration of Charles II. Yet during this period five years have seldom passed away in which some able book or pamphlet has not been published purporting to prove that the wealth of the nation was fast declining, that the country was depopulated, agriculture neglected, manufactures decaying, and trade ruined.

Nor have all of these publications been political pamphlets, the wretched offspring of falsehood and venality. Many of them have been written by very candid and intelligent people, who wrote nothing but what they believed, and for no other reason but because they believed it.

℃ Yet no one can be found to deny that England was more prosperous and productive in 1660 than at the accession of Queen Elizabeth; more prosperous then than at the Norman Conquest; and more prosperous at the Conquest than at the invasion of Julius Caesar, when the inhabitants were little better than North American savages, painted blue.

℃ In each of these periods there were private and public waste, expensive and unnecessary wars, civil discord, fires, plagues, and constant destruction of capital. Each of these reduced in some degree the productive labor of the people, each retarded to some extent the progress of civilization and wealth.[3] To what heights the real wealth and income might otherwise have risen by this time, it is not easy even to imagine.

But though the extravagance of government must undoubtedly have retarded the natural progress of England towards wealth and improvement, it has not been able to stop it. The annual production of its land and labor is, undoubtedly, much greater at present than it was in 1660 or 1688. The capital, therefore, annually employed in cultivating this land, and in maintaining this labor, must likewise be much greater. In the midst of all the exactions of government, this capital has been silently and gradually accumulated by the private frugality and good management of individuals, by their universal, continual, and uninterrupted effort to better their own condition.

It is this effort, protected by law and allowed by liberty to exert itself in the manner that is most advantageous, which has usually maintained the progress of England towards opulence and improvement, and which, it is to be hoped, will do so in all future times.

It must be said, however, that England has never been blessed with a very parsimonious government, nor has parsimony ever been the characteristic virtue of its inhabitants.

It is the greatest impertinence and presumption, therefore, in political heads of the government, to pretend to watch over the

[3] Foreign war, observes Thorold Rogers, is less destructive than civil war, and civil war less destructive than bad government.

economy of private people, and to restrain their spending, either by sumptuary laws, or by prohibiting imports of foreign luxuries. They are themselves, without any exception, the greatest spend-thrifts in the society. Let them look well after their own expense, and they may safely trust private people with theirs. If their own extravagance does not ruin the nation, that of their subjects never will.

CHAPTER V

*Men spend their money in many ways; the
character and intentions of one man may be
as good as another's, but the results of different kinds of spending have very different
effects on the prosperity of the society.*

As FRUGALITY INCREASES and waste reduces the public capital, so
the conduct of those whose expense just equals their income, without either accumulating or encroaching, neither increases nor
diminishes it. Some kinds of spending, however, seem to contribute more to the growth of public opulence than others.

The income of an individual may be spent either in things
which are consumed immediately, or in things more durable, which
can therefore be accumulated.

A wealthy man, for example, may either spend his income
on a profuse and sumptuous table, and in maintaining a great number of servants and a multitude of dogs and horses; or contenting
himself with a frugal table and few attendants, he may lay out the
rest in adorning his house or his country estate, in useful or ornamental buildings, in useful or ornamental furniture, in collecting
books, statues, pictures; or in things more frivolous, jewels, ingenious trinkets of different kinds; or what is most trifling of all, in
amassing a great wardrobe of fine clothes, like the favorite and
minister of a great prince who died a few years ago.[1]

Were two men of equal wealth to spend their income, the
one chiefly in the one way, the other in the other, the magnificence
of the person whose spending had been chiefly for durable commodities would be continually increasing, every day's expense contributing something to support and heighten the effect of that of

[1] Supposed to be the Count de Bruhl, a minister to the King of Poland, who
left at his death 365 rich suits of clothes.

the following day; that of the other, on the contrary, would be no greater at the end of the period than at the beginning.

The former, too, would be the richer man of the two at the end of the period. He would have a stock of goods of some kind or other, which, though it might not be worth all that it cost, would always be worth something. No trace or vestige of the expense of the latter would remain, but would be as completely annihilated as if it had never existed.

As the one kind of spending is more favorable than the other to the wealth of an individual, so is it likewise to that of a nation. The houses, the furniture, the clothing of the rich, in a little time, become useful to the middle and lower classes of people. They are able to purchase them when their superiors grow weary of them, and the general living standard of the whole people is thus gradually improved.

In countries which have long been rich, you will frequently find poorer people in possession of houses and furniture perfectly good and entire, but of which neither the one could have been built, nor the other have been made for their use. The marriage-bed of James the First of Great Britain, which his Queen brought with her from Denmark, as a present fit for a sovereign to make to a sovereign, was, a few years ago, the ornament of a tavern at Dunfermline.

In some ancient cities, which have made no progress or have even gone somewhat to seed, you will sometimes find scarcely a single house which could have been built for its present inhabitants. And if you go into those houses you will frequently find many excellent though antiquated pieces of furniture, which are still very fit for use, and which could as little have been made for them.

Noble palaces, magnificent villas, great collections of books, statues, pictures, and other curiosities, are frequently both an ornament and an honor to the neighborhood, as well as to the whole country to which they belong. Versailles is an ornament and an honor to France, Stowe and Wilton to England. Italy still continues to command some sort of veneration by the number of monuments of this kind which it possesses, although the wealth which produced them has decayed, and the genius which planned them seems to be extinguished.

The expenditure of surplus income for durable commodities is favorable, not only to accumulation, but to frugality. If a person should at any time go too far in it, he can easily reform without exposing himself to the curiosity and criticism of the public. To reduce very much the number of his servants, to reform his table from great profusion to great frugality, to lay down his equipage after he has once set it up, are changes which cannot escape the observation of his neighbors, and which are supposed to imply some acknowledgment of bad management or reverses.

Few of those who have once been so unfortunate as to launch out too far into this sort of extravagance have afterwards the courage to reform, until ruin and bankruptcy force it.

But if a person has been at too great an expense in building, in furniture, in books or pictures, no imprudence can be inferred from his changing his habits. These are things in which further expense is frequently rendered unnecessary by former expense; and when a person stops short, he appears to do so, not because he has exceeded his income, but because he has satisfied his fancy.

It is probable, furthermore, that spending for durable commodities gives maintenance to a greater number of people than that which is employed in the most profuse hospitality. Of the two or three hundredweight of provisions, which may sometimes be served up at a great festival, one-half, perhaps, goes into the garbage, and there is always a great deal wasted.

But if the expense of this entertainment had been employed in setting to work masons, carpenters, upholsterers, mechanics, etc., a quantity of provisions, of equal value, would have been distributed among a still greater number of people, who would have bought them by the single pound or dozen, and not have lost or thrown away a single ounce of them.

In the one way, besides, this expense maintains productive, in the other unproductive workers. In the one way, therefore, it increases, in the other it does not increase, the exchangeable value of the annual produce of the land and labor of the country.

I would not, however, by all this be understood to mean, that the one kind of spending always betokens a more liberal or generous spirit than the other. When a wealthy man spends his income chiefly in hospitality, he shares the greater part of it with his friends and companions; but when he employs it in purchasing such durable commodities, he often spends the whole upon his own person, and gives nothing to anybody without an equivalent.

[196]

The latter kind of spending, therefore, especially when directed towards frivolous objects—ornaments of dress and furniture, jewels, trinkets, gewgaws—frequently indicates, not only a trifling, but a base and selfish disposition.

All that I mean is, that the one sort of expense, as it always results in some accumulation of valuable commodities, as it is more favorable to private frugality, and, consequently, to the increase of the national capital, and as it maintains productive rather than unproductive workers, conduces more than the other to the growth of public opulence.

CHAPTER VI

A study of the lending of capital (usually in the form of money) at interest; showing that in a prosperous country the rate of interest tends to fall, because the price paid for the use of money is regulated by the profit that can be made by the use of it; also that the ordinary market price of land depends upon the ordinary market rate of interest.

WHEN CAPITAL is lent at interest, the lender expects that in due time it is to be paid back to him, and that in the meantime the borrower is to pay him a certain annual rent for the use of it.

The borrower, however, may have no such idea; he may use it either as capital, or as a stock reserved for immediate consumption. If he uses it as capital, he employs it in the maintenance of productive laborers, who reproduce the value with a profit. He can, in this case, both pay back the loan and pay the interest, without alienating or encroaching upon any other source of income. But if he uses it for immediate consumption, he acts the part of a prodigal, and dissipates in the maintenance of the idle, what was intended for the support of the industrious. He can, in this case, neither pay back the capital nor pay the interest, without encroaching upon some other source of income, such as the rent of land.

Capital which is lent at interest is, no doubt, sometimes employed in one way, sometimes in the other, but in the former much more frequently than in the latter. The man who borrows in order to spend will soon be ruined, and he who lends to him will generally have good reason to repent of his folly.

To borrow or to lend for such a purpose, therefore, is in all cases (except those of gross usury), contrary to the interest of both parties; and though it no doubt sometimes happens that people do both the one and the other, yet, from the solicitude that all men have for their own interest, we may be assured that it cannot happen so very frequently as we are sometimes apt to imagine.

Ask any rich man of common prudence, to which of the two sorts of people he has lent the greater part of his capital—to those who, he thinks, will employ it profitably, or to those who will spend it idly—and he will laugh at you for proposing the question.

Even among borrowers, therefore, not the people in the world most famous for frugality, the number of the frugal and industrious must considerably surpass that of the prodigal and idle.

In most cases, therefore, the borrower considers the loan as capital, and uses it as capital. In the case of some of the English country gentlemen, however, who have gone into debt for purchases of various kinds, the loan is used to pay off these old debts. It is therefore not really borrowed to be spent, but to replace capital which had previously been spent.

Almost all interest-bearing loans are made in money, either paper or gold and silver. But what the borrower really wants, and what the lender really supplies him with, is not money, but the money's worth, or the goods which it can purchase. If he wants it for immediate consumption, it is such goods only which he can buy for this use.

If he wants it as capital for employing industry, it is from those goods only that the industrious can be furnished with the tools, materials, and maintenance, necessary for carrying on their work.

By means of the loan, the lender, as it were, assigns to the borrower his right to a certain portion of total production of the land and labor of the country, to be employed as the borrower pleases.

The amount of capital, therefore, or, as it is commonly expressed, of money which can be lent, does not depend on the value of the money which serves as the instrument of the different loans, but by the value of that part of the total production which the owner does not need to replace capital, and does not want to go to the trouble of employing himself.

As such capital is commonly lent out and paid back in

[*199*]

money, it constitutes what is called the monied interest. It is distinct from the landed and from the trading and manufacturing interests, as in these last the owners themselves employ their own capital.

Even in the monied interest, however, the money is, as it were, only a deed of assignment, which conveys from one hand to another capital which the owners do not care to employ themselves.

That the loan is a loan of purchasing power, not of money itself, may be easily shown, since the total of loans made may be far greater than the amount of money used in making them.

Thus A may lend to X a thousand dollars, with which X buys from B a thousand dollars' worth of goods. B, having no immediate use for the money, lends it to Y, who immediately buys another thousand dollars' worth of goods from C. C in turn lends the money to Z, who buys from D, and so on indefinitely; the same original thousand dollars being sufficient for all these transactions, totalling perhaps thirty times that original amount.

The money is altogether different from the real loan, which is a claim on a particular part of the total production of the country—a smaller part for the interest on the loan, and a much larger part for repaying the principal. As the total production increases, that part of it which the owners would like to invest, rather than being at the trouble of employing it themselves, naturally grows larger also. In other words, as the wealth of the country increases, the capital available for lending likewise grows greater and greater.

As the quantity of capital to be lent at interest increases, the interest, or the price which must be paid for the use of that capital, necessarily diminishes, not only from those general causes which make the market price of things commonly diminish as their quantity increases, but for other reasons which are peculiar to this particular case.

As capital increases in any country, the profits which can be made by employing it necessarily diminish. It becomes gradually more and more difficult to find within the country a profitable investment for new capital. There arises in consequence a competition between different capitals, the owner of one endeavoring to get business away from somebody else.

But as a rule he can hope to jostle the other man out of this employment only by dealing upon more reasonable terms. He must not only sell what he deals in somewhat cheaper, but in order to get it to sell, he must sometimes buy it dearer.

The demand for productive labor, by the increase of the funds which are available for maintaining it, grows every day greater and greater. Laborers easily find employment, but the owners of capital find it difficult to get laborers to employ. Their competition raises the wages of labor, and lowers the profits of capital. But when the profits which can be made by the use of capital are thus, as it were, cut down at both ends, the price which can be paid for the use of it, that is, the rate of interest, must necessarily be cut down with them.

℄ Over a period of years, interest rates have fallen considerably, as remarked in an earlier chapter, and some writers have supposed that this has been due to an increase in the supply of gold and silver, which made money of less value.

℄ This, however, is a fallacious idea. If the production of real wealth in a country remained the same, an increase in the supply of money would reduce the purchasing power of each piece of gold or silver. But it would reduce the purchasing power of a dollar of interest in exactly the same proportion as of a dollar of principal, and the relation between the two, or rate of interest, would not necessarily change.

℄ The goods in the country would exchange for a larger number of money units—that is, prices would rise—but there would be no more real wealth and capital in the country than before.

℄ The loans, or assignments of purchasing power, would indeed read in higher amounts, like the conveyances of a verbose lawyer, but they would actually assign and convey no more real value than before.

℄ The fund available for maintaining productive labor not having increased, the demand for labor would be no greater. Its price, or wage scale, would indeed seem higher, but the real wages would be the same. They would be paid in more dollars, but the larger number of dollars would buy only the same amount of goods and services as before.

But the profits of capital are not computed by the number of pieces of money with which they are paid, but by the proportion which those pieces bear to the whole capital employed. Thus in a particular country forty dollars a week is said to be the common wages of labor, and ten per cent the common profit of capital. But if the money supply should increase, the whole capital of the country being the same as before, the competition between the different capitals of individuals would likewise be the same. They would all trade with the same advantages and disadvantages as before.

The common proportion between capital and profit, therefore, would be the same, and consequently the rate of interest on loans; what can commonly be paid as interest for the use of money being necessarily regulated by the profit which can commonly be made by the use of it.

Any increase in the quantity of commodities annually produced and distributed within the country, while that of the money which circulated them remained the same, would, on the contrary, produce very different and important results.

The capital of the country, though it might nominally be the same, would really be increased. It might continue to be expressed by the same quantity of money, but it would command a greater quantity of labor. The quantity of productive labor which it could maintain and employ would be increased, and consequently the demand for that labor. Wages would naturally rise with the demand, and yet might appear to sink. They might be paid with a smaller quantity of money, but that smaller quantity might purchase a greater quantity of goods than higher money wages had done before.

The profits of capital would be diminished, both really and in appearance. The whole capital of the country being enlarged, the competition between the different capitals of different owners would naturally be augmented along with it. Owners of capital would be obliged to content themselves with a smaller proportion of the produce of that labor which their capital employed. The interest rate of money, keeping pace always with the profits of capital, might, in this manner, be greatly diminished, though the value of money, or the quantity of goods which any particular sum could purchase, was greatly increased.

In some countries the interest of money has been prohibited by law. But as something can everywhere be made by the use of money, something ought everywhere to be paid for the use of it. This regulation, instead of preventing, has been found from experience to increase the evil of usury; the debtor being obliged to pay, not only for the use of the money, but for the risk which his creditor runs by lending it. He is obliged, if one may say so, to insure his creditor against the penalties of usury.

In countries where interest is permitted, the law, in order to prevent the extortion of usury, generally fixes the highest rate which can be taken without incurring a penalty. This rate ought always to be somewhat above the lowest market price, or the price which is commonly paid for the use of money by those who can give the most undoubted security.[1] If this legal rate should be fixed below the lowest market rate, the effect of this must be nearly the same as a total prohibition of interest. The creditor will not lend his money for less than the use of it is worth, and the debtor must pay him for the risk which he runs by accepting the full value of that use.

If the rate is fixed precisely at the lowest market price, it ruins the credit of all those who cannot give the very best security, and obliges them to have recourse to exorbitant usurers.

In a country such as Great Britain, where money is lent to government at three per cent, and to private people upon good security at four and four and a half, the present legal rate, five per cent, is perhaps as proper as any.

The legal rate, though it ought to be somewhat above, ought not to be much above the lowest market rate. If the legal rate of interest in Great Britain, for example, was fixed so high as eight or ten per cent, the most of the money which was to be lent would be lent to prodigals and promoters, who alone would be willing to promise this high interest. Sober people, who will give for the use of money no more than a part of what they are likely to make by the use of it, would not venture into the competition. A

---

[1] Here we meet a short passage in W. N. which has been universally criticized by economists. In these paragraphs A. S. appears to approve regulation of interest rates, and to advocate the fixing of the maximum legal rate of interest at a point somewhat above the lowest market price. As this certainly violates one of the basic teachings of W. N.—that the highest degree of freedom inevitably results in the greatest private and public benefit—it has been assailed on all sides, and indeed was immediately attacked and disproved by Jeremy Bentham in his "Defense of Usury." A. S. is said to have admitted to Bentham that his position was incorrect.

In his defense, it might be suggested that A. S. meant only to say that the establishment of a legal interest rate was unnecessary, but as nearly all governments feel it incumbent on them to do it, the maximum rate should at all events be higher than the going market price for money.

great part of the capital of the country would thus be kept out of the hands which were most likely to make a profitable use of it, and thrown into those which were most likely to waste and destroy it.

Where the legal rate of interest, on the contrary, is fixed but a very little above the lowest market rate, sober people are universally preferred, as borrowers, to prodigals and promoters, and a great part of the capital of the country is thus thrown into the hands in which it is most likely to be employed with advantage.

The ordinary market price of land, it is to be observed, depends everywhere upon the ordinary market rate of interest. The person who has capital from which he wishes to obtain income, without taking the trouble to employ it himself, deliberates whether he should buy land with it, or lend it at interest. The greater security of land, together with some other advantages which almost everywhere attend upon this species of property, will generally induce him to content himself with a smaller income from land, than he might have by lending out his money at interest.

These advantages are sufficient to compensate a certain loss of income, but they will not compensate for much difference; and if the rent of land should fall short of the interest of money by a greater difference, nobody would buy land, which would soon reduce its ordinary price.

On the other hand, if the advantages should much more than compensate the difference, everybody would rush to buy land, which again would soon raise its ordinary price.

CHAPTER VII

*How capital may be profitably employed in
the production of raw materials, in manufacturing, in wholesale trade and distribution, and in retailing; of which the use most
beneficial to any country is in agriculture,
and that least beneficial is in the carrying
trade between foreign countries; but all
great fortunes have been built on manufacture and trade.*

THOUGH ALL CAPITAL is destined for the maintenance of productive labor only, yet the quantity of that labor which a given amount
of capital is capable of putting into motion varies widely according
to how it is employed; and so does also the value which that employment adds to the annual production of the country.

Capital may be employed in four different ways: in producing raw materials; in processing these raw materials; in transporting them before and after processing; and in dividing up and
distributing them to purchasers.

In the first class is the capital of farmers, miners, lumber-
men, and fishermen; in the second, manufacturers; in the third,
jobbers and wholesalers;[1] in the fourth, the retailers.

Each of these four is necessary and essential to the functioning of the other three, for obvious reasons. It may be observed
that the prejudices of some people against shopkeepers and tradesmen have no foundation, and are most unjust.

Unless capital were employed in breaking up and dividing

---

[1] Once more, because A. S. sniffed at "unproductive" workers and the
capital that employs them, he here ignores large amounts of service capital which
could as easily be included; in the third class, for example, railroad workers and
truckers as well as wholesalers.

raw materials and manufactured goods, into such small parcels as suit the occasional demands of those who want them, every man would be obliged to buy more of the goods he wanted than his immediate needs called for.

If there were no such trade as a butcher, for example, every man would be obliged to purchase a whole steer or sheep at a time. This would be inconvenient even to the rich, and much more so to the poor.

Nothing can be more convenient for such a person than to be able to purchase his subsistence from day to day, or even from hour to hour, as he wants it. He is thereby enabled to employ almost his whole resources as capital in his own trade. He is thus enabled to furnish work to a greater value, and the profit which he makes by it in this way much more than makes up for the higher price which the profit of the retailer imposes upon the goods.

So far is it from being necessary to tax retailers, or to restrict their numbers, that they can never be multiplied so as to hurt the public, though they may very easily hurt one another.

The quantity of groceries, for example, which can be sold in a particular town, is limited by the demand of that town and its neighborhood. The capital, therefore, which can be employed in the grocery trade cannot exceed what is sufficient to purchase that quantity. If this capital is divided between two different grocers, their competition will tend to make both of them sell cheaper than if there were only one; and if it were divided among twenty, their competition would be just so much the greater, and the chance of their combining together, in order to raise the price, just so much the less.[2]

Their competition might perhaps ruin some of themselves; but to look out for this is the business of the parties concerned, and it may safely be trusted to their discretion. Retail competition can never hurt either the consumer or the producer; on the contrary, it must tend to make the retailers both sell cheaper and buy dearer, than if the whole trade were monopolized by one or two persons.

Some of them, perhaps, may sometimes decoy a weak customer to buy what he has no occasion for. This evil, however, is of

[2] This is certainly questionable, at least; the more severe the competition, the greater the pressure on retailers to form combinations to maintain prices, in defiance of laws and regardless of the public welfare. But it is true that a small number find it easier to get together and hold together.

too little importance to attract the public attention, nor would it necessarily be prevented by restricting their numbers. It is not the multitude of tap-rooms and saloons, to give the most suspicious example, that promotes drunkenness among the common people; but that disposition arising from other causes necessarily gives employment to a multitude of tap-rooms.

The persons whose capital is employed in any of those four ways are themselves productive laborers. Their labor, when properly directed, fixes and realizes itself in the subject or salable commodity upon which it is bestowed, and generally adds to its price the value at least of their own maintenance and consumption. The profits of the farmer, of the manufacturer, of the wholesaler and the retailer, are all drawn from the price of the goods which the first two produce, and the last two buy and sell.

An equal amount of capital, however, employed in each of those four different ways, will directly put into motion very different quantities of productive labor, and the value of this employment in the whole total production of the country is much greater in some cases than in others.

℄ Thus the capital of a retailer employs only himself and his clerks, but that of the wholesale merchant employs all kinds of transportation workers as well. A still greater amount of productive labor is put in motion by manufacture; and the greatest of all by the farmer, or any producer of raw materials. Such primary capital produces a much larger part of the whole total production of the country than any other employment.

℄ Of all the ways in which capital can be employed, this is by far the most advantageous to the general welfare of society.

℄ As to the places where capital is employed, there are again great differences in different employments. The capital of agriculture and of retail trade must always be at a fixed spot within the community. But the capital of the manufacturer may be almost anywhere; it may be far distant from its raw materials, and equally distant from its customers. But it must always, or most of it, be where the manufacture is actually carried on.

℄ One class, the wholesale merchant, may have his capital employed almost anywhere, and it does in fact wander from place to place, wherever goods may be bought and sold. The capital of many of these merchants is employed in the export and import trade, and it is worth noting that if the capital is so employed, it

makes almost no difference whether the capital itself is owned by
a native or a foreigner. It is the trade itself which is valuable to a
country, and where the trader is a foreigner, the value to the country is diminished only by the profit of one man.

℃   The capital of the manufacturer will put into motion more
native labor if the manufacture is carried on within the country;
but even when carried on somewhere else, it is still of some
advantage.

The capital of the British manufacturers who work up the
flax and hemp imported from the coasts of the Baltic, is surely
very useful to the countries which produce these materials. They
are a part of the surplus produce of those countries, which, unless
exchanged for something which is in demand there, would be of
no value, and would soon cease to be produced.

The merchants who export it, replace the capital of the
people who produce it, and thereby encourage them to continue
the production; and the British manufacturers replace the capital
of those merchants.

Just as a particular person may not have enough capital to
carry on a business efficiently, so a whole country may frequently
not have enough capital at once to improve and cultivate all its
lands, to manufacture and prepare these raw materials for immediate use and consumption, and to transport any surplus to
distant markets where it can be exchanged for something for which
there is a demand at home.

The inhabitants of many different parts of Great Britain
have not enough capital to improve and cultivate all their lands.
The wool of southern Scotland is manufactured in Yorkshire, for
want of capital to manufacture it at home. There are many little
manufacturing towns in Great Britain, of which the inhabitants
have not enough capital to move the produce of their own industry to those distant markets where there is demand and consumption for it.

The question arises, in such cases, as to how the capital of
the community ought to be employed—whether in agriculture,
which employs the most labor and adds the greatest value to the
production, or in manufacture, which is next best, or in transportation, which is least valuable.[3]

[3] As always, A. S. sees in agriculture not only the most inviting but the most
valuable of human occupations.

The country which has not capital sufficient for all those purposes, has not arrived at that degree of opulence for which it seems naturally destined. But to attempt, prematurely and with insufficient capital, to do all the three, is certainly not the shortest way for a society, no more than it would be for an individual, to acquire more. The quickest way to build up capital is to employ what capital there is in the way that is the most profitable for the most people.

It has been the principal cause of the rapid progress of our American colonies towards wealth and greatness, that almost their whole capital has hitherto been employed in agriculture. They have no manufactures, those household and coarser manufactures excepted which necessarily accompany the progress of agriculture, and which are the work of the women and children in every private family.

Most of the export and coasting trade of America is carried on by the capital of merchants who reside in Great Britain. Even the stores and warehouses from which goods are retailed, in some provinces, particularly in Virginia and Maryland, belong largely to merchants who reside in the mother country, and afford one of the few instances of the retail trade of a society being carried on by the capital of those who are non-residents.

Were the Americans, either by combination or by any other sort of violence, to stop the importation of European manufactures, and, by thus giving a monopoly to such of their own countrymen as could manufacture the like goods, divert any considerable part of their capital into this employment, they would retard instead of accelerating the further increase in the value of their production, and would obstruct instead of promoting the progress of their country towards real wealth and greatness.[4] This would be still more the case, were they to attempt, in the same manner, to monopolize their whole export trade.

The course of human prosperity, indeed, seems scarcely ever to have continued long enough to enable any great country to save up enough capital for all those three purposes; unless, perhaps, we could believe the wonderful accounts of the wealth

[4] It would, perhaps, have that immediate result, but as a long-term policy it would be highly profitable, as the history of the United States since 1787 has abundantly shown.

and cultivation of China, of those of ancient Egypt, and of the ancient state of Hindustan.

Even those three countries, the wealthiest, according to all accounts, that ever were in the world, were chiefly renowned for their superiority in agriculture and manufactures. They do not appear to have been eminent for foreign trade. Most of the surplus produce of all those three countries seems to have been always exported by foreigners, who gave in exchange for it something else for which they found a demand there, frequently gold and silver.

It is thus that the same capital will in any country put into motion a greater or smaller quantity of productive labor, and add a greater or smaller value to the production of its land and labor, according to the different proportions in which it is employed in agriculture, manufacture, and wholesale trade.

There are also great variations within the wholesale trade itself. There are three general divisions of this business—the home trade, the foreign trade of consumption, and the carrying trade. The home trade is employed in buying in one part of the country, and selling in another, the produce of the industry of that country. The foreign trade of consumption buys foreign goods for home consumption. The carrying trade transacts the commerce of foreign countries, or carries surplus produce of one to another.

The capital which is employed in buying commodities in one part of the country in order to sell in another, generally replaces in this way two distinct capitals that had both been employed in the agriculture or manufactures of that country, and thereby enables them to continue that employment. The capital which sends Scotch manufactures to London, and brings back English grain and manufactures to Edinburgh, necessarily replaces, by every such operation, two British capitals which had both been employed in the agriculture or manufactures of Great Britain.

The capital employed in buying foreign goods for home consumption also replaces two distinct capitals; but one of them only is employed in supporting domestic industry. The capital which sends British goods to Portugal, and brings back Portuguese goods to Great Britain, replaces by every such operation only one British capital. The other is Portuguese.

Even if the returns of the foreign trade of consumption should be as quick as those of the home trade, the capital employed in it will give but one-half the support to the industry or productive labor of the country.

But the returns of foreign trade are very seldom as quick as those of the home trade. Capital employed in the home trade will sometimes make twelve operations, or be turned over twelve times, before capital employed in the foreign trade has made one. If the capital is equal, therefore, the one will give twenty-four times more encouragement and support to the industry of the country than the other.[5]

❡ The returns from foreign trade are even slower, and the capital required even larger, when that trade is not directly with a single country, but a "three-cornered" transaction, or one even more roundabout.

❡ If the flax and hemp of Riga are bought with tobacco from Virginia, which was bought with Bacardi rum, which was bought with some goods of British manufacture, the merchant must wait for all these transactions to be completed before his own venture is complete.

❡ This will require still more capital, and as it employs and supports less British labor, it is even less advantageous to Britain than a trade deal with a single foreign country.

❡ Foreign trade cannot be anything but an exchange of one commodity for another, whether the transaction be direct or roundabout. Sometimes, but not very often, goods are exported and imported, but are paid for in gold or silver.

❡ In such cases, the metal is only a different kind of commodity; for the merchant who pays the gold must have obtained it by exchanging some kind of goods or services for it. In no other way (unless indeed he himself mined the gold) could he have become its owner.

❡ Gold is used for this purpose, on the occasions when it is so used, chiefly for the same reasons that make it the best kind of money—its durable nature, small bulk, and great value. It can

[5] This statement is true enough, but all it means is that to carry on a given volume of business in domestic trade will need only one twenty-fourth as much capital as the same volume of foreign business done on three-year credit. It does not mean that the one kind of business is twenty-four times more profitable or advantageous to the country than the other. As A. S. has himself shown, the rate of profit of capital tends to be equal in all employments; foreign trade on long-time credit must therefore carry a rate of profit enough higher to make it as attractive as if the capital were employed at home.

be shipped much more cheaply than tobacco, for example, and the insurance on it is no greater. An equal quantity of foreign goods can often be bought more cheaply with gold than with other commodities, for this reason.

That part of the capital of any country which is employed in the carrying trade, is altogether withdrawn from supporting the productive labor of that particular country, to support that of some foreign countries. Though it may replace by every operation two distinct capitals, yet neither of them belongs to that particular country.

The capital of the Dutch merchant, which carries the grain of Poland to Portugal, and brings back the fruits and wines of Portugal to Poland, replaces by every such operation two capitals, neither of which had been employed in supporting the productive labor of Holland; but one of them is supporting that of Poland, and the other that of Portugal.

Only the profits return regularly to Holland, and constitute the whole addition which this trade necessarily makes to the whole production of the land and labor of that country. It is only when the carrying trade of a particular country is carried on with the ships and sailors of that country, that part of the capital employed in it is distributed among, and puts into motion, a certain number of productive laborers of that country. Almost all nations that have had any considerable share of the carrying trade have, in fact, carried it on in this manner.[6]

₵ While capital in domestic trade supports more productive labor than in foreign trade, and foreign trade more than in the carrying trade, it does not follow that one is more advantageous to the country than another, much less that a government should encourage or discourage one or another. It ought not to force or tempt more capital into any of these employments than what would naturally flow there of its own accord.

₵ All of these branches of trade are good and necessary, under particular circumstances, and the circumstances will create

[6] The carrying trade has long formed a large part of the productive economy of Great Britain, because of its island position. In the United States, it forms an insignificant part, and can be maintained only by mail and other subsidies. The principal reason for this is the high cost of building and operating ships, which are quite unable to compete in the overseas trade; even our coastwise shipping can be maintained only by forcibly excluding foreign ships by law.

the trade when and where it is needed, without constraint or violence.

When there is a surplus of some commodity, this must be sent abroad, and exchanged for something for which there is a demand at home. Without such export, a part of the productive labor of the country must cease, and the value of its annual produce diminish.[7]

The land and labor of Great Britain produce generally more grain, woolens, and hardware, than the demand of the home market requires. The surplus, therefore, must be sent abroad, and exchanged for something for which there is a demand at home. It is only by means of such export that this surplus can acquire a value sufficient to compensate the labor and expense of producing it.

The neighborhood of the sea-coast, and the banks of navigable rivers, are advantageous situations for industry, only because they facilitate the export and exchange of such surplus produce for something else which is more in demand.

When the foreign goods which are thus bought with the surplus produce of domestic industry exceed the demand of the home market, the surplus part of them must be sent abroad again, and exchanged for something more in demand at home.

About 96,000 hogsheads of tobacco are annually purchased in Virginia and Maryland, with a part of the surplus produce of British industry. But the demand of Great Britain does not require, perhaps, more than 14,000. If the remaining 82,000 therefore could not be sent abroad and exchanged for something more in demand at home, the importation of them must cease immediately, and with it the productive labor of all those British workers who are at present employed in preparing the goods with which these 82,000 hogsheads are annually purchased.

When the capital stock of any country is increased to such a degree, that it cannot be all employed in supplying the consumption, and supporting the productive labor of that particular country, the surplus part of it naturally disgorges itself into the carrying trade, and is employed in performing the same offices to other countries.

The carrying trade is the natural effect and symptom of

[7] But of course only temporarily; the labor should and would be diverted as rapidly as possible to producing "something for which there is a demand at home."

[213]

great national wealth; but it does not seem to be the natural cause of it. Those statesmen who have been disposed to favor it with particular encouragement, seem to have mistaken the effect and symptom for the cause. Holland, in proportion to the extent of its land and the number of its inhabitants by far the richest country in Europe, has, accordingly, the greatest share of the carrying trade of Europe.

England, perhaps the second richest country of Europe, is likewise supposed to have a considerable share of it; though what commonly passes for the carrying trade of England, will frequently, perhaps, be found to be no more than a roundabout foreign trade of consumption.

The extent of the home trade and of the capital which can be employed in it, is necessarily limited by the value of the surplus produce of all those distant places within the country which exchange their respective productions with one another. That of the foreign trade of consumption is limited, by the value of the surplus produce of the whole country, and of what can be purchased with it.

The extent of the carrying trade, however, is limited only by the value of the surplus produce of all the different countries in the world. Its possible extent, therefore, is in a manner infinite in comparison with that of the other two, and is capable of absorbing the very largest capital.

In concluding this book, it must be recognized that the sole motive which determines the owner of any capital to employ it in agriculture, in manufacture, or in some particular branch of the wholesale or retail trade, is the consideration of his own private profit.[8]

The different quantities of productive labor which it may put into motion, and the different values which it may add to the country's total production, according as it is employed in one or another of those different ways, never enter his head.

In countries, therefore, where agriculture is the most profitable of all employments, and farming and improving form the most direct roads to a fortune, the capital of individuals will

[8] The capitalist is in fact an example of the beneficial division of labor, says Thorold Rogers. The person who really sustains labor is not the employer but the consumer. The capitalist is a mere intermediary, a convenience to laborer and consumer alike.

naturally be employed in the manner most advantageous to the whole society.

But it would be difficult to find such a country. All great fortunes have been built up on trade and manufacture, sometimes from a very small capital to begin with, sometimes indeed on no capital at all.

Yet there is much uncultivated land; and the only explanation is that while the rate of profit in agriculture may be as high as elsewhere, yet there are other disadvantages which in every country prevent agriculture from attracting all the capital which it could profitably use.

The nature and causes of these disadvantages will be examined in the next book.

BOOK III

The progress of civilization has been the story of the conflicting interests of the towns and agriculture; in most cases, but not all, policies of governments have tended to favor the towns over the country, although this is not the natural order, nor the one most conducive to justice and prosperity.

CHAPTER I

*A short chapter opening a short book, and
devoted to an explanation of the interde-
pendence of the towns and the country;
how industry would naturally progress from
agriculture to manufactures and trade, and
finally to foreign trade, if left to itself.*

THE REALLY important commerce of every civilized society, is
that carried on between the inhabitants of the town and those of
the country. It consists in the exchange of raw materials for manufactured articles, either directly, or by the medium of money, or
of some sort of paper which represents money.

The country supplies the town with the means of subsistence, and the materials of manufacture. The town repays this
supply by sending back a part of the manufactured goods to the
inhabitants of the country. The town, in which there neither is
nor can be any reproduction of material things, may very properly
be said to gain its whole wealth and subsistence from the country.

We must not, however, upon this account, imagine that
the gain of the town is the loss of the country. The gains of both
are mutual and reciprocal, and the division of labor is in this case,
as in all others, advantageous to all the different persons employed
in the various occupations into which it is subdivided.

The country people buy from the town a greater quantity
of goods, with the expenditure of a much smaller quantity of their
own labor, than they must have expended in attempting to prepare
them themselves. The town affords a market for the surplus
produce of the country, or what is over and above the maintenance of the farmers, and it is there that the inhabitants of the
country exchange it for something else they need.

The greater the number and the larger the incomes of

townspeople, the more extensive is the market which it offers to country people; and the more extensive that market, the wider its benefits are extended.

The grain which grows within a mile of the town sells there for the same price as that which comes from twenty miles away. But the price of the latter must generally cover not only the expense of raising and bringing it to market, but the ordinary profits of agriculture to the grower. The proprietors and cultivators of land in the neighborhood of the town, gain not only the ordinary profits of agriculture, but in addition, the whole value of the transportation of the produce that is brought from more distant parts; and they save, besides, the element of freight in the price of what they buy.

Compare the cultivation of the lands in the neighborhood of any considerable town, with those which lie at some distance from it, and you may easily satisfy yourself how much the country is benefited by the commerce of the town. Among all the absurd speculations that have been put forth concerning the balance of trade, it has never been pretended that either country or town is the loser by their commerce with each other.

As food always comes before refinements and luxury, so agriculture must always have preceded the industries of the towns. And as the towns live only on the surplus production of the land, they could increase only as fast as this surplus. It is true, however, that the town does not necessarily draw its support from the land in its own neighborhood; it may sometimes come from great distances and from other countries.

This order of things is formed by the natural impulse of mankind to cultivate the land. The man who puts capital into this employment has it always under his own eye and management, and it is much less liable to damage or destruction than that of the trader, for example. The latter must often put his fortune at the peril of winds and waves, and at much greater danger through the elements of human folly and injustice.

The capital of the landlord, on the contrary, as it is fixed in the improvement of his land, seems to be as secure as the nature of human affairs ever permits. Furthermore, the beauty of the country, the pleasures of rural life, the tranquility of mind which it promises, and (wherever the injustice of human laws does not disturb it) the independence which it really affords, have charms that attract all men to some extent. As to cultivate the soil was the original destination of man, so in every stage of his existence he seems to retain a predilection for this primitive employment.

Without the assistance of some artificers, however, the cultivation of land can be carried on only with great inconvenience and continual interruption. Smiths, carpenters, wheelwrights, masons, bricklayers, tanners, shoemakers, and tailors, are people whose service the farmer often needs. Such artificers also need the assistance of one another; and as their residence is not, like that of the farmer, necessarily tied down to a precise spot, they naturally settle near each other, and thus form a small town or village.

The butcher, the brewer, and the baker soon join them, together with many other artificers and retailers, necessary or useful for supplying their occasional wants, and who contribute still further to enlarge the town.

Thus the inhabitants of the town and those of the country are mutually the servants of each other. The town is a continual fair or market, to which the inhabitants of the country resort, in order to exchange their products for manufactured goods. The quantity of finished goods which townspeople sell to the inhabitants of the country, necessarily regulates the quantity of the materials and provisions which they buy. Neither their employment nor subsistence, therefore, can increase any faster than the demand from the country for finished work; and this demand can increase only in proportion to the extension of improvement and cultivation.

Had human institutions, therefore, never disturbed the natural course of things, the progressive wealth and increase of the towns would everywhere be the result of and in proportion to the improvement and cultivation of the soil.

℀ In new countries where there is much uncultivated land available, manufactures are not easily established. A workman who has accumulated some capital is very apt to go into farming, where he will be his own master, rather than to enlarge his manufacture.

℀ But this is not so easy in countries where most good land is already occupied. Accumulated capital is more likely to be invested in the manufacture of more goods, which, as the nearby market is already supplied, must be sold at a distance. Such manufactures and sales would first be on a small scale, for safety if for no other reason, but eventually this trade would be expanded to foreign countries and to all parts of the world.

℃   Again, if a community has not enough capital both to cultivate all its lands and to manufacture all its raw materials, it is to its advantage to sell its surplus of raw materials for export, so that at least the whole capital of the community will be employed.

According to the natural course of things, therefore, most of the capital of every growing society is directed first to agriculture, afterwards to manufactures, and last of all to foreign commerce. This order of things is so very natural, that in every society that had any territory, it has always, I believe, been in some degree observed.

But though this natural order of things must have taken place in some degree in every such society, it has, in all the modern states of Europe, been entirely inverted. The foreign commerce of some of their cities has introduced all their finer manufactures; and manufactures and foreign commerce together have brought about the principal improvements of agriculture.

This has been the result of the manners and customs which the nature of their original government introduced, which remained after that government was greatly altered, and which necessarily forced them into this unnatural and retrograde order.

CHAPTER II

The rise and fall of the feudal system left European agriculture in a deplorable condition, the farm people little better than slaves; how this retarded the improvement of nations.

To UNDERSTAND why the state of agriculture in Europe has for many centuries been less advantageous than that of the towns, we must go far back to the period following the fall of the Roman Empire.

℃   The invasions of the German and Scythian tribes, which overran the western provinces, were marked by violence and rapine. Towns were ruined and destroyed, the country left uncultivated, and these provinces, once wealthy and civilized, were reduced to the lowest state of poverty and barbarism.

℃   Under such lawless conditions, the land came to be engrossed almost entirely by a small number of great land-owners. On his own land, each was a kind of petty prince, who ruled his tenants, dispensed a kind of justice, and with their help waged war against his neighbors and sometimes against his sovereign.

℃   To maintain his position in peace and his security in war, the domain had to be as large and populous as possible. Hence it was bad policy to let it be divided on the death of the proprietor. From this principle arose the practice of primogeniture and entail, by which the entire property was made to descend to the eldest son, or at least to some one person within the family.

Whatever their value at one time, these practices are now absurd; being based on the untenable theory that the ownership of land in this generation should be dictated by persons who may have died five hundred years ago. However, vast tracts of uncultivated land were, in this manner, not only engrossed by particular families, but the possibility of their being divided again was as far as possible precluded forever.

It seldom happens, however, that a great land-owner is a great improver. In the disorderly times which gave birth to those barbarous institutions, the great proprietor was sufficiently employed in defending his own territories, or in extending his jurisdiction and authority over those of his neighbors. He had no leisure to attend to the cultivation and improvement of land.

When the establishment of law and order afforded him this leisure, he often lacked the inclination, and almost always the requisite abilities. If the expense of his house and person equalled or exceeded his income, as it frequently did, he had no capital to employ in improvements. If he was economical, he generally found it more profitable to employ his annual savings in new purchases, than in the improvement of his old estate.

To improve land with profit, like all other commercial projects, requires an exact attention to small savings and small gains, of which a man born to a great fortune, even though naturally frugal, is very seldom capable. He is much more inclined to attend rather to ornament which pleases his fancy, than to profit for which he has so little occasion. The elegance of his dress, of his equipage, of his house and household furniture, are objects which from his infancy he has been accustomed to have some anxiety about.

The turn of mind which this habit naturally forms, follows him when he comes to think of the improvement of land. He embellishes perhaps four or five hundred acres in the neighborhood of his mansion, at ten times the expense which the land is worth after all his improvements; and finds that if he were to improve his whole estate in the same manner (and he has little taste for any other), he would be a bankrupt before he had finished the tenth part of it.

If little improvement was to be expected from such great land-owners, still less was to be hoped for from those who cultivated land under them. In the ancient state of Europe, these were all tenants at will. They were all or almost all slaves; but their slavery was of a mild kind.

They were supposed to belong more directly to the land than to their masters. They could, therefore, be sold with the land, but not separately. They could marry, provided it was with the consent of their master; and he could not afterwards dissolve the marriage by selling the man and wife to different persons. If he maimed or murdered any of them, he was liable to some penalty, though generally only to a small one.

They were not, however, capable of acquiring property. Whatever they acquired belonged to their master, and he could take it from them at pleasure. Such slaves could acquire nothing but their daily maintenance. It was properly the proprietor himself, therefore, who occupied his own lands, and cultivated them by his own bondmen.

But if great improvements are seldom to be expected from great proprietors, they are least of all to be expected when they employ slaves for their workmen. The experience of all ages and nations, I believe, demonstrates that the work done by slaves, though it appears to cost only their maintenance, is in the end the dearest of any.

A person who can acquire no property can have no other interest but to eat as much and to labor as little as possible. Whatever work he does beyond what is enough to secure his own maintenance, can be squeezed out of him by violence only, and not by any interest of his own.

In ancient Italy, how much the cultivation of grain degenerated, how unprofitable it became to the master when it fell under the management of slaves, is remarked by both Pliny and Columella. In the time of Aristotle it had not been much better in ancient Greece.

Yet the pride of man makes him love to domineer, and nothing mortifies him so much as to be obliged to condescend to persuade his inferiors. Wherever the law allows it, and the nature of the work can afford it, therefore, he will generally prefer the service of slaves to that of freemen.

ℂ   This species of serfdom, called in England villeinage, was gradually succeeded by another, less arbitrary and more profitable. This was a kind of share-cropping, by which the tenant was permitted to acquire property, and to share in the produce of the land. It was to his advantage, therefore, to increase production, since his own share was thus increased.

    ¶   But it was not to the interest of the share-cropper to invest his own capital in farm improvements, since the landlord, who invested nothing, would get a share of the increase. What improvements were made, therefore, were altogether at the expense of the proprietor.

    To this species of tenancy succeeded, though by very slow degrees, farmers properly so called, who cultivated the land with their own capital, paying a fixed rent to the landlord. When such farmers have a lease for a term of years, they may sometimes find it to their interest to invest part of their capital in the further improvement of the farm; because they may hope to recover it, with a large profit, before the expiration of the lease.

    But the possession of such farmers was long extremely precarious, and is still so in many parts of Europe. If they were turned out illegally by the violence of their master, the action by which they obtained redress was extremely imperfect. It did not always reinstate them in the possession of the land, but gave them damages which never amounted to the real loss.

    ¶   Even in England, where the yeoman has long been held in much greater respect than the peasant of continental Europe, the tenant was under many disadvantages, and only in relatively recent times have English leases been made in terms long enough to justify the tenant in making important permanent improvements to the land. In other parts of Europe, no equal security to the tenant existed.

    ¶   In addition to the payment of rent, the farmers of ancient times were subjected to many abuses and vexations. They performed many services for the landlord, they were made to maintain the roads, they had to furnish horses and provisions for the sovereign and his officials who might happen to pass through that part of the country.

    Still worse, the farmer was subject to a special tax. The ancient lords, though themselves extremely unwilling to grant any pecuniary aid to their sovereign, easily allowed him to tallage, as they called it, their tenants, and had not knowledge enough to foresee how much this must in the end affect their own income.

    The taille, as it existed in France until abolished by the

Revolution, may serve as an example of those ancient tallages. It was a tax upon the supposed profits of the farmer, which was estimated by the stock that he had upon the farm. It was to his interest, therefore, to appear to have as little as possible, and consequently to employ as little as possible in cultivation, and none in improvement. Should any capital happen to accumulate in the hands of a French peasant, the taille practically guaranteed that it never would be expended in improving the land.

This tax besides was supposed to dishonor whoever was subject to it, and to degrade him, not only below the rank of a gentleman, but that of a townsman; and whoever rented the lands of another became subject to it. This tax, therefore, not only hindered the capital which accumulated upon the land from being employed in its improvement, but drove away all other capital from it.

℃ Under all these discouragements, including that inferior social status which was universal in Europe (and of which many traces still exist), it is not to be wondered at that the farms have not been an attractive field for the investment of capital in improvements. The land-owner was by nature not inclined to do so; and the tenant could do so only slowly, since so much of the produce was consumed in the rent that capital accumulated slowly.

℃ Finally, to all these obstacles must be added the governmental regulations and laws, such as prohibition of the export of grain, which have hampered agriculture even in fertile countries, and far more so in those less favorably situated.

CHAPTER III

The fall of feudalism left the towns little better off than the country; how they escaped from this servitude much earlier than agriculture, and partly at its expense.

THE CONDITION of townspeople after the fall of Rome seems to have been almost as servile and degraded as that of the villeins of the country; but they emerged from that situation much more quickly than the latter.

They seem, indeed, to have been a very poor, mean set of people, who used to travel about with their goods from place to place, and from fair to fair, like the hawkers and peddlers of the present day. Taxes used to be levied upon the persons and goods of travelers, when they passed through certain manors, when they crossed certain bridges, when they carried about their goods from place to place in a fair, when they erected a booth or stall for the sale of them.

But sometimes the king, sometimes a great lord, would grant to particular traders, particularly such as lived in their own demesnes, a general exemption from such taxes, and such traders, called free-traders, in return usually paid to their protector a sort of annual poll-tax. This tax might, perhaps, be considered as compensation for what their patrons might lose by their exemption from other taxes.

That part of the king's revenue which arose from such poll-taxes in any particular town, used commonly to be "farmed out" during a term of years for a fixed rent, sometimes to the sheriff of the county, and sometimes to other persons.

To collect rents in this manner was quite customary with European land-owners, who used frequently to let whole manors to all the tenants of those manors, they becoming jointly and severally answerable for the whole rent. In return they were allowed to collect it and pay it over in their own way, being thus altogether freed from the insolence of the king's officers; a circumstance in those days regarded as of the greatest importance.

❦ From such beginnings, the townspeople received successively the perpetual right to collect all their own taxes, perpetual rights to own property, with other advantages equivalent to what we call freedom, and eventually their own municipal governments and courts.

❦ They might have had more difficulty in this process of emancipation, had it not been for the fact that the kings of that time were frequently at war with their barons and lords, and in such struggles the towns were their natural allies.

The wealth of the townspeople never failed to provoke the envy and indignation of the great land-owners, and they plundered them at every opportunity without mercy or remorse. The townspeople naturally hated and feared the lords. The king hated and feared them too; but though perhaps he might despise townspeople, he had no reason either to hate or fear them.

Mutual interest, therefore, disposed them to support the king, and the king to support them against the lords. They were the enemies of his enemies, and it was his interest to render them as secure and independent of those enemies as he could. By granting them magistrates of their own, the privilege of making laws for their government, of building walls for their own defense, and of reducing all their inhabitants under a sort of military discipline, he gave them all the means of security and independence of the barons which it was in his power to bestow.

The princes who lived upon the worst terms with their barons, seem accordingly to have been the most liberal in grants of this kind to their towns. King John of England, for example, appears to have been a most munificent benefactor.

It was during the unprosperous reigns of the princes of the house of Suabia that most of the free towns of Germany received the first grants of their privileges, and that the famous Hanseatic League first became formidable.

The militia of the cities seems, in those times, not to have been inferior to that of the country, and as they could be more readily assembled upon any sudden occasion, they frequently had the advantage in their disputes with the neighboring lords. In

[*229*]

countries such as Italy and Switzerland, in which for various reasons the sovereign came to lose all his authority, the cities generally became independent republics, and conquered all the nobility in their neighborhood; obliging them to pull down their castles in the country, and to live, like other peaceable inhabitants, in the city.

This is the short history of the republic of Berne, as well as of several other cities in Switzerland. If you except Venice, for of that city the history is somewhat different, it is the history of all the important Italian republics, of which so great a number arose and perished, between the end of the 12th and the beginning of the 16th Century.

In France and England the cities reached such a stage of independence that they could not be taxed (beyond the usual rent-tax of the whole town) without their own consent; their representatives were generally called to the great council of the country, to counterbalance the influence of the nobility.

Order and good government, and along with them the liberty and security of individuals, were thus established in cities, at a time when the farm peasantry were exposed to every sort of violence. Men in this defenseless state naturally content themselves with a bare subsistence; because to acquire more might only tempt the injustice of their oppressors.

On the contrary, when they are secure in the enjoyment of the fruits of their industry, they naturally exert it to better their condition, and to acquire not only the necessaries, but the conveniences and elegances of life. That industry, therefore, which aims at something more than a bare existence, was established in cities long before it was commonly practiced in the country.

If a poor cultivator succeeded in saving up a little capital, he would naturally conceal it with great care from his master, to whom it would otherwise have belonged, and would take the first opportunity of running away to a town.

The law was at that time so indulgent to the inhabitants of towns, and so desirous of diminishing the authority of the lords over their serfs, that if he could conceal himself there from the pursuit of his lord for a year, he was free forever. Whatever capital, therefore, accumulated in the country, naturally took refuge in cities, as the only sanctuaries in which it could be safe in the hands of its owner.

The inhabitants of a city, it is true, must always ultimately derive their subsistence, and the whole materials and means of their industry, from the country. But those of a city situated near the seacoast, or on the banks of a navigable river, are not necessarily confined to getting them from the country in their own neighborhood. They have a much wider range, and may draw them from the most remote corners of the world, either in exchange for the manufactured produce of their own industry, or by performing the office of carriers between distant countries, and exchanging the produce of one for that of another.

A city might in this manner grow up to great wealth and splendor, while not only the country in its neighborhood, but all those with which it traded, were in poverty and wretchedness. Each of those countries, perhaps, taken singly, could afford the trading city but a small part of its subsistence or employment, but all of them taken together could make it rich.

The cities of Italy seem to have been the first in Europe which were thus raised by commerce to any considerable degree of wealth. Italy lay in the center of what was at that time the improved and civilized part of the world. The Crusades, which by the great waste of capital and destruction of population which they caused must necessarily have retarded the progress of much of Europe, were extremely favorable to that of some Italian cities.

The great armies which marched from all parts to the conquest of the Holy Land were immensely profitable to the shipping of Venice, Genoa, and Pisa, sometimes in transporting them, and always in supplying them with provisions. They were the commissaries, so to speak, of those armies; and the most destructive madness that ever befell the European nations was a source of opulence to those republics.

ℂ   The cities which grew rich by foreign trade rather than by manufacture nevertheless soon established manufactures of their own. As they became acquainted with the finer products of foreign countries, these were soon imitated by enterprising manufacturers, and sold to the neighboring land-owners for increased amounts of raw materials.

ℂ   Sometimes, too, these improved manufactures were themselves sold to foreign countries, in competition with those foreigners who originally developed them. Raw materials were imported, the goods manufactured, and re-exported. Venice, originally a trading city, became a manufacturer by buying raw silk from Sicily and the Near East, and exporting the product.

❡   But the manufactures and wealth of towns and cities far from the seacoast, and sometimes without even water transportation, also grew up, although more slowly, through development and refinement of earlier rude manufactures. No country or neighborhood is ever wholly without manufactures, however coarse and rude. And where the surrounding country is fertile, food correspondingly plentiful and cheap, workmen are attracted by the prospect that their labor will exchange for more of the necessaries and conveniences of life than elsewhere.

They work up whatever materials of manufacture the land produces, and exchange their finished work, or what is the same thing, the price of it, for more materials and provisions. They give a new value to the surplus part of the raw materials, by saving the expense of carrying it to the seacoast, or to some distant market; and they furnish the farmers with something in exchange for it that is useful or agreeable to them, upon easier terms than they could have obtained it before.

The farmers get a better price for their surplus produce, and can purchase other conveniences more cheaply. They are thus encouraged and enabled to increase this surplus produce by a further improvement and better cultivation of the land; and as the fertility of the land had given birth to the manufacture, so the progress of the manufacture reacts upon the land, and increases still further its fertility.

The manufacturers first supply the immediate neighborhood, and afterwards, as their work improves and refines, more distant markets. For though neither the raw materials, nor even the coarse manufacture, could without great difficulty support the expense of transportation to a distance, the refined and improved manufacture easily may. In a small bulk it frequently contains the price or equivalent of a great quantity of raw materials.

It is in this way that the wealth and vigor of the towns has been built up, contrary to the natural order, first foreign commerce, and later by development of local manufacture. How this process resulted eventually in the extension and improvement of agriculture, I shall explain in the next chapter.

CHAPTER IV

Contrary to the natural order, the towns ultimately achieved independence and wealth, and in turn improved the country, but only because of the childish vanity of the great land-owners, and the selfish pursuit of their own interests by manufacturers and artisans; the capital invested in agricultural improvement is the most durable and profitable.

THE RICHES of commercial and manufacturing towns contributed to the improvement and cultivation of the countries in which they were situated in three different ways.

As I remarked in the last chapter, by affording a ready market for the produce of the farms, they gave encouragement to their cultivation and further improvement. This benefit was not even confined to the countries in which they were situated, but extended more or less to all those with which they had any dealings. To all of them they afforded a market for some part of their production, and consequently gave some encouragement to the industry and improvement of all.

Their own country, however, on account of its proximity, necessarily derived the greatest benefit from this market. Its produce being charged with smaller carrying costs, the traders could pay the growers a better price for it, and yet sell it as cheaply to the consumers as that of more distant countries.

In the second place, the wealth acquired by the inhabitants of cities was frequently employed in buying land, much of which would frequently be uncultivated. Merchants are commonly ambitious of becoming country gentlemen, and when they do, they are generally the best of all improvers.

A merchant is accustomed to employ his money chiefly in profitable projects; whereas a mere country gentleman does nothing but spend it. The one often sees his money go from him and return to him again with a profit; the other, when once he parts with it, very seldom expects to see any of it again.

These different habits naturally affect their temper and disposition in every sort of business. A merchant is commonly a bold entrepreneur; a country gentleman a timid one. The one is not afraid to invest much money in the improvement of his land, because he has a probable prospect of raising the value of it in proportion to the expense. The other, if he has any capital, which is not always the case, seldom ventures to risk it in this manner. If he improves his land at all, it is commonly not with his capital, but with what little he can save out of his income.

Whoever has had the fortune to live in a mercantile town in the midst of an unimproved country, must have frequently observed how much more enterprising the operations of merchants were with their land, than those of mere country gentlemen. Besides, the habits of order and attention, to which business naturally trains the merchant, render him much fitter to execute with profit and success any project of improvement.[1]

Finally, commerce and manufactures gradually introduced order and good government, and with them, the liberty and security of individuals, among the country population, who had before lived almost in a continual state of war with their neighbors, and of servile dependence upon their superiors. This, though it has been the least noticed, is by far the most important of all their effects. Mr. Hume is the only writer who, as far as I know, has hitherto called attention to it.

In a country which has neither foreign commerce nor any of the finer manufactures, a great land-owner, having nothing for which he can exchange the surplus produce of his lands, has no choice but to consume the whole in rustic hospitality at home. If this surplus is enough to maintain a hundred or a thousand men, he can make use of it in no other way than by maintaining a hundred or a thousand men.

He is at all times, therefore, surrounded with a multitude of retainers and dependents, who, having no equivalent to give in

---

[1] Let us insert another question mark at this point. Some, but not all "city farmers" deserve this commendation.

return for their support, but being fed entirely by his bounty, must obey him, for the same reason that soldiers must obey the government that pays them.

Before the extension of commerce and manufactures, the hospitality of the rich and great in Europe, from kings down to the smallest baron, exceeded anything we can nowadays easily conceive. Westminster Hall was the dining-room of William Rufus, and might frequently, perhaps, not be too large for his company. It was reckoned a piece of magnificence in Thomas à Becket, that he strewed the floor of his hall with clean hay or rushes in the season, in order that the knights and squires, who could not get seats, might not spoil their fine clothes when they sat down on the floor to eat their dinner.

The great Earl of Warwick ("the King-maker") is said to have entertained every day at his different manors thirty thousand people; and though the number here may have been exaggerated, it must, however, have been very great to admit of such exaggeration. A hospitality nearly of the same kind was exercised not many years ago in many different parts of the Highlands of Scotland, and it seems to be common in all nations to whom commerce and manufactures are little known.

The peasant farmers were in every respect as dependent upon the great land-owners as his retainers. Even such of them as were not in a state of villeinage were tenants at will, who paid a rent by no means equivalent to the subsistence which the land afforded them. A crown, half a crown, a sheep, a lamb, was some years ago in the Highlands of Scotland a common rent for land which maintained a whole family. In some places it is so to this day; nor will money at present purchase a greater quantity of commodities there than in other places.

The reason for this is that where the surplus produce of a large estate must be consumed somehow, it will frequently be more convenient for the proprietor that part of it be consumed at a distance from his own house, provided that they who consumed it are still wholly dependent upon him. He is thereby saved from the embarrassment of too large a company or family.

Such a proprietor, as he feeds his servants and retainers at his own house, so he feeds his tenants at their houses. The subsistence of both is derived from his bounty, and its continuance depends upon his good pleasure.

Upon the authority which the great proprietors necessarily held in this way over their tenants and retainers, was founded the power of the ancient barons. They necessarily became the judges in peace, and the leaders in war, of all who dwelt upon their land.

They could maintain order and execute the law here, because each of them could turn the whole force of all the inhabitants against the injustice of any one. No other person had enough authority to do this.

The king in particular had not. In those ancient times he was little more than the chief land-owner in his dominions, to whom, for the sake of common defense against their common enemies, the other great proprietors paid certain respects. To have enforced payment of a small debt within the lands of a great noble, where all the inhabitants were armed and accustomed to stand by one another, would have cost the king as much effort as to extinguish a civil war.

He was, therefore, obliged to abandon the administration of justice through most of the country, to those who were capable of administering it; and for the same reason to leave the command of the rural militia to those whom that militia would obey.

It is a mistake to imagine that these local jurisdictions took their origin from the feudal law. Not only the supreme civil and criminal jurisdiction, but the power of levying troops, of coining money, and even that of making general laws for their own people, were all rights possessed by the great land-owners several centuries before even the name of the feudal law was known in Europe.

The authority and jurisdiction of the Saxon lords in England appear to have been as great before the Conquest, as that of any of the Norman lords after it. But the feudal law is not supposed to have become the common law of England till after the Conquest. And the situation in France was similar.

The introduction of the feudal system was in fact an attempt to limit the authority of the great lords, not to extend it. It established a regular line of subordination, accompanied with a long train of services and duties, from the king down to the smallest proprietor.

But the authority of government still continued to be, as before, too weak in the head and too strong in the inferior members, and the excessive strength of the inferior members was the cause of the weakness of the head. The great lords still continued to make war according to their own discretion, almost continually upon one another, and very frequently upon the king; and the open country still continued to be a scene of violence, rapine, and disorder.

But what all the force and violence of the feudal institutions could never have effected, the silent and insensible operation of foreign commerce and manufactures gradually brought about. These occupations were able to supply the great proprietors with something for which they could exchange the surplus produce of their lands, and which they could consume themselves without sharing it either with tenants or retainers.

All for ourselves, and nothing for other people, seems in all ages to have been the vile maxim of the masters of mankind. As soon, therefore, as they discovered a method of consuming the whole value of their rents themselves, they abandoned any idea of sharing them with anyone else.

For a pair of diamond buckles, perhaps, or something else as frivolous and useless, they exchanged the maintenance, or what is the same thing, the price of the maintenance of a thousand men for a year, and with it the whole weight and authority which that maintenance could give them. The buckles, however, were all their own, and no other human creature was to have any share of them; whereas in the former arrangement they must have divided up with at least a thousand people.

As the person who acquired the buckles was the one who made the decision, the result was not in doubt; and thus, for the gratification of the most childish, the meanest, and the most sordid of all vanities, they gradually bartered away their whole power and authority.

This profound change from ancient times does not mean that the income of the wealthy no longer supports many of the population. Where a great baron maintained perhaps a thousand families, a man of the same wealth now supports directly perhaps not more than twenty people. But indirectly he maintains as many as the feudal baron ever did.

The things for which he spends his income require the labor of many persons in collecting and preparing them. But what he thus pays to each of these workmen is only a small part of the annual income of any one of the workmen—seldom more than a tenth, more often not a thousandth or ten-thousandth of it.

Though he contributes something to the maintenance of all, however, they are all more or less independent of him, because all can if necessary get along without him.

The luxuries and personal expense of the great landowners having thus gradually increased, it was impossible that the number of their retainers should not as gradually diminish, until at last they were dismissed altogether. The same cause gradually led them to dismiss all the tenants not actually needed.

Farms were enlarged, and the farmers, notwithstanding the complaints of depopulation, were reduced to the number necessary for cultivating the land, according to the imperfect state of cultivation and improvement in those times. By getting rid of the unnecessary mouths, and by exacting from the farmer the full value of the farm, a greater surplus, or what is the same thing, the price of a greater surplus, was obtained for the proprietor; and the merchants and manufacturers soon furnished him with a method of spending this increased income upon his own indulgence in the same manner as he had done the rest.

As these same forces continued to operate, the landlord was desirous to raise his rents above what his lands, in the actual state of their improvement, could afford. His tenants could agree to this upon one condition only—that they should be secured in their possession, for a term of years long enough to give them time to recover with profit whatever they should invest in the further improvement of the land. The expensive vanity of the landlord made him willing to accept this condition; and hence the origin of long leases and the complete independence of the modern tenant who has one.

The tenants having in this manner become independent, and the retainers and men-at-arms being sent away to hunt jobs, the great proprietors no longer could interrupt the regular administration of justice, or disturb the peace of the country. Having sold their birthright, not like Esau for a mess of pottage in time of hunger and necessity, but in the wantonness of plenty, for trinkets and baubles, fitter to be the playthings of children than the serious pursuits of men, they became as insignificant as any substantial business man or tradesman in a city. A regular government was established in the country as well as in the city, nobody having sufficient power to disturb its operations in either place.

It does not, perhaps, bear on this subject, but I cannot help remarking that very old families, who have inherited wealth for many generations, are very rare in commercial countries. A wealthy man in ancient times, who had to spend his income on the support of retainers and tenants, could never ruin his fortunes by so doing. But where he spends his income on himself and his vanities and indulgences, he frequently has no trouble at all in spending himself to his own ruin and that of his family.

Thus a revolution of the greatest importance to the public happiness was brought about by two different orders of people who had not the slightest interest or intention of doing so. To gratify the most childish vanity was the sole motive of the great land-owners. The merchants and artisans, much less ridiculous, acted merely from a view to their own interest, and in pursuit of their own shop-keeping principle of turning a penny wherever a penny was to be got. Neither of them had any inkling of that great revolution which the folly of the one, and the industry of the other, was gradually bringing about.

It is thus that through most of Europe the commerce and manufactures of cities, have been the cause and occasion, instead of the effect, of the improvement and cultivation of the country.

This process, however, being contrary to the natural course of things, is necessarily both slow and uncertain. Compare the slow progress of those European countries whose wealth depends very much upon their commerce and manufactures, with the rapid advances of our North American colonies, of which the wealth is founded altogether in agriculture.

In Europe the law of primogeniture, and perpetuities of different kinds, prevent the division of great estates, and thereby hinder the multiplication of small land-owners. But a small land-owner, who knows every part of his little property, who views it all with the affection which property, especially small property, naturally inspires, and who upon that account takes pleasure not only in cultivating but in adorning it, is generally of all improvers the most industrious, the most intelligent, and the most successful.

Everywhere in Europe the purchase of land is a most unprofitable employment of a small capital. For the sake of the superior security, indeed, a man of moderate circumstances, when he retires from business, will sometimes choose to lay out his little capital in land. A professional man, too, whose income is derived from another source, often loves to secure his savings in the same way.

But a young man who should put ten or fifteen thousand dollars into the purchase and cultivation of a small piece of land, might indeed expect to live very happily, and very independently, but must bid farewell forever to all hope of either great wealth or great fame, which by a different employment of his capital he might have had the same chance of acquiring with other people.

⟮ In North America before the Revolution, on the contrary, the purchase and improvement of uncultivated land was the most profitable employment of the smallest as well as of the greatest capital, and the most direct road to all the fame and fortune which can be acquired in that country. Such land, indeed, would then be had almost for nothing, or at a price much below the value of the natural produce; a thing impossible in Europe, or, indeed, in any country where all lands have long been private property.

⟮ England has been favored by a fertile soil and excellent water communication, yet the progress of improvement of agriculture has been slow, and would have been still slower had it not been for laws which in many ways fanned this occupation.

⟮ France, Spain, and Portgual, whose laws have been on the whole unfavorable to agriculture, have progressed far less.

The capital that a country accumulates by commerce and manufactures remains very precarious and uncertain, until some part of it has been secured and made permanent in the cultivation and improvement of its lands. A merchant, it has been said very properly, is not necessarily the citizen of any particular country. It makes little difference to him from what headquarters he carries on his trade; and a very trifling disgust may induce him to remove his capital, and together with it all the industry which it supports, from one country to another.

No capital can really be said to belong to any particular country until it has been spread as it were over the face of that country, in buildings or in the lasting improvement of lands. No vestige now remains of the great wealth, said to have been possessed by many of the Hanse towns, except in the obscure histories of the 13th and 14th Centuries. It is even uncertain where some of them were situated, or to what towns the Latin names given to some of them belong.

But though the misfortunes of Italy in the 15th and 16th

Centuries greatly diminished the commerce and manufactures of the cities of Lombardy and Tuscany, those countries still continue to be among the most populous and best-cultivated in Europe.

The ordinary revolutions of war and government easily dry up the sources of that wealth which arises from commerce only. That which arises from the more solid improvements of agriculture is much more durable; it can be destroyed only by the depredations of hostile and barbarous nations continued for a century or two together, such as those that preceded and followed the fall of the Roman Empire in the western provinces of Europe.

BOOK IV

Turning from the behavior of individuals in the production and distribution of wealth (insofar as their activities are not regulated and injured by governments), this book takes up the necessary functions of governments themselves; government being, on the whole, an evil, but a necessary one.

CHAPTER I

*The first evil but necessary function of gov-
ernment is to protect the society from violence and invasion, by military force; why
the defense of a country becomes constantly
more expensive.*

THE FIRST DUTY of the state—that of protecting the society from
violence and invasion—can be performed only by means of a military force. But the expense both of preparing this military force
in time of peace, and of employing it in time of war, is very different in the different states of society, and in the different stages of
improvement.

Among nations of hunters, the lowest and rudest state of
society, it costs nothing. Every man is a warrior, and fights in the
same manner as he hunts. An army of such warriors could never
be more than a few hundred men.

Among nations of shepherds, a more advanced state of
society, such as we find among the Tartars and Arabs, every man
is, in the same manner, a warrior. Such nations have commonly
no fixed habitation, but live either in tents, or in a sort of covered
wagons which are easily transported from place to place. The
whole tribe or nation changes its location according to the different seasons of the year, as well as for other reasons.

When its herds and flocks have consumed the forage of one
part of the country, it removes to another, and from that to a third.
In the dry season, it comes down to the banks of the rivers; in the
wet season it retires to the uplands.

When such a nation goes to war, the warriors will not trust
their herds and flocks to the feeble defense of their old men, their
women and children, nor will they leave the latter behind without
defense and without subsistence. The whole nation, being accus-

tomed to a wandering life even in time of peace, easily takes the field in time of war.

Among the Tartars, even the women have been frequently known to engage in battle. If they conquer, whatever belongs to the hostile tribe is the recompense of the victory. But if they are vanquished, all is lost, and not only their herds and flocks, but their their women and children, become the booty of the conqueror.

But whatever happens, the chief or sovereign (for those nations all have chiefs or sovereigns) is at no sort of expense in preparing for the field; and when the Tartar or Arab warrior is at war, the chance of plunder is the only pay which he either expects or requires.

In a more advanced state of society, among those nations of farmers who have little foreign commerce, and no other manufactures but those coarse and household ones which almost every private family can prepare for its own use, every man, in the same manner, either is a warrior, or easily becomes such.

They who live by agriculture generally pass the whole day in the open air, exposed to all the inclemencies of the seasons. The hardiness of their ordinary life prepares them for the fatigues of war, to some of which their necessary occupations bear a strong analogy.

The ordinary pastimes of such husbandmen are the same as those of shepherds, and are in the same manner the images of war. But as the farmers have less leisure than shepherds, they are not so frequently employed in those pastimes. Such as they are, however, it seldom costs the sovereign or state any expense to prepare them for the battlefield.

Agriculture, even in its rudest and lowest state, supposes some sort of fixed habitation which cannot be abandoned without great loss. When a nation of husbandmen goes to war, therefore, the old men, the women and children, at least, must remain at home to take care of the habitation. All the men of military age, however, may take the field, and in small nations of this kind have frequently done so.

In every nation the men of military age are supposed to amount to about a fourth or a fifth part of the whole body of the people. If the campaign should begin after seed-time, and end before harvest, both the husbandman and his principal laborers can be spared from the farm without much loss. He trusts that the work which must be done in the meantime can be well enough carried on by the old men, the women and the children. He is not unwilling, therefore, to serve without pay during a short campaign, and it frequently costs the government as little to maintain him in the field as to prepare him for it.

In the European monarchies, which were founded upon the ruins of the Roman Empire, both before and for some time after the establishment of what is properly called the feudal law, the great lords, with all their immediate dependents, used to serve the crown at their own expense. In the field, in the same manner as at home, they maintained themselves by their own revenue, and not by any pay which they received from the king upon that particular occasion.

In a still more advanced state of society, two different causes contribute to render it altogether impossible that soldiers should maintain themselves at their own expense. Those two causes are, the progress of manufactures, and the improvement in the art of war.

Though a farmer should be employed in a campaign, provided it begins after seed-time and ends before harvest, the interruption of his business will not usually hurt it. Without his labor Nature herself does most of the work which remains to be done.

But the moment that an artisan, a smith, a carpenter, or a paperhanger, for example, quits his job, the sole source of his revenue is completely dried up. Nature does nothing for him, he must do all for himself. When he goes to war, therefore, in defense of the public, he must necessarily be maintained by the public. In a country of which a large part of the inhabitants are artisans and workmen, most of the fighting men must be drawn from those classes, and must therefore be maintained by the public as long as they are in its service.

Furthermore, when the art of war has gradually grown to be a very intricate and complicated science, when the event of war ceases to be determined, as in the first ages of society, by a single irregular skirmish or battle, but when the contest is generally spun out through several different campaigns, each of which lasts during the greater part of the year, it becomes universally necessary that the public should maintain the armed forces.

The number of those who can go to war, in proportion to the whole number of the people, is necessarily much smaller in a civilized society. Since the soldiers are maintained altogether by the labor of the rest of the population, the number of the former can never exceed what the latter can maintain, in addition to maintaining themselves.

In the little agrarian states of ancient Greece, a fourth or a fifth part of the whole body of the people considered themselves as soldiers, and would sometimes, it is said, take the field. Among the civilized nations of modern Europe, it is commonly computed that not more than one per cent of the inhabitants of any country can be employed as soldiers, without ruin to the country.

℄ Similarly, the expense of military training has had to be undertaken by the public in the modern state, and as war has become more technical and complicated, so the expense of this training has greatly increased. The weapons and supplies of the armed forces have become far more intricate and expensive.[1]

℄ At the same time, civilized life, the division of labor, and the progress of the arts have given civilized men little time or inclination for military training and exercise. The citizen becomes most unwarlike at a time when the soldier requires far greater training and equipment than ever.

℄ The civilized nations have provided for their defense in two ways: either by a militia system, under some form of state compulsion, or by a standing army, in which the soldier comes to practice a particular trade, separate and distinct from all others.

℄ The invention of firearms made the physical strength and agility of the individual soldier of much less importance, and vastly increased the importance of training and discipline. Accordingly, the militia has always shown itself greatly inferior to the trained and disciplined standing army.

Those militias which, like the Tartar or Arab militia, go to war under the same chieftains whom they are accustomed to obey in peace, are by far the best. In respect for their officers, in the habit of ready obedience, they approach nearest to standing armies. The Scottish Highland militia, when it served under its own chieftains, had some advantage of the same kind.

As the Highlanders, however, were not wandering, but stationary shepherds, as they all had a fixed habitation, and were

---

[1] It is perhaps needless to emphasize how much the history of the world since 1776 has expanded and fortified these general principles; the whole cost of the total war of 1939–1945 seems beyond human computation.

not, in peaceable times, accustomed to follow their chieftain from place to place; so in time of war they were less willing to follow him to any considerable distance, or to continue for any long time in the field. When they had acquired any booty they were eager to return home, and the chief's authority was seldom sufficient to detain them. In point of obedience they were always much inferior to what is reported of the Tartars and Arabs.

A militia of any kind, it must be observed, however, which has served for several successive campaigns in the field, becomes in every respect equal to a standing army. The soldiers are every day exercised in the use of their arms, and, being constantly under the command of their officers, are habituated to the same prompt obedience which is the rule in standing armies. What they were before they took the field, is of little importance.

❡ All history shows this to be true. The standing army of Philip of Macedon easily defeated the militias of the Greek republics, and the effeminate and ill-trained militia of the great Persian empire. The armies of Carthage, under three great generals, subdued Spain and almost annihilated the militia of Italy at Trebia, Lake Trasimene, and Cannae. But when the Romans had learned through adversity the art of war, and Hannibal had lost most of his veterans, Rome reconquered Italy, subdued the Carthaginian militia in Spain, and destroyed Carthage.

❡ The conquering legions of Rome easily overthrew the other Mediterranean nations. But the militia of the barbarous nations of the region of the Black and Caspian Seas resisted with better success, and the fierce horsemen of the Parthian empire ruined two Roman expeditions, and to the end defied the mercenaries of Italy.

❡ After the fall of the Roman republic, the conquering legions of Rome again deteriorated. In the course of centuries those who were not stationed on the frontiers came to be quartered in small bodies in garrison towns, where many became themselves artisans and workmen. The civil came to predominate over the military character; and the standing armies of Rome gradually degenerated into a corrupt, neglected, and undisciplined militia, incapable of resisting the attack of the German and Scythian militia, which soon afterwards invaded the West.[2]

[2] The degenerate Roman militia of the empire were themselves, Thorold Rogers observes, victims of the oppressive taxation of the imperial government.

It was only by hiring the militia of some of those nations to oppose that of others, that the Roman emperors were for some time able to defend themselves.

The fall of the Western Empire is the third great revolution in the affairs of mankind, of which ancient history has preserved any distinct or circumstantial account. It was brought about by the irresistible superiority which the militia of a barbarous, has over that of a civilized nation; which the militia of a nation of shepherds has over that of a nation of farmers and workmen.

The victories which have been gained by militias have generally been, not over standing armies, but over other militias inferior to themselves in exercise and discipline. Such were the victories which the Greek militia gained over that of the Persian empire; and such too were those which in later times the Swiss militia gained over that of the Austrians and Burgundians.

In a word, a well-regulated standing army is superior to every militia. Such an army, as it can best be maintained by a wealthy and civilized nation, so it alone can defend such a civilization.

A standing army establishes, with an irresistible force, the law of the state through the remotest provinces of the empire, and maintains some degree of regular government in countries which could not otherwise admit of any.

Whoever examines with attention the improvements which Peter the Great introduced into the Russian empire, will find that they resolve themselves almost entirely into the establishment of a well-regulated standing army. That degree of order and internal peace which that empire has ever since enjoyed, is altogether owing to the influence of that army.[3]

Men of republican principles have been jealous of a standing army as dangerous to liberty. It certainly is so, wherever the interest of the generals and principal officers are not necessarily connected with the support of the constitution of the state. The standing army of Caesar destroyed the Roman republic. The

[3] But order and internal peace are by no means all a society requires. Government by an army is invariably corrupt and oppressive; the order and peace of Russia came to its logical fruition in the October Revolution of 1917. A general determination to obey and uphold the law, says Thorold Rogers, is a far stronger guarantee of liberty and order than any standing army. Will, not force, is the basis of the state, says T. H. Green.

standing army of Cromwell repeatedly turned the Long Parliament out of doors.

But where the sovereign is himself the commander-in-chief, and the principal nobility and gentry of the country the chief officers of the army; where the military force is placed under the command of those who have the greatest interest in the support of the civil authority, because they have themselves the greatest share of that authority, a standing army can never be dangerous to liberty.

The first duty of the state, therefore, that of defending the society from the violence and injustice of other independent societies, grows gradually more and more expensive, as the society advances in civilization.

The military force of the society, which originally cost the government no expense either in time of peace or in time of war, must, in the progress of improvement, first be maintained in time of war, and afterwards even in time of peace.

CHAPTER II

The second necessary function of govern-
ment is in protecting every citizen from the
violence and oppression of every other citi-
zen—the administration of justice; how the
magistrate ordinarily acquires his authority
and the respect of society; and how the cost
of justice could best be defrayed.

THE SECOND DUTY of the state—that of protecting, as far as possible, every member of the society from the injustice or oppression
of every other member of it, or the duty of establishing an exact
administration of justice—requires two very different degrees of
expense in the different periods of society.

Among nations of hunters, as there is scarcely any property, or at least none that exceeds the value of two or three days'
labor, so there is seldom any established magistrate or any regular
administration of justice.

Men who have no property can injure one another only
in their persons or reputations. But when one man kills, wounds,
beats, or defames another, though he to whom the injury is done
suffers, he who does it receives no benefit.

It is otherwise with injuries to property. The benefit of
the person who does the injury is often equal to the loss of him who
suffers it. Envy, malice, or resentment, are the only passions
which can prompt one man to injure another in his person or reputation. But few men are frequently under the influence of those
passions; and the very worst men are so only occasionally. Men
may live together in society with some tolerable degree of security,
though there is no civil magistrate to protect them from the injustice of those passions.

But avarice and ambition in the rich, hatred of work and the love of present ease and enjoyment in the poor, are the passions which prompt men to invade property—passions much more steady in their operation, and much more universal in their influence.

Wherever there is great property, there is great inequality. For one very rich man, there must be at least five hundred poor, and the affluence of the few must imply the poverty of the many.[1] The affluence of the rich excites the indignation of the poor, who are often driven by want, and prompted by envy, to invade his possessions.

It is only under the protection of the civil magistrate that the owner of valuable property, which is acquired by the labor of many years, or perhaps of many successive generations, can sleep a single night in security. He is at all times surrounded by unknown enemies, from whose injustice he can be shielded only by the powerful arm of the magistrate. The acquisition of valuable and extensive property, therefore, necessarily requires the establishment of civil government.

The causes or circumstances which naturally introduce subordination, or which naturally give some men some superiority over most of their brethren, seem to be four in number.

The first of those causes or circumstances is the superiority of personal qualifications, of strength, beauty, and agility of body; of wisdom, of virtue, of prudence, justice, fortitude, and moderation of mind. The qualifications of the body, unless supported by those of the mind, can give little authority in any period of society. He must be a very strong man who by mere strength can force two weak ones to obey him.

The qualifications of the mind can give very great authority. They are, however, invisible qualities; always disputable, and generally disputed. No society, whether barbarous or civilized, has ever found it convenient to settle the rules of precedence of rank and subordination, according to those invisible qualities; but according to something that is more obvious and tangible.

The second of those causes or circumstances is the superiority of age. An old man, provided his age is not so far advanced

---

[1] An idea that sounds very like Malthus and Henry George; but A. S. does not say that the affluence of the few necessarily *requires* the poverty of the many. The actual word in W. N. is "supposes."

as to give suspicion of dotage, is everywhere more respected than a young man of equal rank, fortune, and abilities.

In the most opulent and civilized nations, age regulates rank among those who are in other respects equal, and among whom, therefore, there is nothing else to regulate it. Among brothers and among sisters, the eldest always take place; and in the succession of the paternal estate everything which cannot be divided, but must go entire to one person, such as a title of honor, is in most cases given to the eldest. Age is a plain and palpable quality which admits of no dispute.

The third of those causes is the superiority of fortune. The authority of riches, however, though great in every age of society, is perhaps greatest in the rudest age of society which admits of any considerable inequality of fortune.

A Tartar chief, the increase of whose herds and flocks is sufficient to maintain a thousand men, cannot well employ that increase in any other way than in maintaining a thousand men, and he thus necessarily becomes their general and their judge.

In an opulent and civilized society a man may possess a much greater fortune, and yet not be able to command a dozen people.

The authority of fortune, however, is very great even in an opulent and civilized society. That it is much greater than the prestige of age or personal qualities, has been the constant complaint of every period of society.

The fourth of those circumstances is superiority of birth, which implies an ancient superiority of fortune in the family of the person who claims it. All families are equally ancient; and the ancestors of the prince, though they may be better known, cannot well be more numerous than those of the pauper. Antiquity of family means everywhere the antiquity either of wealth, or of that greatness which is commonly founded upon wealth, or accompanied by it. Upstart greatness is everywhere less respected than ancient greatness. There never has been, I believe, a great family in the world whose fame and influence was derived only from the inheritance of wisdom and virtue.

Birth and fortune, therefore, are evidently the two circumstances which principally set one man above another. They are the two great sources of personal distinction, and are therefore the principal causes which naturally establish authority and subordination in any society.

It is in the age of shepherds, in the second period of society, that the inequality of fortune first begins to appear, and introduces among men a degree of authority and subordination which could not possibly exist before. It thereby introduces some degree of that civil government which is indispensably necessary for its own preservation: and it seems to do this naturally, and even before there seems any necessity for it.

The consideration of that necessity comes no doubt afterwards to contribute very much to maintain and secure that authority and subordination. The rich, in particular, are necessarily interested in supporting that order of things, which can alone secure them in the possession of their own advantages. Poorer men combine to defend those of superior wealth in the possession of their property, so that the rich may combine to defend them in the possession of theirs.

All the inferior shepherds and herdsmen feel that the security of their own small herds and flocks depends upon the security of those of the chief shepherd or herdsman; that the maintenance of their lesser authority depends upon that of his greater authority, and that upon their subordination to him depends his power of keeping their inferiors in subordination to them.

Civil government, therefore, so far as it is instituted for the security of property, is in reality instituted for the defense of the rich against the poor, and of those who have a little property against those who have none.

The judicial authority of such a sovereign, however, far from being a cause of expense to him, was for a long time a source of income to him. The persons who applied to him for justice were always willing to pay for it, and a present never failed to accompany a petition.

After the authority of the sovereign was thoroughly established, too, the person found guilty, over and above the satisfaction which he was obliged to make to the other party, was likewise forced to pay an amercement to the sovereign. He had given trouble, he had disturbed, he had broken the peace of his lord the king, and for those offenses an amercement was thought due.

Originally both the sovereign and the inferior chiefs used to exercise jurisdiction in their own persons. Afterwards they universally found it convenient to delegate it to some substitute, bailiff, or judge. This substitute, however, was still obliged to account to his principal for the profits of the jurisdiction.

Whoever reads the instructions which were given to the English judges of the circuit in the time of Henry II will see clearly that they were a sort of itinerant factors, sent round the country for the purpose of collecting certain branches of the king's revenue.

The sale of the king's justice, therefore, came in much the same class as the sale of his deer or timber.

This scheme of making the administration of justice subservient to the purposes of revenue, could not fail to be productive of several very gross abuses. The person who applied for justice with a large present in his hand, was likely to get something more than justice; while he who applied for it with a small one, was likely to get less or none. Again, justice might frequently be delayed, in order that this present might be repeated. That such abuses were far from uncommon, the ancient history of every country in Europe bears witness, and this was true whether the sovereign exercised his authority in person or by deputy.

In all barbarous governments, accordingly, and especially in all those ancient governments of Europe which were founded upon the ruins of the Roman empire, the administration of justice appears to have been extremely corrupt; far from being equal and impartial, even under the best monarchs, and altogether scandalous under the worst.

As long as presents, the emoluments of justice, or what may be called the fees of court, constituted in this manner a large part of the revenue which the sovereign derived from his sovereignty, it could not well be expected, it could not even decently be proposed, that he should give them up altogether.

It might be proposed, and frequently was, that he should regulate and ascertain them. But after they had been so regulated and ascertained, how to hinder a person who was all-powerful from extending them beyond those regulations was still very difficult, not to say impossible. During the continuance of this state of things, therefore, the corruption of justice, naturally resulting from the arbitrary and uncertain nature of those presents and court fees, could not be remedied.

But when from different causes, chiefly from the continually increasing expense of defending the nation against its enemies, the private estate of the sovereign had become altogether insufficient for defraying the expense of the sovereignty; and when it had become necessary that the people should, for their own security, contribute towards this expense by taxes, it seems to have been very commonly stipulated, that no present for the administration of justice should, under any pretense, be accepted, either by the sovereign or by his judges.

It appeared easier to abolish the system altogether than to try to regulate it.

Fixed salaries were then appropriated to the judges, which were supposed to compensate them for the loss of whatever might have been their share of the ancient emoluments of justice. Justice was thereafter said to be administered free.

Justice, however, never was in reality administered free in any country. Lawyers and attorneys, at least, must always be paid by the parties; and, if they were not, they would perform their duty still worse than they actually perform it. The fees annually paid to lawyers and attorneys amount, in every court, to a much greater sum than the salaries of the judges.

That these salaries are now universally paid by the government can nowhere much diminish the necessary expense of a lawsuit. But it was not so much to diminish the expense, as to prevent the corruption of justice, that the judges were prohibited from receiving any present or fee from the parties.

The office of judge is in itself so very honorable, that men are willing to accept it, though accompanied with very small emoluments. The inferior office of justice of the peace, though attended with a good deal of trouble, and in most cases with no emoluments at all, is an object of ambition to many.

The salaries of all the different judges, high and low, together with the whole expense of the administration and execution of justice, even where it is not economically managed, makes, in any civilized country, but a very inconsiderable part of the whole expense of government.

℃   A. S. now digresses somewhat to consider whether the ancient practice of compensating the judges by some sort of fee system would not result in speeding up the courts and reducing the cost of justice.

℃   His conclusion is that it would, provided the fees and costs were fixed and plainly made known to all parties to suits at law. He suggests that the judges might be maintained partly in this way and partly by salaries, so that a diligent judge would earn a larger income than a slothful one. The courts might even be endowed with money or property; but this source of income seems scarcely stable enough.

A stamp duty upon the law proceedings of each particular court, to be levied by that court, and applied towards the maintenance of the judges and other officers belonging to it, might, in the same manner, afford a revenue sufficient for defraying the expense of the administration of justice, without bringing any burden upon the general revenue of the society. But it is true that the judges might, in this case, be under the temptation of multiplying unnecessarily the proceedings upon every cause, in order to increase as much as possible the yield of such a stamp-duty.

It has been the custom in Europe to regulate, upon most occasions, the payment of the attorneys and clerks of court, according to the number of pages which they had occasion to write; the court, however, requiring that each page should contain so many lines, and each line so many words. In order to increase their incomes, the attorneys and clerks have therefore contrived to multiply words beyond all necessity, to the corruption of the law language of, I believe, every court of justice in Europe. A like temptation might perhaps occasion a like corruption in the form of law proceedings.

The separation of the judicial from the executive power seems originally to have arisen from the increasing business of the society, in consequence of its increasing improvement. The administration of justice became so laborious and so complicated a duty as to require the undivided attention of the persons to whom it was entrusted. The person entrusted with the executive power, not having leisure to attend to the decision of private suits himself, a deputy was appointed to decide them in his stead.

In the progress of the Roman greatness, the consul was too much occupied with the political affairs of the state to attend to the administration of justice. A praetor, therefore, was appointed to administer it in his stead.

In the progress of the European monarchies which were founded upon the ruins of the Roman Empire, the sovereigns and great lords came universally to consider the administration of justice as an office too laborious and too ignoble for them to bother with. They universally evaded it by appointing a deputy, bailiff, or judge.

When the judicial is united to the executive power, it is scarcely possible that justice should not frequently be sacrificed to what is vulgarly called politics. The persons entrusted with the great interests of the state may, even without any corrupt views, sometimes imagine it necessary to sacrifice to those interests the rights of a private man.

But upon the impartial administration of justice depends the liberty of every individual, the sense which he has of his own security. In order to make every individual feel himself perfectly secure in the possession of every right which belongs to him, it is not only necessary that the judicial should be separated from the executive power, but that it should be rendered as much as possible independent of that power.

The judge should not be liable to be removed from his office according to the caprice of the executive, nor should the regular payment of his salary depend upon the good-will or even upon the good management of that power.

CHAPTER III

The third function of government is to build and maintain public works which private enterprise, for one reason or another, cannot be expected to undertake; of which the principal ones are the post-office, roads, bridges, and canals.

THE THIRD AND LAST DUTY of the state is that of erecting and maintaining those public institutions and public works which, though they may be in the highest degree advantageous to a great society, are of such a nature that the profit could never repay the expense to any individual or small number of individuals, and which they, therefore, cannot be expected to erect or maintain.[1]

The works and institutions of this kind are chiefly those for facilitating the commerce of the society, and those for promoting the instruction of the people, the latter including both the education of youth, and the instruction of people of all ages.

That the erection and maintenance of the public works which facilitate commerce, such as roads, bridges, canals, harbors, etc., must require very different degrees of expense in the different periods of society, is self-evident.

It does not seem essential that the expense of those public works should be defrayed from the public revenue, as it is commonly called. Most such public works may easily be so managed as to yield income sufficient for defraying their own expense, without bringing any burden upon the general revenue of the society.

[1] There is a fairly definite principle, says Carver, which determines which enterprises can and which can not be carried on by private enterprise. Those whose products or services can be sold to voluntary buyers at prices which will at least cover costs, belong in the first class. Those in which coercion is necessary to raise the money or get the work done, belong in the second.

A highway, a bridge, a navigable canal, for example, may in most cases be built and maintained by a small toll upon the traffic which makes use of them: a harbor, by a moderate port-duty upon the tonnage of the shipping which load or unload there.

The coinage, another institution for facilitating commerce, in many countries not only defrays its own expense, but affords a small income or seignorage to the state. The post office, another institution for the same purpose, over and above defraying its own expense, affords in almost all countries a very considerable profit.[2]

When the vehicles which pass over a highway or a bridge, and the barges which sail upon a canal, pay toll in proportion to their weight or their tonnage, they pay for the maintenance of those public works exactly in proportion to the wear and tear which they cause. It seems scarcely possible to invent a more equitable way of maintaining such works.

Furthermore, this toll or tax, though it is advanced by the carrier, is finally paid by the consumer, to whom it must always be charged in the price of the goods. As the expense of transportation, however, is very much reduced by means of such public works, the goods are actually cheaper to the consumer than they could otherwise have been, notwithstanding the toll; their prices not being so much raised by the toll, as they are lowered by the cheapness of transportation.

The person who finally pays this tax, gains more than he loses by the payment of it. His payment is exactly in proportion to his gain. It is in reality no more than a part of that gain which he is obliged to give up in order to get the rest. It seems impossible to imagine a more equitable method of raising a tax.

When the toll upon luxury travel is made somewhat higher in proportion to weight than upon commercial freight, the indolence and vanity of the rich is made to contribute in a very easy manner to the relief of the poor, by rendering cheaper the transportation of heavy goods throughout the country.

When highways, bridges, canals, etc. are thus made and supported by the commerce which is carried on by means of them, they can be built only where that commerce requires them, and

---

[2] It is not so apt to do so in countries of great distances and insatiable political demands; yet even in such countries this essential institution can and should pay its own way.

consequently where it is proper to make them. Their character and cost must be suited to what that commerce can afford to pay.

℃ A magnificent highway cannot be built through a desert country where there is little or no commerce, or merely because it happens to lead to the country villa of the local political boss, or to that of some wealthy man who co-operates closely with him.

A great bridge cannot be thrown over a river at a place where nobody passes, or merely to embellish the view from the windows of a neighboring palace—things which sometimes happen, in countries where works of this kind are built out of public revenues or loans.[3]

In various parts of Europe the toll or lock-duty upon a canal is the property of private persons, whose private interest obliges them to maintain the canal. If it is not kept in tolerable order, the navigation necessarily ceases altogether, and along with it the whole profit which they can make by the tolls.

The canal of Languedoc cost the king of France and the province upwards of thirteen millions of livres, the equivalent of about $12,500,000. When the great work was finished, the most likely method of keeping it in repair, it was found, was to make a present of the tolls to Riquet, the engineer who planned and built it.

Those tolls still constituted, a century later, a very large property to the different branches of the family of that gentleman, who have, therefore, a great interest to keep the canal in constant repair.

But had those tolls been put under the management of some government bureau, which had no such interest, they might perhaps have been dissipated in ornamental and unnecessary expenses, while the most essential parts of the work were allowed to go to ruin.

The tolls for the maintenance of a highroad cannot with any safety be made the property of private persons. A highroad,

[3] In the United States, public policy has long followed the theory that transportation should precede traffic—that roads and railways should be the instruments of future development, not wait until demand has been built up.

Such a policy has in some cases resulted in construction and maintenance of public roads in whatever areas residents demanded them, regardless of their probable utility. This has led to absurdities and losses. There are some signs, such as the rural zoning laws in Wisconsin, that this over-sanguine policy may be corrected hereafter.

though entirely neglected, does not become altogether impassable, though a canal does. The proprietors of the tolls, therefore, might neglect altogether the repair of the road, and yet continue to levy very nearly the same tolls.[4] It is proper, therefore, that the tolls for the maintenance of such work should be put under the management of some public body.

In France, the funds destined for the repair of the main highways were [5] under the immediate direction of the government. Those funds consisted partly in a certain number of days' labor which the country people were obliged to give to work on the highways, and partly in such portion of the general revenue of the state as the king chose to spare from his other expenses.

By the ancient law of France, as well as by that of most other parts of Europe, the labor of the country people was under the direction of a local jurisdiction, which had no immediate dependence upon the king's council. But later both the labor of the country people, and whatever other funds the king expended on highway repairs, were entirely under the management of the intendant—an officer appointed and removed by the king's council, who received his orders from it, and was in constant correspondence with it.

In the progress of despotism the authority of the executive power gradually absorbs that of every other power in the state, and assumes to itself the management of every branch of revenue which is destined for any public purpose.

In France, the great post-roads, the roads which made the communication between the principal towns of the kingdom, were in general kept in good order; and in some provinces were a good deal superior to most of the turnpike roads of England.

But what we call the backroads—that is, the far greater part of the roads in the country—were entirely neglected, and were in many places absolutely impassable for any heavy travel. In some places it was even dangerous to travel on horseback, and mules were the only conveyance which could safely be trusted.

The proud minister of an ostentatious court may frequently take pleasure in executing a work of splendor and mag-

[4] Which is almost precisely what happened on hundreds of American turnpikes, and was one reason for their general abolition. The new toll-roads and bridges now being built have nearly all some quasi-public nature.

[5] Were before the French Revolution, that is.

nificence, such as a great highway, which is frequently seen by the principal nobility, whose applause not only flatters his vanity, but may even contribute to support his interest at court.

But to execute a great number of little works, in which nothing that can be done can make any great display, or excite the smallest degree of admiration in any traveler, and which, in short, have nothing to recommend them but their extreme utility, is a business which appears much too mean and paltry to merit the attention of so great an official. Under such an administration, therefore, such works are almost always entirely neglected.

In China, and in several other governments of Asia, the executive power charges itself both with the repair of the highways, and with the maintenance of the navigable canals. In the instructions which are given to the governor of each province, those objects, it is said, are constantly recommended to him, and the judgment which the government forms of his conduct is very much regulated by the attention which he appears to have paid to this part of his duties.

This branch of public service accordingly is said to be very well attended to in all those countries, but particularly in China, where the highroads, and still more the navigable canals, it is pretended, very much exeed anything of the same kind in Europe.

The accounts of those works, however, which have been transmitted to Europe, have generally been drawn up by weak and wondering travelers, and frequently by stupid and lying missionaries. If they had been examined by more intelligent eyes, and reported by more faithful witnesses, they would not, perhaps, appear to be so wonderful.

⁋ But if we assume those reports to be partly true, one reason for the excellence of these public works is that the chief revenue of many of the governments of Asia arises from a kind of land tax or land rent, which is based on the agricultural production. It is, therefore, greatly to the interest of the government that production should be large and its value high.

⁋ To accomplish this it is necessary to cultivate the markets, and to establish the freest, easiest, and cheapest communication between all parts of the country; and this can best be done by good roads and canals.

⁋ When a government does not get its revenue directly from the land (although in most countries the largest part of it comes

[*264*]

directly from this source) there is no such obvious and compelling motive for keeping roads and canals constantly in good repair.

Even those public works which are of such a nature that they cannot earn any income for maintaining themselves, but of which the convenience is confined to some particular place or district, are always better maintained by a local or provincial revenue, under the management of a local administration, than by the general revenue of the state.

Were the streets of London to be lighted and paved at the expense of the British Treasury, is there any probability that they would be so well lighted and paved as they are at present, or even at so small an expense?

The abuses which sometimes creep into the administration of a local and provincial revenue, however flagrant they may appear, are in reality almost always very trifling, in comparison with those which commonly take place in the administration and expenditure of the revenue of a great nation. They are, besides, much more easily corrected.

Under the local administration of the justices of the peace in Great Britain, the six days' labor which the country people were obliged to give to the repair of the highways was not always perhaps very judiciously applied, but it was scarcely ever exacted with any circumstance of cruelty or oppression.

In France, under the administration of the intendants, the application was not always more judicious, and the exaction was frequently cruel and oppressive. Such Corvées, as they are called, made one of the principal instruments of tyranny by which those officers chastised any community which had the misfortune to fall under their displeasure.

CHAPTER IV

*In addition to public works of general util-
ity, governments have habitually taken
measures for encouraging commerce and
manufacture, or some particular branches
thereof, such as the East India Company
and other great trading companies, with
very indifferent success and satisfaction; the
fields in which joint stock companies may
operate with success.*

THE OBJECT OF the public works and institutions I have discussed
in the previous chapter is to facilitate commerce in general. But in
order to facilitate some particular branches of it, particular institutions are necessary, which again require a particular and extraordinary expense to the state.

Some particular branches of commerce, which are carried
on with barbarous and uncivilized nations, require extraordinary
protection. An ordinary store could, for example, give little security to the goods of the merchants who trade to the western coast
of Africa.

Among other nations, whose vigorous government will not
permit any strangers to occupy any fortified place within their
territory, it may be necessary to maintain some ambassador, minister, or consul, who may decide the differences arising among his
own countrymen, according to their own customs, and, in their
disputes with the natives, may, by means of his public character,
interfere with more authority, and afford them a more powerful
protection, than they could expect from any private person.

The interests of commerce have frequently made it necessary to maintain ministers in foreign countries, where no other interest would have required any. The commerce of the Turkey Company first occasioned the establishment of a British ambassador at Constantinople. The first English embassies to Russia arose altogether from commercial interests. This custom, now universal, was unknown to ancient times, and seems not to be older than the end of the 15th or the beginning of the 16th Century; that is, than the time when commerce first began to extend itself to the nations of Europe, and when they first began to pay attention to its interests.

It seems not unreasonable that the extraordinary expense, which the protection of any particular branch of commerce may require, should be defrayed by a moderate tax upon that particular branch; by a moderate fee, for example, to be paid by the traders when they first enter into it. Or, what is fairer, by a particular duty of so much per cent upon the goods which they import into, or export out of, the particular countries with which it is carried on.

The protection of trade in general, from pirates and freebooters, is said to have been the original motive for imposing customs duties. But, if it was thought reasonable to lay a general tax upon trade, in order to defray the expense of protecting trade in general, it should seem equally reasonable to lay a particular tax upon a particular branch of trade, in order to defray the extraordinary expense of protecting that branch.

The protection of trade in general has always been considered as essential to the defense of the commonwealth, and for that reason a necessary part of the duty of the executive power. The collection and application of the customs, therefore, have always been left to that power.

But the protection of any particular branch of trade is a part of the general protection of trade; a part, therefore, of the duty of that power. And if nations always acted consistently, the particular duties levied for such particular protection would always have been left equally at its disposal.

But in this respect, as well as in many others, nations have not always acted consistently; and in most of the commercial states of Europe, particular companies of merchants have been able to delude the legislature into entrusting to them the performance of this part of the duty of the sovereign, together with all the powers which are necessarily connected with it.[1]

Though these companies may, perhaps, have been useful for the first introduction of some branches of commerce, by making at their own expense an experiment which the state might not think it prudent to make, they have in the long run proved universally burdensome or useless, and have either mismanaged or handicapped the trade itself.

℃ The great trading companies which in the 17th and 18th Centuries carried on a very large part of the foreign commerce of the world were of two kinds.

℃ What were called regulated companies resembled the incorporated trades which were so common in the cities and towns, and differed from them only in being monopolies on a larger scale. Admission to them was in theory open to anybody. But the monopolistic spirit which always prevails, when not suppressed by law, provided that membership in these companies should be difficult to obtain, in order to keep down the competition. The directors often tried to grant membership only to their own friends, and in general the companies were hampered by all kinds of burdensome restrictions. When the law restrained them from these practices, they became altogether useless and insignificant.[2]

The object of most of the by-laws of all regulated companies was not so much to oppress those who were already members, as to discourage others from becoming so; which could be done not only by a high entrance fee, but by many other contrivances.

The constant object of such companies was always to raise the rate of their own profit as high as they could; to keep the market for the goods which they handle as much understocked as they could: which could be done only by restraining the competition, or by discouraging new adventurers from entering into the trade.

In all trades, the regular established traders, even though

[1] "There is nothing," says Thorold Rogers, "in which an over-governed country is more mischievously over-governed than in taking the initiative in industrial enterprises." Certainly the next most mischievous is government intrusion into commerce, as history has abundantly shown.

[2] The five "regulated companies" in foreign commerce in A. S.'s day were the Merchant Adventurers of England, commonly called the Hamburg Company, the Russia Company, the Eastland Company, the Turkey Company, and the African Company.

not incorporated, naturally combine to raise profits, which are by no method so likely to be kept at all times down to their proper level, as by the occasional competition of speculative adventurers.

More important were the great joint stock companies like the East India Company, which was not only a trading concern, but actually waged war, conquered territory, and acted in many ways as a sovereign power. Such companies differed in several respects, not only from regulated companies, but from private partnerships.

In a private partnership, no partner, without the consent of the company, can transfer his share to another person, or introduce a new member. Each member, however, may, upon proper notice, withdraw from the partnership, and demand payment from the others of his share of the common stock. In a joint stock company, on the contrary, no member can demand payment of his share from the company; but each member can, without their consent, transfer his share to another person, and thereby introduce a new member.

The value of a share in a joint stock company is always the price which it will bring in the market; and this may be either greater or less than the sum which its owner stands credited for in the stock of the company, or the par value.

In a private partnership, each partner is bound for the debts contracted by the enterprise to the whole extent of his fortune. In a joint stock company, on the contrary, each partner or stockholder is liable only to the extent of his share.

The trade of a joint stock company is always managed by a board of directors. This board, indeed, is supposed to represent, and be subject to, the general body of stockholders. But the greater part of those owners seldom pretend to understand anything of the business of the company; and when the spirit of faction happens not to prevail among them, give themselves no trouble about it, but receive contentedly such dividends as the directors think proper to make to them.

This total exemption from trouble and risk, beyond a limited sum, encourages many people to invest in joint stock companies, who would not think of risking their fortunes in any private partnership. Such companies, therefore, commonly draw to themselves much greater capital than any private partnership can boast.

The working capital of the South Sea Company amounted at one time to upwards of £33,800,000. The directors of such companies, however, being the managers of other people's money rather than of their own, it cannot reasonably be expected that they should watch over it with the same anxious vigilance with which the partners in a private partnership naturally watch over their own. Like the stewards of a rich man, they are apt to consider attention to small matters as beneath their master's dignity. Negligence and extravagance, therefore, must always prevail, more or less, in the management of the affairs of such a company.

It is upon this account that joint stock companies for foreign trade have seldom been able to withstand the competition of private adventurers. They have, accordingly, very seldom succeeded except with the aid of special privileges, and indeed have not always succeeded even then. Without exclusive privileges they have commonly mismanaged their business. With them, they have both mismanaged and limited it.

℃ A. S. here proceeds to describe at great length the experience of the Royal African Company and the Hudson's Bay Company, both of which claimed exclusive trading privileges in their own territories.

℃ The former, after trying all kinds of trade, including the sale of African slaves to the West Indies, losing money all the time, finally became hopelessly bankrupt, as had three successive companies in that field before them.

℃ The Hudson's Bay Company, on the contrary, was successful on a moderate scale. Its capital was small, its employes few, and its stockholders still fewer. It resembled, therefore, a private partnership, with the partnership's efficiency and economy. It is probable that the actual net profit of the company did not much exceed the ordinary profit of trading capital, if it exceeded it at all.

℃ But the most instructive case was that of the South Sea Company, which had no exclusive privileges, but had an immense capital contributed by an immense list of stockholders. It was naturally to be expected, therefore, that folly, negligence, and extravagance should be the rule in its enterprises, and this was in fact the case.

℃ Besides the slave trade, which lost money, the company was permitted by the Spanish government to send one ship a year to trade with the Spanish West Indies. Of ten of these annual voyages, only one made any money.

℃ The loss was attributed, by the company's own agents, to

the extortion and oppression of the Spanish authorities; but was no doubt principally due to the extravagance and dishonesty of the agents themselves, some of whom were said to have acquired great fortunes in a single year.

⊂ Later the South Sea Company tried whaling, with even worse results, and eventually it went out of foreign trading altogether. Its experience showed, as most such enterprises have done, that where they come into direct competition with private traders operating on their own account, they have been unable to make expenses in foreign trade.

⊂ The case of the famous United Company of Merchants Trading to the East Indies, commonly known as the East India Company, is in quite another class. A. S. describes at length the early successes of the old East India Company, the rise of competition, and the long contests for the favor of Parliament and the right to the East Indian trade.

⊂ Eventually, the course of events led to the waging of wars and the partial conquest of Hindustan, an event of such momentous importance to Great Britain and the world, to this day. The conclusion, however, is the same—that a great foreign trading company is nearly always incompetent, extravagant, and a failure, even when supported by state aid and exclusive privileges.

⊂ Such privileges it might be reasonable to grant in the case of a company undertaking at their own risk and expense to establish some new enterprise in a remote and barbarous land. But such privileges should be only temporary; and experience shows that they tend to become perpetual.

By a perpetual monopoly, all the other citizens are taxed very absurdly in two different ways: first, by the high price of goods, which otherwise they could buy much cheaper; and, secondly, by their total exclusion from a branch of business, which it might be convenient and profitable for many of them to carry on.

And it is for the most worthless of all purposes that they are taxed in this manner. It is merely to enable the company to support the negligence, extravagance, and malversation of their own employees, whose disorderly conduct seldom allows the earnings of the company to exceed the ordinary rate of profit in trades which are altogether free, and very frequently makes it fall even a good deal short of that rate.

To buy in one market, in order to sell with profit in another, when there are many competitors in both; to watch over, not only the occasional variations in the demand, but the much greater and more frequent variations in the competition, or in the supply which that demand is likely to get from other people, and to adjust with dexterity and judgment both the quantity and quality of each assortment of goods to all these circumstances, is a type of warfare of which the conditions are continually changing, and which can scarcely ever be conducted successfully, without such an unremitting exertion of vigilance and attention, as cannot long be expected from the directors of a stock company.

The only trades which it seems possible for a joint stock company to carry on successfully, without any special privilege, are those of which all the operations are capable of being reduced to a routine, or to such a uniformity of method as admits of little or no variation. Of this kind is, first, the banking business; second, the trade of insurance from fire, and from sea risk and capture in time of war; third, the trade of building and maintaining a navigable cut or canal; and, fourth, the similar trade of supplying water for a great city.[3]

Though the principles of banking may appear somewhat abstruse, the practice is capable of being reduced to strict rules. To depart from those rules, in pursuit of some flattering speculation of extraordinary gain, is almost always extremely dangerous, and frequently fatal to the bank which attempts it. But the constitution of joint stock companies makes them in general tenacious of established rules, and such companies, therefore, seem extremely well fitted for this business.

The principal banking companies in Europe, accordingly, are stock companies, many of which manage very successfully without any monopolistic privilege. The Bank of England has no

---

[3] The experience of the last 170 years has shown that this idea is fallacious; there is hardly any form of human activity not now carried on by some corporation with success. Boards of directors are not, in general, as lacking in vigilance and attention as A. S. supposes; but the factor with which he was unacquainted is the invention and development of professional management able to compete on even terms with the economy and efficiency of the partnership or the individual entrepreneur.

Again, this increase in corporate efficiency has made it unnecessary to obtain from the state the special privileges which were formerly demanded and often granted; and with this reform the objections of A. S. to corporations would doubtless largely disappear. But it must be added that the vast extension of corporate enterprise has brought new problems, with which we do not yet seem wise enough to cope fully.

other exclusive privilege, except that no other banking company in England shall consist of more than six persons.

The value of the risk from fire, or from loss by sea, or by capture, although it cannot, perhaps, be calculated very exactly, admits of such a gross estimation as renders it, to some degree, reducible to strict rule and method. The trade of insurance, therefore, may be carried on successfully by a joint stock company, without any exclusive privilege.

When a navigable canal has been once made, the management of it becomes quite simple and easy, and is reducible to strict rule and method. Even the building of it is simple, as it may be built under contract at so much a mile, and so much a lock. The same thing may be said of an aqueduct and the great water mains for supplying a great city. Such enterprises, therefore, may be, and accordingly frequently are, very successfully managed by joint stock companies.

To establish a stock company for a particular undertaking, however, merely because such a company might be capable of managing it successfully; or to exempt a particular group of dealers from the general laws which govern all their neighbors, merely because they might be capable of thriving if they had such an exemption, would certainly not be reasonable.

To render such a project perfectly reasonable, two other circumstances ought to concur. First, it ought to appear with the clearest evidence that the undertaking is of greater and more general utility than most common trades; and second, that it requires a greater capital than can easily be raised by a private partnership. If a moderate capital were sufficient, the great utility of the undertaking would not be a sufficient reason for establishing a joint stock company; because, in this case, the demand for what it was to produce would readily and easily be supplied by individuals. In the four trades above mentioned, both those circumstances concur.

The English copper company of London, the leading smelting company, the glass-grinding company, have not even the pretext of any great or singular utility in the object which they pursue; nor does the pursuit of that object seem to require any expense too great for the resources of many private men. Whether the trade which those companies carry on is reducible to such strict rule and method as to render it fit for the management of a joint stock company, or whether they have any reason to boast of their extraordinary profits, I do not pretend to know.[4] The mine-adventurers company has long been bankrupt. A share in the stock of the British Linen Company of Edinburgh sells, at present, very much below par, though less so than it did some years ago.

The companies which are established for the public-spirited purpose of promoting some particular manufacture, besides managing their own affairs ill, to the diminution of the general capital of the society, can in other respects scarcely ever fail to do more harm than good.

Notwithstanding the most upright intentions, the unavoidable partiality of their directors to particular branches of the manufacture is a real discouragement to the rest. It necessarily breaks, more or less, that natural proportion which would otherwise establish itself between judicious industry and profit, and which, to the general industry of the country, is of all encouragements the greatest and most effective.

[4] Nor do we; but these activities and ten thousand others have long been carried on successfully and profitably under the corporate form.

CHAPTER V

An activity of government not hitherto mentioned is education; this can and should be imparted, at least in the case of children, by the state at its expense; but heavily endowed institutions are frequently of little educational value; why an educated population is advantageous to the society.

INSTITUTIONS FOR THE education of youth may, as with other public works, furnish revenue sufficient for defraying their own expense. The fee or honorarium which the scholar formerly paid to the master naturally constituted a revenue of this kind. Even where the reward of the instructor does not arise altogether from this natural revenue, it still is not necessary that it should be derived from general public funds.

Through the greater part of Europe, accordingly, the endowment of schools and colleges makes either no charge upon the public treasury, or but a very small one. It everywhere arises chiefly from some local revenue, from the rent of some estate, or from the interest of some sum of money held in trust for this particular purpose.

Have those great endowments contributed in general to promote the end of their institution? [1] Have they contributed to encourage the diligence, and to improve the abilities of the teachers? Have they directed the course of education toward objects more useful, both to the individual and to the public, than those

[1] The justification for endowments, observes Thorold Rogers, is that it is a means of supporting learned men, who would not otherwise be hired. It selects and puts forward competent persons. A. S. himself owed his learning and fame to the seven years' leisure which his "exhibition" at Balliol College gave him.

to which it would naturally have gone of its own accord? It should not seem very difficult to give at least a probable answer to each of those questions.

In every profession, the exertion of most of those who exercise it is always in proportion to the necessity they are under. This necessity is greatest with those to whom the emoluments of their profession are the only source from which they expect to become rich, or even to get their ordinary income and subsistence.

In order to acquire this fortune, or even to get this subsistence, they must, in the course of a year, execute a certain quantity of work of a known value; and, where the competition is free, the rivalry of competitors, all endeavoring to jostle one another out of employment, obliges every man to execute his work with the greatest possible degree of exactness.

The greatness of the rewards of success in some particular professions may, no doubt, sometimes stimulate the exertion of a few men of extraordinary spirit and ambition. But great rewards are evidently not essential to the greatest exertions.

The fact is that rivalry and emulation are far more potent than the hope of wealth, even in the meanest professions, in calling forth all the powers and exertions of a man. Few men born to wealth and ease have ever become, for example, famous and successful lawyers.

Somewhat the same principle applies to the profession of teaching, where it is possible for some few men of spirit and ambition to become famous, but where few or none ever become rich.

The endowments of schools and colleges have necessarily diminished to some extent the necessity of application in the teachers. Their subsistence, so far as it arises from their salaries, is evidently derived from a source altogether independent of their success and reputation as teachers.

In some universities the salary makes but a part, and frequently but a small part, of the emoluments of the teacher, the great part arising from the honorariums or fees of his pupils. The necessity of application, though always more or less diminished, is not in this case entirely taken away.

Reputation in his profession is still of some importance to him, and he is still somewhat dependent upon the affection, gratitude, and favorable report of those who have received his instructions; and these favorable sentiments he is likely to gain in no way so well as by deserving them—that is, by the ability and diligence with which he discharges every part of his duty.

In other universities the teacher is prohibited from receiving any payment or fee from his pupils, and his salary constitutes the whole of his income. His interest is, in this case, set as directly in opposition to his duty as it is possible to set it.

It is the interest of every man to live as much at his ease as he can; and if his emoluments will be precisely the same, whether he does or does not perform some very laborious duty, it is certainly his interest, at least as interest is vulgarly understood, to neglect it altogether. Or, if he is subject to some authority which will not allow him to do this, to perform it in as careless and slovenly a manner as that authority will permit.

Even if a man is naturally active and a lover of labor, it is his interest to employ that activity in some way from which he can derive an advantage, rather than in the performance of his duty, from which he can derive none.

℃ A. S. goes on to criticize Oxford and other English universities for sloth and neglect, principally because the great endowments made the teachers indifferent to the students, and sometimes (as at Oxford) because the faculties, being all members of the corporate body, were in a kind of tacit agreement that no one need work hard.

℃ In the French universities, on the contrary, control was from without, such as by the bishops, the governor of the province, or some minister of state. Such external control would generally be ignorant and capricious, and the teacher, being wholly dependent on this authority for his position and his sustenance, would not scruple to sacrifice to his own safety the interests of his pupils and even of his university itself.

℃ Any restrictions upon the students, in the same way, tend to reduce the value of the instruction. If a student is obliged to attend a particular college, or to study under a particular teacher, the teacher will generally take advantage of this position to reduce to a minimum the exertion he puts forth.

The discipline of colleges and universities is in general contrived, not for the benefit of the students, but for the interest, or more properly speaking, for the ease of the masters. Its object is, in all cases, to maintain the authority of the master, and whether he neglects or performs his duty, to oblige the students in all cases to behave to him as if he performed it with greatest diligence and ability. It seems to presume perfect wisdom and virtue in the one order, and the greatest weakness and folly in the other.

Where the masters, however, really perform their duty, there are no cases, I believe, in which the greater part of the students ever neglect theirs. No discipline is ever requisite to force attendance upon lectures which are really worth the attending, as is well known wherever any such lectures are given.

Force and restraint may be in some degree requisite, no doubt, in order to oblige children, or very young people, to acquire what is really necessary during that early period of life. But after twelve or thirteen years of age, provided the teacher does his duty, force or restraint can scarcely ever be necessary to carry on any part of education.

Such is the generosity of most young men, that, so far from being disposed to neglect or despise the instructions of their master (provided he shows some serious intention of being of use to them), they are generally inclined to pardon a great deal of incorrectness in the performance of his duty, and sometimes even to conceal from the public a good deal of gross negligence.

Those parts of education, it is to be observed, for the teaching of which there are no public institutions, are generally the best-taught.[2] When a young man goes to a fencing or a dancing school, he does not indeed always learn to fence or to dance very well; but he seldom fails of learning to fence or to dance in some fashion.

The three most essential parts of literary education—reading, writing, and arithmetic—it still continues to be more common to acquire in private than in public schools; and it very seldom happens that anybody fails of acquiring them to a sufficient degree.

℃ A. S. now devotes a long passage to a discussion of the English school and university system of 1776; a discussion which, while interesting in itself, is even less germane to the general subject of economics than what has just been quoted.

℃ He traces the rise of the European universities, originally instituted for the education of churchmen, and explains how the

[2] Carver thinks that the best schools are, in general, those which have no support from the state. But it is obvious that in order to give every child the rudiments of an education, however poor or stingy his parents, compulsory state-supported schools are indispensable.

Reformation forced on them the study of the Greek and Hebrew languages. He then turns to ancient Greek philosophy, and from this back to the teaching of philosophy in medieval times, and finally in the 18th Century universities. This passage concludes with the following caustic remarks upon English university teachings, which, he thinks, brought about the even worse practice of sending English upper-class youth to the Continent for study and travel.

The improvements which, in modern times, have been made in the several branches of philosophy, have not, for the most part, been made in universities; though some no doubt have.

Most universities have not even been very forward to adopt those improvements, after they were made; and several of those learned societies have chosen to remain, for a long time, the sanctuaries in which exploded systems and obsolete prejudices found shelter and protection, after they had been hunted out of every corner of the world.

In general, the richest and best-endowed universities have been the slowest in adopting those improvements, and the most averse to permitting any considerable change in the established plan of education. Those improvements were more easily introduced into some of the poorer universities, in which the teachers, depending upon their reputation for the greater part of their subsistence, were obliged to pay more attention to the current opinions of the world.

But though the public schools and universities of Europe were originally intended only for the education of a particular profession, that of churchmen; and though they were not always very diligent in instructing their pupils even in the sciences which were supposed necessary for that profession, yet they gradually drew to themselves the education of almost all other people, particularly of almost all gentlemen and men of fortune.

No better method, it seems, could be hit upon of spending, with any advantage, the long interval between infancy and that period of life at which men begin to apply themselves in good earnest to the real business of the world, which is to occupy them during the remainder of their days.

Most of what is taught in schools and universities, however, does not seem to be suitable preparation for that business.

In England, it becomes every day more and more the

[279]

custom to send young people to travel in foreign countries immediately upon their leaving school, and without sending them to any
university.

Our young people, it is said, generally return home much
improved by their travels, and no doubt they do. A young man
who goes abroad at seventeen or eighteen, and returns home at
twenty-one, returns three or four years older than he was when
he went abroad; and at that age it is very difficult not to improve
a good deal in three or four years.

In the course of his travels, he generally acquires some
knowledge of one or two foreign languages; a knowledge, however, which is seldom sufficient to enable him either to speak or
write them with proficiency.

In other respects, he commonly returns home more con-
ceited, more unprincipled, more dissipated, and more incapable of
any serious application to study or business, than he could possibly
have become in so short a time, had he lived at home. By traveling
so very young, by spending in the most frivolous dissipation the
most precious years of his life, at a distance from the observation
and control of his parents and relatives, every useful habit which
his early education might have had some tendency to form in him,
instead of being riveted and confirmed, is almost necessarily either
weakened or effaced.

Nothing but the discredit into which the universities are
allowing themselves to fall, could ever have brought into popularity so very absurd a practice as that of traveling at this early
period of life. By sending his son abroad, a father delivers himself, at least for some time, from so disagreeable an object as that
of a son unemployed, neglected, and going to ruin before his eyes.

Such have been the effects of some of the modern institutions for education.

❡ With these opinions off his chest, A. S. now arrives by this
roundabout route at the real subject under examination—the
extent to which the state is justified in spending its revenues for
public education.

❡ Several pages are devoted to the systems of the ancient
Greeks and Romans—the subjects taught, the effects of study upon
the morals of the people, public and private, and particularly the
excellence of the instruction and the great influence of the instruc-
tors. Reading, writing, and arithmetic were taught privately,

philosophy and rhetoric were taught in schools not supported by the state—indeed were for a long time barely tolerated.

℄ Not until the time of Marcus Antonius was any teacher supported, even in part, by taxes; his only authority lay in the superior virtue and ability which attracted and held his pupils.

The abilities, both civil and military, of the Greeks and Romans will readily be allowed to have been equal, at least, to those of any modern nation. Our prejudice is perhaps rather to overrate them. But except in what related to military exercises, the state seems to have been at no pains to form those great abilities: for I cannot be induced to believe, that the musical education of the Greeks could be of much consequence in forming them.

Schoolmasters, however, had been found, it seems, for instructing the better sort of people in every art and science necessary in the circumstances of their society. The demand for such instruction produced, what it always produces, the talent for giving it; and the emulation which an unrestrained competition never fails to excite, appears to have brought that talent to a very high degree of perfection.

In the attention which the ancient philosophers aroused, in the empire which they acquired over the opinions and principles of their listeners, in the faculty which they possessed of giving a certain tone and character to the conduct and conversation of those listeners, they appear to have been much superior to any modern teachers.

In modern times, the diligence of public teachers is more or less corrupted by the circumstances which render them more or less independent of their success and reputation in their particular professions.

Their government salaries, too, put the private teacher who might attempt to compete with them, in the same state as a merchant who attempts to trade without a bounty, in competition with those who trade with a considerable one.

If he sells his goods at nearly the same price, he can make less profit, and poverty and beggary, if not bankruptcy and ruin, will infallibly be his lot. If he attempts to sell his goods dearer, he is likely to have so few customers that his circumstances will not be much better.

The endowments of schools and colleges have, in this manner, not only corrupted the diligence of public teachers, but have rendered it almost impossible to have any good private ones.[3]

Ought the public, therefore, to pay no attention, it may be asked, to the education of the people? Or if it ought to give any, what are the different parts of education which it ought to attend to in the different orders of the people? and in what manner ought it to attend to them?

In the progress of the division of labor, the employment of most of those who live by labor—that is, of the great body of the people—comes to be confined to a few very simple operations, frequently to one or two. But the understandings of most men are necessarily formed by their ordinary employment.

The man whose whole life is spent in performing a few simple operations has no occasion to exert his understanding, or to exercise his ingenuity in finding out expedients for removing difficulties which never occur. He naturally loses, therefore, the habit of such exertion, and generally becomes as stupid and ignorant as it is possible for a human creature to become.

The torpor of his mind renders him not only incapable of relishing or bearing a part in any rational conversation, but of conceiving any generous, noble, or tender sentiment, and consequently of forming any just judgment concerning even the ordinary duties of private life.

Of the great and extensive interest of his country he is altogether incapable of judging; and unless very particular pains have been taken to render him otherwise, he is equally incapable of defending his country in war.

His dexterity at his own particular trade seems, in this manner, to be acquired at the expense of his intellectual, social, and warlike virtues. But in every improved and civilized society this is the state into which the laboring poor, that is, the great body of the people, must necessarily fall, unless government takes pains to prevent it.[4]

[3] True, says Thorold Rogers; the actual effect of endowments is to lower the remuneration of teachers in unendowed institutions.

[4] "The statements in this paragraph are as unfounded as can well be imagined," says M'Culloch. "Dr. Smith has suffered his judgment to be swayed by ancient prejudices." Indeed, even the most illiterate ditch-digger often will be found much superior to A. S.'s doleful estimate.

It was the exclusion of the mass of artisans from political power in the 18th Century, not the nature of their work, that made them "stupid," says Thorold Rogers; and they were not nearly so stupid as A. S. asserts.

It was otherwise in barbarous societies, or even among nations of farmers, where necessity kept the capacities active. Nor is public education necessary for the wealthy, who can readily look after their own interests.

But though the common people cannot, in any civilized society, be so well instructed as people of some position and fortune, the most essential parts of education can be acquired at so early a period of life, that most of those who are to be bred to the lowest occupations, have time to acquire them before they must go to work. For a very small expense the public can facilitate, can encourage, and can even impose upon the whole body of the people, the necessity of acquiring at least reading, writing, and arithmetic.

The public can do this by establishing in every parish or district a school where children may be taught for a fee so moderate that even a common laborer may afford it, the teacher being partly, but not wholly, paid by the public; because, if he were wholly, or even principally paid by it, he would soon learn to neglect his business.

If in those little schools the books by which the children are taught to read, were a little more instructive than they commonly are; and, if instead of a smattering of Latin, which can scarce ever be of any use to these children, they were instructed in elementary geometry and mechanics, the literary education of this class of people would perhaps be as complete as it can be made.[5]

The public can impose upon almost the whole body of the people the necessity of acquiring those most essential parts of education, by obliging every man to undergo an examination in them before he can obtain the freedom in any incorporated trade, or be allowed to set up any trade in a village or town.

It was in this very way, by facilitating the acquisition of their military and gymnastic exercises, by encouraging it, and even by imposing upon the whole body of the people the necessity of learning those exercises, that the Greek and Roman republics maintained the martial spirit of their citizens.

Even though the martial spirit of the people were of no use towards the defense of the society, yet to prevent that sort of mental mutilation, deformity, and wretchedness, which cowardice

[5] How far the practice of every civilized and even the semi-civilized state has gone beyond A. S. and his 18th Century England it is superfluous to point out.

necessarily involves, from spreading through the great body of the people, would still deserve the most serious attention of government. In the same manner it would deserve its most serious attention to prevent leprosy or any other loathsome and offensive disease, though neither mortal nor dangerous, from spreading itself among them.

The same thing may be said of the gross ignorance and stupidity which, in a civilized society, seems so frequently to benumb the understandings of the lower classes.

A man without the proper use of the intellectual faculties of a man is, if possible, even more contemptible than a coward, and seems to be mutilated and deformed in a still more essential part of the human character. Though the state were to derive no advantage from the instruction of the people, it would still deserve its attention that they should not be altogether uninstructed.

The state, however, derives no inconsiderable advantage from their instruction. The more they know, the less liable they are to the delusions of enthusiasm and superstition, which, among ignorant nations, frequently occasion the most dreadful disorders.

An instructed and intelligent people are always more decent and orderly than an ignorant and stupid one. They feel themselves each individually more respectable, and more likely to obtain the respect of their lawful superiors, and they are therefore more disposed to respect those superiors. They are more disposed to examine, and more capable of seeing through, the agitation of faction and sedition, and they are, upon that account, less apt to be misled into any wanton or unnecessary opposition to the measures of government.

In free countries, where the safety of government depends very much upon the favorable judgment which the people may form of its conduct, it must surely be of the highest importance that they should not be disposed to judge it rashly or capriciously.

CHAPTER VI

A short paraphrase of a long chapter deal-
ing with religious instruction in an estab-
lished church, as part of the expense of the
state; with a brief review of the reform of
the Roman Catholic church; and some
remarks as to the impolicy of terror as an
instrument of government.

THIS LONG CHAPTER in W. N. is devoted to the "expense of the institutions for the instruction of people of all ages," by which A. S. meant principally religious instruction. It analyzes the relations between the churches and the state, with the historical development of many of them.

⊄   As the American Constitution of 1787 has up to this time forbidden anything resembling an "established church" in this country, most of the chapter is inapplicable to our conditions. But the passage is interesting and deserves a brief paraphrase.

⊄   Religious teachers are like other teachers in being far more energetic if they are not endowed. The clergy of a safely established church, while frequently men of learning, eloquence, and virtue, gradually lose the qualities which originally gave them their influence and established their church.

⊄   Such clergy, when attacked by popular and bold, though perhaps stupid and ignorant enthusiasts, feel themselves perfectly defenseless, and have commonly no resource but to call on the civil power to persecute, destroy, or drive out their adversaries.

⊄   The lower clergy of the Roman Catholic church are more dependent for their incomes on their parishioners than are the clergy of the established Protestant churches, and they are correspondingly more energetic. The Franciscan and other mendicant orders are entirely dependent on their own efforts for subsistence, and to them the Catholic church owes the revival of faith and devotion in the 13th and 14th Centuries.

℃   David Hume thought that a church should be established, or supported by the state, specifically to discourage the excessive zeal of the clergy, and their efforts to build up their own church by attacking other sects.

℃   The establishment of state churches has not, however, come about through such philosophical reasoning, but almost always through the alliance of a particular church with a political faction. A party engaged in some political struggle would enlist the aid of a sect, would be victorious, and would then be obliged to reward the sect (generally much against the will of the politicians) by silencing its enemies and settling a permanent income on itself.

℃   If the politicians had never done this, no one sect would have such a peremptory claim, there would be many independent sects, and they would have to learn to get along amicably. Even if they did not, their squabbles could do no real harm.

℃   In every civilized society, a strict system of morals is advocated by the common people (although not necessarily practiced by them), and a looser system by people of wealth and fashion. As nearly all religious sects have started among the common people, so their systems of morals have at first been very strict, if not disagreeably rigorous and unsocial. Indeed, this extravagant austerity is sometimes cultivated for the admiration it draws.

℃   Whether the state should interfere in such cases is doubtful; but if it were decided to do so, it could probably correct these excesses by requiring a knowledge of science and philosophy from candidates for the learned professions, and by encouraging the arts and public discussions.

℃   An established church becomes in effect an incorporated monopoly, whose interest is never exactly the same as that of the state, and sometimes is opposed to it. This is particularly the case where the church feels itself threatened by heresy, and the state interferes to protect the alleged heretics. In such cases the full power of the church hierarchy may be turned against the government, and not even a powerful standing army has always been able to prevent its overthrow.

℃   To prevent such violence, the state must retain some

control over the established clergy, but this should not be done by threatening to deprive the clergy of their positions, but by controlling their original appointments and their advancement.

Fear is in almost all cases a wretched instrument of government, and ought in particular never to be employed against any order of men who have the smallest pretensions to independency. To attempt to terrify them serves only to irritate their bad humor, and to confirm them in an opposition which more gentle usage perhaps might easily induce them to soften, or to lay aside altogether.

℣ The violence which the French government usually employed to force their courts to reverse any unpopular decision very seldom succeeded, although the refractory judges were imprisoned. In England the Stuart kings sometimes attempted similar coercion against members of Parliament, but found them equally intractable.

℣ Gentler tactics of management have usually succeeded, but have seldom been persevered with.

For though management and persuasion are always the easiest and safest instruments of government, as force and violence are the worst and the most dangerous, yet such, it seems, is the natural insolence of man, that he almost always disdains to use the good instrument, except when he cannot or dare not use the bad one.

There is no order of men, it appears, I believe, from the experience of all ages, upon whom it is so dangerous, or rather so perfectly ruinous, to employ force and violence, as upon the respected clergy of any established church.

⊂   But though this order of men can scarcely ever be forced, they may be managed as easily as any other class; and the means of management consist principally in the power of appointment which the government may possess.

⊂   Originally the bishops of the Christian church were elected jointly by the clergy and the people, later by the clergy alone, and still later this power gradually was drawn into the hands of the Pope. The civil power had at this stage no real influence with the Christian clergy. Ultimately the Pope succeeded in getting a large measure of control over the appointment of the inferior clergy, leaving to the bishop little more than enough power to give him a decent authority with his own clergy.

⊂   Thus the Pope came to be at the head of an immense and powerful army, quartered in every civilized nation, supported by that nation, and yet commanded from Rome. This organization, with the great wealth of the church, made it a formidable enemy, feared by sovereigns and nobles alike. One natural result—which in the unsettled times of the Middle Ages can hardly be complained of—was what was called in England "benefit of clergy." This was the system under which the clergy were made answerable for crimes and misdemeanors only in their own courts.

⊂   On the whole, the Church of Rome was at that time a powerful combination for spreading gross superstition, opposing and undermining civil authority, and conspiring against the liberty, reason, and happiness of mankind.[1]

⊂   The breakdown of this system came about through precisely the same cause as the decline of the feudal barons—through the

---

[1] Here I have abbreviated and slightly softened A. S.'s harsh language, which (with some other passages) has caused the Roman Catholic church to take a somewhat dim view of W. N. The work has never, however, been placed on the Index of disapproved books, so I am informed; its importance to every economist and sociologist is too great.

Macaulay takes much the same view of the failings of the medieval church; but he says, very justly: "She retained enough of the sublime theology and benevolent morality of her earlier days to elevate many intellects and to purify many hearts. . . . That which in an age of good government is an evil may, in an age of grossly bad government, be a blessing. It is better that mankind should be governed by wise laws . . . than by priestcraft: but it is better that men should be governed by priestcraft than by brute violence. . . . Had not [the cloisters of the medieval church] been scattered here and there, among the huts of a miserable peasantry, and the castles of a ferocious aristocracy, European society would have consisted merely of beasts of burden and beasts of prey."

gradual improvement of arts, manufactures, and commerce. The increase in consumable goods caused a reduction in personal service, an increase in rents, and the emancipation of tenants. The ties of interest which bound the lower classes to the clergy were thus gradually dissolved and disappeared, so that by the 15th Century the church had ceased to have much influence except through its spiritual offices.

℃ The sovereigns of Europe seized upon this decay to deprive the Pope of the disposal of the great church offices, and in England and France they were successful. This took place just as the Reformation was sweeping northern Europe, when the common people were readily convinced by the zeal of the new teachers, and many of the smaller sovereigns were at odds with the Pope, and adopted the reformed faith as a political measure.

℃ In other countries, friendly to the Pope, notably Spain and Austria, the Reformation was suppressed or obstructed. In Scotland, where the government was weak and unpopular, the Reformation overturned not only the church, but also the state for attempting to support it.

℃ The reformed churches developed many forms in different nations, dividing into two general groups of Lutherans and Calvinists, sometimes retaining the episcopal system and sometimes abandoning it. Where the congregations elected their own pastors, factions and disorder necessarily arose, and the civil powers frequently had to intervene to establish some sort of peace and order. In this day the Presbyterian system, by which the authority of all clergy is equal, and the differences between benefices not very great, makes the ministers of this sect respectable, and gives them unusual influence with the common people.

℃ The income of every established church is of course a branch of the general public revenue, except for that part which is the interest on endowments. It follows that the richer a given church, the poorer will be the state or the mass of people, or both. A wealthy church is therefore apt to be both an indolent one, and a burden upon the progress and wealth of its people.

The proper performance of every service seems to require that its pay or recompense should be, as exactly as possible, proportioned to the nature of the service. If any service is very much under-paid, it is very apt to suffer by the meanness and incapacity of most of those who are employed in it. If it is very much over-paid, it is apt to suffer, perhaps, still more by their negligence and idleness.

A man of large income, whatever may be his profession, thinks he ought to live like other men of large incomes, and to spend a great part of his time in festivity, in vanity, and in dissipation.

But in a clergyman this mode of life not only consumes the time which ought to be employed in the duties of his function, but in the eyes of the common people destroys almost entirely that sanctity of character which can alone enable him to perform those duties with proper weight and authority.

CHAPTER VII

A brief summing-up of the previous six chapters.

OVER AND ABOVE the expense necessary for enabling the head of the state to perform his several duties, a certain expense is requisite for the support of his dignity.

In a rich and cultured society, where all the different orders of people are growing every day more expensive in their houses, in their furniture, in their food, in their dress, and in their equipage, it cannot well be expected that the ruler should alone hold out against the fashion. He too naturally, or rather necessarily, becomes more expensive in all these respects. His dignity even seems to require this.

As in point of dignity a monarch is supposed to be more raised above his subjects than the chief magistrate of any republic is ever supposed to be above his fellow-citizens, so a greater expense is necessary for supporting that higher dignity. We naturally expect more splendor in the court of a king, than in the mansion of a burgomaster.[1]

The expense of defending the society, and that of supporting the dignity of the chief of state, are both laid out for the general benefit of the whole society. It is reasonable, therefore, that they should be defrayed by the general contribution of the whole society, all the different members contributing, as nearly as possible, in proportion to their abilities.

The expense of the administration of justice, too, may no doubt be considered as laid out for the benefit of the whole society. There is no impropriety, therefore, in its being defrayed by the general contribution of the whole society, all the different members contributing, as nearly as possible, in proportion to their abilities.

[1] Or the White House of a President.

Those individuals, however, who make this expense necessary, are those who by their injustice in one way or another, make it necessary to seek redress or protection from the courts. Again, the persons most immediately benefited by this expense, are those whom the courts either restore to their rights, or maintain in their rights.

The expense of the administration of justice, therefore, may very properly be defrayed by the particular contribution of one or the other, or both of those two different sets of persons, according to the circumstances—that is, by payment of the court costs. It cannot be necessary to rely on the general contribution of the whole society, except for the conviction of criminals who may be wholly unable to pay anything.[2]

Those local expenses of which the benefit is local (what is spent, for example, upon the police of a particular town or district) ought to be defrayed by a local revenue, and ought to be no burden upon the general revenue of the society. It is unjust that the whole society should contribute towards an expense of which the benefit is confined to a part of the society.

The expense of maintaining good roads and communications is, no doubt, beneficial to the whole society, and may, therefore, without any injustice, be defrayed by the general contribution of the whole society. This expense, however, is most immediately and directly beneficial to those who travel or transport goods from one place to another, and to those who consume such goods, and the impost of tolls on roads and bridges is therefore quite proper, where it is in effect.

The expense of the institutions for education and religious instruction is likewise, no doubt, beneficial to the whole society, and may, therefore, without great injustice, be defrayed by the general contribution of the whole society.

But this expense might perhaps, with equal propriety, and even with some advantage, be defrayed altogether by those who receive the immediate benefit of such education and instruction, or by the voluntary contribution of those who think they have occasion for the one or the other.

[2] This is surely less than justice. Thorold Rogers observes that a man who defends his just rights in court would not be there unless the state had in some way failed to secure them. Hence the state, not the defendant, should pay the costs or most of them.

When beneficial institutions or public works cannot, or at all events are not maintained altogether by the contribution of those members of the society who are most immediately benefited by them, the deficiency must in most cases be made up by the general contribution of the whole society. The sources of this general or public revenue, I shall try to explain in the following chapters.

CHAPTER VIII

The next ten chapters take up the perennial problem of governments—where to raise the cash for their necessary and unnecessary expenses; why most of this revenue, in a modern state, has to come from taxes of various sorts; and the famous four principles to which all good taxes must conform.

THE SOCIETY OR STATE, like any other owner of property, may obtain income from it, either by engaging in business itself, or by lending it out at interest.

℃   The revenue of a Tartar or Arabian chief consists in profit; he is indeed the principal shepherd or herdsman of his tribe. Some small republics have at times operated such enterprises as wine cellars and drug stores, and some larger states, like Venice and Amsterdam, have engaged in commercial banking with success.

℃   Nearly all states operate post offices, which are strictly mercantile undertakings, and nearly always at a profit.[1]

℃   Sovereigns of nations have generally been unsuccessful as business men, the extravagance with which their affairs are always managed by their agents making it impossible to earn profits.

℃   There are a few cases, too, where states have lent property, usually money, and have collected some small revenue from the interest.

℃   The colonial government of Pennsylvania, with no precious metals available, invented a method of lending paper money to its citizens at a considerable profit. The plan was to advance paper bills of credit upon the security of land, the bills to be redeemable

---

[1] Except of course in a political democracy such as the United States, where political subsidies of various sorts generally eat up what profit there might be.

after fifteen years, and meanwhile to be legal tender within the province.

❡ This ingenious scheme depended for its success on the scarcity of metal currency, on the good credit of the government of the colony, and on careful restriction of the amount of such bills put in circulation. The same plan in other colonies failed because of violation of some one of these requirements, producing much more disorder than convenience.

❡ None of these devices can compare, as a source of large income for the society, with income from land, and the rent of crown lands was for a long time the principal source of revenue of the sovereigns of Europe. True, their expenses were small; wars, which now swallow up such vast sums, were then carried on at very small expense to the state; and other national expenses were negligible.

❡ But in a modern society the rent of all the lands in the country would fall far short of ordinary peacetime expenditure, to say nothing of war costs.[2] This would be true even under the best management, and much more under the negligent, expensive, and oppressive management of government bureaus.

❡ In short, the revenue from the rent of land, like that from business undertakings and from interest, is a very unsuitable and totally inadequate source of public revenue. The only adequate source of the funds necessary for the purposes described in the previous chapters is from taxes.

The private revenue of individuals, as has been shown in the first book of this inquiry, arises ultimately from three different sources—one or other of those three different sorts of revenue, or from all of them indifferently. Many of the taxes which I shall presently describe, intended to fall upon some one of these sources of income, are not finally paid from that source at all.

Before I enter upon the examination of particular taxes, it is necessary to premise the four following principles with regard to taxes in general.[3]

I. *The citizens of every state ought to contribute towards*

[2] This is contradicted, I believe, by the followers of Henry George, who maintain that the complete collection of economic rent would cover all public expense in peacetime.

[3] This very famous passage could be condensed materially, but because of its great importance I print it practically as it appears in W. N.

the support of the government, as nearly as possible in proportion to their respective abilities; that is, in proportion to the incomes which they respectively enjoy under the protection of the state. The expense of government to the individuals of a great nation, is like the expense of management to the joint tenants of a great estate, who are all obliged to contribute in proportion to their respective interests in the estate.

Every tax, it must be observed once for all, which falls· finally upon one only of the three sorts of revenue above mentioned, is necessarily unequal, in so far as it does not affect the other two. In the following examination of different taxes I shall seldom take much further notice of this sort of inequality, but shall, in most cases, confine my observations to that inequality which is occasioned by a particular tax falling unequally even upon that particular sort of private revenue which is affected by it.

II. *The tax which each individual is bound to pay ought to be certain, and not arbitrary.* The time of payment, the manner of payment, the amount to be paid, ought all to be clear and plain to the taxpayer, and to every other person. Where it is otherwise, every person subject to the tax is put more or less in the power of the tax collector, who can either increase the tax upon any obnoxious contributor, or extort, by the terror of such increase, some present or perquisite to himself.

The uncertainty of taxation encourages the insolence and favors the corruption of an order of men who are naturally unpopular, even where they are neither insolent nor corrupt. The certainty of what each individual ought to pay is, in taxation, a matter of so great importance, that a very considerable degree of inequality, I believe, is not near so great an evil as a very small degree of uncertainty.

III. *Every tax ought to be levied at the time, or in the manner, in which it is most likely to be convenient for the citizen to pay it.* A tax upon the rent of land or of houses, payable at the same term at which such rents are usually paid, is levied at the time when it is most likely to be convenient for the contributor to pay; or, when he is most likely to have wherewithal to pay.

Taxes upon such consumable goods as are articles of luxury, are all finally paid by the consumer, and generally in a manner that is very convenient for him. He pays them a little at a time, as he has occasion to buy the goods. As he is at liberty, too, to buy or not to buy, as he pleases, it must be his own fault if he ever suffers any considerable inconvenience from such taxes.

IV. *Every tax ought to be so contrived as to take out and keep out of the pockets of the people as little as possible, over and above what it brings into the public treasury.*

A tax may either take out or keep out of the pockets of the people a great deal more than it brings into the treasury, in the four following ways:

First, the levying of it may require a great number of officials, whose salaries may eat up most of the produce of the tax;

Second, it may obstruct the industry of the people, and so reduce their ability to employ labor, and to pay their own taxes more easily;

Third, by the forfeitures and other penalties which those unfortunate individuals incur who attempt unsuccessfully to evade the tax, it may frequently ruin them, and thereby put an end to the benefit which the community might have received from the employment of their capital. An injudicious tax offers a great temptation to smuggling and bootlegging. But the penalties of these practices must rise in proportion to the temptation. The law, contrary to all ordinary principles of justice, first creates the temptation, and then punishes those who yield to it; and it commonly enhances the punishment in proportion to the very circumstances which ought certainly to alleviate it, the temptation to commit the crime.

Fourth, by subjecting the people to the frequent visits and the odious examinations of the tax collectors, it may expose them to much unnecessary trouble, vexation, and oppression; and though vexation is not, strictly speaking, expense, it is certainly equivalent to the expense at which every man would be willing to protect himself from it.

It is in some one or other of these four different ways that taxes are frequently so much more burdensome to the people than they are beneficial to the government.

The evident justice and utility of the foregoing principles of taxation have recommended them more or less to the attention of all nations. All nations have endeavored, to the best of their judgment, to render their taxes as equal as they could contrive; as certain, as convenient to the contributor, both in the time and in the mode of payment, and in proportion to the revenue which they brought to the government, as little burdensome to the people.

The following short review of some of the principal taxes which have been imposed in different ages and countries will show that the results have not in all cases been happy.

CHAPTER IX

A chapter devoted to taxes on farm land,
listing various forms of such taxes, good and
bad, and concluding that a tax on land rent,
with compulsory registry of land leases,
would be the best.*

℃ A. S. TAKES UP FIRST the land tax in Great Britain, which was
a tax levied on each district according to a fixed scale of rents, and
remained unchanged for long periods.

℃   He points out that while the tax would theoretically be
equal at the beginning (actually it was unequal even then), it
becomes unequal according to the improvement or neglect of the
land. It was, however, all right in the other three qualities: it
was perfectly certain; it was convenient to pay; and it was not
burdensome.

℃   This, however, was due rather to good fortune than to the
virtues of the fixed tax itself, since the country had prospered
and rents had risen, while the value of money varied very little.
It could have been very burdensome under other circumstances.

℃   The French school of "Economists," whom we shall meet
again toward the end of the next book, recommended a land tax
varying with the rent. Indeed, they taught that all taxes fall
ultimately upon rent; but it will sufficiently appear a little later
which taxes do fall upon rent and which do not.

℃   Any tax on rent is more equitable than if levied directly
on land, but is not so certain in amount, and is apt to be more

* This chapter is somewhat technical, is not very applicable to modern
taxation practices, and in short might very well be skipped by the general reader.
The same applies in varying degrees to all the next five chapters: I was of two minds
whether or not to omit them entirely.

troublesome and expensive to collect. It could be used to discourage certain abuses in rental, such as fees for renewing leases,
conditions of cultivation,[1] and rents payable in kind, which are
always more hurtful to the tenant than beneficial to the landlord.

℃	It is to the public advantage that the landlord should
cultivate at least a part of his own land, and a partial abatement
of the tax might be allowed to landlords who do this.

℃	They should not, however, be encouraged to farm all of
their land, which would have the effect of filling the country with
idle and profligate bailiffs, whose abusive management would soon
degrade the cultivation of the land and reduce its yields.[2] The
value of improvements should be, for a fixed term, exempt from
the operation of such a tax, in order not to penalize improvements.

The object of the government ought to be to encourage,
by every means in its power, the attention both of the landlord
and of the farmer: by allowing both to pursue their own interest
in their own way, and according to their own judgment; by giving
to both the most perfect security that they shall enjoy the full
fruits of their labor; and by making available the widest market
for every part of their produce, through the easiest and safest
communications by land and water, throughout the country, and
unbounded freedom of export to foreign nations.

In all the variations of the state of the society, in the improvement and in the decline of agriculture, in all the variations in
the value of money, a tax levied on the actual rent of land would,
of its own accord and without any attention of government, readily
adjust itself to the actual situation of things, and would always be
just and equitable.

Some states, instead of determining a land tax by the simple
and obvious expedient of a register of leases, have had recourse to

---

[1] Of which A. S. says that the cause is generally the landlord's conceit of
his own superior knowledge, in most cases very ill-founded. M'Culloch questions the
whole idea, pointing out that toward the end of a land lease the tenant's motive for
following the best cultivation methods naturally decreases. Experience in the United
States favors the use of cultivation conditions in land leases; but of course the only
real point is whether the methods specified are good agriculture or bad.

[2] Here it must be emphasized again that A. S. is considering the English
agricultural system, where the landlord is generally what we would call an absentee
landlord.

the laborious and expensive one of an actual survey and valuation of all the lands in the country. They have suspected, probably, that the lessor and lessee, in order to defraud the Treasury, might combine to conceal the real terms of the lease. Doomsday-book seems to have been the result of a very accurate survey of this kind.

⟨ In the dominions of Frederick the Great of Prussia the land tax was based on actual appraisals, continually revised according to the revenue received. Church lands were taxed higher than those of laymen, and in Silesia the tax paid by nobles was 3 per cent higher than that of commons. But in most European countries these discriminations were reversed.[3]

Taxes upon the produce of farm land are in reality taxes upon the rent; and though they may be originally advanced by the tenant, are finally paid by the landlord. When a certain portion of the produce must be paid in as taxes, the farmer computes, as well as he can, what the value of this portion is likely to amount to one year with another, and he makes a proportionate reduction in the rent which he agrees to pay to the landlord. There is no farmer who does not make such a deduction beforehand for the church tithe, which is a land tax of this type.

The tithe, and every other such land tax, under the appearance of perfect equality, is a very unequal tax—a certain portion of the produce being, in different situations, equivalent to a very different portion of the rent. On some very rich lands production is so large that a half of it is fully sufficient to replace to the farmer his capital employed in cultivation, together with the ordinary profits of farming in the neighborhood. The other half, or, what comes to the same thing, the value of the other half, he could afford to pay as rent to the landlord, if there were no tithe.

But if a tenth of his production is taken from him by the tithe, he will have to have his rent reduced by a fifth, otherwise he cannot get back his capital with the ordinary profit. In this case the rent of the landlord, instead of amounting to five-tenths of the whole produce, will amount only to four-tenths of it.

On poorer lands, on the contrary, production is sometimes

[3] M'Culloch thinks that A. S. should have made more distinction, in his discussion of land taxes, between the rent of the land itself and that part of the rental which is for building and improvements.

so small, and the expense of cultivation so great, that it requires
four-fifths of the crops to replace to the farmer his capital with the
ordinary profit. In this case, though there were no tithe, the rent
of the landlord could amount to no more than a fifth of the production. But if the farmer pays one-tenth of it on the tithe, the
rent of the landlord is likewise reduced to a tenth.

Thus upon a land tax like the tithe the rent of rich lands
may sometimes be a tax of no more than 20 per cent; whereas
upon that of poorer lands, it may sometimes be a tax of 50 per cent.

As I have mentioned in another place, the chief source of
state income in China and some other countries was a tax upon
the produce of land. Accordingly, the rulers of these countries are
said to give particular attention and care to roads and canals, in
order to enlarge the markets and increase production as much as
possible.

ℂ   In China, too, a part of the tax is said to be paid "in kind";
but this system is suitable only for very small districts, where the
collectors of the tax and disposal of the produce are under the immediate eye of the ruler. In a larger state, this form of tax would
be impracticable. The servants of the most careless private person
are, perhaps, more under the eye of their employer than those of
the most careful prince; and a public revenue, which was paid
in kind, would suffer so much from the mismanagement of the
collectors, that a very small part of the collection would ever
arrive at the treasury of the prince.

It is perhaps for this reason that the Chinese Mandarins
and other tax collectors find otheir advantage in continuing the
practice of a payment which is so much more liable to abuse than
any payment in money.

A tax upon farm produce which is levied in money may be
levied either according to the variations of the market price; or
according to a fixed valuation—a bushel of wheat, for example,
being always valued at the same money price, whatever may be
the state of the market.

The yield of a tax levied in the former way will vary only
according to the variations in the real produce of the land, according to the improvement or neglect of cultivation. The yield of a
tax levied in the latter way will vary, not only according to the
variations in the produce of the land, but also according to variations in the value of the precious metals, and variations in the

quantity of those metals which is at different times contained in the coinage.

The yield of the former will always bear the same proportion to the value of the real produce of the land. The yield of the latter may, at different times, bear very different proportions to that value.

CHAPTER X

*The previous chapter having covered taxes
on farm land and its products, this takes up
taxes on the rent of houses, as distinct from
farm property; and shows that the rent of
a house is really two rents—that on the
dwelling, and that on the ground on which
it stands; taxes on both are proper.*

THE RENT OF a house really is composed of two parts, of which
the one may very properly be called the building rent; the other
is commonly called the ground rent.

The building rent is the interest or profit of the capital
expended in building the house. In order to put the trade of a
builder upon an equal basis with other trades, this rent has to be
large enough to pay him, first, the same interest which he could
have gotten for his capital if he had lent it upon good security; and
second, to keep the house in constant repair, or, what comes to the
same thing, to replace, within a certain term of years, the capital
which had been employed in building it.

The building rent, or the ordinary profit of building, is,
therefore, everywhere regulated by the ordinary interest rate of
money.

Where the market rate of interest is 4 per cent, the rent of
a house which, over and above paying the ground rent, affords 6
or 6½ per cent upon the whole expense of building, may perhaps
afford a sufficient profit to the builder. Where the market rate
of interest is 5 per cent it may perhaps require 7 or 7½ per cent.

If, in proportion to the interest of money, the trade of the
builder affords a much greater profit than this, it will soon draw
so much capital from other trades as will reduce the profit to its

proper level. If it affords at any time much less than this, other trades will soon draw so much capital from it as will again raise that profit.

Whatever part of the whole rent of a house is over and above what is sufficient for affording this reasonable profit, naturally goes to the ground rent; and where the owner of the ground and the owner of the building are two different persons, the owner of the ground will receive all of it. This surplus rent is the price which the inhabitant of the house pays for some real or supposed advantage of the situation.

In country houses, at a distance from any large town, where there is plenty of ground, the ground rent is almost nothing, or no more than what the land which the house stands upon would pay if employed in agriculture.

In country villas in the neighborhood of some town or city, it is sometimes a good deal higher; and the peculiar convenience or beauty of situation is there frequently very well paid for.

Ground rents are generally highest in the capital, and in those particular parts of it where there happens to be the greatest demand for houses, whatever be the reason of that demand, whether for trade and business, for pleasure and society, or for mere vanity and fashion.

A tax upon house rent, payable by the tenant and proportioned to the whole rent of each house, could not, for any considerable time at least, affect the rent paid for the building. If the builder did not get his reasonable profit, he would be obliged to quit the trade; which, by raising the demand for building, would in a short time bring back his profit to its proper level with that of other trades. Neither would such a tax fall altogether upon the ground rent; but it would divide itself in such a manner as to fall, partly upon the occupant of the house, and partly upon the owner of the ground.

Let us suppose, for example, that a particular person judges that he can afford for house rent an expense of $600 a year; and let us suppose too that a tax of 20 per cent, payable by the inhabitant, is laid upon house rent. A house renting for $600 will in this case cost him $720 a year, which is more than he thinks he can afford.

He will, therefore, content himself with a worse house,

say one renting for $500, which, with the additional tax, will make up the $600 a year which he judges he can afford; and in order to pay the tax he will give up a part of the additional convenience which he might have had from the better house he wanted.

He will give up, I say, only a part of this additional convenience; for he will seldom be obliged to give up all of it, but will, in consequence of the tax, get a better house for $500 a year, than he could have gotten if there had been no tax.

For a tax of this kind, by taking away this particular competitor, must diminish the competition for houses of $600 rent, and in the same manner for those of all other rents, except the very lowest, for which it would for some time increase the competition. But the rents of every class of houses for which the competition was diminished, would necessarily be more or less reduced.

As no part of this reduction, however, could, for any considerable time at least, affect the building rent, the whole of it must in the long run necessarily fall upon the ground rent. The final payment of this tax, therefore, would fall, partly upon the tenant of the house, who, in order to pay his share, would be obliged to give up a part of his convenience; and partly upon the owner of the ground, who, in order to pay his share, would be obliged to give up a part of his income.

In what proportion this final payment would be divided between them, it is not perhaps very easy to ascertain. The division would probably be very different in different circumstances, and a tax of this kind might, according to those different circumstances, affect very unequally both the occupant of the house and the owner of the ground.

The inequality with which a tax of this kind might fall upon different owners of ground rents, would arise altogether from the accidental inequality of this division. But the inequality with which it might fall upon the occupants of different houses would arise, not only from this, but from another cause.

The proportion of the expense of house rent to the whole cost of living is different in different degrees of fortune. It is perhaps highest in the highest class, and it diminishes gradually through the inferior degrees, so as in general to be lowest in the lowest degree.

The poor spend most of their incomes on the necessaries of life. They find it difficult to get food, and most of their small revenue is spent in getting it. The luxuries and vanities of life occasion the principal expense of the rich; and a magnificent house embellishes and sets off to the best advantage all the other luxuries and vanities which they possess.

A tax upon house rents, therefore, would in general fall heaviest upon the rich; and in this particular inequality there would not, perhaps, be anything very injurious.

It is not very unreasonable that the rich should contribute to the public expense, not only in proportion to their incomes, but something more than that proportion.

The rent of houses, though it resembles in some respects the rent of land, is in one respect essentially different from it. The rent of land is paid for the use of a productive subject. The land which pays it produces it. The rent of houses is paid for the use of an unproductive subject. Neither the house nor the ground which it stands upon produce anything. The person who pays the rent, therefore, must draw it from some other source of revenue.[1]

A tax upon the rent of houses, so far as it falls upon the occupants, must be drawn from the same source as the rent itself, and must be paid from their income, whether derived from the wages of labor, the profits of capital, or the rent of land. So far as it falls upon the occupants, it is one of those taxes which fall, not upon one only, but indifferently upon all the three sources of revenue; and is in every respect of the same nature as a tax upon any other consumable commodity.

If the tax indeed were very high, most people would endeavor to evade it, as much as they could, by contenting themselves with smaller houses, and using their incomes for other expenses.

---

[1] Here that familiar bugaboo of A. S., "unproductive expenditure," once more raises its head; M'Culloch says, once more, that a dwelling house is most certainly productive, if only indirectly. The workman's food is not more necessary to his labor than is his dwelling. But of course these things are relative. Carver asks: to what extent is a house a necessity, to what extent a luxury? There are very few things that are wholly one or the other. Pride of possession is not income, but may frequently take its place.

⟨ The discussion of taxes on ground rents, which follows, is of little importance in modern times, and may be briefly summarized thus:

⟨ Ground rent is a subject for taxation still more proper than the rent of buildings, as such a tax does not in any way reduce the production and incomes of the great body of the population. It falls entirely on the income of the landlord. A tax on ground rent is even more proper than a tax on ordinary land rent.

⟨ Such a tax is, however, almost unknown. In England what was called the annual land tax was assessed on land and building rents together; and this tax, being at a fixed rate on all districts, was unequal to start with, and became still more unequal as time went on.

The contrivers of the various taxes which in England were, at different times, imposed upon houses, seem to have imagined that there was some great difficulty in ascertaining, with tolerable exactness, what was the real rent of every house. They regulated their taxes, therefore, according to some more obvious circumstance, such as they probably imagined would, in most cases, bear some reasonable proportion to the rent.

The first tax of this kind was "hearth-money"—or a tax of two shillings upon every hearth. In order to ascertain how many hearths were in the house, the tax collector had to enter every room in it. This odious visit rendered the tax odious. Soon after the revolution of 1688, therefore, it was abolished as a badge of slavery.

The next attempt was a tax of two shillings upon every inhabited dwelling house; a house with ten windows to pay four shillings more, and a house with twenty windows and upwards to pay eight shillings. The number of windows can, in most cases, be counted from the outside, and, in all cases, without entering every room in the house. The visit of the tax collector, therefore, was less offensive than in the case of hearth-money.

This tax was later repealed, and replaced by a direct tax on windows, which was altered several times, but survived a long time.

The principal objection to all such taxes is their inequality, an inequality of the worst kind, as they must frequently fall much heavier upon the poor than upon the rich. Such taxes are, therefore, directly contrary to the first of the four principles of sound taxation. They do not seem to offend much against any of the other three.

The natural tendency of the window tax, and of all other taxes upon houses, is to lower rents. The more a man pays for the tax, the less, it is evident, he can afford to pay for the rent. But where there has been a continual increase in the demand for houses, that demand has raised rents more than the taxes could sink them; were it not for the tax, rents would probably have risen still higher.

CHAPTER XI

*Taxes on the profit of capital have to fall
on that part of the profit which represents
interest, not the earnings of the entrepreneur; or, in the case of agriculture, on the
land-owner's rent; but the interest of money
can never be taxed equitably or with certainty.*

THE REVENUE OR profit arising from capital naturally divides
itself into two parts—that which pays the interest, which belongs
to whoever owns the capital; and anything that remains after
paying the interest.

This latter part of profit is evidently a subject not taxable
directly. It is the compensation, and in most cases it is no more
than a very moderate compensation, for the risk and trouble of
employing the capital. The entrepreneur must have this compensation, otherwise he cannot, in his own interest, continue the
business. If he were taxed directly, therefore, in proportion to
his whole profit, he would be obliged either to raise the rate of
his profit, or to shift the tax upon the interest of money; that is,
to pay less interest.

But if he raised the rate of profit in proportion to the tax,
the whole tax, though it might be advanced by him, would be
finally paid by one or the other of two different sets of people,
according to the different ways in which his capital is employed.

If he employed it in the cultivation of land, he could raise
the rate of profit only be retaining a larger part, or, what comes
to the same thing, the price of a larger part of the produce of the
land; and as this could be done only by a reduction of rent, the
final payment of the tax would fall upon the landlord.

[*310*]

If he employed it as a mercantile or manufacturing capital, he could raise the rate of his profit only by raising the price of his goods; in which case the final payment of the tax would fall altogether upon the consumers of those goods.

On the other hand, if he did not or could not raise the rate of his profit, he would be obliged to charge the whole tax upon that part of it which was allotted for the interest of money. He could afford to pay less interest for whatever capital he borrowed, and the whole weight of the tax would in this case fall ultimately upon the interest of money. So far as he could not relieve himself from the tax in the one way, he would be obliged to relieve himself in the other.

The interest of money seems at first sight a subject equally capable of being taxed directly as the rent of land. Like the rent of land, it is a net margin which remains after completely covering the whole risk and trouble of employing the capital. As a tax upon the rent of land cannot raise rents, so, for the same reason, a tax upon the interest of money could not raise the rate of interest.

The ordinary rate of profit is everywhere regulated by the quantity of capital to be employed, in proportion to the quantity of the employment, or of the business which must be done by it. But the quantity of the employment, or of the business to be done, could neither be increased nor diminished by any tax upon the interest of money.

If the quantity of the capital to be employed, therefore, was neither increased nor decreased by it, the ordinary rate of profit would necessarily remain the same. But the portion of this profit necessary for repaying the risk and trouble of the entrepreneur would likewise remain the same; that risk and trouble being in no respect altered. The residue, therefore—that portion which belongs to the owner of the capital, and which pays the interest of money, would necessarily remain the same too.

At first sight, therefore, the interest of money seems to be a subject as fit to be taxed directly as the rent of land. There are, however, two reasons why this is not true.

First, the quantity and value of a piece of land can never be a secret, and can always be ascertained with great exactness. But the whole amount of the capital which a man possesses is almost always a secret, and can scarcely ever be ascertained with tolerable exactness. It is liable, besides, to almost continual variations. A year seldom passes away, frequently not a month, sometimes scarcely a single day, in which it does not rise or fall more or less.

An inquisition into every man's private circumstances, and an inquisition which, in order to adjust the tax to them, watched over all the fluctuations of his fortune, would be a source of such continual and endless vexation as no people would endure.

Secondly, land is a subject which cannot be removed, whereas capital can be, very easily. The owner of capital is necessarily a citizen of the world, and is not necessarily attached to any particular country. He could and would abandon the country in which he was exposed to a vexatious inquisition, in order to be subjected to a burdensome tax, and would remove his capital to some other country where he could carry on his business, or enjoy his fortune, more at his ease.

By removing his capital he would put an end to all the industry which it had maintained in the country which he left. Capital cultivates land; capital employs labor. A tax which tended to drive away capital from any particular country, would so far tend to dry up every source of revenue, both to the government and to the society. Not only the profits of capital, but the rent of land and the wages of labor, would necessarily be more or less diminished by its loss.

Those nations, accordingly, which have attempted to tax the revenue arising from capital, instead of any severe inquisition of this kind, have been obliged to content themselves with some very loose, and, therefore, more or less arbitrary estimate. The extreme inequality and uncertainty of a tax assessed in this manner, can be compensated only by its extreme moderation, in consequence of which every man finds himself assessed so far below his real revenue, that he gives himself little concern even though his neighbor should be assessed somewhat lower. This is the system formerly used in England, by which capital was taxed under the so-called land tax, but at a low rate.

In all countries a severe inquisition into the circumstances of private persons has been carefully avoided.

In some small countries the inhabitants formerly assessed themselves, on oath, as at Hamburg and in some Swiss countries, but this is a plan suited only to a very small republic.

In Holland, in the 18th Century, a tax of 2 per cent was imposed upon the whole property of every citizen. Every citizen assessed himself, and paid his tax in the same manner as at Hamburg; and it was in general supposed to have been paid with great fidelity.

But that was at a time when the people had the greatest affection for their new government, which they had just established by a general insurrection. The tax was to be paid but once, in order to relieve the state in a particular emergency.

It was, indeed, too heavy to be permanent. In a country where the market rate of interest seldom exceeds 3 per cent, a tax of 2 per cent amounts to more than half of the highest net revenue which is commonly drawn from capital. It is a tax which very few people could pay without encroaching more or less upon their capital.

At a time of crisis the people may, from great public zeal, make a great effort, and give up even a part of their capital, in order to relieve the state. But it is impossible that they should continue to do so for any considerable time; and if they did, the tax would soon ruin them so completely as to make them incapable of supporting the state at all.

CHAPTER XII

Taxes on the profits of capital, however laid, are never paid by the entrepreneur, but in the case of agriculture are actually paid by the land-owner, and in all other cases by the consumer of the goods and services; taxes on farm equipment, etc., are particularly unwise; the poll tax a badge of liberty.

IN SOME COUNTRIES special taxes are imposed upon the profits of capital; sometimes when employed in particuar branches of trade, and sometimes when employed in agriculture.

Of the former kind are taxes upon peddlers, on vehicles for hire, and the fees for liquor-dispensing licenses.

But a tax upon the profits of capital employed in any particular branch of trade can never fall finally upon the dealers (who must in all ordinary cases have their reasonable profit, and, where the competition is free, can seldom have more than that profit), but always upon the consumers, who are obliged to pay in the price of the goods the tax which the dealer advances; and generally with some overcharge.

A tax of this kind, when proportioned to the trade of the dealer, is finally paid by the consumer, and is not oppressive to the dealer. When it is not so proportioned, but is the same upon all dealers, though in this case too it is finally paid by the consumer, yet it favors the large business and oppresses the small one.

Thus a tax upon each taxicab, as far as it is advanced by the owners, is proportioned closely enough to the extent of their respective dealings. It neither favors the great, nor oppresses the smaller operator. But a uniform tax or fee for selling liquor, being the same upon all retailers, must necessarily give some advantage to the great, and occasion some oppression to the small dealers. The former must find it more easy to get back the tax in the price of their goods than the latter.

If the license fee is small, however, this inequality is of less importance, and it may appear, to many people, not improper to give some discouragement to the multiplication of small taverns and saloons.

What in France was called the personal taille was, perhaps, the most important tax upon the profits of capital employed in agriculture.

In the disorderly state of Europe under the feudal system, the sovereign was obliged to content himself with taxing those who were too weak to refuse to pay taxes. The great lords, though willing to assist him upon particular emergencies, refused to subject themselves to any constant tax, and he was not strong enough to compel it.

The occupants of the land were, for the most part, bondsmen. As they were gradually emancipated, some of them acquired the property of landed estates, which they held by some base or ignoble tenure, sometimes under the king, and sometimes under some other great lord, like the ancient copyholders of England. Others, without acquiring the property, obtained long-term leases of the lands which they occupied under their lord, and thus became less dependent upon him.

The great lords seem to have beheld with a malignant and contemptuous indignation, what prosperity and independency this inferior order of men had thus come to enjoy, and willingly consented that the sovereign should tax them.

In some countries this tax was confined to the lands which were held in property by an ignoble tenure; and, in this case, the taille was said to be "real." In other countries, the tax was laid upon the supposed profits of all those who operated lands belonging to other people, whatever might be the tenure by which they were held; and in this case the taille was said to be "personal."

The real taille, as it was imposed only upon a part of the lands of the country, was necessarily an unequal tax, but not always an arbitrary one, though it was so upon some occasions.[1] The

[1] The French taille was one of the shocking injustices which were swept away by the French Revolution. I omit a long paragraph explaining the very unjust and oppressive manner in which it was administered.

personal taille, as it was intended to be proportioned to the profits of a certain class of people, which could only be guessed at, was necessarily both arbitrary and unequal.

When a tax is imposed upon the profits of capital in a particular branch of trade, the traders are all careful to bring no more goods to market than what they can sell at a price sufficient to reimburse them for advancing the tax. Some of them withdraw a part of their capital from the trade, and the market is more sparingly supplied than before. The price of the goods rises, and the final payment of the tax necessarily falls upon the consumer.

But when a tax is imposed upon the profits of capital employed in agriculture, it is not to the interest of the farmers to withdraw any part of their capital from that employment. Each farmer occupies a certain quantity of land, for which he pays rent. For the proper cultivation of this land a certain quantity of capital is necessary; and by withdrawing any part of this the farmer is not likely to be more able to pay either the rent or the tax.

In order to pay the tax, it can never be his interest to diminish the quantity of his produce, nor consequently to supply the market more sparingly than before.[2] The tax, therefore, will never enable him to raise the price of his produce, so as to reimburse himself by throwing the final payment upon the consumer.

The farmer, however, must have his reasonable profit like any other entrepreneur, otherwise he must give up the trade. After the imposition of a tax of this kind, he can get this reasonable profit only by paying less rent to the landlord. The more he is obliged to pay in the way of tax, the less he can afford to pay in rent. A tax of this kind imposed during the currency of a lease may, no doubt, distress or ruin the farmer. Upon the renewal of the lease it must always fall upon the landlord.[3]

[2] A. S. here skirts the edges of the basic distinction between the producers of raw materials, of which agriculture is the largest, and the manufacturers and merchants. Where the prices of agricultural products fall, or what is the same thing, are made less remunerative by a tax, the result is not immediately to reduce the supply coming to market, but for a time, at least, to increase it, and so bring about a further fall in prices.

[3] In this passage A. S. shows a trace of the influence of the French Physiocrats, whom we shall meet in the last chapter of Book V. They held that, as every tax was ultimately shifted onto the owners of land, it would be far better to collect them directly from land-owners in the first place, in the form of the "impôt unique"—the single tax.

In the countries where a tax is imposed on the supposed profit of agriculture, the farmer is commonly assessed in proportion to the capital which he appears to employ. He is, therefore, frequently afraid to have a good team of horses or oxen, but endeavors to operate with the meanest and most wretched implements that he can. Such is his distrust of the justice of his assessors, that he counterfeits poverty, and wishes to appear scarcely able to pay anything, for fear of being obliged to pay too much.

By this miserable policy he is, indeed, often worse off, for he probably loses more by his reduced production than the amount of the tax. By his smaller production, the consumer is ill-supplied, and the landlord receives less rent. No part of the population fails to suffer more or less by this unwise tax.

Taxes of so much a head upon the bondsmen employed in cultivation seem, in ancient times, to have been common all over Europe. It is probably upon this account that poll taxes of all kinds have often been represented as badges of slavery. Every tax, however, is to the person who pays it a badge, not of slavery, but of liberty. It denotes that he is subject to government, indeed, but that, as he has some property, he cannot himself be the property of a master. But of course this does not apply to a poll tax upon slaves.

Taxes upon the profits of capital in particular employments can never affect the interest of money. Nobody will lend his money for less interest to those who are in a business that is taxed, than to those who are not subject to it.

But taxes upon the revenue arising from capital in all employments, where the government attempts to levy them with any degree of exactness, will, in many cases, fall upon the interest of money.[4]

[4] One wonders what A. S. would have said of the modern corporation income or profits tax. Here is a case where an enormous amount of money is collected impartially from the wages of labor, the profit of capital, and the rent of land, not a cent coming from the corporation itself, which merely advances the tax and collects it later, principally from its customers. It is doubtful if any of it comes directly from the corporation's employes and stockholders, over any considerable period. Practically all is charged into the cost of goods and paid by consumers, provided of course the product is something for which there is an effective demand.

The sole advantage of the corporation profits tax appears to be the cheapness and certainty of collection. Even this is dubious, since the complexity of corporation accounting makes difficult a clear agreement on the amount of tax payable; and as a matter of experience the tax collected from any large corporation is generally arrived at by a process of controversy and compromise.

The general public seems entirely ignorant of these basic principles of taxation. Perhaps some improvement might be obtained if it were constantly emphasized that all taxes are borne by individuals; that a so-called "tax" is not a tax unless it comes out of some individual's pocket, and to that extent reduces his other expenditures or standard of living; that any agency that advances money to the government and reimburses itself from others is not a taxpayer but a tax collector.

Obviously, if every real tax must come out of somebody's standard of living, a corporation, having not only no soul but no standard of living, does not and cannot "pay" any tax; it can only collect it from those who have both.

CHAPTER XIII

Direct taxes on capital are rare, but taxes on the transfer of capital in the form of property are very common; such taxes generally fall on the purchaser as a part of the price, but in the case of land, and old houses, on the seller; but most such taxes are unequal, and all more or less injurious.

WHILE PROPERTY REMAINS in the possession of the same person, whatever permanent taxes may have been imposed upon it, they have never been intended to diminish or take away any part of its capital value, but only some part of the revenue arising from it.[1]

But when property changes hands, when it is transmitted either from the dead to the living, or from the living to the living, such taxes have frequently been imposed upon it as necessarily take away some part of its capital value.

The transfer of all sorts of property from the dead to the living, and that of immovable property, of lands and houses, from the living to the living, are transactions which are in their nature either public and notorious, or such as cannot be long concealed. Such transactions, therefore, may be taxed directly.

The transfer of capital or movable property, from the

[1] "Capital levies" have been proposed from time to time, and still are. One instance in Holland was touched upon in a previous chapter. But none has ever been imposed, at least on a universal basis, partly because the theory is offensive to justice, but more particularly because the project could not be carried out. Such a levy could not be paid in money; a violent fall in the prices of all capital goods and property would prevent sales; and if government seized property itself, it could not readily dispose of it except perhaps to foreigners. Yet such proposals are heard not infrequently.

living to the living, by the lending of money, is frequently a secret transaction, and may always be made so. Thus it cannot easily be taxed directly. It has been taxed indirectly in two different ways: first, by requiring that the deed, containing the obligation to repay, should be written upon paper or parchment which had paid a certain stamp duty, otherwise not to be valid; secondly, by requiring, under the like penalty, that it should be recorded in a public or secret register, and by imposing certain costs upon such registration.

Stamp duties and registration fees have frequently been imposed likewise upon the deeds transferring property of all kinds from the dead to the living, and upon those transferring immovable property from the living to the living, transactions which might easily have been taxed directly.

Of the same kind was the Dutch tax upon successions. Collateral successions were taxed, according to the degree of relation, from 5 to 30 per cent upon the whole value of the succession. Testamentary donations, or legacies to collaterals, were subject to the same taxes. Those from husband to wife, or from wife to husband, at 7½ per cent to the fifteenth penny. Direct successions, or those of descendants to ascendants, paid no tax.

The death of a father, to such of his children as live in the same house with him, is seldom attended with any increase, and frequently with a considerable loss of income; by the loss of his industry, or his position, or of some life rent estate, of which he may have been in possession. That tax would be cruel and oppressive which aggravated their loss by taking from them any part of his estate.

It may, however, sometimes be otherwise with those children who, in the language of the Roman law, are said to be emancipated (what the Scots call "foris-familiated"); that is, who have received their portion, have got families of their own, and are supported by funds separate and independent of those of their father. Whatever part of his estate might come to such children would be a real addition to their fortune, and might therefore, perhaps, without more inconvenience than belongs to all duties of this kind, be liable to some tax.

Taxation by stamp duties and by fees upon registration are of very modern invention. In the course of little more than a century, however, stamp duties have, in Europe, become almost universal, and registry fees extremely common.

There is no art which one government sooner learns of another, than that of draining money from the pockets of the people.

Taxes upon the transfer of property from the dead to the living, fall finally as well as immediately upon the person to whom the property is transferred. Taxes upon the sale of land fall altogether upon the seller. The seller is almost always under the necessity of selling, and must, therefore, take such a price as he can get. The buyer is scarcely ever under the necessity of buying, and will, therefore, only give such a price as he likes. He considers what the property will cost him in tax and price together. The more he is obliged to pay in the way of tax, the smaller the price he will be disposed to give. Such taxes, therefore, fall almost always upon a necessitous person, and must, therefore, be frequently very cruel and oppressive.

Taxes upon the sale of newly-built houses, where the building is sold without the ground, fall generally upon the buyer, because the builder must generally have his profit; otherwise he could not stay in the business. If he advances the tax, therefore, the buyer must generally repay it to him.

Taxes upon the sale of old houses, for the same reason as those upon the sale of land, fall generally upon the seller, who in most cases is under some necessity to sell. The number of old houses which happen at any time to come on the market is regulated by accidents, of which the greater part have no relation to the demand. Two or three great bankruptcies in a mercantile town will bring on the market many houses which must be sold for what they will bring.

Taxes upon the sale of ground rents fall altogether upon the seller; for the same reason as those upon the sale of land. Stamp duties, and fees for the registration of bonds and contracts for borrowed money, fall altogether upon the borrower, and, in fact, are always paid by him. Charges of the same kind upon law proceedings fall upon the suitors. They reduce to both the capital value of the subject in dispute.

All taxes upon the transfer of property of every kind, so far as they reduce the capital value of that property, tend to diminish the funds available for the maintenance of productive labor. Every tax that increases the revenue of the government, which seldom maintains any but unproductive laborers, at the expense of the capital of the people, which maintains none but productive, must be to some extent injurious.[2]

Such taxes, even when they are proportioned to the value of the property transferred, are still unequal; the frequency of transfer not being always equal, in property of equal value. When they are not proportioned to this value, which is the case with most of the stamp duties, and registration fees, they are still more so. They are in no respect arbitrary, but are or may be in all cases perfectly clear and certain. Though they sometimes fall upon a person who is not very able to pay, the time of payment is in most cases sufficiently convenient for him. When the payment becomes due, he must in most cases have the money available. They are levied at very little expense, and in general subject the contributors to no other inconvenience besides always the unavoidable one of paying any tax.

The recording of mortgages, and in general of all rights upon immovable property, as it gives great security both to creditors and purchasers, is extremely advantageous to the public. That of most deeds of other kinds is frequently inconvenient and even dangerous to individuals, without any advantage to the public.

No secret registers should be permitted, for the credit of individuals ought certainly never to depend upon so very slender a security as the probity and religion of a minor clerk in a registry office.

Such stamp taxes as those upon cards and dice, upon cigarettes and tobacco, etc., are properly taxes upon consumption; the final payment falls upon the persons who use or consume such commodities. License fees upon liquor wholesalers and retailers, though intended, perhaps, to fall upon the profits of the merchants, are likewise finally paid by the consumers of those liquors.

[2] Indeed, it may be said that every tax is injurious, unless every taxpayer receives some direct benefit equal to the amount of the tax; but A. S.'s old false distinction between "productive" and "unproductive" labor is not the real reason.

CHAPTER XIV

*Taxes upon wages are common; they are,
in general, actually paid by the consumers
of goods or out of the rent of land; but taxes
upon larger salaries may fall upon the taxpayer himself.*

THE WAGES OF common workmen, I have endeavored to show in
the first book, are everywhere necessarily regulated by two factors: the demand for labor, and the ordinary or average price of
food.

The demand for labor, according as it happens to be either
increasing, stationary, or declining, or to require an increasing, stationary, or declining population, regulates the subsistence of the
laborer, and determines in what degree it shall be liberal, moderate, or scanty.

The ordinary or average price of provisions determines the
quantity of money which must be paid to the workman in order
to enable him, one year with another, to purchase this liberal,
moderate, or scanty subsistence.

As long as the demand for labor and the price of provisions
remain the same, therefore, a direct tax upon wages can have no
other effect than to raise them by an amount somewhat greater
than the tax.[1] Let us suppose, for example, that in a particular
place the demand for labor and the price of provisions were such as
to render $40 a week the average wage; and that a tax of 20 per cent
was imposed upon wages. If the demand for labor and the price of
provisions remained the same, it would still be necessary that the
workman should in that place earn such a subsistence as could be

[1] The personal income tax in the United States plays so large a part in the
tax scheme, that this analysis of its effect on wages deserves to be read with particular
care.

bought only for $40 a week, or that after paying the tax he should still have this amount clear.

But in order to leave him such free wages after paying such a tax, the price of labor must in that place soon rise, not to $48 a week only, but to $50. In other words, to enable him to pay a tax of one-fifth, his wages must necessarily rise, not one-fifth only, but one-fourth. Whatever was the proportion of the tax, the wages of labor must in all cases rise, not only in that proportion, but in a higher proportion. If the taxes were one-tenth, wages must necessarily soon rise, not one-tenth part only, but one-eighth.[2]

A direct tax upon wages, therefore, though the workman might perhaps pay it out of his hand, could not properly be said even to be advanced by him; at least not if the demand for labor and the average price of provisions remained the same after the tax as before. In all such cases, not only the tax, but something more than the tax, would in reality be advanced by the employer.

The final payment would in different cases fall upon different persons. The rise which such a tax might occasion in the wages of manufacturing labor would be advanced by the manufacturer, who would not only be entitled but obliged to charge it, with a profit, upon the price of his goods. The final payment of this rise of wages, therefore, together with the additional profit of the manufacturer, would fall upon the consumer.

The rise which such a tax might occasion in the wages of farm labor would be advanced by the farmer, who, in order to maintain the same number of hired men as before, would be obliged to employ a greater capital. In order to get back this greater investment, together with the ordinary profits of capital, it would be necessary that he should retain a larger portion, or what comes to the same thing, the price of a larger portion, of the produce of the land, and consequently that he should pay less rent to the landlord.

The final payment of this rise in wages, therefore, would in this case fall upon the landlord, together with the additional profit of the farmer who had advanced it.

In all cases a direct tax upon the wages of labor must, in

[2] Whether taxes on wages would operate in just this way would depend on whether the wage rate was at the lowest or bare subsistence level. If it were higher, the workman would certainly bear at least a part of it. Our "Social Security" tax is surely borne partly by the workers, in most cases.

the long run, cause both a greater reduction in the rent of land, and a greater rise in the price of manufactured goods, than would have followed from the direct levy of a sum equal to the produce of the wage tax, partly upon the rent of land, and partly upon consumable commodities.

If direct taxes upon the wages of labor have not always occasioned a proportionate rise in those wages, it is because they have generally caused a considerable fall in the demand for labor. The decline of industry, the decrease of employment, a falling-off in the annual produce of the land and labor of the country, have generally been the effects of such taxes. In consequence of them, however, the price of labor must always be higher than it otherwise would have been in the actual state of the demand; and this enhancement of price, together with the profit of those who advance it, must always be finally paid by the landlords and the consumers.

Absurd and destructive as such taxes are, however, they are found in many countries. In France that part of the taille which was charged upon the industry of workmen and day-laborers in country villages, was properly a tax of this kind.

The recompense of ingenious artists and of men of liberal professions, I have endeavored to show in the first book, necessarily maintains a certain proportion to the emoluments of inferior trades. A tax upon this recompense, therefore, could have no other effect than to raise it somewhat higher than in proportion to the tax. If it did not rise in this manner, the ingenious arts and the liberal professions, being no longer upon a level with other trades, would be so much deserted that they would soon return to that level.

The emoluments of government officials, national and local, are not, like those of trades and professions, regulated by the free competition of the market, and do not, therefore, always bear a just proportion to what the nature of the employment requires.

They are, perhaps, in most countries, higher than necessary; the persons who have the administration of government being generally disposed to reward both themselves and their immediate dependents rather more than enough. The emoluments of officials, therefore, can in most cases very well bear to be taxed.

Those persons, besides, who enjoy public offices, especially the more lucrative, are in all countries the objects of general envy; and a tax upon their emoluments, even though it should be somewhat higher than upon any other sort of revenue, is always a very popular tax.

In England, for example, when by the land tax every other sort of revenue was supposed to be assessed at four shillings in the pound, it was very popular to lay a real tax of five shillings and sixpence upon the salaries of officials which exceeded a hundred pounds a year; the pensions of the younger branches of the royal family, the pay of the officers of the army and navy, and a few others less obnoxious to envy excepted.

CHAPTER XV

Poll taxes are arbitrary and unequal, and a
"capitation" tax based on the supposed
wealth of the taxpayer even more so, and
very difficult to collect; governments do not
(in 1776) know how to tax income, hence
they often turn to taxes on commodities,
which have varying effects, depending on
whether the commodities are necessaries or
luxuries.

THE TAXES WHICH, it is intended, should fall indifferently upon every kind of income are capitation taxes, or taxes on persons, and taxes upon consumable commodities. These must be paid indifferently from whatever income the taxpayer may possess; from the rent of his land, from the profits of his capital, or from the wages of his labor.

If it is attempted to proportion a capitation tax to the estimated fortune or income of each contributor, it becomes altogether arbitrary. The state of a man's fortune varies from day to day, and without an inquisition more intolerable than any tax, and renewed at least once every year, can only be guessed at. His assessment, therefore, must in most cases depend upon the good or bad humor of the assessors, and must, therefore, be altogether arbitrary and uncertain.[1]

If such a tax is proportioned not to the supposed wealth or income, but to the rank or occupation of each contributor, it becomes altogether unequal.

[1] This is very nearly the case with the personal income tax; except where the tax is large enough to justify a Treasury audit (and sometimes even then) the tax actually paid is often arbitrary and uncertain.

If it is attempted to make it equal, it becomes altogether arbitrary and uncertain; and if it is attempted to make it certain and not arbitrary, it becomes altogether unequal. Let the tax be light or heavy, uncertainty is always a great grievance. In a light tax a considerable degree of inequality may be endured; in a heavy one it is altogether intolerable.

In England the different poll taxes imposed from time to time never produced the sum which had been expected from them, or which, it was supposed, they might have produced, had they been exactly levied. The mild government of England contented itself with whatever the tax happened to produce, and required no compensation for the loss which the state might sustain either by those who could not pay, or by those who would not pay (for there were many such), and who, by the indulgent execution of the law, were not forced to pay.

Capitation taxes, so far as they are levied upon the common people, are direct taxes upon the wages of labor, and are attended with all the inconveniences of such taxes.

They are, however, levied at little expense; and, where they are rigorously exacted, afford a very sure revenue to the state. It is upon this account that in countries where the ease, comfort, and security of the people are of little or no consequence, capitation taxes are very common.

In general, however, but a small part of the public revenue in any great empire has ever been drawn from such taxes; and the greatest sum which they have ever yielded might always have been found in some other way much more convenient to the people.[2]

The impossibility of taxing people in proportion to their incomes by any capitation, seems to have suggested as an alternative taxes upon consumable commodities. The state not knowing how to tax directly and in proportion the revenue of its subjects,[3] endeavors to tax it indirectly by taxing their expense, which, it is supposed, will in most cases be nearly in proportion to incomes. This expense is taxed by taxing the consumable commodities upon which it is laid out.

[2] A. S. thus ranges himself on the side of those who prefer excise taxes, which he next proceeds to consider.

[3] The state of 1776 certainly showed remarkably little ingenuity; the state of 1947 knows very well how, and makes the fullest use of its knowledge.

Consumable commodities are either necessaries or luxuries.

By necessaries I mean not only the commodities which are indispensably necessary for the support of life, but whatever the custom of the country renders it indecent for people, even of the lowest order, to be without. A linen shirt, for example, is, strictly speaking, not a necessary of life. The Greeks and Romans lived, I suppose, very comfortably, though they had no linen.

But in the present times, a respectable day laborer would be ashamed to appear in public without a linen shirt, the want of which would be taken to indicate such a disgraceful degree of poverty, as, it is presumed, nobody can well fall into without extreme bad conduct.

Custom, in the same manner, has rendered leather shoes a necessary of life in England. The poorest respectable person of either sex would be ashamed to appear in public without them. In Scotland, custom has rendered them a necessary of life to the poorest of men; but not to the same order of women, who may, without any discredit, walk about barefoot. In France, they are necessaries neither to men nor to women; the lowest classes of both sexes appearing there publicly, without any discredit, sometimes in wooden shoes, and sometimes without any.

Under necessaries, therefore, I include not only those things which nature requires, but those things which the established rules of decency have rendered necessary to people. All other things I call luxuries; without meaning by this term to throw the smallest degree of reproach upon the temperate use of them.

Beer and ale, for example, in Great Britain, and wine, even in the wine countries, I call luxuries. A man of any rank may, without any reproach, abstain totally from tasting such liquors. Nature does not render them necessary for the support of life; and custom nowhere renders it indecent to live without them.

As remarked above, since the wages of labor are everywhere regulated, partly by the demand for it, and partly by the average price of the necessary articles of subsistence, whatever raises this average price must necessarily raise those wages, so that the workman may still be able to purchase those necessary articles which the state of the demand for labor, whether increasing, stationary, or declining, requires that he should have.

A tax upon those articles necessarily raises their price by somewhat more than the amount of the tax, because the dealer who advances the tax must generally get it back with a profit. Such a tax must, therefore, cause a rise in the wages of labor proportionable to the rise of price.

It is thus that a tax upon the necessaries of life operates exactly the same as a direct tax upon the wages of labor. The workman, though he may pay it out of his hand, cannot, for any considerable time at least, be properly said even to advance it. It must always in the long run be made good to him by his employer in the advanced rate of his wages.

If that employer is a manufacturer, he will add into the price of his goods this rise of wages, together with a profit; so that the final payment of the tax, together with this overcharge, will fall upon the consumer. If the employer is a farmer, the final payment, together with a like overcharge, will fall upon the rent of the landlord.

It is otherwise with taxes upon what I call luxuries; the rise in their prices will not necessarily cause any rise in the wages of labor. A tax upon tobacco, for example, though a luxury of the poor as well as of the rich, will not raise wages. The same thing may be said of the taxes upon tea and sugar, which in England and Holland have become luxuries of the poorest people; and of those upon chocolate, which in Spain is said to have become so.

The different taxes which in Great Britain were in the course of the century imposed upon spirituous liquors, do not appear to have had any effect upon the wages of labor.

The high price of such luxuries does not necessarily diminish the ability of working people to bring up families. Upon the sober and industrious poor, taxes upon such commodities act like sumptuary laws, inducing them to moderate or to refrain altogether from the use of superfluities which they can no longer easily afford.

Their ability to bring up families, in consequence of this forced frugality, instead of being reduced, is frequently, perhaps, increased by the tax. It is the sober and industrious poor who generally bring up the most numerous families, and who principally supply the demand for useful labor.

Not all the poor are indeed sober and industrious, and the dissolute and disorderly might continue to indulge themselves in the use of such commodities after this rise of price in the same manner as before, without regarding the distress which this indulgence might bring upon their families. Such disorderly persons, however, seldom bring up numerous families, their children generally perishing from neglect, mismanagement, and the scantiness or unwholesomeness of their diet. If by the strength of their constitutions they survive the hardships to which the bad conduct of their parents exposes them, yet the example of that bad conduct commonly corrupts their morals; so that, instead of being useful to society by their industry, they become public nuisances by their vices.

Though the advanced price of the luxuries of the poor, therefore, might increase somewhat the distress of such disorderly families, and thereby diminish somewhat their ability to bring up children, it would probably not diminish the useful population of the country.

Any rise in the average price of necessaries, however, unless it is compensated by a proportionate rise in the wages of labor, must necessarily diminish more or less the ability of the poor to bring up numerous families, and consequently to supply the demand for useful labor.

Taxes upon luxuries, on the other hand, have no tendency to raise the price of any commodities except those taxed. Taxes upon necessaries, by raising the wages of labor, necessarily tend to raise the price of all manufactures, and consequently to diminish the extent of their sale and consumption.[4] Taxes upon luxuries are finally paid by the consumers of the commodities taxed, without any recourse. They fall indifferently upon every kind of income.

Taxes upon necessaries, so far as they affect the poor, are finally paid, partly by landlords in the diminished rent of their lands, and partly by rich consumers, whether landlords or others, in the advanced price of manufactured goods; and always with a considerable overcharge.

The advanced price of such manufactures as are themselves real necessaries of life, destined for the consumption of the poor, must be compensated to the poor by a farther increase of their wages. The middle and upper classes of people, if they understood their own interest, ought always to oppose all taxes upon the necessaries of life, as well as all direct taxes upon the

[4] M'Culloch disputes this.

wages of labor, the final payment of both falling altogether upon themselves, and always with a considerable overcharge.

They fall heaviest upon the landlords, who always pay in a double capacity as landlords, by the reduction of their rent; and as rich consumers, by the increase of their expense. The observation of Sir Matthew Decker, that certain taxes are, in the price of certain goods, sometimes pyramided four or five times, is perfectly just with regard to taxes upon the necessaries of life.

Such sales or excise taxes, though they raise the cost of living, and consequently the wages of labor, yet they do yield a considerable revenue to government, which it might not be easy to find in any other way. There may, therefore, be good reasons for continuing them.

Consumable commodities, whether necessaries or luxuries, may be taxed in two different ways. The consumer may either pay an annual sum on account of his using or consuming goods of a certain kind; or the goods may be taxed while they remain in the hands of the dealer, and before they are delivered to the consumer.[5]

Consumable goods which last a considerable time before they are consumed altogether, are most properly taxed in the one way. Those of which the consumption is either immediate or more speedy, in the other. The coach tax and plate tax are examples of the former method; excise taxes and customs, of the latter.

It was the well-known proposal of Sir Matthew Decker, that all commodities, even those of which the consumption is either immediate or very speedy, should be taxed under a kind of license system; the dealer advancing nothing, but the consumer paying a certain annual sum for the license to consume certain goods. The object of his scheme was to promote all foreign trade, particularly the carrying trade, by taking away all tariff duties upon im-

---

[5] The despised wartime "use tax" on automobiles is an example of the former; the cigarette excise tax of the latter. A. S. does not seem to have heard or thought of the simple tax on retail sales at the time of sale, to which so many of our states and municipalities are turning.

A very persuasive case can be made for basing the tax system principally on the personal income tax and the retail sales tax. The first is borne by individuals, and hence does not directly enter into the cost of goods and services. The second, where it is collected separately at the time of sale of goods, likewise does not directly tend to raise their cost. Since nearly all taxes are borne ultimately by the same individuals, there seems no reason why they should not be directly collected, except the additional difficulty and expense of collection.

portation and exportation, and thereby enabling the merchant to employ his whole capital and credit in the purchase of goods and the freight of ships, no part of either being diverted towards the advancing of taxes.

C   A. S. goes on to analyze this scheme, and to point out the four obvious objections to it. As such a plan has never been tried, at least on any important scale, it need not detain us.

Excise duties or taxes are imposed chiefly upon goods of home production intended for home consumption. They are imposed only upon a few kinds of goods of the most general use. There can never be any doubt either concerning the goods which are subject to them, or concerning the particular tax which each species of goods is subject to. They fall almost altogether upon what I call luxuries, including liquor and tobacco.

CHAPTER XVI

Customs duties on imports are an all-but-universal form of taxation; rates have often been made too high, which thereupon causes smuggling; an improved system recommended.

CUSTOMS DUTIES or tariffs are much more ancient than those of excise. They seem to have been called customs, as denoting customary payments which had been in use from time immemorial. They appear to have been originally considered as taxes upon the profits of merchants.

During the barbarous times of feudal anarchy, merchants, like all the other inhabitants of towns, were considered as little better than emancipated bondsmen, whose persons were despised, and whose profits envied. The great nobility, who had consented that the king should tallage the profits of their own tenants, were not unwilling that he should tallage likewise those of an order of men whom it was much less their interest to protect.

In those ignorant times, it was not understood that the profits of merchants are a subject which can not be taxed directly; or that the final payment of all such taxes must fall, with a considerable overcharge, upon consumers.

The gains of foreign merchants were looked upon even more unfavorably than those of English merchants. It was natural, therefore, that those of the former should be taxed even more heavily. This distinction between the duties upon foreigners and those upon English merchants, which was begun from ignorance, has been continued from the spirit of monopoly, or in order to give our own merchants an advantage both in the home and the foreign market.

On this theory, the ancient customs duties were imposed equally upon all sorts of goods, necessaries as well as luxuries, goods exported as well as goods imported. Why should the dealers in one sort of goods, it seems to have been thought, be more favored than those in another? or why should the merchant exporter be more favored than the merchant importer?

The ancient customs were divided into three branches. The first, and perhaps the most ancient of all those duties, was that upon wool and leather. It seems to have been chiefly or altogether an export duty. The second, called tonnage, was upon wine; and the third, called poundage, upon all other goods.

℃ The rise and general adoption of the principles of the Mercantile System, which I shall have occasion to consider in the next book, led to the gradual removal of most export duties. Those that were retained were rather for some purpose related to regulation of trade than to the revenue of the state.

For the same reason, the management of import duties has frequently been unfavorable to state revenues. In consequence of that system, importation of several sorts of goods was prohibited altogether. This prohibition in some cases entirely prevented, and in others very much reduced, the importation of those commodities, by reducing the importers to the necessity of smuggling. It entirely prevented the importation of foreign woolens; and it very much diminished that of foreign silks and velvets. In both cases it entirely annihilated the customs revenue which might have been collected upon such importation.

The high duties imposed upon the importation of many different sorts of foreign goods, in order to discourage their consumption in Great Britain, in many cases served only to encourage smuggling; and in all cases reduced the revenue from the customs below what more moderate duties would have yielded.

The saying of Dr. Swift, that in the arithmetic of the customs two and two, instead of making four, make sometimes only one, holds perfectly true with regard to such heavy duties, which never could have been imposed, had not the mercantile system taught us, in many cases, to employ taxation as an instrument, not of revenue, but of monopoly.

Heavy duties being imposed upon almost all goods imported, our merchant importers smuggle as much, and make entry of as little as they can. Our merchant exporters, on the contrary, report more than they export; sometimes out of vanity, and to pass for great dealers, and sometimes to gain a bounty or a drawback.

Our exports, in consequence of these different frauds, appear upon the customhouse books greatly to overbalance our imports; to the unspeakable comfort of those politicians who measure the national prosperity by what they call the balance of trade. I shall consider this subject at length in the next book.

High import and excise taxes, sometimes by diminishing the consumption of the taxed commodities, and sometimes by encouraging smuggling, frequently yield a smaller revenue to the government than what might be drawn from more moderate taxes.

When the loss of revenue is the effect of the reduction of consumption, there can be but one remedy, and that is the lowering of the tax. When it is the effect of the encouragement given to smuggling, it may be remedied in two ways, either by diminishing the temptation to smuggle, or perhaps by increasing the difficulty of smuggling. The temptation to smuggle can be diminished only by the lowering of the tax; and the difficulty of smuggling can be increased only by establishing such system of administration as is most proper for preventing it.

The excise laws, it appears, I believe, from experience, obstruct and embarrass the operations of the smuggler much more effectually than those of the customs. By introducing into the customs a system of administration as nearly like the excise as the nature of the different duties will admit, the difficulty of smuggling might be very much increased. This alteration, it has been supposed by many people, might very easily be brought about.

❏   The system of warehousing and bonding, which A. S. here goes on to outline, together with a reduction in the number of commodities subject to duty, was actually adopted, and proved eminently successful. As the "bonded warehouse" system, it is now freely used in all countries.

If by such a change of system the public revenue suffered no loss, the trade and manufactures of the country would certainly gain a very considerable advantage. The trade in those commodities not taxed, by far the greatest number, would be perfectly · free, and might be carried to and from all parts of the world with every possible advantage. Among those commodities would be included all the necessaries of life, and all the raw materials of manufacture.

[336]

So far as the free importation of the necessaries of life reduced their average money price in the home market, it would reduce the money price of labor, but without reducing in any respect its real earnings.

The value of money is in proportion to the quantity of the necessaries of life which it will purchase. That of the necessaries of life is altogether independent of the quantity of money which can be had for them. The reduction in the money price of labor would necessarily be attended with a proportionate decrease in that of all domestic manufactures, which would thereby gain some advantage in all foreign markets. The price of some manufactures would be reduced in a still greater proportion by the free importation of the raw materials.

The cheapness of their goods would secure to our own workmen, not only the possession of the home, but a very great command of the foreign market.

Even the trade in those commodities still taxed would be carried on with much more advantage than at present. If those commodities were delivered out of the public warehouse for foreign export, being in this case exempt from all taxes, the trade in them would be perfectly free. The carrying trade in all sorts of goods would under this system enjoy every possible advantage.

The duties upon foreign luxuries imported for home consumption, though they occasionally fall upon the poor, fall principally upon people of middling or more than middling fortune.

The duties upon the cheaper luxuries of home production destined for home consumption, fall pretty equally upon people of all classes in proportion to their respective expense. The poor pay these excise taxes upon their own consumption; the rich, upon both their own consumption and that of their servants.

The whole consumption of the lower classes of people, or of those below the middle class, it must be observed, is in every country much greater, not only in quantity, but in value, than that of the upper classes. The whole expense of the inferior is much greater than that of the superior ranks.

In the first place, almost the whole capital of every country is annually distributed among the people, as the wages of productive labor. Secondly, a great part of the revenue arising from both the rent of land and the profits of capital is annually distributed among the same class, in the wages and maintenance of servants, and other unproductive laborers. Thirdly, some part of the profits of capital also belongs to them, as a revenue arising from the employment of their small capitals. Fourthly, and lastly, some part even of the rent of land belongs to them—a considerable part to those who are somewhat below the middling rank, and a small part even to the lowest class. Common laborers sometimes possess in property an acre or two of land.

Though the expense of those common people, therefore, taking them individually, is very small, yet the whole mass of it, taking them collectively, amounts always to by far the largest portion of the whole expense of the society; what remains being always much less, not only in quantity but in value.

The taxes upon expense, therefore, which fall chiefly upon the upper classes, upon the smaller portion of the annual produce, are likely to be much less productive than those which fall indifferently upon all ranks, or even those which fall chiefly upon the bottom class.

The excise tax upon the materials and manufacture of home-made fermented and spirituous liquors is accordingly, of all the different taxes upon expense, by far the most productive, since this falls very much, perhaps principally, upon the common people.

It must always be remembered, however, that it is the expenditure for luxuries, not for the necessaries of common people, that ought ever to be taxed. The final payment of any such tax upon necessaries would fall altogether upon the superior ranks of people.

This is because such a tax must in all cases either raise the wages of labor, or lessen the demand for it. It could not raise the wages of labor, without throwing the final payment of the tax upon the upper classes. It could not lessen the demand for labor, without lessening the annual produce of the land and labor of the country, the fund from which all taxes must be finally paid. Whatever might be the degree to which a tax of this kind reduced the demand for labor, it must always raise wages higher than they otherwise would be in that condition; and the final payment of this enhancement of wages must in all cases fall upon the upper classes.

℃   A long discussion of the proper method of assessing the excise tax on malt and distilled liquors follows; a few passages showing the effect of such taxation on land growing barley and on vineyards seems scarcely important enough to summarize here.

Among minor sources of revenue for the state, which have at times been levied in different countries, are the duties which in French are called Péages, which in old Saxon times were called Duties of Passage, and which seem to have been originally established for the same purpose as our turnpike tolls, or the tolls upon our canals and navigable rivers, for the maintenance of the road or of the navigation.

Those duties, when applied to such purposes, are most properly imposed according to the bulk or weight of the goods. As they were originally local duties, applicable to local purposes, the administration of them was in most cases entrusted to the particular town, parish, or lordship in which they were levied; such communities being in some way or other supposed to be accountable for the application.

The sovereign, who is altogether unaccountable, has in many countries assumed to himself the administration of those duties; and though he has in most cases greatly increased the duty, he has in many entirely neglected the application. If the turnpike tolls of Great Britain should ever become one of the resources of government, we may learn, by the example of many other nations, what would probably be the consequence.[1]

Such tolls are no doubt finally paid by the consumer; but the consumer is not taxed in proportion to his expense when he pays, not according to the value, but according to the bulk or weight of what he consumes. When such duties are imposed, not according to the bulk or weight, but according to the supposed value of the goods, they become properly a sort of internal customs or excises, which obstruct very much the most important of all branches of commerce, the domestic commerce of the country.

In some small states duties similar to those passage duties are imposed upon goods carried across the territory, either by land or by water, from one foreign country to another. These are in some countries called transit-duties.

Some of the little Italian states, which are situated upon

[1] The nationalization of the railways of Europe offers an instructive example.

the Po, and the rivers which run into it, derive some revenue from duties of this kind, which are paid altogether by foreigners, and which are perhaps the only duties that one state can impose upon the subjects of another, without obstructing in any respect the industry or commerce of its own.

CHAPTER XVII

*Of all taxes, sales or excise taxes upon "lux-
ury goods" are the most equitable, certain,
and convenient; but their collection is
wasteful, and they have several harmful
effects, particularly if the rate of tax is un-
reasonably high.*

SUCH TAXES upon luxuries as most of the customs duties and
excise, though they all fall indifferently upon every different kind
of income, and are paid finally by whoever consumes the commodities taxed, yet they do not always fall equally or propor-
tionately upon the income of every individual.

As every man's choice or fancy regulates his consumption,
every man contributes taxes rather according to his humor than in
proportion to his income; the profuse contribute more, the parsimonious less, than their proper proportion.

During the minority of a man of great fortune, he contributes commonly very little, by his consumption, towards the
support of that state under whose protection he derives a large
income. Those who live in another country contribute nothing,
by their consumption, towards the support of the government of
that country from which their income arises. If in this latter
country there should be no property tax, nor any considerable duty
upon the transfer of property, as is the case in Ireland, such
absentees may derive a large income from the protection of a
government to the support of which they do not contribute a
penny.

This inequality is likely to be greatest in a country of which
the government is in some respects subordinate to and dependent
upon that of some other. The people who possess the most extensive property in the dependent country will in this case generally

choose to live in the governing country. Ireland is precisely in this situation, and we cannot therefore wonder that the proposal of a tax upon absentees should be so very popular in that country.

If you except, however, this very peculiar situation, any inequality in the contribution of individuals, which can arise from taxes upon luxuries, is much more than compensated by the very circumstance which causes that inequality—the fact that every man's contribution is altogether voluntary, it being altogether in his power either to consume or not to consume the commodity taxed.

Where such taxes, therefore, are properly assessed, and upon proper commodities, they are paid with less grumbling than any other. When they are advanced by the merchant or manufacturer, the consumer, who finally pays them, soon comes to combine them with the price of the commodities, and almost forgets that he pays any tax.[1]

Such taxes are or may be perfectly certain, or may be assessed so as to leave no doubt concerning either what ought to be paid, or when it ought to be paid; concerning either the amount or the time of payment. Whatever uncertainty there may sometimes be, must arise only from the inaccurate or obscure language in which the law that imposes them is expressed.

Taxes upon luxuries generally are, and always may be, paid piecemeal, or in proportion as the taxpayers have occasion to purchase the goods. In the time and mode of payment they are, or may be, of all taxes the most convenient. Upon the whole, therefore, such taxes are perhaps agreeable to the first three of the four general maxims concerning taxation. They offend in every respect against the fourth.

Such taxes, in proportion to what they bring into the public treasury, always take out or keep out of the pockets of the people more than almost any other taxes. They seem to do this in all the four different ways in which it is possible to do it.

First, the levying of such taxes, even when imposed in the most judicious manner, requires a great number of customs and excise officers, whose salaries are a real tax upon the people, which brings nothing into the treasury of the state.

Secondly, such taxes necessarily create some obstruction or

---

[1] As for example the fantastic excise taxes upon cigarettes and gasoline levied in this country, and the even more fantastic tax on tobacco in England.

discouragement to certain branches of industry. As they always raise the price of the commodity taxed, they so far discourage its consumption, and consequently, its production. If it is a commodity of home growth or manufacture, less labor comes to be employed in raising and producing it. If it is a foreign commodity, the commodities of the same kind made at home may thereby, indeed, gain some advantage in the home market, and a greater quantity of domestic industry may thereby be turned toward preparing them.

But though this rise of price in a foreign commodity may encourage domestic industry in one particular branch, it necessarily discourages almost every other. All taxes upon consumable commodities tend to reduce the quantity of productive labor below what it otherwise would be, either in producing the commodities taxed, if they are home commodities; or in producing those with which they are purchased, if they are foreign imports.

Such taxes, too, always alter, more or less, the natural direction of national industry, and turn it into a channel always different from, and generally less advantageous than that in which it would have run of its own accord.[2]

Thirdly, the hope of evading such taxes by smuggling[3] results frequently in forfeitures and other penalities, which entirely ruin the smuggler; a person who, though no doubt highly blamable for violating the laws of his country, is frequently incapable of violating those of natural justice, and would have been, in every respect, an excellent citizen, had not the laws of his country made that a crime which nature never meant to be so.

In those corrupted governments where there is at least a general suspicion of extravagant and unnecessary expense, and great misapplication of the public revenue, the laws which guard it are little respected. In such countries not many people are scrupulous about smuggling, when, without perjury, they can find any easy and safe opportunity of doing so.

To pretend to have any scruple about buying smuggled goods, though that encourages violation of the revenue laws, and the perjury which almost always attends it, would in most countries

---

[2] Which, as applied both to import duties and excise taxes, is the real milk in the coconut.

[3] And moonshining and bootlegging.

be regarded as one of those pedantic pieces of hypocrisy which, instead of gaining respect for anybody, serve only to expose the pretender to the suspicion of being a greater knave than most of his neighbors.

By this indulgence of the public, the smuggler is often encouraged to continue a trade which he is thus taught to consider as in some measure innocent; and when the severity of the revenue laws is ready to fall upon him, he is frequently disposed to defend with violence, what he has been accustomed to regard as his just property. From being at first, perhaps, rather imprudent than criminal, he at last too often becomes one of the hardiest and most determined violators of the laws of society.

Finally, such taxes, by subjecting business men to the frequent visits and odious examination of the tax collectors, expose them sometimes, no doubt, to some degree of oppression, and always to much trouble and vexation. And though vexation, as has already been said, is not expense, strictly speaking, it is certainly equivalent to the expense at which every man would be willing to redeem himself from it. The laws of excise, though more effectual for the purpose for which they were instituted, are, in this respect, more vexatious than those of the customs.

In consequence of the notion that duties upon consumable goods were taxes upon the profits of merchants, those duties have, in some countries, been repeated upon every successive sale of the goods. If the profits of the importer or manufacturer were taxed, equality seemed to require that those of all the middle buyers, who intervened between either of them and the consumer, should likewise be taxed. The famous Alcavala of Spain seems to have been established upon this principle.[4]

It subjects the dealers in all sorts of goods, every farmer, every manufacturer, every merchant and shopkeeper, to the continual visits and examination of the tax-collectors. Through the greater part of a country in which a tax of this kind is established, nothing can be produced for distant sale, and the production of every part of the country can therefore be no greater than the consumption of the immediate neighborhood.

⊏   Most of the rest of this very long chapter is devoted to a general appraisal of the tax system of Great Britain and other

---

[4] What we would call a transaction or turnover tax.

countries, as A. S. found them in 1776. It was his opinion that the British taxes, although far from perfect, were the best in Europe, particularly because of the uniformity of the tax laws throughout the nation, and the freedom of domestic trade.

⁋ In France, besides other injurious features, the diversity of taxes in different provinces hindered internal trade, the important wine trade being particularly hampered. Some of the small Italian states were further sub-divided, with a different tax structure for each. Under such absurd management only the great fertility of the soil and the favorable climate could save such countries from relapsing into the lowest state of poverty and barbarism.

⁋ In all countries, tax-collecting by government officials was found greatly superior to the common European custom of "farming out" the taxes. Where the latter system was in use, the taxes did indeed come in punctually, but the amount received by the government was far below what it should be, while the amounts exacted from the people were far higher.

⁋ Furthermore, farmed taxes had to be enforced by laws which grew steadily more sanguinary. Even a bad sovereign felt more compassion for his people than could be expected of the farmer of the revenue.

⁋ In some cases not only was the tax farmed out, but the tax-farmer was given a monopoly of the commodity, as with tobacco and salt in France. Salt being an absolute necessity, and the taxes on both being exorbitant, smuggling was very profitable and very common. The laws were consequently very severe, several hundred people being sent every year to the galleys, and a considerable number being hanged.

⁋ The whole financial system of France was at that time in a deplorable condition, and A. S. makes several sensible suggestions for its improvement. (As we know, it took the Revolution to accomplish this.) With a population of less than 8,000,000, Great Britain collected £10,000,000 annually in taxes, while in France, a larger and richer country, with about 23,000,000 inhabitants, the annual revenue did not amount to £15,000,000.

⁋ In Holland, the heavy taxes on the necessities of life were said to have ruined their manufacture, but the situation of Holland was admittedly difficult. Besides its heavy debt, due to many wars, which in turn were forced on the nation by its exposed position, Holland had its never-ending and costly contest with the sea.

❡   After all the proper subjects of taxation have been exhausted, under such conditions, if the state requires still more revenue, taxes must be imposed upon improper subjects. This was the case with Holland; and A. S. suggests that only because it was a republic, where the wealthier men also hold the places of honor in the government, could the exorbitant taxation in that country be continued for any length of time.

❡   So far in this book we have examined the expenses of the state, and the meeting of these expenses by annual contributions called taxes and duties. Another resource, quite as universal, is the borrowing of money by the government from its citizens. The last chapter of the book will examine this dangerous and often disastrous practice.

CHAPTER XVIII

The expense of the state can usually be met by taxes as long as peace is maintained; war, however, increases expense suddenly and very greatly, and in a modern state this means borrowing from the citizens on a vast scale; the forms of such borrowings, and the institution of "sinking funds."

IN THAT rude state of society which precedes commerce and manufactures, when those expensive luxuries which commerce and manufactures can alone create are altogether unknown, a person with a large income can, as I have shown, enjoy or employ that income only by spending nearly all of it on the support of other people.

A large income may at all times be said to consist in the command of a large quantity of the necessaries of life. In early times it was commonly paid in a large quantity of those necessaries, in the materials of plain food and coarse clothing, in grain and cattle, in wool and raw hides.

When neither commerce nor manufacture furnish anything for which the owner can exchange the commodities which are over and above his own consumption, he can do nothing with the surplus but feed and clothe relatives, servants, and retainers.

This form of spending is one by which people are not very apt to ruin themselves. There is not, perhaps, any selfish pleasure so frivolous, of which the pursuit has not sometimes ruined even sensible men. A passion for cock-fighting has ruined many. But it is uncommon, I believe, for people to be ruined by hospitality, whereas luxury and ostentation have ruined many. Among our feudal ancestors, the long time during which estates used to continue in the same family sufficiently demonstrates the general disposition of the people of those times to live within their incomes.

Our ancestors were usually able to sell a part of their wool and raw hides for money. Some part of this money, perhaps, they spent in purchasing the few objects of vanity and luxury which could be found in the markets; but some part of it they seem commonly to have hoarded.

They could not well indeed do anything else but hoard whatever money they saved. To trade was disgraceful to a gentleman, and to lend money at interest, which at that time was considered as usury and prohibited by law, would have been still more so.

In those times of violence and disorder, besides, it was convenient to have a hoard of money at hand, so that if they should be driven from their own home, they might have something of known value to carry with them to some place of safety.

The same violence which induced them to hoard, made it equally useful to conceal the hoard. The frequency of treasure-trove, or of hoards found of which no owner was known, sufficiently demonstrates the frequency in those times both of hoarding and of concealing the hoard. In these times such discoveries are rare, if not altogether unknown.

❡ A. S. then goes on to point out that in ancient times kings and rulers generally followed the same course as the private subject. They devoted their revenues to the support of tenants and retainers; and when they had a surplus of income in money, it was necessarily hoarded.

❡ When, however, manufacture and trade began to produce and offer for sale objects of art and luxury, the surplus revenue of rulers turned in that direction. Money was lavished on brilliant and dissipated courts, and in pageantry, with the result that not only kingdoms, but even republics like the Netherlands and some of the Swiss cantons, customarily spent all their incomes, even in time of peace.

This want of parsimony in time of peace makes it necessary to contract debt in time of war. When war comes, there is no money in the treasury not already appropriated for carrying on the ordinary expense of the peace establishment. War expense greatly exceeds that of peace times.

Supposing that the government should have, what it scarcely ever has, the immediate means of increasing its revenue in proportion to war demands, still the tax money will not begin to come into the treasury for some weeks or months.

But the moment war begins, or rather the moment in which it appears likely to begin, the army must be augumented, the fleet must be fitted out, defenses must be manned. Army, fleet, and garrisons must be furnished with arms, ammunition and provisions. An immediate and great expense must be incurred which will not wait for the returns of the new taxes. In this emergency government can have no other resource but in borrowing.

The same commercial state of society which thus forces the government to borrow, also gives private interests the ability and inclination to lend.

A country abounding with merchants and manufacturers, necessarily abounds with a class of people through whose hands pass not only their own capital but the capital of all those who either lend them money, or trust them with goods. Such a country, therefore, necessarily includes many people who have it at all times in their power to advance, if they choose to do so, very large sums of money to the government.

Commerce and manufactures can seldom flourish long in any state which does not enjoy a regular administration of justice, in which the people do not feel themselves secure in the possession of their property, in which the faith of contracts is not supported by law, and in which the authority of the state does not uniformly require the payment of debts from all those who are able to pay.

Commerce and manufactures, in short, will not flourish in any state in which there is not a certain degree of confidence in the justice of the government. The same confidence which disposes wealthy people to rely on the protection of a particular government disposes them, in an emergency, to trust that government with the use of their property.

By lending money to government, they do not even for a moment diminish their ability to carry on their businesses. On the contrary, they commonly increase it.

The necessities of the state usually make the government willing to borrow upon terms extremely advantageous to the lender. The security which it issues to the original creditor, is made transferable to any other creditor, and, where there is confidence in the justice of the state, it generally sells in the market for more than was originally paid for it.

The government of such a state is very apt to rely upon this ability and willingness of its citizens to lend it their money in emergencies. It foresees the ease of borrowing, and therefore does not bother itself with saving in advance.

In a rude state of society those individuals who hoard whatever money they can save, and who conceal their hoard, do so from a distrust of the justice of government, from a fear that if it were known that they had a hoard, and where that hoard was to be found, they would quickly be plundered.

In such a state of things few people would be able, and nobody would be willing, to finance the government in extraordinary exigencies. The lawless sovereign feels that he must provide for such exigencies by saving, because he foresees the absolute impossibility of borrowing.

The progress of the enormous debts which at present oppress all the great nations of Europe, and will in the long run probably ruin them, has been pretty uniform. Nations, like private men, have generally begun to borrow upon what may be called personal credit, without assigning or mortgaging any particular fund for the payment of the debt; and when this resource has failed them, they have gone on to borrow upon assignments or mortgages of particular funds.

What is called the unfunded debt of Great Britain, was contracted in the former of those two ways.

⧗   A. S. then proceeds to explain the details of Great Britain's unfunded debt as it stood in 1776.

When this resource is exhausted, and it becomes necessary, in order to raise money, to assign or mortgage some particular part of the public revenue for the payment of the debt, government has at different times done this in two different ways. Sometimes it has made this assignment or mortgage for a year, or a few years; and sometimes for perpetuity.

In the one case, the fund was supposed sufficient to pay, within the limited time, both principal and interest of the money borrowed. In the other, it was supposed sufficient to pay the interest only, or a perpetual annuity equivalent to the interest, the government being at liberty to redeem this annuity at any time, upon paying off the principal. When money was raised in the one way, it was said to be raised by anticipation; when in the other, by perpetual funding, or, more shortly, by "funding."

In Great Britain the annual land and malt taxes were regularly (in 1776) anticipated every year, by virtue of a borrowing clause constantly inserted into the tax laws. The Bank of England generally advanced the amount the tax was expected to produce, being reimbursed as the tax came in. If there was a deficiency, which there always was, it was provided for in the next tax bill. The only considerable branch of the public revenue which yet remained unmortgaged was thus regularly spent before it came in.

Like an improvident spendthrift, who cannot wait for the regular payment of his income, the state constantly has to borrow from its own agents, and pay interest for the use of its own money. ❡ The next few paragraphs explain the successive steps by which various government loans between 1697 and 1717 were consolidated in the so-called General Fund of the British government; this amounting to about £725,000 by 1717.

Had money never been raised but by anticipation, the course of a few years would have liberated the public revenue, without any other attention of government besides that of not overloading the fund by charging it with more debt than it could pay within the limited term, and of not anticipating a second time before the expiration of the first anticipation.

But most European governments have been incapable of such prudence. They have frequently overloaded the fund, even upon the first anticipation; and when this happened not to be the case, they have generally taken care to overload it, by anticipating a second and a third time before the expiration of the first anticipation.

The incoming revenue becoming in this manner altogether insufficient for paying both principal and interest of the loan, it became necessary to charge it with the interest only, and such improvident anticipations necessarily gave birth to the more ruinous practice of perpetual funding.

But though this practice necessarily postpones the liberation of the public revenue to a time so indefinite that it is not very likely ever to arrive, yet as more money can always be raised in this way than by anticipations, the former, when men have once become familiar with it, has in the great emergencies of the state always been preferred to the latter.

To relieve the present exigency is always the object which principally interests those immediately concerned in the administration of public affairs. The future liberation of the public revenue, they leave to the care of posterity.

During the reign of Queen Anne, a fall in the market rate of interest led to a surplus of tax revenue over what was needed for interest on the public debt. This gave rise to what is called the "Sinking Fund."

Such a sinking fund, though instituted for the payment of old debts, makes it far easier to contract new ones. It is a subsidiary fund always at hand to be mortgaged, in case the yield of other taxes seems doubtful.

Besides those two methods of borrowing, by anticipations and by perpetual funding, there are two other methods, which hold a sort of middle ground between them. These are, that of borrowing upon annuities for terms of years, and that of borrowing upon annuities for lives.

ℂ These methods of borrowing on annuities, used by the government of Great Britain, were never transplanted to the United States, and so need not be considered here. Some further paragraphs at this point explain the differences between annuity borrowing practices in Great Britain and in France under the Bourbon kings. A. S. attributes this difference in method partly to the fact that in England most lenders were merchants, whereas in France they were the collectors and "farmers" of taxes, who were chiefly bachelors.

The ordinary expense of most modern governments in time of peace being equal or nearly equal to their ordinary revenue, when war comes they are neither willing nor able to increase their revenue in proportion. They are afraid to offend the people, who by so great and so sudden an increase of taxes, would soon be disgusted with the war; and they cannot easily calculate what taxes would be sufficient to produce the revenue wanted.

The ease of borrowing delivers them from all these embarrassments. By means of borrowing they can, with a very moderate increase of taxes, raise enough money to carry on the war, and by the practice of making the loans perpetual they can, with the smallest possible increase of taxes, raise the largest possible sum of money.

In great empires the people who live in the capital, and in sections remote from the scene of action, feel, many of them, scarce any inconvenience from the war; but enjoy, at their ease, the amusement of reading in the newspapers the exploits of their fleets and armies.[1]

To them this amusement makes up for the small difference between the taxes which they pay on account of the war, and those which they had been accustomed to pay in time of peace. They are commonly dissatisfied with the return of peace, which puts an end to their amusement, and to a thousand visionary hopes of conquest and national glory, which might result from a continuance of the war.[2]

The return of peace, indeed, seldom relieves taxpayers from the taxes imposed during the war. These are mortgaged for the interest of the debt contracted in order to carry it on.

If, over and above paying this interest and ordinary expense of government, the old and new taxes produce some surplus revenue, it may perhaps be converted into a sinking fund for paying off the debt.

But, in the first place, this sinking fund, even supposing it should not be diverted, is generally altogether inadequate for paying off the whole debt within any period during which it can reasonably be expected that peace should continue. And, in the second place, this fund is in fact almost always diverted to other purposes.

Even during the most profound peace, various events occur which require an extraordinary expense, and the government always finds it easier to meet this expense by misapplying the sinking fund than by imposing a new tax.

Every new tax is immediately felt more or less by the

[1] The worst of it is that a war which is financed by borrowing creates an illusion of prosperity that deceives even very acute minds; if all war costs had to be met by taxes, the illusion of wealth would quickly disappear.

[2] The advent of "total war," as experienced in 1939–1945, has greatly weakened the force of these remarks, without entirely destroying it.

people. It always causes some murmur, and meets with some opposition.

The more taxes may have been multiplied, the higher they may have been raised, the more loudly the people complain of every new tax, and the harder it becomes either to find new subjects of taxation, or to raise higher the taxes already imposed.

A temporary suspension of the payment of debt is not immediately felt by the people, and causes neither murmur nor complaint. To borrow from the sinking fund is thus always an obvious and easy expedient for getting out of a tight spot.

The more the public debt may have accumulated, the more urgent it is to reduce it, the more dangerous and ruinous it may be to misapply any part of the sinking fund. The less likely the public debt is to be reduced, the more certainly will the sinking fund be misapplied to meet extraordinary peacetime demands.

When a nation is already overburdened with taxes, nothing but the necessities of a new war, nothing but national vengeance, or fears for national security, can induce taxpayers to submit, with tolerable patience, to a new tax. Hence the usual misapplication of the sinking fund.

In Great Britain, from the time that we had first recourse to the ruinous expedient of perpetual funding, the reduction of the public debt in time of peace, has never borne any proportion to its accumulation in time of war.

It was in the war which began in 1688, and was concluded by the treaty of Ryswick in 1697, that the foundation of the present enormous debt of Great Britain was first laid.

¶   This war left a debt of £21,516,000. This was reduced by five millions by 1701, increased to £53,681,000 by 1714, and to £122,603,000 by 1763. Even during one period of seventeen years of peace, only £8,328,000 was paid off, while a war of only nine years added £31,339,000.

¶   A. S. here adds, in the third edition of W. N., after the end of the war of the American Revolution, that a previous period of eleven years of peace had reduced the public debt by not much more than ten million pounds; the American war increased it by more than a hundred million.

¶   From these considerations of the causes of public debt, and its particular history in Great Britain, A. S. now turns to analyze its effects on the economic structure and the general welfare.

[354]

CHAPTER XIX

Why public debts resulting from war are
seldom reduced except by repudiation; the
sources of money lent to the government,
and the pernicious effect of the debt on the
economy of the nation; the various open and
concealed methods by which great public
debts have usually been repudiated, and
their effects.

THE PUBLIC DEBTS of different nations, particularly those of
England, have by one author been wrongly represented as the
accumulation of large capital super-added to the other capital of
the country, by means of which its trade is extended, its manufactures multiplied, and its lands cultivated and improved much
beyond what they could otherwise have been.

He does not consider that the capital advanced to government was, from the moment in which the lenders advanced it, a
certain portion of the annual production of wealth, turned away
from serving as capital to serve as revenue; from maintaining
productive laborers, to maintain unproductive ones; and to be
spent and wasted, generally in the course of the year, without
even the hope of any future reproduction.

In return for the capital which lenders advanced they
obtained, indeed, an annuity in the public funds, in most cases of
more than equal value. This annuity, no doubt, replaced to them
their capital, and enabled them to carry on their trade and business
to the same or perhaps to a greater extent than before.

In other words, they could either borrow of other people
new capital upon the credit of this annuity, or by selling it they

could obtain new capital, as much or more than what they had advanced to government.

But this new capital must have existed in the country before, and must have been employed as nearly all capital is, in maintaining productive labor. When it came into the hands of those who had advanced their money to government, though it was in some respects new capital to them, it was not so to the country; but was only capital withdrawn from certain employments in order to be turned towards others.

Thus though it replaced to the lenders what they advanced to government, it did not replace it to the country. Had they not made their loans to the government, there would have been in the country twice as much capital, two portions of the annual produce, instead of one, employed in maintaining productive labor.

When the whole expense of government is paid out of taxes, a certain portion of the incomes of private people is merely diverted from maintaining one kind of unproductive labor toward maintaining another.

Some part of their tax money might no doubt have been saved and turned into capital, and consequently employed in maintaining productive labor; but most of it would probably have been spent.

When government expenses are paid out of taxes, this no doubt hinders more or less the further accumulation of new capital; but it does not necessarily destroy any capital already existing.

But when the public expense is met by borrowing, this destroys some capital which had before existed in the country, by turning that part of it, which would have maintained some productive labor, to maintaining unproductive labor. As in this case, however, taxes are lighter than they would have been, the private income of individuals is necessarily less burdened, and consequently their ability to save and accumulate capital is a good deal less impaired.

If borrowing destroys more old capital than does taxing, it at the same time hinders less the accumulation or acquisition of new capital. Under the system of borrowing, the frugality and industry of private people can more easily repair the damage which the waste and extravagance of government may occasionally make in the general capital of the community.

[*356*]

It is only while war is going on, however, that the system of borrowing retains this advantage. Were the expense of war to be defrayed always by revenue raised within the year, the taxes would last no longer than the year. The ability of private people to save, though less during the war, would be greater when peace was restored. War would not necessarily have occasioned the destruction of any old capital, and peace would have permitted the accumulation of much more new.

If financed by taxation, wars would in general be more speedily ended, and less wantonly undertaken. The people feeling, during the course of the war, the full burden of it, would soon grow weary of it, and government, in order to humor them, would not carry it on longer than necessary. The prospect of the heavy and unavoidable burdens of war would hinder the people from wantonly calling for it, when there was no real or solid interest to fight for.[1]

When the public debt has grown to a certain point, the multiplication of taxes which it brings along with it sometimes impairs the ability of private people to save, even in time of peace, as much as the pay-as-you-go plan would in time of war. The private income of the inhabitants of Great Britain is now as much encumbered in time of peace, their ability to save as much impaired, as it would have been during the most costly war, had the prenicious system of borrowing and funding never been adopted.

In the payment of the interest on the public debt, it has been said, it is the right hand which pays the left. The money does not go out of the country. It is only a part of the income of one set of the inhabitants which is transferred to another; and the nation is not a cent poorer.

This apology is founded altogether in the sophistry of the Mercantile System, and after the long examination which I bestow upon that system in the next book, it may perhaps be unnecessary to say anything about it here. It supposes, for example, that the whole public debt is owing to the inhabitants of the country, which happens not to be true; the Dutch, as well as several other foreign nations, holding a very considerable share of our debt. But though

[1] Doubtless true when warfare was not much more than the sport of kings, but hardly true in an era of nuclear fission and atomic bombs.

the whole debt were owing to British subjects, it would not on that account be less pernicious.[2]

Land and capital are the two original sources of all earnings, both private and public. Capital pays the wages of productive labor, whether employed in agriculture, manufactures, or commerce. The management of those two original sources of new wealth belongs to two different sets of people: the proprietors of land, and the owners or employers of capital.

The landlord is interested for the sake of his own revenue to keep his property in as good condition as he can, by building and repairing his tenants' houses, by making and maintaining the necessary drains and fencing, and all those other expensive improvements which properly belong to him. But the revenue of the landlord may be so much impaired by land taxes, and this diminished income be rendered of so little real value by taxes and

---

[2] It is disappointing that A. S. here contents himself with damning, as a "sophistry of the Mercantile System," the theory that a great public debt is harmless because "we owe it to ourselves."

M'Culloch says that A. S. "has given no sufficient refutation of this fallacy." It is true, he says, that the interest payments on such a debt are a payment from the right hand to the left—a transfer of wealth from one group to another. But the real burden of the debt on society arises not so much from the interest burden as from the way in which the principal was dissipated.

This principal was not lent by one set of individuals to another set, but to the government, which in most cases spent it (always very wastefully) in waging war. Nearly all that capital, therefore, was totally destroyed; and the lenders, who can derive no income from what has been destroyed, must get it from taxes laid on the labor and income of others.

Paraphrasing M'Culloch further, let us suppose that a nation with 140 millions of people and 200 billions of capital engages in war, and that the government borrows from individuals 30 billions of their capital, which it spends. If the ordinary rate of profit on capital is 10 per cent, the annual income of the owners before the war would have been 20 billions; but after 30 billions of capital was borrowed and spent, at the end of the war the lenders' incomes would be only 17 billions. True, they would in addition receive interest on their loans, but this would come, not from the capital destroyed, but out of the taxes of the people, including their own.

It follows that the borrowing of capital by the government, whether destroyed in war or dissipated by some other unproductive use, can have no other effect than to reduce the real capital of the whole population, and its ability to employ labor.

It is not even true that "we owe it to ourselves," for the fact is that all of us owe it to some of us. But the greatest evil consists in the fact that capital which might have employed labor and produced wealth is destroyed and irretrievably lost.

duties on the necessities and conveniences of life, that he may find himself altogether unable to make or maintain those expensive improvements.

When the landlord thus ceases to do his part, it is altogether impossible that the tenant should continue to do his. As the distress of the landlord increases, the agriculture of the country must necessarily decline.

Similarly, when, by different taxes upon the necessaries and conveniences of life, the owners and employers of capital find that their earnings from it will not, in a particular country, buy the same quantity of those necessaries and conveniences which an equal income would buy in almost any other, they will be disposed to remove to some other.

And when, in order to raise those taxes, the merchants and manufacturers come to be continually exposed to the mortifying and vexatious visits of the tax-collector, this disposition to remove will soon be changed into an actual removal. The industry of the country will necessarily fall with the removal of the capital which supported it, and the ruin of trade and industry will follow the decay of agriculture.

To transfer from the owners of land and capital, from the persons immediately interested in its good condition and management, to another set of persons, the greater part of the revenue arising from either, must, in the long run, cause both neglect of land and the waste or removal of capital.

One who lends to the government has no doubt a general interest in the prosperity of the agriculture, industry, and commerce of the country; and consequently in the good condition of its land, and in the good management of its capital. Otherwise his loan and his interest would no longer be secure.

But a creditor of the public, considered merely as such, has no interest in the good condition of any particular land, or in the good management of any particular capital. He has no knowledge of any such particular portion. He has never seen it. He can have no care about it. Its ruin may be unknown to him, and cannot directly affect him.[3]

[3] A. S. now repeats his pessimistic remark in the last chapter—that enormous war debts will in the long run probably ruin every nation in Europe—and goes on to say that the existence of a funded public debt has always enfeebled the nation which contracted it; and that England, although favored by a superior system of taxation, can not support an unlimited burden. (*Footnote continued on following page.*)

❰ A. S. next goes on to explain the ways by which great public debts are commonly made less burdensome—by what amounts to partial repudiation through depreciation of the currency.

When national debts have once been accumulated to a certain degree, there is scarcely, I believe, a single instance of their having been fairly and completely paid. The liberation of the public revenue, if it has ever been brought about at all, has always been brought about by bankruptcy; sometimes by an avowed one,[4] but always by a real one, though frequently by a pretended payment.

The raising of the denomination of the coin has been the most usual expedient by which a real public bankruptcy has been disguised under the appearance of a pretended payment.

If a nickel, for example, should by law be raised to the denomination of a dime, and ten nickels to that of a dollar, the person who under the old denomination had borrowed ten dimes of silver would, under the new, pay with ten nickels, containing mostly copper.

A national debt of two hundred billions of dollars might in this manner be paid with a hundred billions of our present money. It would indeed be a pretended payment only, and the

---

Since this was written the public debt of England has risen a thousand-fold, and as this is written it is impossible to calculate the fantastic burden with which the British have emerged from World War II.

A. S. has been widely criticized for his pessimism on this point. Lord Macaulay, in Chapter XIX of his History, devotes several pages to a review of the British debt, pointing out its steady growth, during a period when England was passing through its most prosperous and glorious age. "David Hume," he says, "undoubtedly one of the most profound political economists of his time, declared that . . . the road to national ruin was through the national debt . . . Adam Smith saw a little, and but a little further."

"There must have been," says Macaulay, "some great fallacy in the notions of those who uttered and of those who believed that long succession of confident predictions, so signally falsified by a long succession of indisputable facts"; and he finds the fallacy in a twofold mistake: "They greatly overrated the pressure of the burden; they greatly underrated the strength by which the burden was to be borne."

Whether Great Britain has at last reached the limit of its strength, and must resort to open or indirect repudiation of its debt burden, remains, as this is written, uncertain.

[4] As by Germany in 1922–23. The retirement of the debt incurred in our war between the states, after 1865, probably comes as near an example of full payment as history records; but even this was incomplete.

creditors of the government would really be defrauded of half of what was due them.[5]

Such a calamity too would extend much further than to the government creditors; every creditor would suffer a proportionate loss; and this without any advantage, but in most cases with a great additional loss, to the creditors of the state.

If the creditors of the public indeed were generally much in debt to other people, they might to some extent compensate their loss by paying their creditors in the same coin in which the government paid them. But in most countries the creditors of the government are usually the wealthy people, who are more apt to be creditors than debtors.

A pretended payment of this kind, therefore, causes a general and most pernicious subversion of the fortunes of private people; enriching in most cases the idle and profuse debtor, and at the expense of the industrious and frugal creditor, and transferring much of the national capital from hands which were likely to increase and improve it, to those which are likely to dissipate and destroy it.

When it becomes necessary for a state to declare itself bankrupt, a fair, open, and avowed bankruptcy is always the measure which is both least dishonorable to the debtor, and least hurtful to the creditor. The honor of a state is surely very poorly maintained when, in order to cover the disgrace of a real bankruptcy, it has recourse to a juggling trick of this kind, so easily seen through, and at the same time so extremely pernicious.

Almost all states, however, ancient and modern, when reduced to this necessity, have stooped to play this very juggling trick. The Romans, at the end of the first Punic war, reduced the *as*, the coin or denomination by which they computed the value of all their other coins, from twelve ounces of copper to only two ounces; that is, they raised two ounces of copper to a demonination which had always before expressed the value of twelve ounces.

The republic was thus enabled to pay the great debts which it had contracted with the sixth part of what it really owed.

So sudden and so great a bankruptcy, we should expect, must have raised a very violent popular clamor. It does not appear

[5] This is precisely what was done by the American government in 1934, under the pleasant name of "reflation," when the value of the paper dollar was reduced from about one-twentieth of an ounce of gold to one thirty-fifth of an ounce.

to have raised any. The law which enacted it was, like all other laws relating to the coinage, introduced and carried through the assembly of the people by a tribune, and was probably a very popular law.

In Rome, as in all the other ancient republics, the poor people were constantly in debt to the rich and great, who, in order to secure their votes at the annual elections, used to lend them money at exorbitant interest, which, as it could never be paid, soon increased the debt to a sum too great for the debtor to pay, or for anybody else to pay for him. The debtor, for fear of a very severe execution, was thus obliged to vote for the candidate whom the creditor recommended.

To deliver themselves from this subjection, the poorer citizens were continually calling out either for an entire abolition of debts, or for what they called "new tables"; that is, for a law which should square up their debts, upon paying only a certain proportion of the face value.

The law which reduced the coin of all denominations to a sixth part of its former value, since it enabled them to pay their debts with a sixth part of what they really owed, was as good as the most advantageous "new tables." In order to quiet the people, the rich and great were several times obliged to consent to laws both for abolishing debts, and for introducing new tables; and they probably were induced to consent to this law, partly for the same reason, and partly because, by liberating the public revenue, they might restore vigor to that government of which they themselves had the principal direction.

In the course of the second Punic war the *as* was still further reduced, first, from two ounces of copper to one ounce, and afterwards from one ounce to half an ounce; that is, to the twenty-fourth part of its original value.[6]

By means of such expedients the coin of all nations, I believe, has been gradually reduced more and more below its original value, and the same nominal sum has been gradually brought to contain a smaller and a smaller quantity of metal.

Nations have sometimes, for the same purpose, adulterated the standard of their coin; that is, have mixed a greater quantity

[6] Modern criticism has shown, says Cannan, that these transactions were not so simple as represented by A. S. But many other examples could be cited, since most unbearable public debts have been disposed of in some such manner.

of alloy in it. This adulteration of the metal has exactly the same effect as what the French call an "augmentation," or a direct raising of the denomination of the coin.

An augmentation always is, and from its nature must be, open and avowed. By means of it pieces of a smaller weight and bulk are called by the same name which had before been given to pieces of a greater weight and bulk.

The adulteration of the metal, on the contrary, has generally been a concealed operation. By means of it pieces were issued from the mint of the same denominations, and, as nearly as could be contrived, of the same weight, bulk, and appearance, with pieces which had been current before of much greater value.

When King John of France, in order to pay his debts, adulterated his coin, all the officers of his mint were sworn to secrecy.

Both operations are unjust. But a simple augmentation is an injustice of open violence, whereas an adulteration is an injustice of treacherous fraud.

This latter operation, therefore, as soon as it has been discovered (and it could never be concealed very long), has always excited much greater indignation than the former.[7] The coin after any considerable augmentation has very seldom been brought back to its former weight; but after adulterations it has almost always been brought back to its former fineness. It has scarcely ever happened that the fury and indignation of the people could otherwise be appeased.

In the end of the reign of Henry VIII, and in the begin-

[7] A graphic passage in Macaulay's "History" describes the debasement of the metal coinage in Dublin under James II. "James was absurd enough," he says, "to suppose that he could extricate himself from his financial difficulties by the simple process of calling a farthing a shilling. In his view, the right of coining included the right of debasing the coin. Pots, pans, knockers of doors, were carried to the mint, and some lumps of base metal, nominally worth near a million sterling, intrinsically worth about a sixtieth part of that sum, were in circulation. A mortgage for a thousand pounds was cleared off by a bag of counters made out of old kettles. Any man might walk into a shop, lay on the counter a bit of brass worth threepence, and carry off goods to the value of half a guinea. Of all the plagues of that time none made a deeper or a more lasting impression than the plague of the brass money."

ning of that of Edward VI, the English coin was not only raised in its denomination, but adulterated in its standard.[8] The like frauds were practiced in Scotland during the minority of James VI. They have occasionally been practiced in most other countries.

℃   At this point A. S. turns to consider what might be done in the way of tax reform to so increase the revenues of the British government that there might be some prospect that the public debt could be paid off.

℃   This study takes him at once into the intricate tax, trade, and fiscal relationships of England with her colonies, principally Ireland and the American colonies and the islands of the West Indies. His suggestions aroused interest at the time; but as the independence of the American colonies followed almost immediately, these pages are now of not much more than academic interest. They duplicated to a large extent the analysis of the whole colonial system in Chapters XI and XII of the next book.

[8] A considerable part of the troubles of England in the time of Henry VIII and Edward VI resulted from the frequent tampering with the currency of this nation.

BOOK V

This book is devoted to Adam Smith's analysis of the world
and its economic organization as he found it in 1776; to the
set of theories and policies then in practice to which he gave
the name of the Commercial or Mercantile System; to
that famous dissection of those fallacious policies which
within two generations caused them to be generally abandoned by enlightened governments.

CHAPTER I

The function of gold and silver in the society, and why any nation with natural resources can always acquire all the precious metals it needs; the false notion of the "favorable balance of trade," which the Mercantile System made its principal objective.

IN THE PREFACE to Book I, I remarked that the policies which in nearly all countries have been adopted by its statesmen and legislators to provide income and subsistence for the people, have for the most part resulted in what may be called the Mercantile System.

℃   It is now time to examine this system in greater detail, and in particular to point out the many respects in which its policies have obstructed and retarded, if they have not altogether prohibited, the progress of improvement and enrichment of the society.

That wealth consists in money, or in gold and silver, is a popular delusion which naturally arises from the double function of money, as the medium of exchange, and as the measure of value.[1] When we have money we can obtain whatever else we have occasion for more readily than by means of any other commodity. The great affair, we always find, is to get money. When that is obtained, there is no difficulty in buying whatever is for sale.

Since money is also the measure of value, we estimate the value of all other commodities by the quantity of money which they will exchange for. We say of a rich man that he is worth a

---

[1] Modern economics distinguishes other minor functions of money, of which the most important may be called the temporary storage of purchasing power.

great deal, and of a poor man that he is worth very little money. A frugal man, or a man eager to be rich, is said to love money; and a careless, a generous, or an extravagant man, is said to be indifferent about it.

To grow rich is to get money; and wealth and money, in short, are, in common language, considered as in every respect synonymous.

The popular notion is that a rich country, in the same manner as a rich man, is a country abounding in money; and to heap up gold and silver in any country is supposed to be the readiest way to enrich it.

For some time after the discovery of America, the first inquiry of the Spaniards, when they arrived upon any unknown coast, used to be, if there was any gold or silver to be found in the neighborhood? By the information which they received, they judged whether it was worth while to make a settlement there, or if the country was worth conquering.

Plano Carpino, a monk sent as an ambassador from the king of France to one of the sons of the famous Genghis Khan, says that the Tartars used frequently to ask him, if there was plenty of sheep and oxen in the kingdom of France? Their inquiry had the same object as that of the Spaniards. They wanted to know if the country was rich enough to be worth the conquering.

Among the Tartars, as among all nations of shepherds, who are generally ignorant of the use of money, cattle are the instruments of commerce and the measure of value. Wealth, therefore, according to them, consisted in cattle, as according to the Spaniards it consisted in gold and silver. Of the two, the Tartar notion was perhaps the nearer to the truth.

If a nation could be separated from the rest of the world, it is clear that it would not matter how much or how little money circulated in it. The consumable goods which were circulated by means of this money, would only be exchanged for a greater or a smaller number of pieces of metal or paper; but the real wealth or poverty of the country would depend altogether upon the abundance or scarcity of those goods.

But it is not so clear to many people that the same principle applies to countries which have connections with foreign countries, and which are obliged to carry on foreign wars, and to maintain fleets and armies in distant countries.

This, they say, cannot be done except by sending abroad money to pay them with, and a nation cannot send much money abroad, unless it has a good deal at home.

Every such nation, therefore, must endeavor in time of peace to accumulate gold and silver, so that, when occasion requires, it may have the wherewithal to carry on foreign wars.

In consequence of these popular errors, all civilized nations have studied (without much success, indeed) every possible means of accumulating gold and silver in their respective countries. Spain and Portugal, the owners of the principal mines which for a long time supplied those metals, formerly prohibited their exportation under the severest penalties, or subjected it to a considerable export duty.

When those countries developed commerce, the merchants found this prohibition extremely inconvenient. They could frequently buy foreign goods more advantageously with gold and silver than with any other commodity, and they remonstrated, therefore, against this prohibition as hurtful to trade.

℃ Their arguments were that the export of gold and silver to buy foreign goods did not necessarily reduce the precious metal in the country, because what was bought might be sold again in a third country, in return for more gold and silver than what was originally paid out. They pointed out that the export prohibition was futile anyway, since the metals were easily smuggled out if it were profitable to do so.

℃ But the most persuasive argument was found by these merchants in what they named the balance of trade—a term perhaps as much discussed, and as generally misunderstood, as any in economics. They argued that when a country exported more goods than it imported, the difference in value had to be made up by payment in imported gold and silver, and that the laws should therefore be so framed as to bring about this excess of exports over imports.

℃ The legislators should, therefore, busy themselves with expedients for producing this excess, or what they called a "favorable" balance of trade.

Those arguments were partly sound and partly fallacious. They were sound so far as they asserted that the export of gold and silver in trade might frequently be advantageous to the country, and when they said that no prohibition could prevent

[*369*]

their export, when private people found any advantage in doing it.

But they were sophistical in supposing that to preserve or to increase the quantity of those metals needed the attention of government, any more than to preserve or increase the quantity of any other useful commodities, which freedom of trade, without any attention whatever, never fails to supply in the proper quantity.

They were altogether wrong in asserting that an unfavorable balance of trade tended to get worse unless the government interfered; the fact being that the unimpeded operation of foreign exchange of money and goods invariably tends to equalize itself, as it were automatically.

Such as they were, however, these arguments convinced the people to whom they were addressed. They were addressed by merchants to parliaments, to councils, to nobles, and to country gentlemen; by those who were supposed to understand trade, to those who were well aware that they knew nothing about the matter.[2]

That foreign trade enriched the country, the nobles and country gentlemen knew as well as the merchants; but how, or in what manner, none of them could well make out.

The merchants knew perfectly in what manner foreign trade enriched themselves. It was their business to know it. But to know in what manner it enriched the country was none of their affair.

They did not bother their heads with this question, except when they had occasion to apply to their country for some change in the laws relating to foreign trade, when it became necessary to

[2] It is a far cry from the British legislature of 1776 to that of 1947. Instead of a House of Commons guided by the superior knowledge or persuasion of merchants and manufacturers, partial to the land-owning class, and slightly contemptuous of the workman, we see a body dominated by town labor, intolerant of capital in all forms, openly hostile to land-ownership, and disposed to regard agriculture as something of a necessary nuisance.

What the two sets of law-makers have in common is a totally unfounded confidence in their own wisdom and ability to direct the British people in the management of their private affairs.

It may be predicted with considerable assurance that the economic measures adopted by the present Parliament will be found no more necessary, wise, just, nor salutary than those of 1776 under the ministry of Lord North.

devise some story about the beneficial effects of foreign trade, and the manner in which those effects were obstructed by the laws as they then stood.

To the legislators who had to decide the matter, it appeared most satisfactory, when they were told that foreign trade brought money into the country, but that the laws in question hindered it from bringing as much as it otherwise would do.

ℭ Those arguments therefore produced the wished-for effect. The prohibition of the export of gold and silver was generally removed; and governments turned their attention from this fruitless but relatively simple job, to watch over the balance of trade—a task equally fruitless and far more intricate.

ℭ It is in fact no more difficult for a country without mines to acquire gold and silver, than for a country without vineyards to acquire wine. Both are commodities, and both always can be bought if the country has the wherewithal to offer in exchange. Indeed, the small bulk of the precious metals makes them easier to import and export than almost anything else.

When the quantity of gold and silver imported into any country exceeds the demand, no vigilance of government can prevent their export. All the sanguinary laws of Spain and Portugal were not able to keep their gold and silver at home.

If, on the contrary, in any particular country their quantity fell short of the demand, so as to raise their price above that of neighboring countries, the government would have no occasion to take any pains to import them. It could not even prevent their importation if it tried.

When the Spartans had got wherewithal to purchase the precious metals, they broke through all the barriers which the laws of Lycurgus opposed to their importation into Lacedemon.

It is partly owing to the easy transportation of gold and silver from the places where they abound to those where they are wanted, that the price of those metals does not fluctuate continually like most other commodities, which are hindered by their bulk from shifting their situation, when the market happens to be either overstocked or understocked with them.

If, notwithstanding all this, gold and silver should ever fall short in a country which has wherewithal to purchase them, there are more expedients for supplying their lack than that of almost any other commodity.

[371]

If the materials of manufacture are lacking, industry must stop. If provisions are lacking, the people must starve. But if money is lacking, barter will supply its place, though with a good deal of inconvenience. Buying and selling on credit, the different dealers clearing their credits with one another periodically, will supply it with less inconvenience. A well-regulated paper money will supply it, not only without any inconvenience at all, but in some cases with advantage.

Upon every account, therefore, the attention of government never was so unnecessarily employed, as when directed to watch over the preservation or increase of the quantity of money in any country.

No complaint, however, is more common than that of a scarcity of money. Money, like wine, must always be scarce with those who have neither wherewithal to buy it nor credit to borrow it.

Those who have one or the other will seldom lack money or wine, whichever it is they want.

There are, indeed, cases where money is temporarily scarce in a town and its surrounding area. This is due, as a rule, to over-expansion of business, so that many people want to borrow simultaneously more money than is available to be lent in that area. It is a temporary shortage of credit, not a true scarcity of money.

It would be too ridiculous to go about seriously to prove that wealth does not consist in money, or in gold and silver; but in what money purchases, and is valuable only for purchasing. Money, no doubt, makes always a part of the national capital; but it has already been shown that it generally makes but a small part of it, and always the most unprofitable part.

The merchant finds it generally more easy to buy goods with money, than to buy money with goods; and this is because money is the known and established instrument of commerce, for which everything is readily given in exchange, but which is not always with equal readiness to be got in exchange for other things.

But though a particular merchant, with abundance of goods

[*372*]

in his warehouse, may sometimes be ruined by not being able to sell them in time, a nation is not liable to the same accident.

The whole capital of a merchant frequently consists in perishable goods destined for purchasing money, but it is but a very small part of the total production of a country which can ever be destined for purchasing gold and silver from foreigners. Most of it is circulated and consumed among themselves; and even of the surplus which is sent abroad, the greater part is generally destined for the purchase of other foreign goods. Though gold and silver, therefore, could not be had in exchange for the goods intended to purchase them, the nation would not be ruined.

Goods can serve many other purposes besides buying money, but money can serve no other purpose except to buy goods. Money, therefore, necessarily runs after goods, but goods do not always or necessarily run after money. The man who buys, does not always mean to sell again, but frequently to use or consume; whereas he who sells always means to buy again. The one may frequently have done the whole of his business, but the other can never have done more than half of it. It is not for its own sake that men desire money, but for the sake of what they can purchase with it.

❡ It has sometimes been argued that gold and silver, being very durable, should be imported in preference to consumable goods; they might be thus accumulated for ages together, and the country thus become incredibly rich.

❡ No idea could be more absurd. Pots and pans for cooking are also durable; but no one would therefore argue that more of them should be accumulated than are actually needed for cooking. Similarly, it is absurd to accumulate more gold and silver than is actually needed as a medium of exchange for commodities and services; and in fact such an unnecessary accumulation cannot take place, or rather cannot be maintained for any considerable time in a free country.

The transportation of these metals is so easy, and the loss which attends their lying idle and unemployed so great, that no law could prevent their being immediately sent out of the country.

❡ Here A. S. proceeds to examine another argument advanced for the accumulation of the precious metals—that they are necessary as a resource for the expense of possible foreign wars. Without going into his elaborate analysis, he shows that the ex-

[*373*]

penses of armies in distant fields are not, in fact, paid with gold or money of any kind, but with commodities, principally the finer manufactures. The precious metals are perhaps paid out to the soldiers and for supplies, but manufactures must previously have been exported to obtain the metals for this purpose.

There is therefore no more reason for importing gold and silver in excessive amounts for this purpose than for any other; a nation unable to export manufactured goods to obtain gold and silver for the expense of distant armies being obviously in no condition to wage war at all.

The real benefits of foreign trade are twofold. Trade carries out that surplus part of the produce of the land and labor for which there is no demand, and brings back in return for it something else for which there is a demand. It gives a value to their superfluities, by exchanging them for something else, which may satisfy a part of their wants, and increase their enjoyments.

By means of it, the narrowness of the home market does not hinder the division of labor in art or manufacture from being carried to the highest perfection. By opening a more extensive market for whatever part of the produce of their labor may exceed the domestic demand, it encourages them to improve its productive powers, and to increase its annual produce to the utmost, and thereby to increase the real income and wealth of the society.

These great and important services foreign trade is continually performing, to all the different countries between which it is carried on. They all derive great benefit from it, though that in which the merchant resides generally derives the greatest.[3]

It was not by the importation of greatly increased supplies of gold and silver that the discovery of America enriched Europe. By the abundance of the American mines, those metals became cheaper. Silverware can now be purchased for about a third part of the grain, or a third part of the labor, which it would have cost in the 15th Century.

With the same annual expense of labor and commodities, Europe can annually purchase about three times the quantity of silverware that it could at that time. But when a commodity

---

[3] While foreign trade is usually beneficial (more so between regions than between nations), it has no inherent superiority over domestic trade, or vice versa. Thorold Rogers says that whichever suits best the peculiar circumstances of a given nation will be best for that nation.

comes to be sold for a third part of what had been its usual price, not only those who bought it before can purchase three times as much, but it is brought down to the level of a much larger number of purchasers, perhaps to ten, perhaps to more than twenty times the former number.

The cheapness of gold and silver renders those metals rather less fit for the purposes of money than they were before. In order to make the same purchases, we must load ourselves with a greater quantity of them, and carry about a quarter in our pocket where a dime would have done before. It is difficult to say which is most trifling, this inconvenience, or the opposite convenience. Neither of them could have made any very essential change in the state of Europe.

The discovery of America, however, certainly changed Europe in an essential way.

By opening a new and inexhaustible market to all the commodities of Europe, it gave occasion to new divisions of labor and improvement of art, which, in the narrow circle of the ancient commerce, could never have taken place for want of a market. The productive powers of labor were improved, and its produce increased in all the different countries of Europe, and the real income and wealth of the inhabitants increased with it.

The commodities of Europe were almost all new to America, and many of those of America were new to Europe. A new set of exchanges, therefore, began to take place which should naturally have proved as advantageous to the new world as it certainly did to the old. It was only the savage injustice of the Europeans that rendered an event, which ought to have been beneficial to all, ruinous and destructive to several of those unfortunate countries.

℄ The discovery of the passage to the East Indies by the Cape of Good Hope, about the same time, should have been still more advantageous. The American natives were, with the exception of the Mayas and Incas, mere savages, while the nations of the Far East were by comparison rich and civilized.

℄ But the Far Eastern trade had the misfortune to fall under the domination of great private trading companies, beginning with the Portuguese and Dutch. Not until the 19th Century did Europe begin to receive the benefit of free commerce, in this great market.

CHAPTER II

The theory of the "balance of trade" examined further, and shown to be the result of one or another form of monopoly; why the state should not permit monopolies, much less encourage them; the evil effects of endeavoring forcibly to turn the capital of a country out of the channels in which it would naturally flow, and the benefits of free exchange of products between nations.

AT THE RISK OF BEING exceedingly tiresome, I have thought it necessary to examine at full length this popular delusion that wealth consists in money, or in gold and silver. As I have already observed, money is commonly spoken of as the same as wealth, because it will nearly always exchange for wealth; and this ambiguity of expression has rendered this popular notion so familiar to us, that even people who know better are very apt to forget their own principles, and in the course of their reasonings to take it for granted as a certain and undeniable truth.

However that may be, there were eventually established these two principles, both of which were false: that wealth consisted in gold and silver, and that those metals could be brought into a country only by the balance of trade, or by exporting to a greater value than it imported. This necessarily made it the great object of political economy to diminish as much as possible the importation of foreign goods, and to increase as much as possible the exportation of the produce of domestic industry. Its two great

[*376*]

engines for enriching the country, therefore, were restraints upon imports, and encouragements to exports.[1]

The restraints upon importation were of two kinds: restraints upon importing foreign goods which could be produced at home; and restraints upon importing any goods from particular countries with which the balance of trade was supposed to be unfavorable.

Those different restraints consisted sometimes in high duties, and sometimes in absolute prohibitions.

On the other side, exportation was encouraged sometimes by drawbacks, sometimes by bounties, sometimes by advantageous treaties of commerce with foreign states, and sometimes by the establishment of colonies in distant countries.

All these together constitute the six principal means by which the commercial system proposes to increase the quantity of gold and silver in any country by turning the balance of trade in its favor. I shall consider each of them in turn, and shall examine chiefly what are the effects of each of them upon the annual produce of a country's industry. According as they tend either to increase or diminish the value of its production, they must evidently tend either to increase or decrease the real wealth and income of the nation.

By restraining by high duties, or by absolute prohibitions, the importation of such goods as can be produced at home, the monopoly of the home market is more or less secured to the domestic industry employed in producing them.

[1] Here we enter on the famous and devastating analysis of the system of law-enforced tariffs and bounties, drawbacks, preferences, and prohibitions, which together make up the Mercantile System, with which W. N. in a few years overturned that system, and in a literal sense changed the world.

"The life of everyone in England," said Walter Bagehot, "—perhaps of everyone—is different and better in consequence of it."

It took the principle of freedom of production and exchange out of the realm of speculation, and made the governments of the world, for the first time, defend their right to interfere in the business of the people. It set England on the road that led eventually to a century of "free trade" and the leadership of the civilized world.

In an era which has seen the steady resurrection of all the old delusions and fallacies of the Mercantile System, with a few new ones thrown in for good measure (including the apostasy of England herself in the matter of protective tariffs and freedom of commerce), these chapters deserve to be read once more with anxious attention.

Many lines of manufacture have obtained in Great Britain a complete or nearly complete monopoly against their country-men. The variety of goods of which the importation into Great Britain is prohibited, either absolutely, or under certain circumstances, greatly exceeds what those who are not well acquainted with the customs laws would suspect.

That this monopoly of the home market frequently gives great encouragement to those particular lines of industry which enjoy it, and frequently turns towards that employment a greater share of both the labor and capital of the society than would otherwise have gone to it, cannot be doubted. But whether it tends either to increase the general industry of the society, or to give it the most advantageous direction, is not, perhaps, altogether so evident.[2]

The general industry of the country can never exceed what its capital can employ. As the number of workmen that can be kept in employment by any particular person must bear a certain proportion to his capital, so the number of those that can be employed by all the members of a great nation must bear a certain proportion to its whole capital, and never can exceed that proportion.[3]

No regulation of commerce can increase the quantity of industry in any society beyond what its capital can maintain. It can only divert a part of it into a direction into which it might not

[2] There is no special advantage of a monopoly of the home market, observes Thorold Rogers, unless there is a monopoly *within* the market. If competition is maintained among domestic producers, the interests of consumers are safe, even when there are no imports. But it is the exclusion of imports which makes domestic monopoly so much the easier to establish, and monopoly is already too easy.

[3] A re-statement of the very mild form of wage-fund theory as found in W. N. At any given moment, employment certainly depends on the capital (from whatever source derived) available to pay wages at that moment. But the proportion between total capital and total employment will be constantly changing, through development of better methods and many other causes.

otherwise have gone; and it is by no means certain that this artificial direction is likely to be more advantageous to the society
than that into which it would have gone of its own accord.

Every individual is continually exerting himself to
find the most advantageous employment for whatever
capital he can command. It is his own advantage, indeed,
and not that of the society, which he has in view. But
the study of his own advantage naturally, or rather
necessarily, leads him to prefer that employment which
is most advantageous to the society.

First, every individual will try to employ his capital as
near home as he can, and consequently as much as he can in the
support of domestic industry; provided always that he can thereby
obtain the ordinary, or not much less than the ordinary, profits of
capital.

❦ Thus a wholesale merchant, because he can keep his capital
close at home and under his own eye, will naturally prefer a
domestic business to foreign trade, and domestic business is the
most advantageous to the society as a whole. For the same reason
he will prefer direct foreign trade to the carrying trade, which
latter is the least favorable to the nation.

Again, every individual who employs his capital in the
support of domestic industry, necessarily tries to direct that industry so that its product may be of the greatest possible value, or will
exchange for the greatest quantity of money or of other goods.

But the annual income of every society is always precisely
equal to the exchangeable value of the whole annual produce of
its industry—one is the same as the other.[4]

As every individual, therefore, endeavors as much as he
can both to employ his capital in the support of domestic industry,

[4] This brings up the subject of "purchasing power," which should be better
understood. Purchasing power is actually an end-product of production; distribution
of money and credit appear to produce purchasing power, and do actually confer it
upon the individuals who receive such a hand-out. But for the society as a whole, this
is an illusion; real purchasing power is created only when some article or service is
sold to a consumer.   (*Footnote continued on following page.*)

and so to direct that industry that its produce may be of the greatest value, every individual necessarily labors to render the annual income of the society as great as he can.

It makes no difference that he neither intends to promote the public interest, nor knows how much he is promoting it. By preferring the support of domestic to that of foreign industry, he intends only his own security; and by directing that industry so as to produce the greatest value, he intends only his own gain.

In this, as in many other cases, he is led by an invisible hand to promote an end which was no part of his intention.[5] I have never known much good done by those who affected to trade for the public good. It is an affectation, indeed, not very common among merchants, and very few words need be employed in dissuading them from it.

The amount thus created is equal to the price at which the sale is made, and this amount is then divided up among all who have contributed in any way to the production and distribution of the article. As the share of any contributor cannot be increased except at the expense of the others, the size of these shares is a prolific source of disputes.

Thus it is production, and production only, which can create real purchasing power, and the purchasing power created is exactly sufficient to purchase everything that is produced, provided there is an effective demand for it.

[5] This is the famous sentence that so infuriates all Marxists and their fellow-travelers, and even occasions some eyebrow-lifting among economists.

Just why the economists should be upset is not clear. To say that the freest play of individual judgment and enterprise, however selfish in motive, will produce the maximum of public prosperity and happiness, is surely good economic doctrine. And why object to the "invisible hand"? The critics who call A. S. "too materialistic" should ponder this reference to a Supreme Power.

As to the Marxist, the case is quite clear. The hand with which he proposes to achieve Utopia is by no means invisible—it is his own. Like many so-called liberals, he secretly visualizes himself in the seat of power, directing the activities of a submissive and grateful people with supreme wisdom and complete success. By no means dare he admit that the collective decisions of millions, each intending only his own gain, will do a better job than he could.

The Marxist state would be a kind of aristocracy, to be sure—the rule of the best—but "the best," as in Russia, would be specifically the most ambitious and ruthless. To this baleful eminence, in the name of the public welfare, every Marxist aspires. It is a form of megalomania.

What line of domestic industry his capital can best employ, and of which the product is likely to be of the greatest value, every individual, it is evident, can judge much better than any statesman or lawgiver can do for him.

The statesman who should attempt to direct private people in what manner they ought to employ their capital would not only load himself with a most unnecessary attention, but assume an authority which could safely be trusted, not only to no single person, but to no council or senate whatever, and which would nowhere be so dangerous as in the hands of a man who had folly and presumption enough to fancy himself fit to exercise it.

To give the monopoly of the home market to a particular branch of manufacture, is in some measure to direct private people in what manner they ought to employ their capital, and must, in almost all cases, be either useless or hurtful. If domestic goods can be brought to the market as cheap as those of foreign industry, the regulation is evidently useless. If they cannot, it must generally be hurtful.

It is the maxim of every prudent master of a family, never to attempt to make at home what it will cost him more to make than to buy. The tailor does not attempt to make his own shoes, but buys them of the shoemaker. The shoemaker does not attempt to make his own clothes, but employs a tailor. The farmer attempts to make neither the one nor the other, but employs those different artificers.

All of them find it for their interest, by the division of labor, to employ their whole industry in a way in which they have some advantage over their neighbors, and to purchase with a part of its produce, or what is the same thing, with the price of a part of it, whatever else they have occasion for.

What is prudence in the conduct of a private family, can scarcely be folly in that of any nation. If a foreign country can supply us with a commodity cheaper than we ourselves can make it, better buy it of them with some part of the produce of our own industry, employed in a way in which we have some advantage.

The general industry of the country, being always in proportion to the capital which employs it, will not thereby be diminished, but only given the task of finding out the way in which it can be employed with the greatest advantage. It is certainly not employed to the greatest advantage, when it is artificially directed toward an object which it can buy cheaper than it can make.

The value of the whole national production is certainly more or less diminished, when it is turned away from producing a commodity evidently of more value toward something of less value. That commodity could be purchased from foreign countries cheaper than it could be made at home. It could, therefore, have been bought with a part only of the commodities, or, what is the same thing, the price of the commodities, which an equal capital would have produced at home, had it been left to follow its natural course.

The industry of the country, therefore, is thus turned away from a more advantageous to a less advantageous employment, and the exchangeable value of its total production, instead of being increased, according to the intention of the law-maker, must necessarily be lowered by every such regulation.

By means of such protective measures, indeed, a particular manufacture may sometimes be established sooner than it would otherwise have been, and after a certain time may be made at home as cheaply as or cheaper than in the foreign country. But it will by no means follow that the sum total of its industry or revenue can ever be augmented by any such expedient.

The industry of the society can grow, only in proportion as its capital grows, and its capital can grow only in proportion to what can be gradually saved out of its income.

But the immediate effect of every such regulation is to reduce its income, and what reduces its income is certainly not very likely to augment its capital faster than it would have grown of its own accord, had both capital and industry been left to find out their natural employment.

The natural advantages which one country has over another in producing particular commodities are sometimes so great, that it is acknowledged by all the world to be in vain to struggle against them. By means of glass, hotbeds, and hotwalls, very good grapes can be raised in Scotland, and very good wine can be made of them, at about thirty times the cost for which equally good wine can be brought from foreign countries.

Would it be a reasonable law to prohibit the importation of all foreign wines, merely to encourage the making of claret and burgundy in Scotland?

But if there would be a manifest absurdity in turning toward any employment thirty times more of the capital and industry of the country, than would be necessary to purchase the same commodities from foreign countries, there must be an absurdity, not altogether so glaring, yet exactly of the same kind, in turning toward any such employment twice as much, or even a thirtieth or a three-hundredth part more.

Whether the advantages which one country has over another be natural or acquired, is of no consequence. As long as the one country has those advantages, and the other lacks them, it will always be more advantageous for the latter to buy of the former. The advantage which one artificer has over his neighbor in another business is also acquired; and yet they both find it more advantageous to buy of one another, than to make what does not belong to their particular trades.

CHAPTER III

A further examination of monopolies, which were in 1776 and still are the peculiar favorite of merchants and manufacturers, not farmers; some particular cases where it may be justifiable, nevertheless, to place restrictions on some imports; while freedom of trade is best, it is an Utopian ideal scarcely to be hoped for in any nation of would-be monopolists governed by politicians; it is sometimes even dangerous to advocate it.

MERCHANTS AND MANUFACTURERS are the people who derive the greatest advantage from this monopoly of the home market. Agriculture can derive very little benefit from it. The prohibition of the importation of foreign cattle, together with the high duties upon foreign grain, which in times of moderate plenty amount to a prohibition, are not nearly so advantageous to the stock raisers and farmers of Great Britain, as other regulations of the same kind are to its merchants and manufacturers.

In manufactures, a very small price advantage will enable foreigners to undersell our own workmen, even in the home market. It will require a very great one to enable them to do so in farm products. If the free importation of foreign manufactures were permitted, some home manufactures would probably suffer, and perhaps go to ruin altogether, and a considerable part of the capital and industry at present employed in them, would be forced to find some other employment. But the freest importation of farm products could have no such effect upon the agriculture of the country.

℃ Here A. S. devotes a couple of pages to a discussion of the effect of free import of cattle from Ireland, and also of salt meat and grain, upon British farmers. His conclusion is that it would affect their interests little if at all.

Country gentlemen and farmers are, to their great honor, of all people the least subject to the wretched spirit of monopoly. The great manufacturer is sometimes alarmed if another plant of the same kind is established within twenty miles of him. The Dutch manufacturer of woolens at Abbeville stipulated that no factory of the same kind should be established within thirty leagues of that city.

Farmers and country gentlemen, on the contrary, are generally disposed rather to promote than to obstruct the cultivation and improvement of their neighbors' farms and estates. They have no trade secrets, but are generally rather fond of communicating to their neighbors, and of extending, as far as possible, any new practice which they have found to be advantageous.

Country gentlemen and farmers, dispersed in different parts of the country, cannot so easily combine as merchants and manufacturers, who, being concentrated in towns, and accustomed to that exclusive spirit which prevails in them, naturally endeavor to obtain against all their countrymen, the same exclusive privilege which they generally possess against their own townspeople. They accordingly seem to have been the original inventors of those restraints upon the importation of foreign goods, which secure to them the monopoly of the home market.[1]

It was probably in imitation of them, and to put themselves upon a level with those who, they found, were disposed to oppress them, that the country gentlemen and farmers of Great Britain so far forgot the generosity which is natural to their station, as to demand the exclusive privilege of supplying their countrymen with grain and meat. They did not perhaps take time to consider, how much less their interest could be affected by the freedom of trade, than that of the people whose example they followed.

To prohibit by a perpetual law the importation of foreign grain and cattle, is in reality to enact that the population and industry of the country shall at no time exceed what the products of its own soil can maintain.

[1] By the time of the Corn Law agitation in England, the farm interests had become violent supporters of the "protective" system, while the mercantile classes, influenced by W. N., generally repudiated it.

There seem, however, to be two cases in which it will generally be advantageous to lay some burden upon foreign industry.

The first is, when some particular sort of industry is necessary for the defense of the country. The defense of Great Britain, for example, depends very much upon the number of its sailors and ships. The Act of Navigation, therefore, very properly endeavors to give the sailors and shipping of Great Britain the monopoly of the trade of their own country—in some cases by absolute prohibitions, and in others by heavy burdens upon the shipping of foreign countries.[2]

When this law was passed, though England and Holland were not actually at war, the most violent animosity existed between the two nations. It is not impossible, therefore, that some of its regulations may have proceeded from national animosity. They are as wise, however, as if they had all been dictated by the most deliberate wisdom. National animosity at that particular time aimed at the very same object which the most deliberate wisdom would have recommended, the diminution of the naval power of Holland, the only naval power which could endanger the security of England.[3]

The interest of a nation in its commercial relations with foreign nations is, like that of a merchant with regard to the different people with whom he deals, to buy as cheap and to sell as dear as possible. But it will be most likely to buy cheap, when by the most perfect freedom of trade it encourages all nations to bring to it the goods which it needs; and, for the same reason, it will be most likely to sell dear, when its markets are thus filled with the greatest number of buyers.

The Act of Navigation, it is true, lays no burden upon foreign ships that come to export the produce of British industry. But if foreigners are hindered from coming to sell, they cannot always afford to come to buy; because coming without a cargo, they must lose the freight from their own country to Great Britain. By diminishing the number of sellers, therefore, we neces-

---

[2] This celebrated law, dating from the reign of Charles II, prohibited foreign shipping from trading with the British colonies, and from the coastwise trade; excluded the Dutch and other carrying nations from British ports; prohibited the import of many commodities from any country except where produced—probably another blow at the Dutch; and doubled the tariff duties on fish not caught by British fishermen.

[3] Here speaks, for once, the insular Briton.

sarily diminish that of buyers, and are thus likely not only to buy foreign goods dearer, but to sell our own cheaper, than if there were a more perfect freedom of trade.

As defense, however, is of much more importance than opulence, the Act of Navigation is, perhaps, the wisest of all the commercial regulations of England.[4]

The second case in which it will generally be advantageous to lay some burden upon foreign for the encouragement of domestic industry, is when some tax is imposed at home upon some commodity. In this case, it seems reasonable that an equal tax should be imposed upon imports of this article. This would not give the monopoly of the home market to domestic industry, nor turn toward a particular employment a greater share of the capital and labor of the country than would naturally go to it.

It would only hinder any part of what capital would naturally go to it from being turned away by the tax into a less natural direction, and would leave the competition between foreign and domestic industry, after the tax, as nearly as possible upon the same footing as before.

In Great Britain, when any such tax is laid upon some domestic product, it is usual at the same time, in order to stop the clamor of our merchants and manufacturers that they will be ruined, to lay a much heavier duty upon the importation of all foreign goods of the same kind.

This second limitation of the freedom of trade, according to some people, should sometimes be extended much farther than to the precise foreign commodities which could compete with those which had been taxed at home. When the necessaries of life have been taxed at home, it becomes proper, they pretend, to tax not only the like necessaries of life imported from other countries, but all sorts of foreign goods which can come into competition with anything produced at home.

Subsistence, they say, becomes necessarily dearer in consequence of such taxes; and the price of labor must always rise with the price of the laborer's subsistence. Every domestic commodity, therefore, though not immediately taxed itself, becomes

---

[4] The believers in the protective tariff take great comfort from this passage: "Even A. S. puts national defense ahead of free trade." As a matter of history, when the Navigation Act was abandoned in 1849 and 1854, navigation was not discouraged nor the supply of seamen reduced.

dearer in consequence of such taxes, because the labor which produces it becomes so. Such taxes, therefore, are really equivalent, they say, to a tax upon every particular commodity produced at home. In order to put domestic industry upon the same footing with foreigners, therefore, it becomes necessary, they think, to lay some duty upon every foreign commodity.

Whether taxes upon the necessaries of life, such as soap, salt, leather, candles, etc., necessarily raise the price of labor, and consequently that of all other commodities, I have already discussed in the chapters on taxes. But assuming for the moment that they have this effect (and no doubt they have), this general enhancement of the price of all commodities differs in two ways from that of a particular commodity, of which the price was enhanced by a particular tax.

In the first place, it is impossible to calculate with any accuracy how much general prices would be increased by the tax on a particular commodity; to impose tariff duties on such a basis would be mere guess-work.

Secondly, taxes upon the necessaries of life have nearly the same effect upon the circumstances of the people as a poor soil and a bad climate. Provisions are made dearer by the tax, exactly as if it required extraordinary labor and expense to raise them. Just as under a natural scarcity arising from soil and climate, it would be absurd to direct the people in what manner they ought to employ their capital and industry, so it is likewise under an artificial scarcity arising from such taxes.

They should be left to accommodate, as well as they could, their industry to their situation, and to find out those employments in which, notwithstanding their unfavorable circumstances, they might have some advantage at home or in a foreign market. To lay a new tax upon them, because they are already overburdened with taxes, and because they already pay too much for the necessaries of life to make them likewise pay too much for nearly everything, is certainly a most absurd way of helping them.

Such taxes, when they have grown up to a certain height, are a curse equal to the barrenness of the earth and the inclemency of the heavens; and yet it is in the richest and most industrious countries that they have been most generally imposed. No poor country could support so great a disease.

Only the nations which have the greatest natural and acquired advantages can subsist and prosper under such taxes. Holland is the country in Europe in which they abound most, and which from peculiar circumstances continues to prosper, not because of them, as has been most absurdly supposed, but in spite of them.[5]

[5] As far as I have been able to find, neither A. S. nor any other economist is fully aware of the dominant influence of the public debt of a nation, in setting the market value or purchasing power of its currency.

The purchasing power of money, or the average money prices of goods and services, by whichever name it is called, seems to be determined largely by the amount of revenue which must be raised to support the government, in any nation where capital and labor are reasonably free. Some part of this revenue is necessary for interest and sinking fund payments on the national debt, and these payments are unavoidable unless this debt is to be openly repudiated.

In other words, service of the public debt is the inflexible element in national taxes. When it forms a large element, the total cost of government is increased more than in proportion. The increase cannot usually be compensated by government frugality in other directions, even if frugality were practiced, which it never is for any length of time.

The result is that the taxpayer, feeling the burden of unprecedented taxation, will do everything in his power to increase his income to a point where that burden is no longer seriously felt.

Heavy taxes, recommended to "combat inflation," are actually deflationary over a short term. In the long run, they are highly inflationary.

What is true of one individual is true of the whole body of taxpayers, and the necessary effect is that in no long time the entire structure of prices, wages, salaries, and rents is forced upward. This is the "inflation" which follows every great war.

I do not mean to say that this is the sole cause of post-war inflation. Nor is the fall in the purchasing power of money necessarily in direct proportion to the rise in taxes. Growth of population, increase in productivity, a willingness to accept a lower standard of living, some monetary factors, all modify the process in various ways.

Economists are familiar with the temporary price inflation which results from a great surplus of money and credit in a period of scarcity of goods. This is temporary, though real, and disappears as soon as the supply of goods overtakes the demand. But the much more serious permanent inflation which inevitably follows any great increase in the public debt seems to have escaped their notice.

It is, in fact, a partial and perfectly legal repudiation of the debt, as every holder of government loans becomes painfully aware. Where government bonds can be "monetized," as in the case of the United States at present, their money value may not fall. But the purchasing power of the interest, and of the real asset value of the loan, is subject to the same steady wasting away as that of other money.

A. S. refers in one passage to the debasement of the coinage by various sovereigns, and elsewhere to the repudiation of public debts. But even A. S. did not put two and two together, and find in the cost of government, inflated by debts, usually due to great wars, the true key to the steadily falling purchasing power of money in every great nation.

℃ Besides the two cases where it is reasonable to lay some burden upon foreign imports, there are two others where sound policy would suggest partial exceptions to the general rule of freedom of commerce.

℃ The first is where some foreign country unjustly penalizes domestic industry in some way. Some measure of retaliation, to induce the foreign country to desist from its oppression, might be considered. But it must be said that such measures generally result, not in correction of the evil, but in counter-measures; so that trade relations between the nations go from bad to worse.

℃ To judge whether such retaliation is likely to be effective would seem to belong not to the statesman, whose acts should be governed by unchanging general principles, but to the skill of that insidious and crafty animal, vulgarly called a politician, who is guided by opportunism only.[6]

℃ As I have said, such retaliation generally fails; and it seems a bad method of compensating the injury done to one class of our people, by inflicting a second injury on them, and extending it to almost everybody else besides.

℃ The second consideration is that when particular goods have long paid duties upon importation, so that capital has been attracted to this manufacture and many workmen employed, this protection should be removed with caution and only by slow degrees.

Were those high duties and prohibitions taken away all at once, cheaper foreign goods might be poured into the home market so fast as to deprive many thousands of our people of their ordinary employment and means of subsistence. The distress which this would cause might no doubt be very considerable, but it would in all probability be much less than is commonly imagined.

There would be no distress in the case of goods which are customarily exported, and which are therefore already successfully meeting the competition of foreign goods in the world's markets.

Although many people should, by thus restoring the freedom of trade, be thrown all at once out of their ordinary employ-

---

[6] An interesting example of changes in the use of words. This sentence in W. N. reads: "does not belong so much to the science of a legislator . . . as to the skill of that insidious and crafty animal, vulgarly called a statesman or politician." The synonym of 1776 is the antonym of 1947.

ment, it would by no means follow that they would thereby be deprived either of employment or subsistence. By the reduction of the army and navy at the end of the late war, more than a hundred thousand soldiers and seamen were all at once thrown out of their ordinary employment; but, though they no doubt suffered some inconvenience, they were not thereby deprived of all employment and subsistence.

In most lines of manufacture, there are other collateral manufactures of so similar a nature, that a workman can easily transfer his industry from one of them to another. The capital which employed them in a particular manufacture before, will still remain in the country to employ an equal number of people in some other way. The capital of the country remaining the same, the demand for labor will likewise be the same, or very nearly the same, though it may be exerted in different places and for different occupations.

To expect, indeed, that complete freedom of trade should ever be entirely restored is as absurd as to expect that Utopia should ever be established. Not only the ignorant prejudices of the public, but what is much more unconquerable, the private interests of many individuals, irresistibly oppose it.

Were the officers of the army to oppose any reduction in the armed forces, with the same zeal and unanimity with which large and small manufacturers set themselves against every law that is likely to increase the number of their rivals in the home market—were the former to animate their soldiers, in the same manner as the latter inflame their workmen, to attack with violence and outrage the proposers of any such reform—any attempt to reduce the army would be as dangerous as it has now become to attempt to reduce in any respect the monopoly which our own manufacturers have obtained against us.

This monopoly has so much increased the number of some particular tribes of them, that, like an overgrown standing army, they have become formidable to the government, and upon many occasions intimidate the legislature.

The politician who supports every proposal for strengthening this monopoly, is sure to acquire not only the reputation of understanding trade, but great popularity and influence with an order of men whose numbers and wealth render them of great importance.

[391]

If he opposes them, on the contrary, and still more if he has authority enough to be able to thwart them, neither the most acknowledged probity, nor the highest rank, nor the greatest public services, can protect him from the most infamous abuse and detraction, from personal insults, and even sometimes from real danger, arising from the insolent outrage of furious and disappointed monopolists.[7]

The owners of a great establishment who, by the home markets being suddenly laid open to the competition of foreigners, should be obliged to go out of business, would no doubt suffer very considerably. That part of their capital which had usually been employed in purchasing materials and in paying workmen, might without much difficulty, perhaps, find another employment. But that part of it which was fixed in factories and machinery could scarcely be disposed of without considerable loss.

Justice therefore requires that changes of this kind should never be introduced suddenly, but slowly, gradually, and after a very long warning. The legislature, were it possible that its deliberations could always be directed, not by the clamorous importunity of special interests, but by a broad view of the general good,

[7] It is largely to the forthright and courageous analysis of the system of protective tariff duties, in this and the preceding chapter, that we owe the firm establishment of the principle of free trade in the world. All economists, broadly speaking, are free-traders.

Even those who, like Friedrich List and Henry A. Carey, have supported the protective principle, have agreed that it cannot be defended on economic grounds. They are therefore forced to argue that protection is necessary for the introduction of "infant industries," for military defense, for the conservation of scarce raw materials, or for the development of certain political and metaphysical values.

At different times, social objectives have been emphasized, particularly those relating to agriculture. Protection was formerly urged because a purely agricultural country would be stupid, uninteresting, and barbarous. A century later, protection for farm raw materials is urged to maintain agriculture, regarded as the source of all social health and intellectual force.

Nevertheless, the generalization stands: on purely economic grounds, all economists are free-traders.

ought upon this very account to be particularly careful neither to establish any new monopolies of this kind, nor to extend further those which are already established.

Every such law introduces some degree of dislocation into the constitution of the state, which it will be difficult afterwards to cure without occasioning another equally bad.

CHAPTER IV

Foreign trade may be restrained and har-
assed by unreasonable national dislikes and
animosities as well as by the "mean rapacity,
the monopolizing spirit of merchants and
manufacturers"; the true principle being
that it is greatly to the advantage of any
nation to be surrounded by prosperous and
wealthy neighbors, provided they are not
military aggressors.

IN ITS ANXIETY to increase the quantity of gold and silver in a country, the commercial or mercantile system had a second expedient to restrain and harass the trade of other countries with which the balance of trade was supposed to be unfavorable.

⊄ The arch-rival of England, for centuries together, was France; and accordingly goods imported from across the Channel were subjected to all kinds of special burdens, so that 75 per cent was in 1776 the lowest rate of duty imposed on most French imports. Upon most commodities this rate amounted to total exclusion.

The French in their turn treated British goods and manufactures just as roughly, and these mutual restraints put an end to almost all fair commerce between the two nations. Smugglers therefore naturally became the principal importers of British goods into France, and of French goods into Great Britain. The principles which I have been examining in the foregoing chapter took their origin from private selfishness and the spirit of monopoly; but these I am now speaking of arose from national prejudice

[*394*]

and animosity. They are accordingly (as might well be expected), still more unreasonable. They are unreasonable even upon the unreasonable principles of the commercial system.

⁋ Even if free trade with France had led to an unfavorable balance of trade with that one country, it would not necessarily have done so with the world in general, which is what would determine the import of gold and silver. Furthermore, some of the imports from France would certainly have been re-exported, the sale price plus a profit possibly bringing back in gold and silver the whole value of all French imports.

⁋ To these possibilities and uncertainties it would have to be added that the question of a "favorable" or unfavorable" balance of trade with a particular country is itself uncertain. Neither the actual statistics of imports and exports, nor the movement of exchange rates with individual countries, can be at all relied upon for this information.[1]

⁋ Another ground for uncertainty as to international trade balances in the 18th Century arose from the varying standards of money itself. The coinage of those days, particularly the silver, varied between different countries, sometimes because of wear and tear, sometimes because the government charged seigniorage upon coinage, raising the value of the coin above the value of bullion it contained. In some nations the paper of the banks bore a different value from that of the metal coinage.

⁋ For these and other reasons, even the open market rates of exchange did not show with any certainty how the balance of trade stood between countries.

⁋ But this situation in the late 18th Century was far better, even so, than in earlier times. It was because small nations were obliged to admit the money of more powerful neighbors, if they

---

[1] The improvements in statistical technique since A. S. have now made it possible to assemble fairly dependable figures on trade balances with particular countries. But even these are apt to be misleading, since so much foreign trade (at least in peacetime) consists of triangular or multilateral exchanges.

It is, indeed, a vain inquiry at best. What all the modern studies have succeeded in proving boils down to one simple fact—that the trade of a particular nation with the rest of the world can not, over a reasonable period of time, be either "favorable" or "unfavorable." Exports and imports, counting all visible and invisible items —commodities, freight charges, insurance, travelers' and immigrants' expenditures and remittances, permanent investments, interest and profits payments, shipments of gold considered as merchandise—must and will, over a reasonable time, exactly balance.

wished to engage in foreign trade, that they were customarily victimized with debased, chipped, and worn coins.

    ❡   Banks were therefore established, whose original purpose was to receive any kind of money at its real or intrinsic value, and pay in good money, in which everyone might have some confidence.

    ❡   The famous Bank of Amsterdam was established in 1609 for this purpose, under the guarantee of the city. The earlier banks of Venice, Genoa, Hamburg, and Nuremberg had a similar origin.

    ❡   A. S. here digresses to explain at considerable length the operations of the Bank of Amsterdam—a subject of interest chiefly, perhaps, to the student of banking. This institution enjoyed for nearly two centuries a very high reputation, principally because it was believed that it was always in a situation 100 per cent liquid—that for every guilder owed a depositor, the bank had in its vaults an actual guilder of coin or bullion.

    ❡   A. S. describes this policy in a way that suggests that he had some doubts as to this perfect liquidity; but as the bank issued no statements, no precise information was obtainable.[2]

    ❡   But if the idea of manipulating the balance of trade in order to promote prosperity in a country was unreasonable even on the principles of the Mercantile System, it was absurd on sound principles, as are almost all other regulations of commerce.

When two places trade with one another, this doctrine supposes that, if the balance be even, neither of them either loses or gains; but if it leans in any degree to one side, one must lose and the other gain in proportion.

Both superstitions are false. A trade which is forced by means of bounties and monopolies may be, and commonly is, disadvantageous to the country in whose favor it is meant to operate; but that trade which, without force or constraint, is naturally and regularly carried on between any two places, is always advantageous, though not always equally so, to both.

---

[2] As a matter of fact, the bank's complete liquidity turned out to be a myth. The directors and the city government of Amsterdam had long been secretly making unsecured advances to the city, to two Dutch provinces, and to the Dutch East India Company; and this fact having been reluctantly made public in 1795, the ruin of the bank followed shortly afterward. Secrecy almost always covers not safety but fraud.

By "advantage" or "gain," I mean not an increase of the quantity of gold and silver, but that of the exchangeable value of the annual produce of the land and labor of the country, or the increase of the annual income of its inhabitants.

If the balance be even, and if the trade between the two places consist altogether in the exchange of their native products, they will, as a rule, not only both gain, but they will gain equally, or very nearly equally; each will in this case afford a market for a part of the surplus produce of the other; each will replace capital which has been employed in raising and preparing for the market this part of the surplus produce of the other, and which had been distributed among and given income and maintenance to a certain number of its inhabitants.

If their trade should be of such a nature that one of them exported to the other nothing but their own products, while the returns of the other consisted altogether in foreign goods, the balance, in this case, would still be even, commodities being paid for with commodities. They would both gain in this case too, but they would not gain equally; and the inhabitants of the country which exported nothing but native commodities would derive the greatest advantage from the trade.

If England, for example, should import from France nothing but the native commodities of that country, and, not having such commodities of its own as were in demand there, should annually repay them by sending thither a large quantity of foreign goods, let us say tobacco; this trade, though it would give some income to the inhabitants of both countries, would give more to those of France than to those of England. The whole French capital annually employed in it would annually be distributed among the people of France. But that part of the British capital only which was employed in producing the English commodities with which those foreign goods were purchased, would be annually distributed among the people of England. The greater part of it would replace the capital which had been employed in Virginia, and which had given income and maintenance to the inhabitants of that colony.

There is not, probably, between any two countries, a trade which consists altogether in the exchange either of domestic products on both sides, or of domestic products on one side and of foreign goods on the other. Almost all countries exchange with one another partly native and partly foreign goods. That country, however, in whose cargoes there is the greatest proportion of domestic, and the least of foreign goods, will always be the principal gainer.

ℂ Nor would this principle be any different in any respect if the exports of a country to pay for imports should be gold and silver instead of other commodities. If a country has no mines, it can nevertheless buy as much gold and silver as it needs with other commodities. And when imports are paid for with purchased gold and silver, the result is precisely the same as if it were paid for with purchased tobacco. The foreign country will gain more, but the trade will still be advantageous to both.

ℂ Even when the products exchanged are themselves of little utility, or even injurious, the principle remains the same. Such is the wine trade, which was burdened with heavy duties when wine was bought from France, on the theory that wine-drinking should be discouraged anyway. This, however, merely had the effect of favoring the wine trade with Portugal—it made no difference in the balance of trade with either nation, nor did it reduce wine-drinking in England.

Merchants, however, found reasons to justify this discrimination. The Portuguese, they said, are better customers for our manufactures than the French, and should therefore be encouraged in preference to them. As they give us their business, we should give them ours.

The sneaking arts of inferior tradesmen are thus erected into political maxims for the conduct of a great empire; for it is the most inferior tradesmen only who make it a rule to buy only from their own customers. A great trader purchases his goods always where they are cheapest and best, without regard to any little interest of this kind.

By such maxims as these, however, nations have been taught that their interest consisted in beggaring all their neighbors. Each nation has been made to look with an envious eye upon the prosperity of all the nations with which it trades, and to consider their gains as its own loss.

Commerce, which ought naturally to be, among nations, as among individuals, a bond of union and friendship, has become the most fertile source of discord and animosity.

The capricious ambition of dictators and politicians [3] has not, during the last two centuries, been more fatal to the repose of Europe, than the impertinent jealousy of merchants and manufacturers.

The violence and injustice of the rulers of mankind is an ancient evil, for which, I am afraid, the nature of human affairs can scarcely admit of a remedy. But the mean rapacity, the monopolizing spirit of merchants and manufacturers, who neither are, nor ought to be, the rulers of mankind, though it cannot perhaps be corrected, may very easily be prevented from disturbing the tranquility of anybody but themselves. [4]

That it was the spirit of monopoly which originally invented and propagated this doctrine, cannot be doubted; and they who first taught it were by no means such fools as they who believed it.

In every country it always is and must be the interest of the great body of the people to buy whatever they want of those who sell it cheapest. The proposition is so very manifest, that it seems ridiculous to take any pains to prove it; nor could it ever have been called in

[3] "Kings and ministers"—W. N.
[4] M'Culloch very properly points out that it was a much more enlightened and far-sighted attitude on the part of merchants and manufacturers that, 50 years after A. S., helped consign the Mercantile System to the scrap-heap.

question, had not the interested sophistry of merchants and manufacturers confounded the common sense of mankind.

Their interest is, in this respect, directly opposite to that of the great body of the people. As it is the interest of the members of an incorporated trade to hinder their neighbors from employing any workmen but themselves, so it is the interest of the merchants and manufacturers of every country to secure to themselves the monopoly of the home market. Hence in many countries the extraordinary duties upon almost all goods imported by alien merchants. Hence the high duties and prohibitions upon all those foreign manufactures which can come into competition with our own. Hence, too, the extraordinary restraints upon imports from those countries with which the balance of trade is supposed to be unfavorable; that is, from those against whom national animosity happens to be most violently inflamed.

The wealth of a neighboring nation, however, though dangerous in war and politics, is certainly advantageous in trade. In a state of hostility it may enable our enemies to maintain fleets and armies superior to our own; but in a state of peace and commerce it must likewise enable them to exchange with us to a greater value, and to afford a better market for the immediate produce of our own industry, or for whatever is purchased with that produce.

As a rich man is likely to be a better customer than a poor one, so is likewise a rich nation. It is true that a rich man, who is himself a manufacturer, is a very dangerous neighbor to all those in the same business. All the rest of the neighborhood, however, who are the great majority, profit by the good market which his expenditure affords them. They even profit by his underselling the poorer workmen who deal in the same goods.

The manufacturers of a rich nation, in the same manner, may no doubt be very dangerous rivals to those of their neighbors. But this very competition is advantageous to the great body of the people.

Private people who want to make a fortune never think of retiring to the remote and poor provinces of the country, but resort to the capital, or to some of the great commercial towns. They know that where little wealth circulates, there is little to be got, but that where a great deal is in motion, some share of it may fall to them.

The same maxims which would in this manner direct the common sense of one, or ten, or twenty individuals, should regulate the judgment of one, or ten, or twenty millions, and should make a whole nation regard the riches of its neighbors as a probable cause and occasion for making itself rich. A nation that would enrich itself by foreign trade, is certainly most likely to do so when its neighbors are all rich and industrious.

℃ A. S. here goes on to deplore the great jealousy between England and France, which led to all kinds of restrictions on trade in both directions. This trade, if left unhindered, would be very profitable to both countries—more so, indeed, than England's very profitable trade with the American colonies.

There is no commercial country in Europe of which the approaching ruin has not frequently been foretold by the pretended doctors of the Mercantile System, from an unfavorable balance of trade. After all the anxiety, however, which they have aroused, after all the vain attempts of many nations to turn that balance in their own favor and against their neighbors, it does not appear that any one nation in Europe has been in any respect impoverished on this account.

Every town and country, on the contrary, in proportion as they have opened their ports to all nations, instead of being ruined by this free trade, as the principles of the Mercantile System would lead us to expect, have been enriched by it.

Though there are in Europe a few towns which in some respects deserve the name of free ports, there is no country which does so. Holland, perhaps, approaches the nearest to this character, though still very remote from it; and Holland, it is acknowledged, not only derives its whole wealth, but a great part of its necessary subsistence, from foreign trade.

I have already explained that there is another balance, very different from the balance of trade, and which, according as it happens to be either favorable or unfavorable, necessarily results in prosperity or decay. This is the balance of the annual production and consumption. If the value of the annual production exceeds that of the annual consumption, the capital of the nation must annually increase in proportion to this excess. The society in this case lives within its income, and what is annually saved out of it is naturally added to its capital, and employed so as to increase still further the annual produce.

If the exchangeable value of the annual produce, on the contrary, falls short of the annual consumption, its capital must necessarily decay, and with it the exchangeable value of the annual produce of its industry.

This balance of produce and consumption is an entirely different thing from what is called the balance of trade. It might take place in a nation which had no foreign trade, but which was entirely cut off from all the world.

The balance of production and consumption may be constantly in favor of a nation, though what is called the balance of trade be generally against it. A nation may import to a greater value than it exports for half a century together; the gold and silver which comes into it during all this time may be all immediately sent out of it; its circulating coin may gradually deteriorate, different sorts of paper money being substituted in its place, and even the debts which it contracts in the principal nations with whom it deals, may be gradually increasing; and yet its real wealth, the exchangeable value of the annual produce of its lands and labor, may, during the same period, have been increasing in a much greater proportion.

CHAPTER V

*The Mercantile System's device of bounties
upon export of certain goods, and their
generally injurious effect upon the society.*

MERCHANTS AND MANUFACTURERS are not contented with the
monopoly of the home market, but desire likewise the most extensive foreign sale for their goods. Their country has no jurisdiction
in foreign nations, and therefore can seldom procure them any
monopoly there. They are generally obliged, therefore, to content themselves with petitioning for certain encouragements to
exportation.

Of these encouragements what are called drawbacks seem
to be the most reasonable. To allow the merchant to draw back,
upon exportation, either the whole or a part of whatever excise or
domestic tax is imposed upon domestic industry, will not cause the
export of more goods than would have been exported had no tax
been imposed. Such an arrangement does not tend to turn toward
any particular employment a greater share of the capital of the
country than would go to that employment of its own accord, but
only to hinder the tax from driving away any part of that share to
other employments. It tends to preserve, rather than to destroy,
what it is in most cases advantageous to preserve, the natural division and distribution of labor in the society.

The same thing may be said of drawbacks upon the re-
exportation of foreign goods imported. They were, perhaps,
originally granted for the encouragement of the carrying trade,
which, as the freight is frequently paid by foreigners in money,
was supposed to be peculiarly fitted for bringing gold and silver
into the country. But though the carrying trade certainly needs

no peculiar encouragement, and though the motive of the institution was abundantly foolish, the institution itself seems reasonable enough.[1]

Such drawbacks cannot force into this trade a greater share of the capital of the country than would have gone to it of its own accord, had there been no import duties. They only prevent its being excluded altogether by those duties. The carrying trade, though it deserves no preference, ought to be left free like all other trades. It is a necessary resource for capital which cannot find employment in the agriculture or in the manufactures of the country, either in its home trade or in its foreign trade of consumption.

The other principal form of encouragement demanded by export interests is what is called the bounty. Bounties upon exports are frequently petitioned for, and sometimes granted to the produce of particular branches of domestic industry. By means of them our merchants and manufacturers, it is pretended, will be enabled to sell their goods as cheap as or cheaper than their rivals in the foreign market. A greater quantity, it is said, will thus be exported, and the balance of trade consequently turned more in favor of our own country. We cannot give our workmen a monopoly in the foreign market, as we have done at home. We cannot force foreigners to buy our goods, as we have done our own countrymen. The next best expedient, therefore, is to pay them for buying.

It is in this manner that the Mercantile System proposes to enrich the whole country, and to put money into all our pockets by means of the balance of trade.

It will be conceded, I suppose, that bounties ought to be given only to those branches of trade which cannot be carried on without them. But every branch of trade in which the merchant can sell his goods for a price which replaces to him, with the ordinary profit of capital, the whole capital employed in preparing and sending them to market, can be carried on without a bounty.

---

[1] I omit at this point a long discussion of the complicated British system of drawbacks as it existed in 1776–83. The institution of drawbacks is generally obsolete, having been superseded by the system of bonded warehouses, which by the way were introduced in England by the younger Pitt (after reading W. N.) against the bitter opposition of British merchants.

The only trades needing bounties are those in which the merchant is obliged to sell his products for less than it really costs him to send them to market.

The bounty is given in order to make up this loss, and to encourage him to continue or perhaps to start a trade of which the expense is supposed to be greater than the returns, of which every transaction eats up a part of the capital employed in it, and which is of such a nature that, if all other trades resembled it, there would soon be no capital left in the country.

Thus it is evident that those trades which are carried on by means of bounties are the only ones which can be carried on between two nations for any considerable time together, so that one of them shall always and regularly lose, or sell its goods for less than it really costs to send them to market.

If the bounty did not repay to the merchant what he would otherwise lose upon the price of his goods, his own interest would soon oblige him to employ his capital in some way that would pay him a profit. The effect of bounties, therefore, like that of all the other expedients of the Mercantile System, can only be to force the trade of a country into a channel much less advantageous than that in which it would naturally run of its own accord.

❡ The bounty which was formerly paid in England upon the export of grain was supposed to be advantageous to England, but this was far from the case. It did not, in fact, increase the average real price of grain, nor encourage greater production, as it was supposed to do.

This particular bounty, as well as every other bounty upon exports, imposed two different taxes upon the people; first, the tax which they were obliged to contribute in order to pay the bounty; and secondly, the tax which arose from the advanced price of the commodity in the home market. Since the whole body of the people were purchasers of grain, the higher price must have been paid by the whole body of the people. It follows, therefore, that this second tax is by far the heavier of the two.

The average proportion of the grain exported to that consumed at home, was not more than that of one to thirty-one. For every five shillings, therefore, which the British consumer contributed to the payment of the first tax, he had to contribute six pounds four shillings to the payment of the second.

❡ Such a tax would operate in precisely the same way as

every other tax—reducing the subsistence level of the poor, or else advancing their money wages, and thereby reducing the ability of capital to employ labor.

❡ The true effect of a bounty on grain export is not so much to raise the value of the grain—it ordinarily raises its money value, but not its real value—as to reduce the real value of money. For it is the money value of grain which regulates that of all other domestic commodities. It regulates the money price of labor, of all raw materials, and of almost all manufactures.[2]

Though in consequence of the bounty, therefore, the farmer should be enabled to sell wheat for a dollar a bushel instead of seventy-five cents, and to pay his landlord a money rent in proportion to this increase; yet if, in consequence, a dollar will buy no more goods than 75 cents would have done before, neither the circumstances of the farmer, nor those of the landlord, will be much improved by this change.

❡ That decrease in the value of gold and silver which results from the opening of rich mines, and which operates equally upon all civilized countries, makes very little difference to any one country. But when money is made cheaper in a particular country by some peculiar condition, or by its political system, it becomes a serious matter; far from making anyone richer, it makes everyone poorer.

❡ At one time Spain and Portugal, both producers of gold and silver, foolishly attempted to restrict the export of these metals. Now when you dam up a stream of water, the flow is temporarily stopped; but when the dam is full, as much water thereafter flows over the spillways as if there were no dam there at all.

❡ Similarly, when Spain and Portugal had as much gold and silver as their own land and labor would naturally employ, the surplus had to flow out of those countries. As it could not do so lawfully, it had to be smuggled out, at considerably greater expense. The result was that the money remaining in these countries was cheaper than it would naturally be, or in other words, the

---

[2] M'Culloch says not: "This is an error. The money price of grain does not regulate the money price of other things."

Certainly not, says Thorold Rogers. No regulation can raise the price of all articles; the money price of grain does not determine or regulate the price of anything else, unless perhaps the wages of the lowest-paid labor.

money value of commodities was higher. In other countries, gold and silver were higher, commodities cheaper.[3]

℃ When these restrictions were removed, the theoretical loss to Spain and Portugal turned out to be nominal and imaginary. A fall in the prices of commodities, expressed in money, was nominal and not real; their real value, the amount of labor they would buy, was precisely the same as before. But the free export of the metals was not for nothing; the gold and silver exchanged for an equal amount of real wealth of one kind or another.[4]

A bounty upon the exportation of grain necessarily operates exactly in the same way as this absurd policy of Spain and Portugal. It renders domestic grain somewhat dearer in the home market than it otherwise would be, and somewhat cheaper abroad; and as the average money price of grain regulates more or less that of all other commodities, it lowers the value of money considerably in the one, and tends to raise it a little in the other.

It enables foreigners not only to eat bread cheaper than they otherwise could do, but sometimes to eat it cheaper than even our own people. It hinders our own workmen from furnishing their goods at as low prices as they otherwise might do; and enables the foreigners to furnish theirs for less. It tends to render our manufactures somewhat dearer in every market, and theirs somewhat cheaper than they otherwise would be, and consequently to give their industry a double advantage over our own.

But when by duties on imports and bounties on exports you raise the nominal or money price of grain, you do not raise its real value. You do not increase the real wealth, the real incomes of farmers or country gentlemen. You do not encourage the growth of grain, because you do not enable them to maintain and employ more laborers in raising it. The nature of things has stamped upon grain a real value which cannot be altered by merely altering its money price. No bounty upon exportation, no monopoly of the

[3] Spain and Portugal present a special and most instructive case in economics. Carver says that the decline of these countries was the result of their obsession over gold and silver, plus the despotism of their governments, plus religious intolerance and savage persecution, all of which conspired to degrade the national mind. Their condition improved as fast as and to the extent that these disorders were removed.

[4] This, says M'Culloch, is the real milk in the coconut: restrictions on the export of metals merely deprive the people of those foreign goods which they could obtain in exchange.

home market, can raise that value. The freest competition cannot lower it.

Throughout the world that value is equal to the quantity of labor which it can maintain in the manner, whether liberal, moderate, or scanty, in which labor is commonly maintained in that place.[5]

Bounties upon the exportation of any domestic commodity are liable, first, to that general objection which may be made to all the expedients of the Mercantile System: the objection of forcing some part of the industry of the country into a channel less advantageous than that in which it would run of its own accord; and, secondly, to the particular objection of forcing it, not only into a channel that is less advantageous, but into one that is actually injurious; the trade which can be carried on only by means of a bounty being necessarily a losing trade.

The bounty upon the export of grain is liable to this further objection, that it can in no way increase the production of that particular commodity. When our country gentlemen, therefore, demanded the establishment of the bounty, though they acted in imitation of our merchants and manufacturers, they did not act with that complete understanding of their own interest which commonly directs the conduct of those two other orders of people.

They loaded the public revenue with a very considerable expense; they imposed a very heavy tax upon the whole body of the people, but they did not, in any sensible degree, increase the real value of grain; and by lowering somewhat the real value of money, they discouraged, in some degree, the general industry of the country, and therefore indirectly the improvement of their own land.

To encourage the production of any commodity, a bounty upon production would be, one would think, more effective than one on exportation. It would, besides, impose only one tax upon the people—that which they must contribute in order to pay the

---

[5] Here A. S. is certainly astray. He is so possessed with the idea of the unique position of grain as the great food of the people, its price regulating all other prices, that he loses sight of the distinction, perfectly well known to him, between "value-in-use" and "value-in-exchange."

A bushel of wheat will, it is true, always feed a given number of slices of bread to a given number of workmen; it will "maintain an equal quantity of labor." But it will certainly not always exchange for an equal quantity of shoes, milk, or silk umbrellas.

bounty. Instead of raising the price of the commodity in the home market, it would tend to lower it; and thereby, instead of imposing a second tax upon the people, it might, at least in part, repay them for what they had contributed to the first.

Bounties upon production, however, have been very rarely granted. The prejudices established by the Mercantile System have taught us to believe that national wealth arises more immediately from export than from production. It has accordingly been more favored as the more immediate means of bringing money into the country.

Bounties upon production, it has been said, have been found by experience more liable to frauds than those upon exports. How far this is true, I do not know. That bounties upon exports have been abused to many fraudulent purposes, is very well known. But it is not to the interest of merchants and manufacturers, the great inventors of all these expedients, that the home market should be overstocked with their goods—a result which a bounty upon production might sometimes produce.

A bounty upon exports, by enabling them to send their surplus abroad, and to keep up the price of what remains in the home market, effectually prevents this. Of all the expedients of the Mercantile System, accordingly, it is the one of which they are the fondest.

⟪ A. S. here proceeds to describe at length the special bounties offered by the British government to encourage the herring and whale fisheries. In spite of determined efforts to promote this production, the projects were on the whole unsuccessful, for reasons which need not detain us.

If indeed any particular manufacture were necessary for the defense of the nation, it might not always be prudent to depend upon foreign nations for the supply; and if such manufacture could not be carried on at home otherwise, it might not be unreasonable that all the other branches of industry should be taxed in order to support it. The bounties upon the export of British-made sail-cloth, and British-made gunpowder, may, perhaps, both be justified upon this principle.

But though it can very seldom be reasonable to tax the industry of the great body of the people, in order to support that of some particular class of manufacturers, yet in the wantonness of great prosperity, when the public enjoys a greater income than it knows what to do with, to give such bounties to favorite manufactures may, perhaps, be as natural as to incur any other idle extravagance.

In public as well as in private, great wealth may, perhaps, frequently be admitted as an apology for great folly. But there must surely be something more than ordinary absurdity, in continuing such extravagance in times of difficulty and distress.

Premiums given by the public to artists and artificers who excel in their particular occupations, are not liable to the same objections as bounties. By encouraging extraordinary dexterity and ingenuity, they serve to keep up the emulation of the workmen, and yet are not large enough to turn toward any one of them a greater share of the capital of the country than what would go to it of its own accord.

Their tendency is not to overturn the natural balance of employment, but to render the work which is done in each as perfect and complete as possible. The expense of premiums, besides, is very trifling; that of bounties very great.

CHAPTER VI

A study of the grain trade, one of those to which the Mercantile System gave special attention; its importance; and why it, of all trades, should be carefully left to itself; absurdity of the regulations of government; Great Britain flourished not because but in spite of its laws relating to grain.

IF THERE IS ONE TRADE in a civilized society which should be carefully left to itself, it is the grain trade, which in former days and in many countries was the source of the people's chief food, and even today is of great importance. Yet nowhere did the Mercantile System more continually interfere, and usually with very injurious results.

℃ The trade as a whole may be considered as including the buyer of domestic grain, the importer, the exporter, and those few who may import to export again. Of these the domestic buyer is much the most important, for it is he who performs the necessary duty of collecting grain from the farms, and through the millers and bakers supplying the people with this important food.

℃ His interest is precisely the same as that of consumers of bread: that the consumption shall be proportioned to the supply available. And yet the grain trader has nearly always suffered from public opprobrium, and has been the object of innumerable well-meant but absurd regulations of governments.

The interest of the trader, indeed, is always in selling grain at the highest price. But without intending the interest of the people, he is necessarily led, by a regard to his own interest, to treat them, even in years of scarcity, pretty much in the same manner as the prudent master of a ship is sometimes obliged to treat his crew.

When he foresees that provisions are likely to run short, he puts them upon short allowance. Though from excess of caution he should sometimes do this without any real necessity, yet all the inconveniences which his crew can thereby suffer are trifling, compared with the danger, misery, and ruin to which they might be exposed by a less provident conduct.

Though from greediness the grain dealer should similarly raise the price of his grain higher than the scarcity of the season requires, yet all the inconveniences which the people can suffer are likewise trifling, compared with the shortage which would result from lower prices and larger consumption.

℄ In time of plenty, on the other hand, it is to the interest of the grain trade to make the price low enough to move all grain into consumption if possible; for otherwise the dealer would be left, at the end of the season, with unsold grain on hand, and a new crop season coming on.

℄ It is true that if grain could be monopolized, the owners might maintain a high price, and destroy any surplus remaining on hand, as the Dutch are said to have done with East Indian spices, and as Brazil does to this day with coffee.

Whoever examines the history of shortages in civilized countries, will find that they have never been the fault of the grain trade, but have been principally from unfavorable weather experience, or from wars; and famines have always arisen from the violence of governments which attempted by improper means to remedy the inconveniences of shortage.[1]

℄ The most common of these improper measures is to order the trade to sell grain at what they call a "reasonable" price, by which they mean a price much lower than what the grain should really bring, considering its scarcity.

℄ The result always is, that either the grain trade does not offer grain for sale at all, or if sold at the low price, consumption is greater than it otherwise would be. In both cases, the ultimate result is to greatly aggravate the very shortage that these measures were meant to remedy.

℄ In such cases it is the grain trade that is blamed, though

[1] Thorold Rogers remarks that it is a fact, noticed by Gregory King and many times confirmed, that when the supply of any prime necessity is short, that supply sells for a higher total sum (volume times price) than the total sum received from an average supply.

wholly innocent, and the government that is praised, very unde-
servedly, for its efforts.

℃   Indeed, in years when prices are high, the common people
regard the grain trader, or "middleman," with hatred and indignation; and in former days he was often in danger of being utterly
ruined, and of having his warehouse plundered and destroyed by
their violence.

It is in years of scarcity, however, when prices are high,
that the grain merchant expects to make his principal profit. This
extraordinary profit, however, is no more than sufficient to put his
trade upon a fair level with other trades, and to compensate the
many losses which he sustains at other times, both from the perishable nature of the commodity itself, and from the frequent and
unforeseen fluctuations of its price, seems evident enough from
this single circumstance—that great fortunes are made no oftener
in this than in any other trade.

It is partly because of this popular dislike of the middleman in the grain trade, a business so necessary and beneficial to
the public, that governments have encouraged the feeling by many
violent and absurd regulations.

For example, our ancestors seem to have imagined that the
people would be able to buy their grain cheaper of the farmers
than of the grain merchant, who, they were afraid, would require,
over and above the price which he paid to the farmer, an exorbitant
profit for himself. They endeavored, therefore, to annihilate his
trade altogether. They even tried to hinder as much as possible
any middleman of any kind from coming between the grower and
the consumer.

But this was the exact opposite of the principles followed
with regard to manufactures, the great trade of the towns. By
leaving the farmer no other customers but the consumers or their
immediate agents, it endeavored to force him to exercise the trade,
not only of a farmer, but of a grain merchant or retailer.

On the contrary, a government often prohibited the manufacturer from exercising the trade of a shopkeeper, or from selling his own goods at retail.

It meant by the one law to promote the general interest
of the country, or to render grain cheap, without, perhaps, its
being well understood how this was to be done. By the other it
meant to promote that of a particular order of men, the shop-

[*413*]

keepers, who would be so much undersold by the manufacturer, it was supposed, that their trade would be ruined if he were allowed to sell at retail at all.

The manufacturer, however, though he had been allowed to keep a shop, and to sell his own goods by retail, could not have undersold the common shopkeeper. Whatever part of his capital he placed in the shop, he must have withdrawn from his manufacture. In order to carry on his business on a level with that of other people, as he must have had the profit of a manufacturer on the one part, so he must have had that of a shopkeeper upon the other.

What the manufacturer was prohibited from doing, the farmer was in some measure ordered to do—to divide his capital between two different employments; to keep one part of it in his granaries, for supplying the occasional demands of the market, and to employ the other in the cultivation of his land. But as he could not afford to employ the latter for less than the ordinary profits of farming capital, so he could as little afford to employ the former for less than the ordinary profits of mercantile capital.

Whether the capital which really carried on the business of a grain merchant belonged to the person who was called a farmer, or to the person who was called a grain merchant, an equal profit was necessary in both cases, in order to repay its owner for employing it in this manner. He must do this to put his business upon a level with other trades, and to prevent him from changing it as soon as possible for some other that would pay him better.

The law which prohibited the manufacturer from exercising the trade of a shopkeeper, sought to force his division in the employment of capital to go on faster than it might otherwise have done. The law which obliged the farmer to exercise the trade of a grain merchant, sought to hinder it from going on so fast.

Both laws were evident violations of natural liberty, and therefore unjust; and they were quite as impolitic as they were unjust.

It is the interest of every society, that things of this kind should never either be forced or obstructed. The man who employs either his labor or his capital in a greater variety of ways than his situation renders necessary, can never hurt his neighbor by underselling him. He may hurt himself, and he generally does so. Jack of all trades will never be rich, says the proverb.

But the law ought always to trust people to take care of their own interest, as in their local situations they must generally be able to judge better of it than any politician can do.

The law, however, which obliged the farmer to exercise the trade of a grain merchant, was by far the more pernicious of the two, since it obstructed not only that division in the employment of capital which is so advantageous to every society, but it obstructed likewise the improvement and cultivation of the land. By obliging the farmer to carry on two trades instead of one, it forced him to divide his capital into two parts, of which only one could be employed in cultivation.

❡ Those laws, therefore, which try to prohibit the business of the middleman in the grain trade (and all food trades are in some degree the same), or to restrain and regulate it by various devices, obstruct that free exercise of trade which is the best preventive of shortages and surpluses. Next to the trade of a farmer, no trade contributes so much to the ample supply of grain and other foods as the food trades.

The two practices of the grain trade against which the most severe laws used to be enacted were called "engrossing" and "forestalling". These were, respectively, the buying of grain to sell it again,[2] and buying up grain before it had actually reached the public market. Neither of these was or is actually hurtful to the public in any way, and the popular fear of engrossing and forestalling can only be compared to the popular terrors and suspicions of witchcraft. The unfortunate wretches accused of this crime were not more innocent of the misfortunes imputed to them, than those who have been accused of the former.

❡ The import and export of grain is of greater or less importance in different countries, according as the agriculture of the country is or is not able to supply the population.

❡ In every country the home market, as it is the nearest and most convenient, so is it likewise the most important market for grain.[3] The trade of the importer evidently contributes to the

[2] Equivalent to the routine trading of today on the grain exchanges.

[3] The important difference between food and other commodities and manufactures is that the buying and use of the latter is optional with the consumer; excessive prices are corrected by reduced demand. But the use of food is not optional, hence the prohibition of food imports or other devices for making food prices excessive, are uncommonly injurious.

supply of this market, and must so far be directly beneficial to the great body of the people.

It tends, indeed, to lower somewhat the average money price of grain, but not to lower its real value, or the quantity of labor which it is capable of maintaining. If importation were always free, farmers would probably get, one year with another, less money for their grain; but the money which they got would be of more value, would buy more goods of all other kinds, and would employ more labor. Their real wealth, their real income, therefore, would be the same as at present, though it might be expressed by a smaller quantity of money.

The trade of the exporter of grain certainly does not contribute directly to the plentiful supply of the home market. It does so, however, indirectly. From whatever source this supply may be usually drawn, whether from home growth or from foreign imports, unless more grain is grown or imported than what is consumed, the supply of the home market can never be very plentiful.

But unless any surplus can be exported, the growers will be careful never to grow more, and the importers never to import more, than what the bare consumption of the home market requires. That market will then generally be understocked—the people whose business it is to supply it, being generally afraid lest their goods should be left upon their hands.

The interest of the domestic grain dealer, it has already been shown, can never be opposed to that of the great body of the people. That of the exporter may, and in fact sometimes is. If, while his own country has a shortage, a neighboring country should be afflicted with a famine, it might be to his interest to ship grain to the latter country in such quantities as might very much aggravate the scarcity at home.

Were all nations to follow the liberal system of free exports and imports, the different states into which the world is divided would so far resemble the different provinces of a great nation.

As among such provinces the freedom of domestic trade is obviously the best insurance against scarcity, so would freedom of the export and import trade be among the different states of the world. The easier the communication through all the different parts of it, both by land and by water, the less would any one particular part of it ever by exposed to scarcity or famine, the scarcity of any one country being more likely to be relieved by the plenty of some other.

But very few countries have entirely adopted this liberal system. The freedom of the grain trade is almost everywhere more or less restrained, and, in many countries, is hampered by such absurd regulations as frequently to aggravate the unavoidable misfortune of a shortage into the dreadful calamity of a famine.

The laws concerning grain may be compared to the laws concerning religion. The people feel themselves so much interested in what relates either to their subsistence in this life, or to their happiness in a life to come, that every government must yield to their prejudices, and, in order to preserve the public tranquility, establish that system which they think they need. It is upon this account, perhaps, that we so seldom find a reasonable system established with regard to either of those two capital objects.

The trade of the importer who brings in foreign grain in order to export it again, contributes to the plentiful supply of the home market. It is not indeed his purpose to sell his grain there, but he will generally be willing to do so, and even for a good deal less money than he might expect in a foreign market; because he saves the expense of loading and unloading, of freight and insurance.

Though the carrying trade might thus contribute to reduce the average money price of grain in the home market, it would not thereby lower its real value. It would only raise somewhat the real value of money.

Any system of laws, therefore, which is connected with the establishment of bounties, seems to deserve no part of the praise which has been bestowed upon it. The improvement and prosperity of Great Britain, which has been so often ascribed to those laws, may very easily be accounted for by other causes.

That security which British laws give to every man, that he shall enjoy the fruits of his own labor, is alone sufficient to make any country flourish, notwithstanding these and twenty other absurd regulations of commerce; and this security was perfected by the revolution of 1688 about the same time that the bounty was established.

[417]

The natural effort of every individual to better his own condition, when suffered to exert itself with freedom and security, is so powerful a principle, that it is alone, and without any assistance, not only capable of carrying on the society to wealth and prosperity, but of surmounting a hundred impertinent obstructions with which the folly of human laws too often encumbers its operations.

Though the period of the greatest prosperity and improvement of Great Britain has followed that system of laws which is connected with the bounty, we must not upon that account credit it to those laws. It has likewise followed the imposition of the national debt. But the national debt has most assuredly not been the cause of prosperity.

CHAPTER VII

*A digression explaining how in earlier
times grain was the principal human food,
and silver the principal money; the prices
of these two commodities have changed
in relation to each other; the price-ratio
between silver and gold has also varied;
which changes are real, and which only
apparent; the scarcity or abundance of the
precious metals is of no real importance.*

IN THE HISTORY of England and France, and of the European
market in general, grain was the principal food of the population,
and silver was the metal in which money prices were universally
expressed.

❡ From the middle of the 14th Century, and probably earlier,
up to about 1570, as far as the records of those times can be
ascertained, the price of grain gradually fell, as the price of silver
rose.

❡ A volume of wheat that sold for four ounces of silver in
1350 would bring only two ounces in 1570. The same fall in the
price of wheat was observed in France.

❡ This changed relationship between the prices of grain and
silver has been misrepresented by many writers, for reasons which
need not concern us here.

❡ It seems probable that the change during this period was
an advance in the price of silver, not a fall in the price of grain,
since the growing of grain in long-established areas requires nearly
always about the same amount of labor.

❡ Labor, it must always be remembered, and not any commodity or set of commodities, is the real measure of the value both
of silver and of all other commodities.

⟨ Grain, however, is for this reason a better measure of value than silver, and hence it may safely be said that silver rose in real value, rather than that grain declined. This could have resulted either from an increased demand for silver or from a falling off in its supply.

⟨ The value of silver does not necessarily fall as its quantity increases in any country. If the increase in quantity comes from the discovery of new, rich mines, this may be the case; but a country rapidly increasing in wealth needs and demands more of the precious metals, and these naturally flow to that market where the highest price is offered.

⟨ Gold and silver, therefore, have the highest real value in rich countries, and the lowest in poor countries; among savages they have no value at all. In passing it may be noted that the higher price of grain and all food in big cities does not mean that silver is cheaper there. It costs no more to bring silver to the city than elsewhere, but the cost of transportation has to be added to the price of food. Hence grain is really higher in price in cities.

⟨ All writers agree that the discovery of the new, rich South American mines about 1570 caused a real fall in the value of silver. By about 1640, when the English Civil War was imminent, wheat which could exchange for two ounces of silver in 1570 would buy six to eight ounces.

⟨ This fall was interrupted by the English Civil War, by a decrease in the production of the silver mines, and by other factors, including a bounty on the export of grain, which was in effect for ten or twelve years after 1688. From about this time, silver ceased to fall in price, and has since (up to 1776) somewhat risen.

⟨ One difficulty in determining the price of silver during the 17th Century was due to the wearing and clipping of the silver coin. This caused a distortion of price quotations, since prices had to be calculated, not by what silver the coin was supposed to contain, but what it actually did contain, on the average, or by actual weight.

⟨ At that time, the silver coin was not kept at its face value by being convertible into gold. By 1695, accordingly, when the silver was called in and re-coined, a gold guinea supposed to exchange for 21 silver shillings actually brought about 30 shillings.

⟨ The rise in the price of silver in terms of grain took place about the same time, and to about the same extent, in France,

[420]

although in England a bounty encouraged the export of grain, while in France exportation was prohibited.

℄ Not only has silver risen in price, but the money wages of labor have risen in England during the 18th Century, whereas in France, a country neither so well-governed nor so prosperous, the wages of labor have fallen.

℄ Meanwhile, mining of the precious metals has become less profitable. It would no doubt have been even less, returning no rent to the owner and little profit to the operator, except for a steady increase in demand, both in Europe, in North and South America, and in the East Indies.

℄ In the East Indies, in China and India, the value of gold and silver is the highest of all countries. It is particularly high for silver, since there the relative value of gold and silver is not more than twelve to one, as compared to about fifteen to one in Europe. It has been remarked, however, that in those countries the real price of labor is very low, China being a stationary, and India a declining country.

℄ In order to keep the price of silver stable, the supply must provide for waste as well as for increased use in coinage and in the arts. The loss by wear and tear, by wearing of coins and even by cleaning of silverware, is considerable.

℄ The price of all metals varies very little from year to year, and this steadiness of price is due principally to their durability. Since a vast volume of a metal is always in existence, the added production of a single year makes little difference in the total supply. And of all the metals gold and silver are the most durable.

℄ The ratio of the prices of these two precious metals has varied from time to time. Before the discovery of America the ratio was from ten to twelve to one—an ounce of fine gold was supposed to be worth from 10 to 12 ounces of fine silver. In China, as remarked above, it still is about this ratio.

℄ It is sometimes thought that the gold-silver ratio is in proportion to the amounts of the two metals in existence, or easily available. But this is not true—it is, indeed, an absurdity. The relative prices of gold and silver, as of any two commodities not under some kind of monopoly, depend on the relative costs of production.

℄ The production of silver is becoming gradually more expensive, and the tax imposed on silver increases its cost still more. Further increase in mining costs would mean a further increase in price, or a reduction in the tax, or both.[1]

℄ While certain circumstances have led many observers to the conclusion that silver has been falling in price, it is my opinion that, on the contrary, it has risen slightly in the present century. I have already shown that the increase in the supply of metal does not necessarily lower its value; and the rise in price of many raw materials appears to be a real increase, not a lowering of the price of silver.

℄ The quantity of the precious metals which is to be found in any country is not limited by anything in its local situation, such as the richness or poorness of its own mines. These metals frequently abound in countries which possess no mines. Their quantity in any particular country seems to depend upon two different circumstances; first, upon its purchasing power, upon the state of its industry, upon its total annual production of wealth, by which it can afford to employ a greater or a smaller quantity of labor and subsistence in bringing or purchasing such superfluities as gold and silver, either from its own mines or from those of other countries; and, secondly, upon the richness of the mines which may happen at that time to supply the commercial world with those metals.

℄ So far as their quantity in any particular country depends upon purchasing power, their real price, like that of all other luxuries and superfluities, is likely to rise with the wealth and improvement of the country, and to fall with its poverty and depression.

℄ So far as it depends upon the condition of the mines, their real price, the real quantity of labor and subsistence which they will purchase or exchange for, will, no doubt, vary according to the condition.

℄ The richness of the producing mines, however, is a cir-

[1] The changes in the methods of mining both gold and silver have been so great since 1776, that the conclusions reached in these paragraphs must be somewhat modified. For example, the production of silver, once mined for itself, is now to a large extent a by-product of the mining of copper, nickel, and other metals. Its price has accordingly ceased to reflect precisely the cost of producing and bringing it to market. The discovery of the rich deposits of gold in California, Alaska, Australia, South Africa, and Siberia has likewise greatly increased the world's stock of this metal, and has greatly lowered its real price.

cumstance which, it is evident, may have no sort of connection with the state of industry in a particular country. It seems even to have no very necessary connection with the prosperity or poverty of the world in general.

℄ As arts and commerce, indeed, gradually spread themselves over the earth, the search for new mines may have a somewhat better chance for being successful, than when confined within narrower bounds.

℄ The discovery of new mines, however, as the old ones come to be gradually exhausted, is a matter of the greatest uncertainty, and such as no human skill or industry can insure. In this search there seem to be no certain limits either to the possible success, or to the possible disappointment of human industry.

℄ In the course of a century or two, it is possible that new mines may be discovered, more fertile than any that have ever yet been known; and it is just equally possible that the most fertile mine then known may be less productive than any that was worked before the discovery of the mines of America.

℄ Whether the one or the other of those two events may happen to take place, is of very little importance to the real wealth and prosperity of the world, to the real value of the annual production of the land and labor of mankind.

℄ Its nominal value, the quantity of gold and silver by which the annual produce could be expressed or represented, would, no doubt, be very different; but its real value, the real quantity of labor which it could purchase or command, would be precisely the same.

℄ A quarter-dollar might in the one case represent no more labor than a nickel does at present; and a nickel in the other might represent as much as a quarter does now. But in the one case he who had a quarter in his pocket, would be no richer than he who had a nickel at present; and in the other he who had a nickel would be just as rich as he who had a quarter now.

℄ The cheapness and abundance of articles of gold and silverware, would be the sole advantage which the world could derive from the one event, and the high price and scarcity of those trifling superfluities the only inconvenience it could suffer from the other.

CHAPTER VIII

A further digression upon coinage, and the
advantage of charging a reasonable seignior-
age for coining gold and silver.

THOUGH THE goldsmiths' trade be very considerable in Great
Britain, the far greater part of the new gold and silverware, which
they annually sell, is made from other old plate melted down; so
that the addition annually made to the whole stock of the nation
cannot be very great, and could require but a very small annual
importation.

It is the same case with the coin. Nobody imagines, I
believe, that as much as half of the annual coinage, amounting to
upwards of eight hundred thousand pounds a year in gold, was
an annual addition to the money before current.

In a country where the expense of the coinage is defrayed
by the government, the value of the coin can never be much greater
than that of an equal quantity of those metals uncoined; because
it requires only the trouble of going to the mint, and a brief delay,
to procure for any quantity of uncoined gold and silver an equal
quantity of those metals in coin.

But in every country, most of the current coin is almost
always more or less worn, or otherwise degenerated from its
standard. When the coin is in this degenerate condition, new coins
fresh from the mint will buy no more goods in the market than any
others, because when they come into the coffers of the merchant,
being confounded with other money, they can not afterwards be
distinguished without more trouble than the difference is worth.

As long as the mint makes no charge for coinage, therefore,
there is an evident profit in melting down new-coined money, and
it is done so instantaneously, that no precaution of government
could prevent it.

The operations of the mint are, upon this account, somewhat like the web of Penelope, the work that is done in the day being undone in the night. The mint is employed not so much in making daily additions to the coin, as in replacing the very best part of it which is daily melted down.

Were private people who carry their gold and silver to the mint obliged to pay for the cost of coinage, it would add to the value of those metals. Coined gold and silver would be more valuable than uncoined. This charge, or seigniorage, if it were not exorbitant, would add to the bullion the whole value of the charge; because, the government having everywhere the exclusive privilege of coining, no coin can come to market cheaper than they think proper.

If indeed the charge were exorbitant, that is, if it were very much above the real value of the labor and expense requisite for coinage, counterfeiters might be encouraged, by the great difference between the value of bullion and that of coin, to pour in so great a quantity of counterfeit money as might reduce the value of the government money.

But the seigniorage charge would have to be very high to have this effect. The dangers to which a false coiner is everywhere exposed, if he lives in the country of which he counterfeits the coin, and to which his agents are exposed if he lives in a foreign country, are far too great to be incurred for a profit of only 6 or 8 per cent.

A scigniorage will in many cases take away altogether, and will in all cases diminish the profit of melting down the new coin. This profit always arises from the difference between the quantity of bullion which the common currency ought to contain, and that which it actually does contain.

If this difference is less than the seigniorage, there will be loss instead of profit. If it is equal to the seigniorage, there will neither be profit nor loss. If it is greater than the seigniorage, there will indeed be some profit, but less than if there was no seigniorage. If for example, there would be a loss of 3 per cent upon the melting down of gold coin which has a seigniorage of five per cent upon the coinage, there is 2 per cent deterioration. If the seigniorage is 2 per cent there would be neither profit nor loss. If the seigniorage is 1 per cent, there would be a profit, but of 1 per cent only.

Wherever money is received by tale, therefore, and not by weight, a seigniorage is the most effectual preventive of the melting down of the coin, and, for the same reason, of its export. It is the best and heaviest pieces that are commonly melted down or exported, because it is upon such that the largest profits are made.

When the tax upon a commodity is so moderate as not to encourage smuggling, the merchant who deals in it, though he advances the tax, he does not properly pay it, as he gets it back in the price of the commodity, when it is sold. The tax is finally paid by the last purchaser or consumer.

But money is a commodity with regard to which every man is a merchant. Nobody buys it but in order to sell it again; and with money there is in ordinary cases no last purchaser or consumer. When the seigniorage or tax upon coinage, therefore, is so moderate as not to encourage counterfeiting, though everybody advances the tax, nobody finally pays it, because everybody gets it back in the advanced value of the coin.

A moderate seigniorage, therefore, does not in any case augment the expense of any private persons who carry their bullion to the mint to be coined, and the want of a moderate seigniorage does not in any case diminish it. Whether there is or is not a seigniorage, if the currency contains its full standard weight, the coinage costs nothing to anybody. If it is short of that weight, the coinage must always cost the difference between the quantity of bullion which ought to be contained in it, and that which it actually does contain.

The government, therefore, when it defrays the expense of coinage, not only incurs some small expense, but loses some small income which it might get; and no private person is in the smallest degree benefited by this useless piece of public generosity.

℃ The laws which pretend to encourage coinage by having bullion coined without charge, therefore, are just one more effect of the vulgar prejudices which have been introduced by the Mercantile System.

Nothing could be more agreeable to the spirit of that system than a sort of bounty upon the production of money, the very thing which, it supposes, constitutes the wealth of a nation. It is one of its many admirable expedients for enriching the country.

CHAPTER IX

A short chapter on treaties of commerce,
which are found to be generally useless
when not injurious.

AMONG THE OTHER expedients by which the politicians attempted, under the Mercantile System, to enrich their respective countries, was the practice of making with particular countries special treaties of commerce, from the terms of which other countries were excluded.

Such treaties, however, can hardly ever be of equal advantage to both parties, but must necessarily be more favorable to one, and less favorable to the other.[1]

When a nation binds itself by treaty to permit the entry of certain goods from one foreign country which it prohibits from all others, or to exempt the goods of one country from duties to which it subjects those of all others, the country, or at least the merchants and manufacturers of the country whose commerce is so favored, must necessarily derive advantage from the treaty.

Those merchants and manufacturers then enjoy a sort of monopoly in the country which is so indulgent to them. That country becomes a market more extensive and more advantageous for their goods: more extensive, because the goods of other nations being either excluded or subjected to heavier duties, it reduces the competition; more advantageous, because the merchants of the favored country, enjoying a sort of monopoly there, can often sell their goods for a higher price than if exposed to the free competition of all other nations.

[1] In the 17th and 18th Centuries most treaties of commerce had political and military objectives; the economic effects were secondary. This was still true up to the beginning of World War II, throughout Europe and Asia. But the commercial treaties or "agreements" made recently by the United States are in a different class; their objective is economic, and they include the "most favored nation" clause. While not without flaws, they are on the whole sound, and enlarge commerce.

Such treaties, however, though they may be advantageous to the merchants and manufacturers of the favored country, are necessarily disadvantageous to those of the other. A monopoly is thus granted against them to a foreign nation; and they must frequently buy the foreign goods they need, dearer than if the free competition of other nations were admitted.

That part of its production with which such a nation buys foreign goods must consequently be sold cheaper, because when two things are exchanged for one another, the cheapness of the one is a necessary consequence, or rather is the same thing as the dearness of the other.

The exchangeable value of its production, therefore, is likely to be diminished by every such treaty, but this reduction can hardly be a real loss, but at most a reduction in the profit which it might otherwise make. Though it sells its goods cheaper than it otherwise might do, it will not probably sell them for less than cost; nor, as in the case of bounties, for a price which will not replace the capital employed in bringing the goods to market, together with the ordinary profits of capital. The trade could not long go on if it did. Even the favoring country, therefore, may still gain by the trade, though less than if there were free competition.

Some treaties of commerce, however, have been regarded as advantageous upon principles very different from these. A commercial country has sometimes granted a monopoly against itself to certain goods of a foreign nation, because it expected that in the whole commerce between them, it would sell more than it would buy, and that the difference would be paid to it in gold or silver; this being a prime object of the Mercantile System.

℅   That this notion is an absurdity we have already seen, since if the trade of nation A with nation B is "favorable," the trade of A with nations C, D, or E, must necessarily be "unfavorable" over a period of time.

Or if this is not immediately the case, and gold and silver are imported to settle the balance with nation B, the metals will not remain in the country where they are not needed, but will presently be exported to pay for something that is needed. The more gold any nation imports from one country, the less it must necessarily import from all others. The effective demand for gold, like that for every other commodity, is in every country limited to a certain quantity. If 90 per cent of this quantity is imported from one country, there remains only 10 per cent to be imported from all others.

The more gold that is annually imported from some particular countries, over and above what is requisite for jewelry and for coin, the more must necessarily be exported to some others; and the more that most insignificant object of modern policy, the balance of trade, appears to be in our favor with some particular countries, the more it must necessarily appear to be against us with many others.

But it was upon the silly notion that England could not exist without the Portugal trade, from which nearly all gold imports into England arose, that in 1762 France and Spain, without pretending offense or provocation, required the king of Portugal to exclude all British ships from his ports, and to enforce this exclusion, to receive into them French or Spanish garrisons.

Had the king of Portugal submitted to those ignominious terms, Britain would have been freed from a much greater inconvenience than the loss of the Portuguese trade—the burden of supporting a very weak ally, so destitute of everything for his own defense, that the whole power of England, had it been directed to that single purpose, could scarcely perhaps have defended him for another campaign.

The loss of the Portuguese trade would, no doubt, have caused considerable embarrassment to the British merchants at that time engaged in it, who might not have found out, for a year or two, perhaps, any other equally advantageous method of employing their capital. But this would probably have been the only inconvenience which England could have suffered from this notable piece of mercantile policy.

CHAPTER X

Pursuing its phantom "balance of trade,"
the Mercantile System in some cases dis-
couraged exports and encouraged imports;
how these restrictions were altogether in
the interest of monopolistic producers,
whereas it is the interest of the consumer
only which should be considered, since
"consumption is the sole end and purpose
of all production."

THOUGH THE ENCOURAGEMENT of exports and the discouragement of imports are the two great engines by which the Mercantile
System proposes to enrich every country, yet with regard to some
particular commodities, it seems to follow an opposite plan: to discourage exports and to encourage imports.

Its ultimate object, however, it pretends, is always the
same—to enrich the country by a "favorable" balance of trade.

It discourages the export of the materials of manufacture,
and of the instruments of trade, in order to give domestic workmen an advantage, and to enable them to undersell those of other
nations in all foreign markets. By restraining, in this manner, the
export of a few commodities, of no great price, it proposes to create
a much greater and more valuable export of others.

It encourages the import of the materials of manufacture,
in order that workmen may be enabled to work them up more
cheaply, and thereby prevent a greater and more valuable import
of the manufactured commodities.

When manufactures have advanced to a certain stage of
success, the fabrication of machinery and tools becomes itself the
object of a great number of very important manufactures. To give

encouragement to the importation of such instruments would interfere too much with the interest of those manufactures. Such importation, therefore, instead of being encouraged, has frequently been prohibited.

The importation of the raw materials of manufacture has sometimes been encouraged by an exemption from the duties to which other goods are subject, and sometimes by bounties.

The private interest of merchants and manufactures may, perhaps, have extorted from the legislature many exemptions, as well as most other commercial regulations. They are, however, perfectly just and reasonable, and if they could be extended to all other raw materials, the public would certainly be a gainer.

⁋ In other cases manufacturers have permitted the free import of semi-manufactured commodities such as yarn. But this is because yarn is itself a raw material for further manufacture; and by importing cheap yarn, it was possible to hold down the wages of spinners of yarn in the country of manufacture.

It is the industry which is carried on for the benefit of the rich and the powerful, that is principally encouraged by our Mercantile System. That which is carried on for the benefit of the poor and the indigent, is too often neglected or oppressed.

The encouragement given to the import of the materials of manufacture by bounties, was in England principally confined to such as were imported from the American plantations.

⁋ They were chiefly on purely American products, such as tar, turpentine, indigo, hemp, raw silk, and barrel staves. When imported from other countries, these commodities were subject to considerable duties, on the theory that the interest of the American colonies was the same as that of the mother country.

Their wealth was considered as England's wealth. Whatever money was sent out to them, it was said, all came back to us by the balance of trade, and we could never become a penny the poorer, by any expense which we could lay out upon them. They were our own in every respect, and it was an expense laid out upon the improvement of our own property, and for the profitable employment of our own people.

It is unnecessary, I apprehend, at present to say anything further, in order to expose the folly of a system which fatal experience has now sufficiently exposed. Had the American colonies really been a part of Great Britain, those bounties might have been considered as bounties upon production; they would still have been open to all the objections to which all bounties are liable, but that is all.

℃   The Mercantile System frequently succeeded in having the export of raw materials stopped, sometimes by absolute prohibitions, sometimes by very high export duties. Thus in England the export of wool and live sheep was forbidden under heavy penalties—at one time, under Queen Elizabeth, actually to a sentence of death for a second offense.

℃   The excuse was that the wool trade was very profitable to England, that foreign wool was inferior, and that therefore British sheep must not be exported to improve foreign flocks. All of these pretenses were entirely false—Spanish wool, indeed, being greatly superior to the British article. But the wool merchants were very successful in convincing the law-makers and the population in general of the justice of their claims, and thus obtained one monopoly against consumers by a prohibition of imports of woolen goods, and another against farmers and wool-growers by the prohibition of exports of wool and live sheep.

℃   Not only the export and import trade, but domestic trade as well was subjected to burdensome restrictions. To discourage smuggling, every owner of wool in districts near the seacoast was obliged to give an account in writing, three days after shearing, of the amount of wool and where it was stored. When he moved it elsewhere he had to give notice of the number and weight of fleeces, the name and address of the purchaser, and of the place to which it was being shipped. Every buyer had to give bond that the wool would not be resold to anyone within fifteen miles of the sea; and these oppressive regulations and many others were enforced by severe penalties.

℃   In spite of all, smuggling of wool was common, wherever the relation of prices was such as to make it sufficiently profitable.

℃   Under the same policies, export of pipe-clay, raw hides, woolen yarn, watch cases, some metals, white cloth, glue, horses, and other articles was for a long time prohibited. And on still other commodities there were heavy export duties. Brass manufactures could be exported, but brass itself could not.

Coal may be considered both as a material of manufacture and as an instrument of trade. Heavy duties, accordingly, were imposed upon its export, amounting to more than five shillings a ton in 1783, which was in most cases more than the original value of the commodity at the mine, or even at the shipping port.

The exportation of machinery and tools, properly so called, was commonly restrained, not by high duties, but by absolute prohibitions. Thus the exportation of frames for knitting gloves or stockings was prohibited under the penalty, not only of the forfeiture of such frames, but of forty pounds, one half to the government, and the other to the informer.

In the same manner the export of any machinery made use of in the cotton, linen, woolen, and silk manufactures, was prohibited under the penalty, not only of forfeiture of the machinery, but of two hundred pounds, to be paid by the offender, and likewise of two hundred pounds to be paid by the master of the ship who should knowingly permit the shipment to be loaded.

When such heavy penalties were imposed upon the export of the dead instruments of trade, it could not well be expected that the living instrument, the skilled workman, should be allowed to go free. Accordingly, it was made a penal offense to entice any skilled workman to go abroad to practice his trade; and if he was suspected of such a plan, he was obliged to give security not to go, and was imprisoned until he did so.

❡ If the workman succeeded in escaping, and practicing his trade abroad, he could be warned to return home. If he were not back within six months, to stay back, he could no longer receive any legacy, nor act as executor or administrator of any estate, nor hold any ownership of land. He forfeited all land, goods, and chattels, and lost his citizenship forever.

It is unnecessary, I imagine, to observe, how contrary such regulations were to the boasted liberty of the British subject; but which, in this case, was so plainly sacrificed to the interests of merchants and manufacturers.

The laudable motive of all such regulations, is to extend domestic manufactures, not by their own improvement, but by the depression of those of neighbors, and by putting an end, as much as possible, to the troublesome competition of such odious and disagreeable rivals. The manufacturers think it reasonable that they themselves should have the monopoly of the ingenuity of all their countrymen.

Consumption is the sole end and purpose of all production; and the interest of the producer ought to be attended to, only so far as it may be necessary for promoting that of the consumer. The maxim is so perfectly self-evident, that it would be absurd to attempt to prove it. But in the Mercantile System, the interest of the consumer is almost constantly sacrificed to that of the producer; and it seems to consider production, and not consumption, as the ultimate end and object of all industry and commerce.

In the restraints upon the importation of all foreign commodities which can come into competition with those of our own production, or manufacture, the interest of the home consumer is evidently sacrificed to that of the producer. It is altogether for the benefit of the latter, that the former is obliged to pay that excess price which this monopoly almost always occasions.

It is altogether for the benefit of the producer that bounties are granted upon the exportation of some of his produce. The home consumer is obliged to pay, first, the tax which is necessary for paying the bounty, and secondly, the still greater tax which necessarily arises from the enhancement of the price of the commodity in the home market.

It cannot be very difficult to determine who have been the contrivers of this whole Mercantile System—not the consumers, we may be sure, whose interest has been ignored, but the producers, whose interest has been so carefully attended to; and among this latter class our merchants and manufacturers have been by far the principal architects.

In the mercantile regulations, which have been sketched in this chapter, the interest of the manufacturers has been most peculiarly attended to; and the interest, not so much of the consumers, as that of some other sets of producers, has been sacrificed to it.

CHAPTER XI

Nowhere was the Mercantile System a
worse failure than in its management of
trade with colonies; although the injustice
of its usual restrictions was less in the case
of England than in that of France, Spain,
and Portugal; in all cases, mother countries
and colonies alike were the victims of the
selfish interests of the merchants who car-
ried on the trade.

THE LONG and exhaustive, if repetitious, study of colonies and the colonial system, which constitutes Chapter VII of Book IV of W. N., was in 1776 one of the most interesting, timely, and closely-read passages of the book.

⟪ The colonial problem in England was painfully acute. The North American colonies, which in spite of the ill-contrived policies of British merchants had been a source of strength and growth to the mother country, were obviously about to break away. They were bursting with life and growth, and resentful of the efforts, timid as these were, to get them to assume a fair share of the costs of their defense.

⟪ For more than a year the non-importation agreement of the colonies had been embarrassing British exporters, and had aroused their terrors out of all proportion to the actual injury they were sustaining. At this moment appeared W. N., with its cool-headed analysis of colonial policy, of the real worth and worthlessness of colonies, and its recommendation of what should be attempted under the existing set of conditions.

⟪ It is no reflection upon A. S. that his advice was not heeded, or rather that the hour was already too late; coercion had been decided on, and events rushed on to their ordained conclusion.

℀ The chapter begins with a review of the motives with which colonies have been established, beginning with the Greeks and Romans.

℀ The Greek colonies were sent out when the home population became too great; the Roman colonies to supply lands to soldiers, and to garrison conquered territory. The former, therefore, were practically independent, and grew rapidly in size, wealth, and culture. The latter remained subject to Rome, and never outgrew this relationship nor attained any great importance.

℀ Toward the end of the Middle Ages, the Portuguese and Spanish respectively opened a new sea route to the East Indies, and discovered the new lands of Central and South America—"the two greatest and most important events," says A. S., "recorded in the history of mankind."

℀ But the colonies established by these nations—by Spain in particular—were perverted to the most cynical exploitation. The cruel and oppressive laws of the home countries were extended to the colonies, together with the most rigid controls of all trade, and the system was necessarily injurious to oppressor and oppressed alike.

℀ The establishment of the European colonies in North America and the West Indies were from no necessity or compulsion, but partly by the hope of finding gold, silver, or diamonds, as the Spanish had done, and partly out of sheer adventure and the expectation of profitable trade. The French, the Swedes, the Dutch, and the Danes were all colonizers, but ultimately their settlements were merged with or dominated by the English.

℀ No colonies anywhere progressed more rapidly than the English settlements in North America, and for this the two great causes were the abundance of good land, and liberty to manage their own affairs in their own way.

℀ The Spanish and Portuguese colonies were as well off in land, if not better; but their political institutions and restrictive and wasteful policies more than neutralized this advantage.

℀ The English colonies were not restricted in the land available for cultivation, as was the case in Europe. Its plenty and cheapness produced prosperity quickly. And taxes, by European standards, were abnormally low.

℀ To these basic advantages, the policies of England added

others; for though they were restrictive and often mistaken, they were far more liberal than those of continental Europe.

℄ Every nation, including England, following the principles of the Mercantile System, tried to monopolize the trade with its own colonies. No foreign vessel could trade with them; no goods could be imported except from the mother country. Some nations set up an exclusive company, with which the colonies had to deal. Others confined the whole commerce to a particular port and to particular licensed ships.

℄ The policy of England was far more liberal. Every person could trade through any port, and colonial goods could be exported to any country, except for a certain number of specified commodities. Timber, cattle, fish, sugar, and rum were unrestricted, not so much out of regard for the colonies, as to prevent gluts in England itself.

℄ The commodities which had to be sold only to England included principally those either not produced in England at all, or produced in small quantities. In the former class were molasses, coffee, tobacco, silk, furs, indigo, and some others; in the latter, resin, ships' spars, turpentine, pig iron, copper ore, hides and skins. The monopoly of the first class was obviously profitable to British merchants; the second not so much so, since they competed somewhat with British producers. But this difficulty was evaded by a system of duties, which made imports from North America somewhat dearer than domestic products, but still cheaper than imports from foreign countries.

℄ This relative liberality of England toward her colonies did not, however, extend to manufactured goods. Here the monopoly of the mother country was jealously guarded, sometimes by high duties, sometimes by absolute prohibitions.[1]

℄ Pig iron could be produced in the colonies, but steel furnaces were prohibited. Copper ore could be dug from the Simsbury mine in Connecticut, but it had to be shipped to England to be smelted—an uneconomic cost which made the mine unprofitable and eventually closed it. Hats, wool, and woolen goods could not be transported from one province to any other.

---

[1] Thorold Rogers observes that the trade between England and the American colonies was not, in fact, under the actual conditions, advantageous to either. The Declaration of Independence, thought to be a terrible blow to British trade, turned out to be actually an advantage.

❡ However unjust these fruits of mercantilism, they were not in fact very hurtful to the colonies. A more irksome restriction was the right assumed by the mother country to supply the colonies with all the European goods they bought. Even this was a little liberalized, since the heavy duties paid on goods imported into England were drawn back when the goods were re-exported to North America.

❡ In all respects except foreign trade, the colonies were largely left at liberty to manage their own affairs their own way. And this contrasted strikingly with the policies of France, Spain, and Portugal, where the absolute government at home extended to the colonies, and because of the distance was exercised there with more than ordinary violence.

The policy of Europe, therefore, had very little to boast of, either in the original establishment, or, as far as concerned their internal government, in the subsequent prosperity of the colonies of America.

Folly and injustice seem to have been the principles which presided over and directed the first project; the folly of hunting after gold and silver mines, and the injustice of coveting a country whose harmless natives, far from having ever injured the people of Europe, had received the first adventurers with every mark of kindness and hospitality.

The adventurers who formed some of the later establishments had indeed other motives more reasonable and more laudable; but even these motives do very little honor to the policy of Europe.

The English Puritans, restrained at home, fled for freedom to America, and established there the four governments of New England. The English Catholics, treated with much greater injustice, established that of Maryland; the Quakers, that of Pennsylvania. The Portuguese Jews, persecuted by the Inquisition, stripped of their fortunes, and banished to Brazil, introduced, by their example, some sort of order and industry among the transported felons and strumpets, by whom that colony was originally peopled.

Upon all these different occasions it was, not the wisdom and policy, but the disorder and injustice of the European governments, which peopled and cultivated America.

In effectuating some of the most important of these proj-

ects, the governments of Europe had as little to do as with plan-
ing them. The conquest of Mexico was the scheme, not of the
council of Spain, but of a governor of Cuba; and it was effectuated
by the spirit of the bold adventurer to whom it was entrusted, in
spite of everything which that governor, who soon repented of
having trusted such a person, could do to thwart it.

The conquerors of Chile and Peru, and of almost all the
other Spanish settlements upon the continent of America, carried
with them only a general permission to make settlements and con-
quests in the name of the king of Spain. Those adventures were
all at the private risk and expense of the adventurers.

When those colonies were planted, and had become so considerable as to attract the attention of the mother country, the first
regulations which she made with regard to them always had in
view to secure to herself the monopoly of their commerce; to confine their market, and to enlarge her own at their expense, and
consequently rather to damp and discourage, than to quicken and
forward the course of their prosperity.

❧ In all these regulations, it must be observed, the principal
advisers who suggested them were the very merchants who carried
on the trade. We must not wonder, therefore, that as a rule it was
their own interest, not that of the mother country or of the colonies,
which was consulted.

In what way, therefore, did the policy of Europe contribute
either to the first establishment, or to the present greatness of the
colonies of America? In one way, and in one way only, it has contributed a good deal—*Magna virum mater!*

It bred and formed the men who were capable of achieving
such great actions, and of laying the foundation of so great an
empire; and there is no other quarter of the world of which the
policy is capable of forming, or has ever actually and in fact
formed such men.

The colonies owe to the policy of Europe the education and
great views of their active and enterprising founders; and some of
the greatest and most important of them owe to it scarcely anything
else.

CHAPTER XII

*The real result of the possession of the
North American colonies by England, with
its trade policies based on monopoly, was
a net deficit; hence the eventual loss of the
colonies was a net gain; some remarks as to
the East India and other trading companies
as colonial managers; and a final word as to
colonies and their trade.*

SUCH ARE THE ADVANTAGES which the colonies of America derived
from the policy of Europe.

What are those which Europe derived from the discovery
and colonization of America?

Those advantages may be divided, first, into the general
advantages which Europe, considered as one great country, derived from those great events; and secondly, into the particular
advantages which each colonizing country derived from the colonies which particularly belonged to it, in consequence of the
authority or dominion which it exercised over them.

℃ The general advantages of the colonizing countries as a
whole may be listed as the increase of their enjoyments, and the
increase of their industry. Even countries with no colonies, but
which traded with neighbors who had, participated in some degree
in these benefits. But these advantages were always less than they
might be, when the mother country attempted to monopolize the
trade with her colonies.

℃ The advantage to a particular country was, at least in
theory, of a different kind; it consisted in the military force which
the colony might furnish for its own defense, and the revenue
which it might furnish to the government of the mother country.

But in fact no colony has ever furnished enough military force to protect itself, and only a few colonies of Spain and Portugal have ever contributed any revenue.

❡ The exclusive trade with the colony is therefore in reality the only real advantage to the mother country; and even this may be said to be dubious, since it consists not so much in improving the trade of the nation which possesses colonies, as in depressing the trade of those nations which have none. By means of it England, for example, obtained Virginia tobacco cheaper than France, but not cheaper than it would have been had there been no monopoly at all.[1]

❡ But in order to obtain this very dubious advantage, England had to make two sacrifices. All trade with the colonies had to be carried on with British capital, and this had the double effect of withdrawing capital from other employments, and raising the rate of profit in all trades higher than it otherwise would have been.

❡ To this extent the colonial monopoly reduced the ability of England to carry on trade with other countries. And as more capital was employed in this way at a higher rate of profit, it reduced England's ability to compete on even terms with her rivals. She could sell less and buy less, and foreign countries were able to undersell her in neutral markets.

❡ Furthermore, the colonial monopoly forced British trade into distant and roundabout channels, which of all foreign trade is the least advantageous. It also forced some capital into the carrying trade, which is not very advantageous, and made the whole trade structure less secure because of being driven into one narrow channel.

But we must always carefully distinguish between the effects of the colony trade itself, and those of the *monopoly* of that trade. The former are always and necessarily beneficial; the latter always and necessarily hurtful. The former are so very beneficial, however, that the colony trade, though subject to a monopoly, and notwithstanding the hurtful effects of that monopoly, is still upon the whole beneficial, and greatly beneficial; though a good deal less so than it otherwise would be.

The effect of colony trade in its natural and free state, like

[1] Probably as much tobacco would have reached England without any monopoly, and possibly much more. The freer the trade, the larger, is the lesson of experience.

all other free trade, is to open a great though distant market for such parts of the produce of industry as may exceed the demand of the markets nearer home. In its natural and free state, the colony trade, without drawing from other markets any part of the produce which has ever been sent to them, encourages a nation to increase the surplus continually, by continually presenting new equivalents to be exchanged for it.

In its natural and free state, the colony trade tends to increase the quantity of productive labor in a nation, but without altering in any respect the direction of that which had been employed there before. In the natural and free state of the colony trade, the competition of all other nations would hinder the rate of profit from rising above the common level, either in the new market, or in the new employment.

The new market, without drawing anything from the old one, would create, if one may say so, a new produce for its own supply; and that new produce would constitute new capital for carrying on the new employment, which in the same manner would draw nothing from the old one.

℃ All of these excellent effects are diminished, although not altogether destroyed, by placing this trade under a monopoly; yet this is what the Mercantile System, in its insidious and malignant determination to exclude all other nations from it, is sure to bring about.

℃ A monopoly does indeed raise the rate of mercantile profit, and therefore the profits of some of the merchants. But as it obstructs the natural increase of capital, it reduces the wages of labor, the rent of land, and the profits of other employment.[2] To promote the little interest of one little order of men in one country, it hurts the interest of all other orders of men in that country, and of all men in all other countries.

To found a great empire for the sole purpose of raising up a people of customers, may at first sight appear a project fit only for a nation of shopkeepers. It is, however, a project altogether unfit for a nation of shopkeepers; but extremely fit for a nation whose government is influenced by shopkeepers.

Say to a shopkeeper: "Buy me a good estate, and I shall

[2] Thorold Rogers thinks not. The rent of land and the value of land rose in England, he says, but probably in spite of the monopoly of colony trade, not because of it.

[443]

always buy my clothes at your shop, even though I should pay somewhat dearer than what I can have them for at other shops," and you will not find him very eager to make such a deal.

But should any other person buy you such an estate, the shopkeeper would be much obliged to your benefactor if he would require you to buy all your clothes at his shop.

England purchased for some of her subjects, who found themselves uneasy at home, a great estate in a distant country. The price, indeed, was very small—it amounted to little more than the expense of the different equipments which made the first discovery, reconnoitered the coast, and took a fictitious possession of the country.

The land was good and of great extent, and the cultivators having plenty of good ground to work upon, and being for some time at liberty to sell their produce where they pleased, became in the course of little more than thirty or forty years so numerous and thriving a people, that the shopkeepers of England wished to secure themselves the monopoly of their custom.

Without pretending, therefore, that they had paid any part of the original purchase-money, or of the subsequent expense of improvement, they petitioned the Parliament that the cultivators of America might for the future be limited to their shop; first, for buying all the goods which they wanted from Europe; and, secondly, for selling all such parts of their own produce as those traders might find it convenient to buy.

❡ With such a system, set up in such a manner, Great Britain derived no great gain from her North American colonies. And since she engaged in several expensive wars to protect them from foreign nations, all of which were paid for by the mother country, the final net result was an enormous loss. That this loss was national, not private, and was invisible to the British shopkeeper, made it no less real.

❡ A. S. therefore recommended that at least the monopoly of the colonial trade be gradually given up. A complete and voluntary separation would, he thought, be advantageous, but he well knew that this was an impossibility. "No nation," he remarks, "ever voluntarily gave up the dominion of any province, how troublesome soever it might be to govern it, and how small soever the revenue it provided might be in proportion to the expense it caused." [3]

℣ He made various suggestions as to better tax policies for the colonies, recommended representation in Parliament in proportion to taxes paid, and warned against military coercion. But, as remarked at the beginning of the last chapter, A. S. was already too late. The Mercantile System and principles had done their work, and were at their peak of apparent success and splendor. The next five years were to show that this glorious structure was built upon sand.

℣ The rest of this long chapter is devoted to a similar analysis of the colonial trade with the islands of the East Indies and India. In this A. S. has occasion to repeat his bitter criticism of colonial monopolies, which in the case of the British and Dutch were aggravated by the system of placing the monopoly in the hands of great private trading companies.

℣ These exclusive corporations seemed to embody in themselves all the characteristic vices of the Mercantile System, including, as has been noticed, the Dutch expedient of destroying any seasonal surplus of spices, in order to maintain the monopoly prices of these commodities. Such a policy was directly opposed to the real interest of the company, which combined the character of trader with that of the sovereign of extensive territories.

℣ The companies, however, preferred the small and transitory profits of monopoly trade to the larger and more permanent revenues of a sovereign power.

℣ A secondary abuse was the common practice by which the agents of the companies traded on their own account, at the expense of their employers. At a distance of thousands of miles this was impossible to control or prevent, and the result was not only great loss to the companies, but corrupt and oppressive dealings with the native peoples.

℣ The conclusion of the chapter may well be quoted, if only

---

[3] This is not strictly true, but such instances are certainly rare. The United States voluntarily gave up Cuba, and at present is trying to divest itself of the Philippines. But the first was very imperfectly accomplished, and it is three to one that the Pacific islands will still hang about our necks like the albatross, *de facto* if not *de jure*, for generations to come. To what extent Great Britain will be able to escape from India is something the next few years will show.

for its good advice to all peoples with colonies or dependent possessions of any type.

From the nature of their situation the servants must be more disposed to support with rigorous severity their own interest, against that of the territory which they govern, than their employers can be to support theirs.

The territory belongs to their masters, who cannot avoid having some regard for the interest of what belongs to them. But it does not belong to the servants. The real interest of their masters, if they were capable of understanding it, is the same with that of the territory, and it is chiefly from ignorance, and the meanness of mercantile prejudice, that they ever oppress it. But the real interest of the servants is by no means the same with that of the territory, and the most perfect information would not necessarily put an end to their oppressions.

The regulations which have been sent out from Europe, though they have been frequently weak, have upon most occasions been well-meaning. More intelligence and perhaps less good-meaning has sometimes appeared in those established by the servants.

It is a very singular government in which every member wishes to get out of the country, and consequently to have done with the government, as soon as he can, and to whom, the day after he has left it and taken his whole fortune with him, it would be perfectly indifferent if the whole country were swallowed up by an earthquake.

I mean not, however, by anything which I have here said, to throw any odious imputation upon the general character of the servants of the East India Company, and much less upon that of any particular persons. It is the system of government, the situation in which they are placed, that I mean to censure; not the character of those who have acted in it.

Such exclusive companies, therefore, are nuisances in every respect; always more or less inconvenient to the colonies in which they are established, and destructive to those which have the misfortune to fall under their government.

℃ Completing his study of the colonial system, A. S. reached the conclusion that unless the American colonies could be directly united with the mother country, given representation in Parliament, and thus made to bear their fair share of the expense of the nation (including the interest on the public debt), they should be allowed to become independent without a contest. (In W. N., the paragraphs which follow constitute the final passage in the book.)

It was because the American colonies were supposed to be provinces of the British empire that the cost of protecting them against Spain and France was incurred. But colonies which contribute neither revenue nor military force towards the support of the mother country cannot be considered as provinces.[4]

They may perhaps be considered as appendages, as a sort of splendid and showy equipage of the empire. But if the empire can no longer support the expense of keeping up this equipage, it ought certainly to lay it down; and if it cannot raise its revenue in proportion to its expense, it ought, at least, to adjust its expense to its revenue.

If the colonies, notwithstanding their refusal to submit to British taxes, are still to be considered as provinces of the British empire, their defense in some future war may cost Great Britain as much as it ever has done in any former war.

The rulers of Great Britain have, for more than a century past, amused the people with the illusion that they possessed a great empire on the western side of the Atlantic. This empire, however, has hitherto existed in imagination only. It has hitherto been, not an empire, but the project of an empire; not a gold mine, but the project of a gold mine; a project which has cost, which continues to cost, and which, if pursued in the same way as it has been hitherto, is likely to cost immense expense, without being likely to bring any profit.

For the effects of the monopoly of the colony trade, it has been shown, are, to the great body of the people, mere loss instead of profit. It is surely now time that our rulers should either realize this golden dream (in which they have been indulging themselves, perhaps, as well as the people), or, that they should awake from it themselves, and endeavor to awaken the people.

If the project cannot be completed, it ought to be given up. If any of the provinces of the British empire cannot be made to contribute towards the support of the whole empire, it is surely time

[4] This is not quite fair to the North American colonies; they did not, to be sure, send military forces to England to support her in her continental wars. But in their own defense area, in such operations as the reduction of Louisburg, the colonies certainly made a respectable contribution.

that Great Britain should free herself from the expense of defending those provinces in time of war, and of supporting any part of their civil or military establishments in time of peace, and endeavor to accommodate her future views and designs to the real mediocrity of her circumstances.

CHAPTER XIII

The Mercantile System, based upon the industry of towns, contrasted with the theoretical Agricultural System of the French Physiocrats, based on the industry of agriculture; flaws in this liberal and ingenious system; the only true policy for wealth and greatness of a nation being to leave capital completely free, without interference from the state—"the obvious and simple system of natural liberty."

MR. COLBERT, the famous minister of Louis XIV, was a man of probity, of great industry and knowledge of detail, of great experience and acuteness in the examination of public accounts; and of abilities, in short, in every way fitted for introducing method and good order into the collection and expenditure of the public revenue.

But that minister had unfortunately embraced all the prejudices of the Mercantile System, in its nature and essence a system of restraint and regulation, and such as could scarcely fail to appeal to a laborious and plodding man of business, who had been accustomed to regulate the different departments of public offices, and to establish the necessary checks and controls for confining each to its proper sphere.

The industry and commerce of a great country he endeavored to regulate upon the same model as the departments of a public office; and instead of allowing every man to pursue his own interest in his own way, upon the liberal plan of equality, liberty and justice, he bestowed upon certain branches of industry extraordinary privileges, while he laid others under as extraordinary restraints.

He was not only disposed, like other European ministers, to encourage the industry of the towns more than that of the country; but, in order to support the industry of the towns, he was willing even to depress and keep down that of the country. In order to render provisions cheap to the inhabitants of the towns, and thereby to encourage manufactures and foreign commerce, he prohibited altogether the export of grain, and thus excluded the principal product of French agriculture from every foreign market.

This prohibition, added to the restraints imposed by the ancient provincial laws of France upon the transportation of grain from one province to another, and to the arbitrary and degrading taxes levied upon the farmers in almost all the provinces, discouraged and kept down the agriculture of that country very much below the state to which it would naturally have risen with so very fertile a soil and so very happy a climate.

This state of discouragement and depression was felt more or less in every part of the country, and many different inquiries were set on foot concerning the causes of it. One of those causes appeared to be the preference given, by the institutions of Mr. Colbert, to the industry of the town above that of the country.[1]

If the rod be bent too much one way, says the proverb, in order to make it straight you must bend it as much the other. The French philosophers who proposed the system which represents agriculture as the sole source of the revenue and wealth of every country, seem to have adopted this proverbial maxim. And as in the plan of Mr. Colbert the industry of the towns was certainly over-valued in comparison with that of the country, so in their system it seems to be as certainly under-valued.

℃ It is unnecessary to examine at length the principles of these French philosophers, since their ideas were never applied to French policy, and consequently their errors have not done, and probably never will do any harm in any part of the world. A brief account of these principles, however, may be of interest.[2]

℃ Under their system there were three classes of people—

[1] After Louis XIV, as we know, the affairs of France went from bad to worse; and the "discouragement and depression" of French agriculture came to a violent climax in 1789 in the French Revolution.

[2] A. S. had studied at first hand this system of the French Physiocrats (who themselves preferred the name "Economists") during his stay of thirty months in Toulouse, Geneva, and Paris, in 1764–66.

land owners, cultivators, and a class of artisans, manufacturers and merchants. It is only the land owners and the cultivators or farmers who are really productive, producing a net gain to the country, and they should for this reason be free from taxes and tithes.

℄ All other orders of people are barren and unproductive, since their labor replaces only the capital which employs them, plus its ordinary profit.

The labor of artificers and manufacturers never adds anything to the value of the whole annual amount of the raw product of the land. It adds greatly indeed to the value of some particular parts of it.

The person who works a piece of fine lace, for example, will sometimes raise the value of perhaps two cents' worth of flax to $150. But though at first sight he appears thereby to multiply the value of the raw material about seven thousand two hundred times, he in reality adds nothing to the value of the whole production. The working of that lace cost him perhaps two months' labor. The $150 which he gets for it when it is finished, is no more than the repayment of the subsistence which he advances to himself during that two months.

Artificers, manufacturers and merchants, can increase the income and wealth of the society, by parsimony only; or, as it is expressed in this system, by privation—that is, by depriving themselves of a part of the funds intended for their own subsistence.

They annually reproduce nothing but those funds. Unless, therefore, they annually save some part of them, unless they annually deprive themselves of the enjoyment of some part of them, the income and wealth of their society can never be in the smallest degree augmented by means of their industry.

℄ Thus artificers, manufacturers, and merchants, while useful to landlords and farmers, are actually maintained at their expense. The former can be useful to the country only by increasing its wealth through parsimony and privation.

℄ As in a particular country these classes are necessary to each other, so different countries of these types are useful to each other. As it is not to the interest of farmers to discourage or oppress townspeople, or vice versa, so it is not to the interest of the productive nations to discourage or oppress the unproductive.

℄ In any case, freedom of trade would be the best policy between nations, either resulting in the unrestrained exchange of raw

[451]

materials for manufactured goods, or by gradual stages the introduction of manufactures into the agricultural countries, to the extent most advantageous to them.

❧ Complete liberty of trade, domestic and international, is indeed an essential for the healthy functioning of the society. By whatever degree this liberty is denied, the society will decline in income and wealth.

❧ But this system, so liberal and ingenious, is certainly in error in several respects. Mr. Quesnay, its very ingenious and profound author, was himself a physician; and it is perhaps for this reason that he attributed to the political body the same characteristics as those of the human body.

❧ He seems to have thought that the health of the human body could be preserved only by a certain perfect regimen of diet and exercise, and that every deviation from this, no matter how small, must result in disease or disorder in proportion. In the political body he thought he saw the same principle, by which a society could flourish only under an exact regimen of perfect liberty and perfect justice.

❧ Experience, however, would seem to show that both the human organism and political societies have within them a principle of flexibility and self-preservation, which enables them to adapt themselves to circumstances, and to maintain their health under a wide variety of handicaps.

❧ If a nation could prosper only under perfect liberty and justice, there is no nation in the world that could ever have prospered. The wisdom of nature has fortunately made ample provision for remedying many of the evil effects of the folly and injustice of man in political affairs, as it remedies the effects of sloth and intemperance in individuals.

❧ The agricultural system of Mr. Quesnay and his followers is in error, too, in representing the class of artisans, manufacturers and merchants as altogether barren and unproductive.

First, this class, it is acknowledged, reproduces annually the value of its own annual consumption, and continues, at least, the existence of the capital which maintains and employs it. Why then should it be called unproductive?

We should not call a marriage barren or unproductive, though it produced only a son and a daughter, to replace the father and mother, and though it did not increase the number of the human species, but only continued it as it was before. As a marriage which affords three children is certainly more productive than one which affords only two; so the labor of farmers and farm labor is certainly more productive than that of merchants, artificers, and manufacturers. But because one is more productive we should not call the other barren or unproductive.

Secondly, it seems altogether improper to consider artificers, manufacturers and merchants, in the same light as menial servants. The labor of menial servants does not continue the existence of the fund which maintains and employs them. Their maintenance and employment is altogether at the expense of their masters, and the work which they perform is not of a nature to repay that expense.[3] The labor of artificers, manufacturers and merchants, on the contrary, naturally does fix and realize itself in some vendible commodity.

Thirdly, it seems upon every supposition improper to say that the labor of artificers, manufacturers and merchants, does not increase the real revenue of the society. It does.[4] An artificer, for example, who, in the first six months after harvest, executes $500 worth of work, though he should in the same time consume $500 worth of food and other necessaries, yet really adds the value of $500 to the annual produce of the land and labor of the society.

Though the value of what the artificer produces, therefore, should not at any one moment of time be greater than the value he consumes, yet at every moment of time the actually existing value of goods in the market is, in consequence of what he produces, greater than it otherwise would be.

Fourthly, farmers can no more increase, without parsimony, the real income, the annual produce of the land and labor of their society, than artisans, manufacturers and merchants. The annual produce of the land and labor of any society can be increased only in two ways—either by some improvement in the productive powers of useful labor, or by some increase in the quantity of that labor.

The improvement in the productive powers of labor de-

[3] A last echo from Chapter III of Book II. To A. S. labor which produces nothing that can be seen, stored, or sold is "unproductive" to the end.

[4] The artisan and manufacturing class must certainly add something to the real wealth of society, says Thorold Rogers. If they did not add more value than their own consumption, on the average, the labor would not have been undertaken, and certainly would not be repeated.

pends, first, upon the improvement in the ability of the workman; and, secondly, upon that of the machinery with which he works. But the labor of artificers and manufacturers, as it is capable of being more subdivided, and the labor of each workman reduced to a greater simplicity of operation, than that of farmers, so it is likewise capable of both these sorts of improvement in a much higher degree. In this respect, therefore, farmers can have no sort of advantage over workmen and manufacturers.

The agricultural system of the Economists is, however, with all its imperfections, perhaps the nearest approximation to the truth that has yet been published upon the subject of political economy, and is upon that account well worth the consideration of every man who wishes to examine with attention the principles of this very important science.

Though in representing the labor which is employed upon land as the only productive labor, the notions which it inculcates are perhaps too narrow and confined; yet in representing the wealth of nations as consisting, not in the unconsumable riches of money, but in the consumable goods annually reproduced by the labor of the society, and in representing perfect liberty as the only effectual method for rendering this annual reproduction as large as possible, its doctrine seems to be in every respect as just as it is generous and liberal.

Its followers are very numerous; and it has been in consequence of their representations, accordingly, that the agriculture of France has been delivered from several of the worst oppressions under which it formerly labored. For example, the term during which a lease can be granted, to remain valid against every future purchaser or proprietor of the land, has been extended from nine to twenty-seven years. The ancient provincial restraints upon the transportation of grain from one province to another have been entirely taken away, and the liberty of exporting it to all foreign countries has been established as the common law in all ordinary cases.

ℂ   While this system has never been put in practice in full, and doubtless never will be—the policy of nations tending generally toward favoring the towns over the country—there are some countries where agriculture has been particularly favored. Such are ancient Egypt, China, and India.

ℂ   In these and some other countries, the revenue of the ruler was obtained largely through some sort of land rent or land tax; and accordingly the prosperity of the farmers was an object of solicitude. Great irrigation systems were at various periods constructed in these countries, and other measures were taken, not so much for the avowed benefit of agriculture as for the ultimate benefit of the ruling classes.

The greatest and most important branch of the commerce of every nation, it has already been observed, is that which is carried on between the inhabitants of the town and those of the country. The inhabitants of the town draw from the country the raw materials which constitute both the materials of their work and the fund of their subsistence; and they pay for this by sending back to the country a certain portion of it, manufactured and prepared for immediate use.

The trade which is carried on between those two sets of people consists ultimately in a certain quantity of raw materials exchanged for a certain quantity of manufactures. The dearer the latter, therefore, the cheaper the former; and whatever tends in any country to raise the price of manufactures tends to lower that of farm products, and thereby to discourage agriculture.

Whatever, besides, tends to diminish in any country the number of workmen and manufacturers, tends to diminish the home market, the most important of all markets for agriculture, and thereby still further to discourage it.

Those systems, therefore, which, preferring agriculture to all other employments, impose restraints upon manufactures and foreign trade in order to help farmers, act against the very end which they propose, and indirectly discourage that very division of industry which they mean to promote. They are so far, perhaps, even more inconsistent than the Mercantile System.

That system, by encouraging manufactures and foreign trade more than agriculture, turns a certain portion of the capital of the society from supporting a more advantageous, to support a less advantageous kind of industry. But still it really and in the end does encourage the industry which it means to promote. Those agricultural systems, on the contrary, really and in the end discourage their own favorite industry.

It is thus that every system which endeavors, whether, by extraordinary encouragements, to draw towards a particular branch of industry a greater share of the capital of the society than would naturally go to it; or, by extraordinary restraints, to force from a particular industry some share of the capital which would otherwise be employed in it, is in reality subversive of the very purpose which it means to promote.

It retards, instead of accelerating, the progress of the society towards real wealth and greatness; and diminishes, instead of increasing, the real value of the annual produce of its land and labor.

If all systems either of preference or of restraint are completely taken away, the obvious and simple system of natural liberty establishes itself of its own accord. Every man, as long as he does not violate the laws of justice, is left perfectly free to pursue his own interest his own way, and to bring both his industry and capital into competition with those of any other man, or order of men.

The state is completely discharged from a duty, in attempting to perform which it must always be exposed to innumerable delusions, and for the proper performance of which no human wisdom or knowledge could ever be sufficient: the impossible task of superintending the industry of private people, and of directing it towards the employments most suitable to the interest of the society.

According to the system of natural liberty, the state has only three duties to attend to—three duties of great importance, indeed, but plain and intelligible to common understandings: first, protecting the society from the violence and invasion of other independent societies; second, protecting, as far as possible, every member of it, or the duty of establishing an exact administration of justice; and, third, erecting and maintaining certain public works and certain public institutions, which it can never be for the interest of any individual, or small number of individuals, to erect and maintain.

❡ Let the state confine itself to these necessary functions, and the natural energies of the people will accomplish whatever else is necessary to the progress and wealth of the nation.

INDEX

Abbeville, monopoly of manufacture of woolens at, 385.

Abraham, weighed out four hundred shekels of silver for field, 46.

Abuses, of local revenue, generally very trifling, 265.

Abyssinia, salt used as money, 44.

Actors, paid exorbitantly because of contempt for their profession, 99.

Adulteration of coin, generally concealed if possible, 363.

Africa, living conditions of powerful king far below poorest European workmen, 35; interior of, backward because commerce must move by land, 42; merchants trading there require special protection, 266.

Age, a source of authority among civilized societies, 253.

Agricultural System, one of those proposed by science of political economy, 26, *Preface*.

Agriculture, does not admit of such subdivision as manufactures, 30; requires much knowledge and experience, 113; materials used are variable, 113; capital employed in, most advantageous to society, 207; caused the prosperity of British colonies in America, 209; while most advantageous to society, not the road to fortune, 215; reasons why capital not attracted to, 215; artificers essential to, 221; charms of, attract all men to some extent, 221; not attended to by destroyers of the Roman Empire, 223; the ancient policy of Europe unfavorable to, 226; was promoted by the commerce and manufactures of towns, 233; favored by laws of England, 240; wealth arising from, more solid and durable than that which proceeds from commerce, 240; supposes some fixed habitation, 246; would be encouraged by an equitable tax on rents, 299; landlords should cultivate some of their own land, 300; effect of taxes on the profit of, 316; impaired by taxes resulting from public debt, 358; can derive little benefit from monopoly, 384; of France, discouraged by policies of M. Colbert, 449; proposals of French philosophers for relief of, 450; over-valued in relation to the towns, 452; is favored over manufactures in China and India, 454; a false policy to check manufactures in order to promote, 455.

Agrippina, price of white nightingale given her by Scio, 145.

Alcavala, a Spanish tax in the nature of a transaction tax, 344.

Ambassadors, commercial, unknown in ancient times, 267.

America, colonization followed coast and rivers, 41; wages in, much higher than in England, 79; not so rich as England, 79; great increase of population there, 79; common rate of interest in, 90; account of paper currency of, 178; causes of the rapid prosperity of, 209; carrying trade of goods to Europe, 209; rapid advance founded on agriculture, 239; improvement of own land, most profitable employment of capital in, 240; first inquiry of Spaniards always for gold and silver, 368; discovery caused a revolution in commerce, 375; only two civilized nations found in, 375; British bounties on imports of raw materials granted to, 431; settled by different motives from Greek and Roman colonies, 437; naval stores to England, 438; success of, not due to policy of Europe, 439; folly and injustice presided over settlement of, 439; Europe *magna virum mater*, 440; colonization of, how advantageous to Europe, 441; contribute no military force to mother country, 442; and little revenue, 442; exclusive trade supposed the principal advantage, 442; ought in justice to help discharge British debt, 447; the British Empire there, a mere project, 447.

Amsterdam, city of, engaged in banking for profit, 294; reputation and ruin of the Bank of, 396.

Animals, do not have conception of contracts, nor barter, 36; can make no use of each others' special talents, 38.

Animosity, between nations, results in trade restrictions, 394.

Anne, Queen of England, rate of interest on money in the time of, 89; retirement of debt in the reign of, 352.

Annuities, a device for management of the public debt, 352.

Anticipation, a device for retiring the public debt, 351.

Apothecary, why rate of profit apparently high, 102.

Apprenticeship, statutes of, tend to raise wages and profit above natural rates, 71; may be harmful to workmen in unprofitable trades, 72; statute of, in England, 109; in France and Scotland, 109; system unknown to the ancients, 110.

Arabian chief, revenue of, all profit, 294.

Arabs, each man a warrior among, 245.

Army, cost of, very different in different stages of society, 245; standing, distinctions between and a militia, 248; historical review of, 248; can perpetuate civilization of a country, 250; greatness of Russia introduced by, 250; under what circumstances dangerous or favorable to

INDEX

Income, object of political economy to provide a plentiful, 25, *Preface*; arises from one or more of wages, profit, and rent, 62, 153; of labor, in necessities and conveniences, increased more than money income, 86; of landlord, calls for no labor or attention, 153; of man with small capital, depends on his labor, 161; capital affords, only when circulating or changing owners, 165; whole gross annual, distinguished from net income, 167; large part of, must be used to maintain or increase capital, 168; not the same as money received, 169; real, is the goods and services a man can buy with it, 170; real, of the whole community, much larger than money in circulation, 172; surplus of, as profit or rent, determines number of unproductive laborers, 182; surplus of, either employs labor directly or indirectly through lending at interest, 183; of inhabitants of a country, reduced by extravagance of the prodigal, 185; of an individual, how spent, 194; surplus of, spent on durable goods, favorable to frugality, 196; of wealthy, always supports many other people, 237; of artisans, ceases when they become soldiers, 247; of an established church, a burden on the public revenue, 289; of the poor, spent principally for food, 306; of the wealthy, should be taxed somewhat more than in proportion to others, 307; taxes upon, examined, 327; of lower classes, far greater than that of the rich, 337; of individuals, how expended in a rude state of society, 347; most persons habitually live within, 348; redistribution of, through interest on public debt, examined, 357; of a nation, increased by foreign trade, 374; of a nation, always equal to exchangeable value of whole annual production, 379; every individual naturally labors to make as great as possible, 380; of farmers, not reduced by import of grain, 416.

India, sea shells used as money in parts of, 44; violent police compels every man to follow the occupation of his father, 72; miserable condition under the East India Company, 81; treasure commonly buried in, 166; wonderful accounts of its ancient cultivation and wealth, 210; partial conquest by the East India Company, 271; value of gold and silver highest in, 421; agriculture favored over manufactures, 454.

Indians, of North America, threw away surplus skins of animals, 133.

Indolence, common trait of landlords, 154.

Industrious people, capital of, transferred to the idle by depreciation of money, 361.

Industry, naturally suited to the demand, 67; is more advantageously exerted in towns than in the country, 111; needs no encouragement but security, 143; volume of, increases with increase of capital, 160; is promoted by the use of paper money, 172; creates capital, but not the increase of it, 184; the natural direction of, diverted by taxes on commodities, 343; quantity of, cannot increase beyond what capital can maintain, 378; every individual will direct so as

to produce greatest possible value, 379; of a nation, in no wise diminished by imports of goods, 382.

Inequalities, of wages and profits, even when employment is free, 103; greater because employment seldom free, 107; in wages and profits, not affected by general condition of nation, 121.

Injustice of European discoveries, fatal to some American countries, 375.

Inn-keeper, trade of, profitable with small capital, 96.

Instruction, of all ages, a duty of the state, 260.

Insurance, the value and profits of, 100; marine, the risks alarming, 100.

Interest, for the use of money, basis explained, 62; varies with the rate of profit, 89; may be raised by defective laws, 92; if altogether prohibited, still not prevented, 92; the lowest ordinary rate of, must compensate for losses, 92; the common proportion between interest and rate of profit examined, 93; surplus of income often lent at, 184; principles relating to loans at, 198; rate of diminishes as money available for increases, 200; not lowered by increase in supply of gold and silver, 201; rate of, regulated by rate of profit which can be made on capital, 202; how the legal rate of, should be fixed, 203; market rate of, regulates the price of land, 204; as a source of public revenue, 311; common rate of, not affected by taxes on particular trades, 317; to lend money at, formerly thought disgraceful, 348; on public debts, secured by mortgage on revenue, 350; pretense that payment of is not a burden, 357.

Interference of state, individual never wholly free from, 25, *Preface*.

Invasion, protection from, one of the three duties of the state, 456.

Invisible hand, directs industry of every individual to advantageous ends, 380.

Ireland, supplies strong porters and beautiful prostitutes, fed on potatoes, to London, 131; proposed absentee tax in, considered, 342.

Iron, used as money by the ancient Spartans, 45.

Irrigation systems, in ancient Egypt, China, and India, 455.

Italy, grain imported during Roman prosperity, 128; cultivation degenerated when given over to slaves, 225; cities became independent, 230; cities raised to opulence by commerce, 231; cultivated and improved throughout by foreign commerce, 240; small states on the Po levy transit duties, 339.

James I, his marriage bed brought from Denmark, 195.

James VI, of Scotland, debasement of coinage under, 364.

Jews, from Portugal, settlement in Brazil, 439.

John, King of England, benefactor of towns, 229.

John, King of France, adulteration of the coinage by, 363.

Joint-stock companies, nature of, 269; how distinguished from partnerships, 269; reduce risks of investors, 269; circum-